HISTORY OF
OR LEAGUE
BASEBALL

THE HISTORY OF MAJOR LEAGUE BASEBALL

JOEL ZOSS & JOHN S. BOWMAN

Crescent Books
New York

This 1992 edition published by Crescent Books,
distributed by Outlet Book Company, Inc.,
a Random House Company,
40 Engelhard Avenue
Avenel, New Jersey 07001

Produced by
Brompton Books Corporation
15 Sherwood Place,
Greenwich, CT 06830

ISBN 0-517-06627-0

8 7 6 5 4 3 2 1

Printed and bound in Hong Kong

Part One

THE NATIONAL LEAGUE

Chapter One: In the Beginning 7

Chapter Two: The Modern Game 25

Chapter Three: The League Takes to the Air 53

Chapter Four: Innovation and Upheaval 71

Chapter Five: Dodger Dynasty 89

Chapter Six: The Unpredictable Decade 111

Chapter Seven: Untraditional Seventies 135

Chapter Eight: The Decade Past and Present 161

Page 1: Doug Drabek pitches for the Pirates.
Pages 2-3: Minnesota's Kent Hrbek bats against the Braves in the seventh game of the 1991 World Series.
This page: The New York Giants' Mel Ott is congratulated as he crosses the plate after hitting a two-run homer against the Yankees in the fifth World Series game, 1937.

CONTENTS

Part Two

THE AMERICAN LEAGUE

Chapter One:
The Beginnings of the American League 198

Chapter Two: The House that Ruth Built 220

Chapter Three: Heroes of the Depression 242

Chapter Four: The Fighting Forties 260

Chapter Five: The Fabled Fifties 278

Chapter Six: The Sensational Sixties 304

Chapter Seven: The Seditious Seventies 328

Chapter Eight: The Unsettled Eighties and Into the Nineties 354

Index and Acknowledgments 389

Part One

THE NATIONAL LEAGUE

CHAPTER ONE

In the Beginning

The wit of man cannot devise a plan or frame a form of government that will control the game of baseball for over five years.

William Ambrose Hulbert, founder of the National League

The National League of Professional Base Ball Clubs was founded on 2 February 1876, almost exactly one hundred years after the founding of the United States. The game had long since become the fledgling democracy's national pastime and obsession, but in 1876 few even of its most ardent supporters would have guessed that by the time another hundred years had passed baseball would be a billion-dollar-a-year business with over 50 million paying spectators annually and star players signing multi-year contracts for upwards of $20 million.

The origins of baseball as an American game are probably as clearly understood now as they are ever likely to be, but the history of games with balls and bats stretches back into prehistory. The first recorded instance of 'batting contests' occurred over 5000 years ago, in North Africa, where rival Egyptian priests engaged in ritual mock combat with sticks designed to promote the fertility of crops and people. In other Egyptian fertility rituals ball games were featured in which the ball represented the sun or the mummified head of Osiris. Pictures of half-naked women playing a ball game on piggyback were carved into the tomb of Beni Hasan sometime before 2000 BC.

The Romans and Greeks played ball mainly in secular and athletic contexts, but religious connotations persisted. Ball playing reached Europe as vestiges of popular Egyptian fertility rites transmitted by the expanding Muslim empire. By the time Islam retreated from Europe, ball games had surfaced in Christian ceremonies from Austria to France. During the Middle Ages, the French Cathedral of Rheims wound up its Easter celebrations with widely anticipated team games in which the ball was kicked or swatted with a stick. Eventually these 'mass' games crossed the Channel into England, where they remained connected to the churchyard but evolved into 'stoolball,' a game in which a pitcher tries to hit an upturned stool with a ball before the batter can bat it away with a stick. Stoolball gradually moved into the countryside and became a favorite among milkmaids, who made the game more interesting by adding more milking stools or 'bases' to be circled after the ball was struck. When the rule was added that a runner could be put out by being struck with a thrown ball, the English children's game of 'rounders' was created. Posts driven into the ground called 'goals' or 'bases'

Far right: This drawing from the ancient tomb of Beni Hasan shows Egyptian women playing a ball game on piggyback.

Below: In 1744 *A Little Pretty Pocket Book* was published in London, describing and illustrating children's games. In stoolball, which dates back to 1300, little stools or upright bases were stationed around the field. Later, stones replaced the stools and the game was called base-ball. These informal games were the forerunners of the British games of rounders and cricket, and ultimately American baseball. Although no-one questions that the sport's origins lie in the United States, the word 'baseball' did come from across the Atlantic.

The *little* i Play.

STOOL-BALL.

THE *Ball* once ſtruck with Art and Care,
And drove impetuous through the Air
Swift round his Courſe the *Gameſter* flies,
Or his *Stool's* taken by Surprize.

RULE *of* LIFE.

Beſtow your Alms whene'er you ſee
An Object in Neceſſity.

The little k *Play.*

BASE-BALL.

THE *Ball* once ſtruck off,
Away flies the *Boy*
To the next deſtin'd Poſt,
And then Home with Joy.

MORAL.

Thus *Britons* for Lucre
Fly over the Main;
But, with Pleaſure tranſported,
Return back again.

TRAP-replaced the stools, and the game was called 'goal ball' or 'base ball' as early as 1700. *A Pretty Little Pocket Book,* published in London in 1744, contained a rhymed description of the game and a picture captioned, 'Base-Ball.' The book was extremely popular, and was republished in America several times between 1762 and 1787.

In the United States the development of baseball is the story of 19th-century America in microcosm. While the country was changing from a rural society into a nation of large cities and giant factories, baseball developed from the children's game of rounders to a highly skilled game of professionals performing for the entertainment of paying spectators. In between, it was played by all kinds and classes of people. Dr. Oliver Wendell Holmes writes of playing baseball on a diamond-shaped field at Harvard in 1829. By the 1840s, the basic pattern of the game was being shaped in amateur clubs founded by young professionals in Eastern cities.

The Knickerbocker Base Ball Club of New York City, one of the first amateur clubs to have a real organization, appointed a committee to standardize the rules of the game for intra- and intermural competition. Their code, adopted on 23 September 1845, stands as something of a landmark in baseball history. Significantly, the Knickerbocker rules decreed that a player could no longer be put out by being hit with a thrown ball. In a game played between the Knickerbockers and the New York Nine in New Jersey in 1846, the Knicks were badly trounced, and player J W Davis was fined six cents for swearing at the umpire. Games played by these early amateur clubs were highly social occasions; often the losing team paid for the banquet that followed.

The rules codified by the Knickerbockers were adopted by many other clubs, and the 'New York Game' became the basis for intercity competition. During the 1850s something like a national mania grew up around these amateur clubs. Seasoned observers of the contemporary scene were amazed at baseball's success, and on 10 March 1858 representatives from 25 of the more than 100 clubs in the North formed the first league, the National Association of Base Ball Players. Brooklyn and Manhattan teams played an All-Star game on 20 July 1858, charging 50

Above: *The Book of Sports*, published in 1834, included illustrations and directions on how to play baseball.
Top: Some New York Knickerbockers, circa 1847.

WILL. P. NOBLE DEL

LEON VAN LOO, PHOTO.

THE FIRST NINE.

Above: The Cincinnati Red Stockings team of 1869 – the first professional baseball team.
Right: The Brooklyn Excelsior baseball club of 1860.

cents admission to cover the costs of preparing the grounds. This was the first time admission was charged in the history of the game. Baseball was still amateur, but was on its way to becoming a commercialized amusement.

The Civil War dampened baseball enthusiasm for a while, and many of the clubs from New York to Chicago went under. But the war also did much to spread the gospel of baseball. On Christmas Day 1862, a throng of 40,000 Union soldiers – probably the largest crowd for any sporting event in the 19th century – watched a game between two Union All-Star teams. After the war, baseball mania returned to top prewar excesses. Professional and commercial interests began to realize that profits could be wrung from baseball promotion. By the late 1860s, the gentlemanly amateur code which governed the sport had given way to the ethic of winning, and gentlemen and children were no longer the only players. As Theodore Roosevelt later remarked, 'When money comes in at the gate, sport flies out the window.' Many businesses hired young men to work in their industries with a view toward using their baseball talents in the teams they sponsored. When such teams began traveling, taking on all comers, amateurism became a sham.

In 1869, Harry Wright, a professional cricket player and English-born son of a cricket professional, organized the first all-salaried professional team, the Cincinnati Reds (Red Stockings). Their astounding success against amateurs transformed baseball in America. Professional interests met in New York to establish the first professional league, the National Association of Professional Base-Ball Players, in 1871. This league was not always able to make players live up to their contracts and clubs to their schedules, but during its five years of existence it did much to broaden the game's appeal.

By the mid-1870s, baseball was booming, but the National Association clubs were so riddled with heavy gambling, game-throwing, drunkenness, player

Left: Al Spalding when he played for Boston in the early 1870s. He later went to Chicago as player-manager. He was inducted into the Hall of Fame in 1939.
Below: A Cincinnati Red Stockings game of 1869.

desertion, contract-jumping and plain rowdiness on both sides of the dugout that public confidence in the integrity and character of the game was reaching a dangerous point. William Ambrose Hulbert, a Chicago businessman and president of the Chicago National Association club, feared for professional baseball's future as much as he was excited by its potential, and decided to do something about it.

Joining forces with Boston superstar pitcher Al Spalding, whom he enticed to his Chicago Club for the 1876 season along with the rest of Boston's famous 'Big Four' infield, Hulbert concluded that the reforms necessary for baseball to survive and thrive could not be effected within the existing structure of the rickety National Association, and decided to form a new league to be called the 'National League of Professional Base Ball Clubs.' At a secret meeting in Louisville in January 1876, Hulbert sold his scheme to representatives of the St Louis, Cincinnati and Louisville baseball clubs. Moving east, on 2 February 1876 he met with representatives of Boston, Hartford, Philadelphia and New York at the Grand Central Hotel in New York. Hulbert reportedly locked the hotel room door while he read the proposed constitution and player contract he and Spalding had prepared. The Easterners, equally worried about the effects of gambling and other evils, unanimously agreed to the formation of a new league. Morgan P Bulkeley of Hartford was chosen president of a five-man committee which would control the new organization, and the National League was born.

Hulbert and Spalding's constitution has provided the basis of the National League – as well as the blueprint for professional sport in this country – for more than a century. The National League's objectives were to encourage, foster and elevate the game of baseball; to enact and enforce proper rules for the exhibition and conduct of the game and to make baseball-playing respectable and honorable. The constitution forbade gambling and the sale of alcohol on the grounds, obligated each team to play a complete schedule, and required each franchise to represent a city of at least 75,000. Above all, Hulbert wanted a league that would be profitable, run in a disciplined, businesslike manner. To this end the control of the game was to be placed firmly in the hands of the owners, rather than the players. Players were bound to one club by an ingenious reserve clause (finally approved in 1879) which guaranteed a club a player's services for as long as it wished, and were no longer to have any voice in the operation of the league. Gone were the days when contracts were broken almost at will, and players convicted of throwing games experienced virtually no difficulty in finding employment with other clubs.

The first game of the new league was played in Philadelphia on 22 April 1876, with Boston defeating Philadelphia, 6-5. Each of the eight charter teams was scheduled to meet every other team ten times between 15 March and 15 November (five games at home and five away), league games taking place three times a week. Admission was set at 50 cents, reduced to ten cents after the third inning. Each club had to provide a sufficient number of police to preserve order. Dues were set at $100 annually, ten times what they had been in the National Association. The team

The championship game of 1866 between the Athletics and the Atlantics.

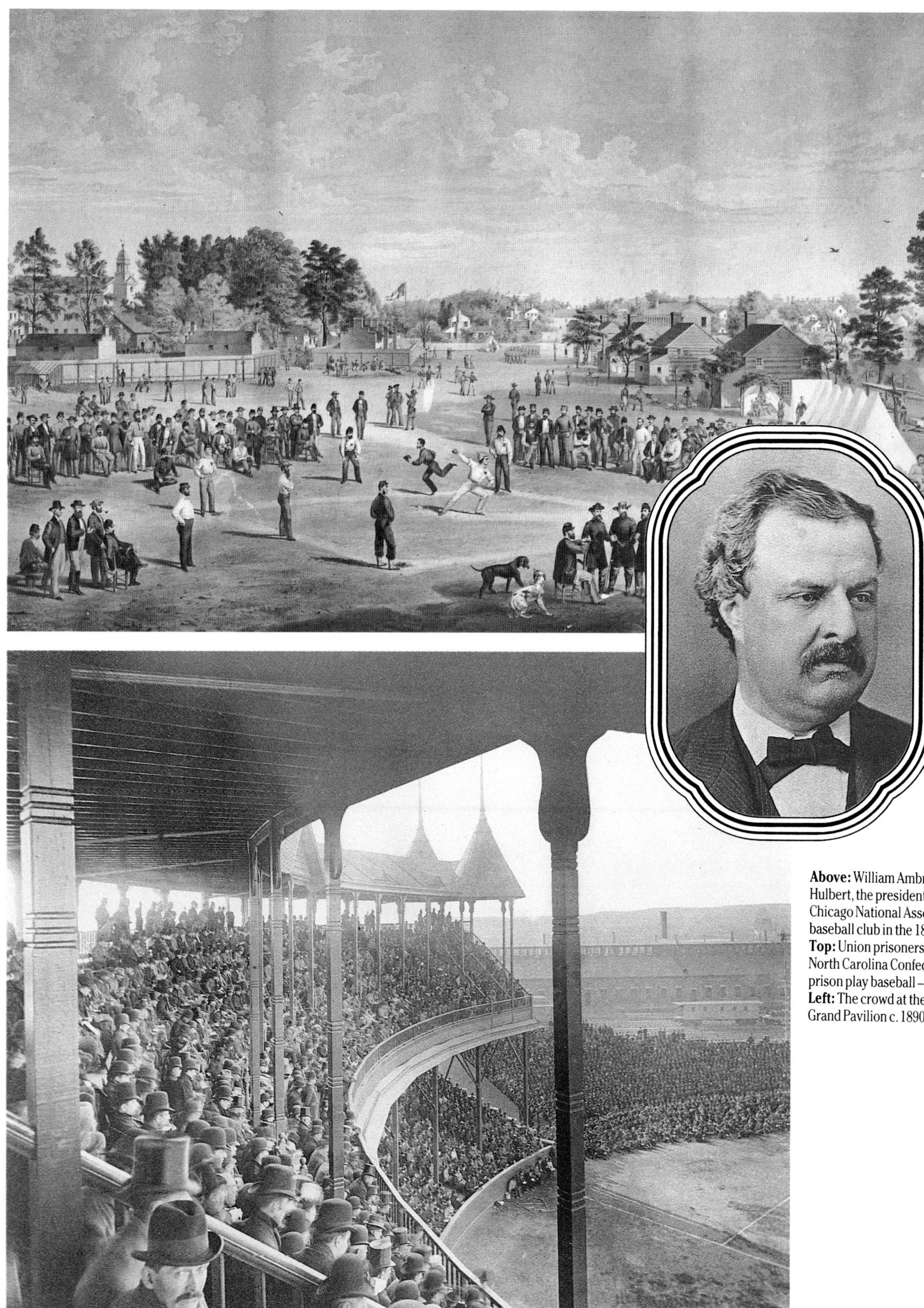

Above: William Ambrose Hulbert, the president of the Chicago National Association baseball club in the 1870s.
Top: Union prisoners in a North Carolina Confederate prison play baseball – 1862.
Left: The crowd at the Boston Grand Pavilion c. 1890.

winning the most games would receive a pennant costing not less than $100.

The first no-hitter in National League history was recorded on 15 July 1876 by George Washington Bradley of St Louis, who blanked Hartford, 2-0. A strong Chicago club took the pennant, followed in order of wins by Hartford, St Louis, Boston, Louisville, New York, Philadelphia and Cincinnati.

Paid attendance was not high enough to ensure financial success that first season, but at least gambling and liquor sales were down. The league's first test occurred when New York and Philadelphia, fearing financial loss, declared themselves more important to the league than the league was to them, and refused to make their final western trip. Much to their astonishment, Hulbert, who had replaced Bulkeley as president in December, proved the league meant business and as his first official action expelled the two clubs from the league.

The 1877 season began with six clubs. The 'fair-foul' rule was eliminated – a ball hit foul but which rolled fair between home and first or third was now forever foul – and the infant league met its second great test when it became clear late in the season that four players from the strong Louisville team were throwing games for big-time New York gamblers. The players confessed, and all were banished forever from organized ball.

Boston and Chicago were the only charter clubs remaining in the league at the start of the 1878 season, but Cincinnati soon made up past dues and bought her way back in, and clubs from Providence, Indian-

Inset: A photograph taken in 1907 of A G Mills, who was the president of the National League in the early 1880s.

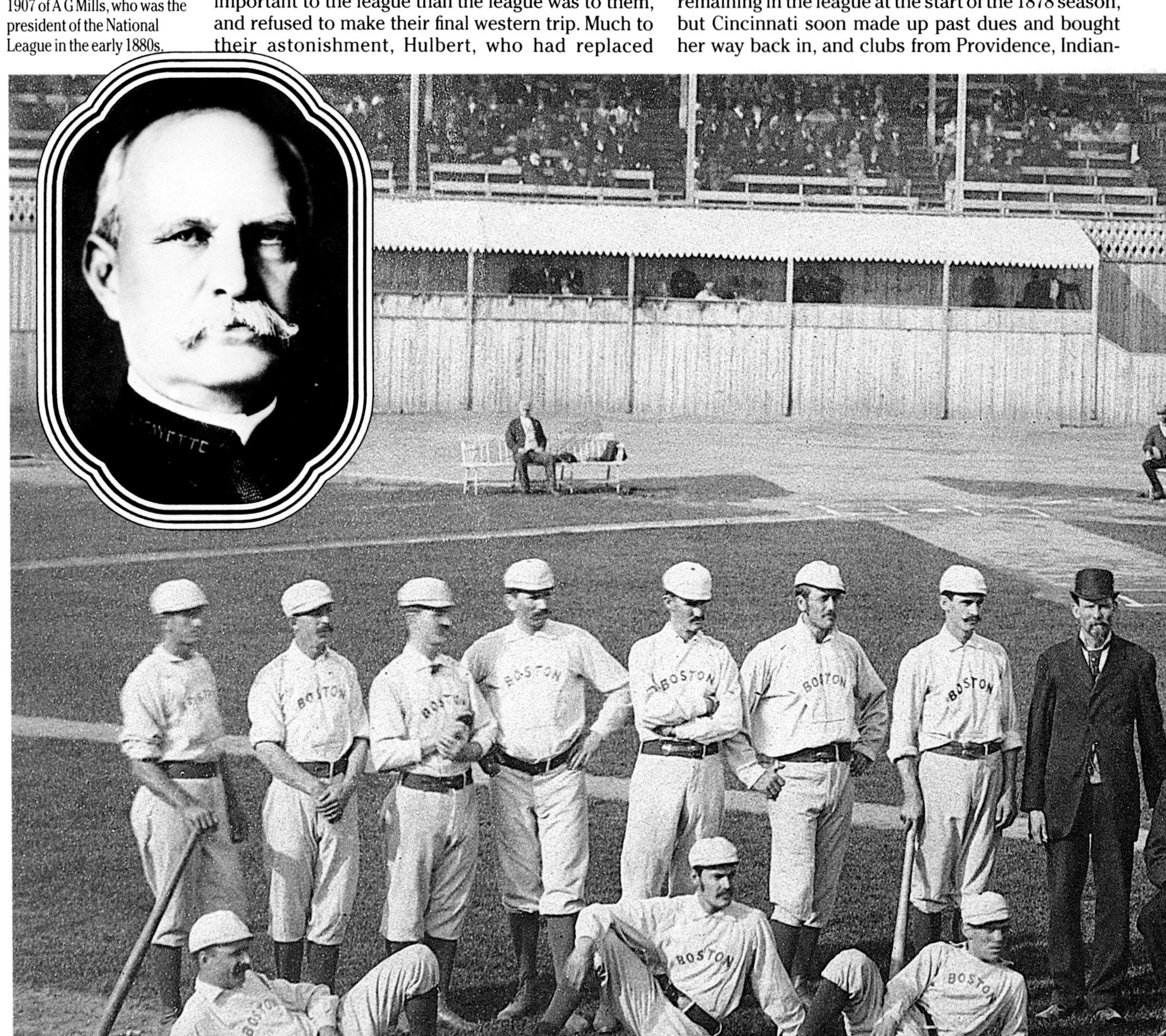

apolis and Milwaukee rounded out the circuit. Because of its swift and firm action against the Louisville gamblers, the league enjoyed a new respect from public and press alike. That year Boston offered season tickets, turnstiles were introduced and the ambiguity surrounding Sunday games was eliminated when the league adopted a rule to expel clubs that violated the Sabbath or failed to expel players who did. Crowds of 6000 fans flocked to see games in Boston and Providence.

The first 25 years tested the courage of the National League's pioneers time and time again. There was a constant shifting of franchises during this period, and many fortunes were made and lost. While Chicago and Boston maintained their uninterrupted presence on the circuit, up until 1900, when the league settled into the same eight franchises it would maintain for the next 53 years, teams from 23 cities came and went, including Providence, Milwaukee, Indianapolis, Buffalo, Cleveland, Troy, Syracuse, Worcester, Detroit, Kansas City, Washington, Baltimore, Brooklyn, Pittsburgh and New York.

The new league also soon found itself involved in costly wars with other organizations. In 1882, the American Association of Base Ball Clubs, also known as the 'Beer-Ball League,' featuring Sunday games, a 25 cent admission, and sale of alcoholic beverages on the grounds, was formed to compete with the National League. Under the farsighted presidency of the National League's President A G Mills, the American Association eventually signed an agreement with the National League, and the two leagues held post-

Below: The players pose for a portrait before a game between Boston (left) and Providence – 1879.

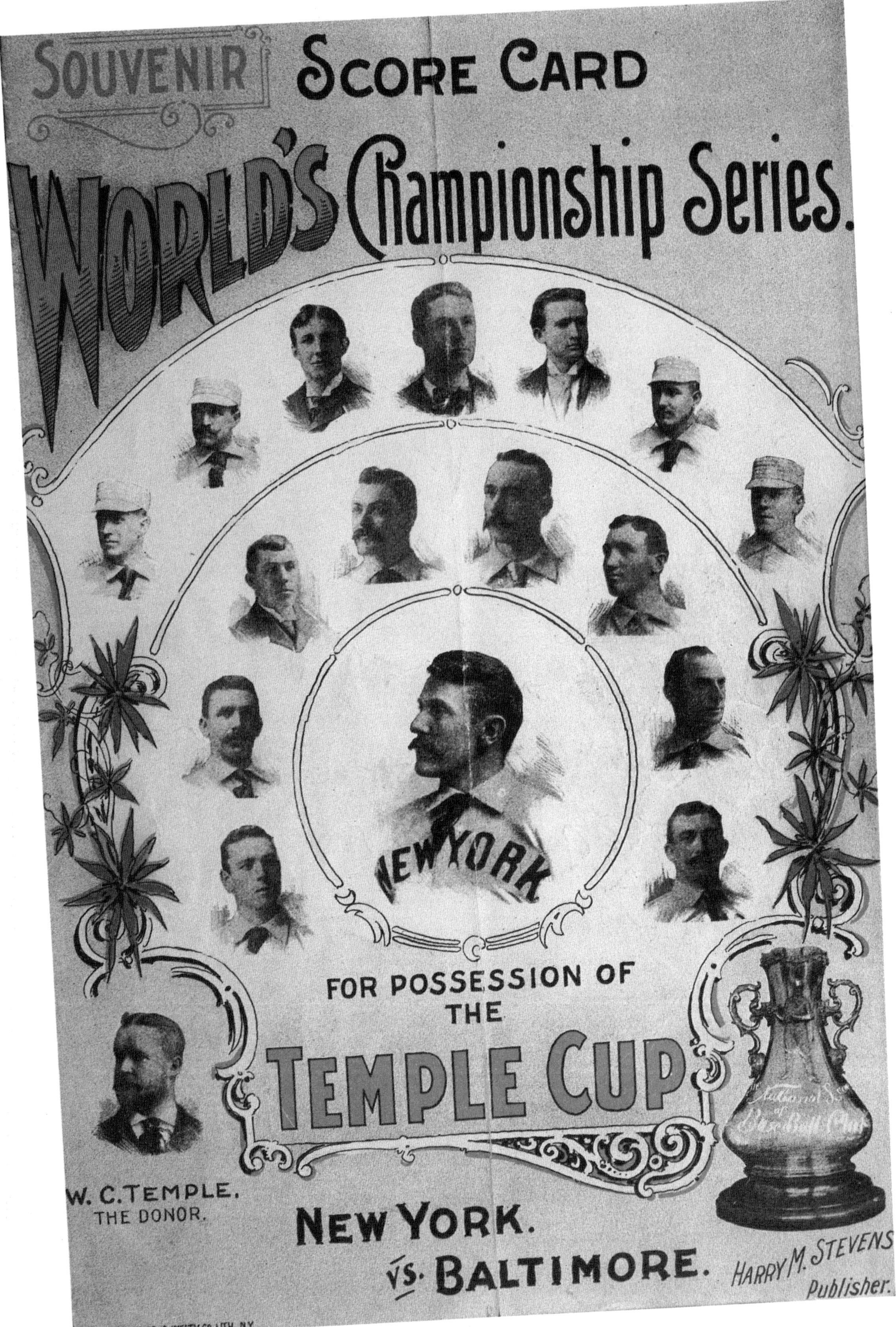
SOUVENIR
SCORE CARD
WORLD'S Championship Series.
NEW YORK
FOR POSSESSION OF
THE
TEMPLE CUP
W. C. TEMPLE.
THE DONOR.
NEW YORK.
VS. BALTIMORE.
HARRY M. STEVENS
Publisher.
THE SPRINGER & WELTY CO. LITH. N.Y.

Opposite: A souvenir scorecard for the championship series between New York and Baltimore in the days of the old Temple Cup.

Left: The Chicago White Stockings ball club of 1888. Pop Anson is third from left, top row.

season World Series which contributed greatly to baseball's popularity.

In 1884, St Louis millionaire Henry V Lucas founded another competitor, the Union Association, but the National League and the American Association raided so many of the Union Association's players that it was reduced to five of its 12 franchises by the end of the year, and folded after a single season.

A more serious threat was mounted in 1890 by the National Brotherhood of Professional Players, a players' benevolent association started in 1885, which responded to owners' plans to grade, classify, reduce and put ceilings on salaries by forming the Players League. An estimated 80 percent of National League players, including most of the headliners and the entire Washington team, left to join the Players League.

The National League responded by rescheduling its games to conflict with the Players League. As a result, attendance slumped badly everywhere, and owners in all three leagues suffered such great losses that major-league baseball nearly ended. But the National League managed to hang on, and by the end of the season the American Association was finished. The Players League, battered and debt-ridden, had no choice but to sue the National League for peace. The National League accepted the Players League's unconditional surrender, and added four American Association teams to its roster, expanding to 12 teams for the remainder of the 19th century. A monopoly again in 1892, National League owners returned with a vengeance to practices even more intolerable than those which had caused the players' rebellion in the first place, cutting club rosters to 13, and salaries by as much as 40 percent.

Baseball didn't really settle into the game it is today until the turn of the century. Before 1887, batters could request a high or a low pitch. After several changes, the distance from pitcher to batter was finally lengthened to the present 60-feet-six-inches in 1893. Pitchers were not permitted to throw overhand

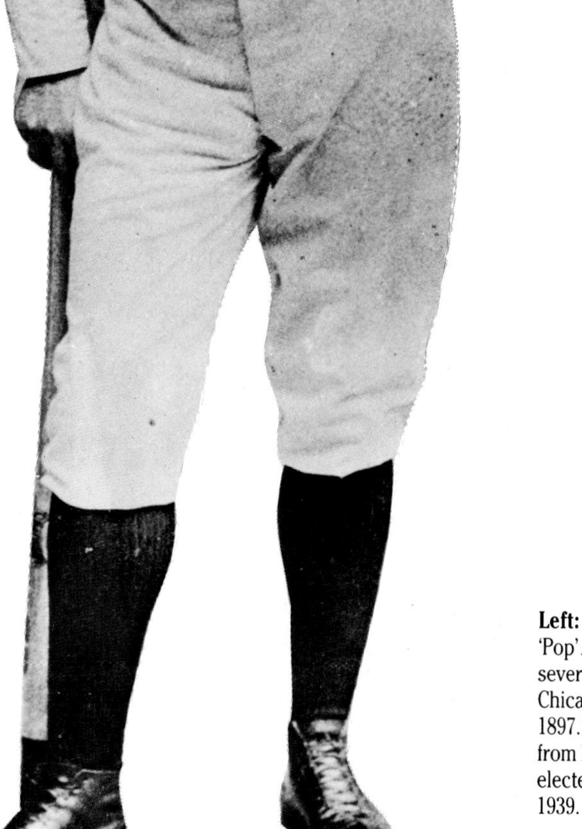

Left: Adrian Constantine 'Pop' Anson, who played several positions for the Chicago team from 1876 to 1897. He was the manager from 1879 to 1898 and was elected to the Hall of Fame in 1939.

until 1883, a date some claim marks the birth of modern baseball, and a staff of umpires with fixed salaries was appointed for the first time in the same year. The nine balls necessary for a batter to walk were reduced to five in 1887, and finally four in 1889. Strikeouts, originally set at five, were reduced to three in 1888, but foul tips did not count as strikes until 1895, and foul balls didn't count as strikes until 1901. In 1903 a foul tip caught after two strikes became an out. Before 1891, substitutions were permitted only in the case of injury or with the other team's permission. Walks were counted as hits the first season, and stolen base statistics credited runners for each base advanced on another player's hit until 1898. The ball itself, of course, was much less lively than it would later become. From 1894 through 1897, first and second place clubs battled for a gaudy trophy known as the Temple Cup.

Changes in regulations made the game more exciting, and it was during the 1880s, a decade of expansion and optimism that saw the economy of America take a dramatic upswing, that National League promoters distilled the formula which was to make baseball a permanent fixture on the American scene. By the mid-1880s, National League clubs were making money. By far the most important ingredient in baseball's success was the new public hero, the baseball star, whose magnetic presence could be counted upon to lure city dwellers to the ball parks.

Primarily a product of keen competition between National League clubs, the baseball hero was also very much the creation of baseball sportswriters. It was this new breed of specialists in American journalism who in the 1880s helped turn major-league baseball into a million-dollar industry. Henry Chadwick long dominated the trade, but it was younger writers who created the breezy, cliché-ridden copy which still characterizes this unique form of American literature.

Chicago and Boston thoroughly dominated the first 11 years of National League life. The Chicago White Stockings took six pennants by 1886, five under the leadership of Adrian Anson, one of the greatest players in baseball history and perhaps the outstanding player in the National League in its first quarter century. Signing with Chicago in 1876, the six-foot-two, two-hundred pound 'Cap' or 'Pop' Anson was a fearsome hitter who batted over .300 for 20 of his 22 seasons with the club, and was as popular as any player until Babe Ruth. Anson lured thousands to games with his genius for showmanship, and was an early adept at vilifying the umpire, a form of ritualized hostility which, to the delight of promoters and writers, flowered in the 1880s, turning umpires into evil black-suited villains who attracted crowds to the park as much as the new baseball heroes.

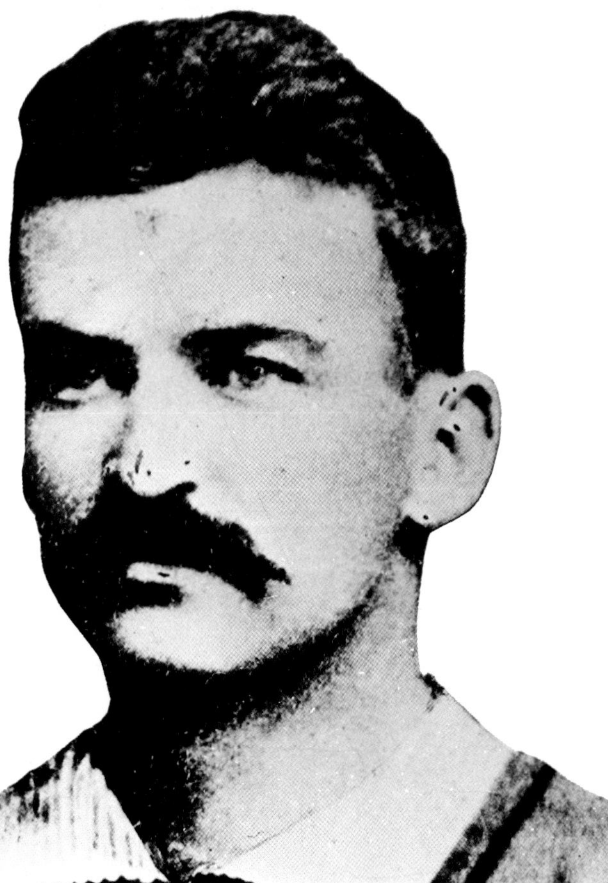

Michael Joseph 'King' Kelly, who broke in with Cincinnati in 1878, then went to Chicago to play from 1880 to 1889. After moving to Boston for three years, he was lured to the Players' League Boston Club, where he was player-manager for two years. In 1892 he returned to the Boston National League club and then switched to New York in 1893 – his final year. He was elected to the Hall of Fame in 1945.

Shortly after the end of his career with Chicago in 1898, Anson entered vaudeville, but at his death in 1922 he was still known as the 'Grand Old Man of Baseball.' His funeral was one of the largest ever accorded an athlete in this country, and he was elected to the Hall of Fame in 1939.

After he was appointed Chicago's playing manager in 1879, Anson's influence on how the game was played became incalculable. The White Stockings won five pennants in his first seven years of management, including three in a row, 1880-1882. Fans of this era thrilled to the deeds of Chicago's pitching ace Larry Corcoran, of third baseman Ed Williamson, who hit an amazing 27 home runs in 1884, of pitcher John Clarkson, catcher Silver Flint, Abner Dalrymple, George Gore, Fred Goldsmith and many others. Cap himself hit five home runs in two consecutive games in 1884, a record that has since been tied but never surpassed. In the 13-year period 1880-1892, Anson's White Stockings never finished lower than fourth place.

Anson was a famous disciplinarian. He instituted a $100 fine for beer drinking on his club and conducted nightly bed checks. Among his many managerial innovations, Anson, who took the White Stockings to Hot Springs, Arkansas in 1885, is generally credited as the first to take a team south for spring training. At a time when baseball strategy was in its infancy, he pioneered the 'scientific' game, drilling his teams in offensive and defensive signals, and experimenting with pitching rotation, alternating fast-baller Larry Corcoran and slow-baller Fred Goldsmith with great effectiveness. He taught his outfielders to back up infielders, sometimes platooned his players, and was among the first, with Mike 'Slide, Kelly, Slide' Kelly, to use the hit-and-run.

Among his heavy hitters and speedy base runners was Fred Pfeffer, who once ran the bases in less than 16 seconds. Billy Sunday, the future evangelist, best at stealing bases in an outstanding 1886 season, and 'King' Kelly captivated crowds with the same flamboyance as their manager. Kelly once won a close game from Boston by cutting from second to home, correctly calculating that the lone umpire used in those days would miss his shortcut.

Not all of Anson's influence on the game was good. His racism left an ugly mark for years to come. In the 1880s, quite a few blacks – at least twenty – played ball with white clubs, despite an 1867 National Association resolution which barred blacks and clubs they played for from membership. The National Association of Professional Base Ball Players, which succeeded the original National Association in 1871, never had a written rule, but an ironclad 'gentlemen's agreement' barred blacks and black clubs. The force

of this unwritten law carried over into the National League. Nevertheless, the color line did not have universal support in the majors. Moses Fleetwood Walker and his brother William Welday Walker, for instance, both played with Toledo in the American Association, which was a major league at the time. Fleetwood Walker later played for a Newark team which included George Stovey, whom some consider the greatest black pitcher of all time.

In 1883, when the White Stockings played an exhibition game against Toledo, Anson saw Fleetwood Walker on the diamond and yelled with characteristic tact, 'Get that nigger off the field!' Anson swallowed his refusal not to play when he was informed that his team would forfeit the gate, but five years later he once again refused to play against a Newark club which included George Stovey. Stovey walked off and refused to play the White Stockings.

In 1887, at a time when it looked like blacks would slowly but surely enter white organized baseball's structure, John Montgomery Ward decided to bring Stovey up to pitch for the Giants, an act that would have broken the color barrier long before Jackie Robinson was born. Anson got wind of his plan, and mustered industry pressure to force Ward to change his mind, using all his tremendous popularity and prestige in baseball circles. Bellowing 'There's a law against that,' Anson succeeded in setting a precedent, and can claim credit for almost singlehandedly excluding the black man from major-league baseball until 1947.

Under baseball pioneer Harry Wright, Boston took the pennant in 1877 and again in 1878. Boston's winning lineup in those years included such outstanding players as Jim O'Rourke, pitcher Tom Bond – who won 40 games in 1877 and in 1878 – George Wright, Jim Morrill and Jim White, top batter of 1877. Boston came back to end Chicago's three-year pennant streak by taking the flag again in 1883.

Providence, which had last taken a pennant in 1879, captured the flag again in 1884, although Anson's White Stockings returned to lead the league in 1885 and 1886. Providence's 1884 win was carried by the incredible pitching of Charles 'Old Hoss' Radbourne, who won 60 of the 75 games he pitched that year, losing 12, for a 1.38 ERA. That season Radbourne had been suspended early on by manager F C Bancroft. Both were difficult men. When Radbourne's services were required, he announced he would pitch every game and Providence would win the flag, but only if

Above: John Montgomery 'Monte' Ward when he was the captain of the New York club. Elected to the Hall of Fame in 1964, he also played for Providence and Brooklyn.
Above left: William Henry 'Harry' Wright of the Boston club, elected to the Hall of Fame in 1953. Oddly enough, he was born in Sheffield, England.
Inset: Charles Gardner 'Old Hoss' Radbourn when he played for the Boston Beaneaters (1886-1889). He also played for Providence, Buffalo, Cincinnati and the Boston Players' League team, and was elected to the Hall of Fame in 1939.

Above: A team portrait of the 1882 Detroit Wolverines.
Far right: Amos Wilson Rusie – 'The Hoosier Thunderbolt' – a pitcher who started with Indianapolis in 1889, then went to New York from 1890 to 1898, finishing his career with Cincinnati in 1901. His lifetime record of 243-160, his earned run average of 3.07 and his 1957 strikeouts earned him a place in the Hall of Fame in 1977.

the directors lifted his suspension and agreed to release him at the end of the season. They did.

Radbourne proceeded to pitch in all but two of his team's last 37 games. From 23 July to 7 August he pitched in nine consecutive games, winning seven and tying one. He took a day off to play right field, then pitched and won six consecutive games. He took off another day to play shortstop, and beginning on 21 August pitched in the next 20 games, winning ten before losing to Buffalo on 9 September, the defeat ending a 16-game winning streak for Radbourne and a 20-game winning streak for his team. Providence finished ten games ahead of second-place Boston, and 'Lord' Radbourne, whose Hall of Fame plaque calls him the 'greatest of the 19th century pitchers,' easily beat the New York Metropolitans in the first official World Series.

The Detroit Wolverines, spearheaded by catcher Charles Bennett and Captain Ned Hanlon, took the pennant in 1887, terrorizing the league with their hitting. Detroit's team batting average for 1887 was .343. The lineup featured Johnny Rowe, Charley Getzein and Charley Ganzel – the 'pretzel battery' – and Dan Brouthers, one of the greatest batters of all times. Brouthers batted over .300 fourteen times, playing professional ball until until he was 48. In the 1887 season both Brouthers and teammate Sam Thompson hit over .400 (in those days a base on balls was credited as a hit), and Brouthers managed at least one base or its equivalent in 107 out of his 122 games.

The New York Giants, who returned to the league with Philadelphia in 1883, took flags in 1888 and 1889 under stovepipe-hatted Jim Mutrie. His teams featured pitcher Jim Keefe, who won 19 in a row, outstanding catcher Buck Ewing, Roger Connor and hurler Micky Welch. Welch, who once fanned the first nine men he faced in a game, credited his pitching prowess to beer: 'Pure elixir of malt and hops/Beats all the drugs and all the drops.'

1889 saw the closest race yet in the National League's 14-year history. The Giants drew 201,662 fans and earned $45,000 profit for their owners, finally taking the pennant and going on to beat Brooklyn in the World Series, 6-3. Brooklyn switched from the American Association to the National League in 1890, and also took the pennant that year.

Hard drinking was a continuing feature of professional baseball, and ruined several prominent careers. Ed Delahanty, who hit .400 in 1884 and .408 in 1889 and had a lifetime average of .346, was one of the best hitters and hardest drinkers in the National League's early history. He had a .376 average in 1902,

and was playing for the American League's Washington club in 1903 with a .333 average in June when he was suspended for drunkenness in Detroit. On the way home to Washington he was put off the train after a drunken brawl. Delahanty tried to reboard, fell into the river near Fort Erie, Ontario, and was swept over Niagara Falls. His broken body was found a week later.

Two outstanding teams whose exploits are now legendary dominated the National League during the 1890s. The Boston Beaneaters took five pennants, 1891-1893 and 1897-1898, relying on outstanding players for their success, while the 'scientific' style of playing perfected by the Baltimore Orioles under manager Ned Hanlon gave his club three pennants, 1894-1896 (they placed second the next two years), and set the style that was to predominate in the National League until the introduction of the lively ball altered baseball's basic offensive concepts.

The Boston Beaneaters, a strong team during most of the National League's first 25 years, flowered under manager Frank Selee in the 1890s. Selee paid little attention to strategy during the game, but had a remarkable knack for spotting and nurturing talent, his eye proving itself again after he left Boston, when he formed the Chicago team which dominated the National League from 1906 to 1910.

In 1890, Selee brought Charles 'Kid' Nichols up to Boston from the Western League. Nichols, who featured an excellent fastball thrown with good control, proceeded to pitch a decade of games unequalled since pitchers began throwing overhand. From 1890 to 1899 Nichol's win totals were 27, 30, 35, 33, 32, 30, 30, 30, 29, and 21. For the first nine years, he averaged over 30 wins a season. He never fell below

Above: The pennant-winning New York Giants of 1889. Manager James J 'Truthful Jim' Mutrie is in civilian clothes at center.

Far left: Charles Augustus 'Kid' Nichols, the star pitcher of the Boston Beaneaters from 1890 to 1901. He finished his career with Philadelphia in 1906. A Hall of Famer (elected in 1949), he had a lifetime record of 360-202 and an earned run average of 2.94.

Far right: William Henry 'Wee Willie' Keeler at the close of his career when he was with the New York Giants. He also played with Baltimore and Brooklyn in the National League and New York in the American. His phenomenal lifetime batting average of .345 and the fact that he struck out only 36 times in his 19-year career (1892-1910) made him a Hall of Famer in 1939.

20 wins for all ten years, during which he pitched as many as 50 complete games a season, and failed to finish only 22 games. Nichols, elected to the Hall of Fame in 1949, ended his career with 360 wins, the seventh best of all time.

Supporting Nichols on those Boston teams were sluggers Bobby Lowe and Hugh Duffy, pitcher Vic Willis, infielders Fred Tenney and Jimmy Collins, and superstars John Clarkson and 'King' Kelly, both purchased from Chicago for an astounding $10,000 each. Bobby Lowe became the first to set the as yet unsurpassed record of hitting four home runs in a single nine-inning game. Showered with silver coins by his fans, Lowe managed a single his last time at bat. Hugh Duffy also established an all-time record, hitting .438 – the highest ever under modern rules – in 1894. The diminutive Duffy hit over .300 in each of his first ten full seasons in the majors. Of his 236 hits in 1894, 18 were home runs, 15 were triples, and 51 were doubles.

Baltimore finished 12th in the first half of the expanded National League's 1892 split season, but under manager Hanlon, who joined the club on 9 May 1892, the Orioles became one of the greatest collections of ball players ever assembled. Hanlon's lineup included six future Hall of Famers: Dan Brouthers, John J McGraw, Hughey Jennings, Wilbert Robinson, Joe Kelley and 'Wee Willie' Keeler, whose famous prescription for batting success was, 'Keep your eye clear and hit 'em where they ain't.'

The Orioles moved from ten games under .500 (60-70) in 1893 to 50 games over .500 (89-39) in 1894, the first of their pennant years. That season the team batted .343, led the league in fielding and stole 343 bases. Brouthers hit .347, McGraw .340 and the star outfield of Brodie, Keeler and Kelley hit .366, .371 and .393! Even without depth in the pitching staff, such batting talent coupled with Hanlon's strategic skill carried the day. When Hanlon took his methods and a few key players to Brooklyn in 1899, the Brooklyn club took pennants in 1899 and 1900.

Before the 1894 season, Hanlon took his Orioles south for spring training, then an unusual move. At a time when the game consisted entirely of individual effort, Hanlon taught his players to back up bases and each other, and to change position to take cutoff throws, He perfected the hit-and-run play, pioneered by Cap Anson and King Kelly, and used it with devastating effect against the Giants in 1894. His Oriole catchers were also the first to feint throws to trap base runners and to become involved in cutoff plays. What became known as 'inside baseball' was born here, the team working together as a unit. Giant manager John Montgomery Ward exclaimed as they devastated his team, 'That's not baseball they're playing.'

Below: Enthusiastic baseball fans of Boston accompanied their 1897 National League Champions to Baltimore for the Temple Cup Series with the Orioles. The scene is the hotel headquarters for the Boston club. This series, which Baltimore won, four games to one, was the last of the Temple Cup Competitions.

True to the spirit of the age, the Orioles were not cowed by the rules of good sportsmanship. An Oriole base runner would happily skip a base if the umpire turned his back, and an opposing base runner might find third baseman McGraw holding on to his belt long enough to upset his dash for home. Pete Browning once scored by unfastening his belt and leaving it in McGraw's hand. Extra balls hidden by Orioles in the tall outfield grass helped prevent extra bases when a ball was hit beyond the outfielders, and Oriole men planted in the stands substituted mushy balls for balls hit foul by the opposing side. Hanlon instructed his groundskeeper to slope the infield to facilitate bunts.

Oriole basemen didn't hesitate to mutilate opposing base runners. Pittsburgh's great shortstop Honus Wagner recalled how the Orioles limited what should have been a home run to a triple when the first baseman gave him the hip as he rounded the base; the second baseman 'almost killed me, Jennings tripped me at shortstop, and when I got around to third McGraw was waiting for me with a shotgun.'

The Orioles and their fans were no kinder to umpires. According to John A Heydler, an umpire who later became president of the National League, 'They were mean, vicious, ready at any time to maim a rival player or umpire . . . they broke the spirits of some very fine men. I've seen umpires bathe their feet after

McGraw and others spiked them through their shoes . . . Other clubs patterned after them, and I feel the lot of the umpire was never worse than in the years when the Orioles were flying high.'

Major-league baseball was not an honorable sport. Winning was important, not how you played the game. Connie Mack, who caught for Pittsburgh in the 1890s, used to mimic the sound of a foul tip with his hands. Sometimes he touched the bat as the batter began his swing, a practice he abandoned when one hitter went for his hand instead of the ball and smashed his fingers.

National League owners played just as rough, especially during the last decade of the century. The country was in a continuing business depression in the 1890s, and clubs such as Chicago, Boston and New York, which had netted annual profits of nearly $100,000 from 1885-1889, never got near those figures. Total National League losses for 1890 were estimated at half a million. In 1898, Boston grossed $50,000, but only five of the league's 12 clubs showed a profit.

Left: Jesse Cale 'The Crab' Burkett, whose lifetime batting average was .340 over his 16 years of playing for New York, Cleveland and St Louis in the National League and St Louis and Boston in the American. He was elected to the Hall of Fame in 1946.

Far left: Cornelius Alexander 'The Tall Tactician' McGillicuddy – better known as Connie Mack – when he played for Pittsburgh from 1891 to 1896. Previously he had been with Washington in the National League and Buffalo in the Players' League. But it was not for his playing (lifetime batting average .247) that he was best known. This former catcher, who was elected to the Hall of Fame in 1937, spent three years as the Pittsburgh manager (1894-1896), then became the manager of the Philadelphia American League club until 1950 – a total managing tenure of 53 years. During that time he won nine pennants and five World Series.

In crushing the American Association, the National League had ended the colorful World Series. The selfish actions of the owners, who now styled themselves 'magnates,' after the captains of industry of the era, alienated fans. Magnate fought magnate, magnates fought players, players fought umpires and league fought league, spewing a wearisome train of lawsuits and slander which taxed the public's patience. Attendance declined.

The most enduring scar etched by the magnates was the so-called 'syndicate' approach to baseball organization. New York Giant owner Andrew Freedman advocated turning the league into a trust, pooling players, franchises and profits under a single organization, shifting players and franchises according to profit opportunities. 'Freedmanism' did not succeed, but it caused serious infighting among the league's clubs, with crippling effects. Baseball pioneer Al Spalding remarked in 1911 that along with gambling and drunkenness, the owners of this era were among the three all-time evils faced by major-league baseball.

It was a National League torn by internal power struggles that refused to recognize the inevitable arrival of a second major league, and chose in 1901 not even to discuss Eastern franchises for Ban Johnson's well-run American League. League war followed. Johnson had little trouble raiding National League players dissatisfied with greedy owners and a league salary ceiling of $2400. In 1901, 111 of the American League's 182 players came directly from the National League. Among the stars who jumped to the American League and never came back were Wee Willie Keeler, Cy Young, Sam Crawford, Jimmy Collins, Elmer Flick, Ed Delahanty, Nap Lajoie and Jesse Burkett of the St Louis Cardinals, who took the National League batting title in 1901 with a .376 average.

When American League attendance climbed to 2,200,000 in 1902, the National League attendance dropped to 1,683,000 and the National League decided to make peace. Early in 1903 the National Agreement finally gave the Americans major league status, reallocated territorial rights for the 16 major franchises and bound both leagues to a common system of schedules, player contracts and playing regulations (with significant but not major differences).

A National Commission was formed to oversee major league baseball, consisting of the presidents of the two leagues, Harry C Pulliam and Ban Johnson; commissioner-at-large August Herrmann of Cincinnati (reelected each year) and a non-voting secretary. American baseball was to find peace and prosperity for 18 years under the National Commission.

In 1903, with the rules and dimensions of baseball the same as they are today, the National League's eight franchises fixed until 1953, the threat of Freedmanism vanquished, the war with the American League over, and the first Modern World Series, the game entered an era of returning prosperity that marks the beginning of baseball's modern age.

Honus Wagner at bat. John Peter Wagner, 'The Flying Dutchman', broke in at Louisville in 1897 and played for Pittsburgh from 1900 to 1917. He was an outstanding shortstop with a .328 lifetime batting average. Wagner was elected to the Hall of Fame in 1936.

CHAPTER TWO

The Modern Game

Oh, it's great to be young and a Giant.

Larry Doyle, second baseman for McGraw's Giants

Opposite left: 'The Flying Dutchman' Honus Wagner taking his swings.
Opposite right: Honus Wagner, the consummate shortstop.
Below: Roderick John Wallace, also known as 'Bobby' or 'Rhody,' was another outstanding shortstop. During his 25-year career (1894-1918) he batted .268 while striking out a mere 79 times – 39 of them in his first three years. Wallace, who was elected to the Hall of Fame in 1953, played with Cleveland and St Louis in the National League and St Louis in the American League.

The war with the American League brought many changes in club rosters, forcing a shift in the National League's balance of power away from the clubs that had dominated the 1890s, to three new centers and a new breed of owners and managers who wrote history their own way. Beginning in 1901, the Pittsburgh Pirates, the New York Giants and the Chicago Cubs were to dominate the National League for the next two decades.

The Cardinals, led by Jesse Burkett and Bobby 'Mr Shortstop' Wallace – both of whom jumped to the American league after the 1901 season – topped the league in attendance in 1901, with almost 380,000 paid admissions. By 1906, Wallace, then with the St Louis Browns, was baseball's highest salaried player at $6000 a year. But the best the Cardinals could do in 1901 was fourth, and it was the Pittsburgh Pirates who took the pennant, as they were to do in 1902 and 1903.

Among Pittsburgh's most valuable players during the opening years of the century were pitcher Deacon Phillippe, third baseman Tommy Leach, playing manager Fred Clarke and of course shortstop Honus Wagner. All were acquired as a unit from Louisville after that club left the league in 1899.

John Peter 'Honus' Wagner, indisputably one of the greatest players of all time, was the good-natured, folksy son of a Pennsylvania coal-mining family of German descent. An extraordinarily versatile player, in the 1901 season, before he settled in to set the standard for shortstop, he played 24 games at third and 54 in the outfield, as well as 61 at shortstop. In later years he even pitched on occasion. Big and awkward-looking, he led the National League in stolen bases five times, and his career total of 772 places him fifth in major-league history. His unorthodox, wide-open batting stance earned him a lifetime average of .329 and a league record for most hits (including four consecutive batting titles) that stood until Stan Musial broke it in 1962. But Honus, who was satisfied when he became a $10,000-a-year-man and never asked for more, was also capable of playing a strong game according to the ruthless standards of the day. In the 1909 World Series – or so legend has it – Ty Cobb, preparing to steal, yelled to Wagner, 'Get ready, Krauthead, I'm coming down.' 'I'll be waiting,' Wagner replied, and tagged Cobb so hard with the ball that he split his lip.

In 1902 Pittsburgh finished 27½ games ahead of second-place Brooklyn, the largest margin by a

Above: Joe McGinnity (left) talks with John McGraw, his manager on the New York Giants. 'Iron Man' McGinnity pitched for Baltimore and Brooklyn before joining the Giants in 1902. At the end of his career in 1908, he had won 247 games with an ERA of 2.64. He was elected to the Hall of Fame in 1946. 'Little Napoleon' McGraw played baseball for 16 years, but it was as a manager that he was elected to the Hall of Fame in 1937. From 1903 to 1932 he was manager of the New York Giants.
Right: McGinnity (left), McGraw (center) and Christy Mathewson. Christopher 'Big Six' Mathewson pitched for the Giants for 17 years (1900-1916). He was elected to the Hall of Fame in 1936 for his 373-188 record and his 2.13 lifetime ERA.

winner in major league history. That year Pittsburgh's Ginger Beaumont led the league in hitting with .357, while Wagner led in stolen bases, runs scored, runs batted in, doubles and slugging average. Tommy Leach was league home run champion with a modest six homers, pitcher Jack Chesbro won 28 games and pitchers Phillippe and Tannehill each won 20. The Pittsburgh pitching staff produced an incredible 130 complete games in 141 starts, winning 103 and losing only 36. Despite the loss of Chesbro, Leach, Tannehill and Conroy to the American League at the end of the season, the club managed to win again in 1903, with Wagner hitting .355 to lead the league and pitchers Phillippe and Sam Leever combining to win 49 games. The Boston Pilgrims took the first American League/National League World Series from the Pirates, 5-3.

A new force had slowly been gathering strength in the National League, and the 1904 and 1905 pennants went to the New York Giants. Under fiery John McGraw, this club was to total ten flags between 1904 and 1924. In 31 years of managing, McGraw's teams added 11 second places to his ten flags, and finished in the first division 27 times. No manager before or since has matched his impact on the game.

In practice, McGraw exercised extremely close

control over his men. Players did almost nothing without his guidance – 'The Little Napoleon' called pitches and gave signals to his batters on every pitch. Tyrannical, brilliant, innovative, 'Muggsy' (a nickname he hated) flamboyantly cursed fans, defied league presidents and was particularly famous for his battles with umpires. As a star player for the great Orioles of the 1890s, McGraw once succeeded in inciting a lynch mob to wait for an umpire after a game with a rope. The umpire wisely waited for the mob to disperse before he left the park. But even those who hated McGraw never questioned his superiority as a manager, and many great players of the era did not consider their careers complete until they had played for him. Second baseman Larry Doyle expressed it best: 'Oh, its great to be young and a Giant.'

In 1902, when McGraw took over the Giants for owner John T Brush, he knew he could not escape the cellar. The Giants finished at the bottom of the league in 1902, as they had in 1900. But McGraw, who had a three-year contract, began drilling his team in the classic deadball style, adding five key men in 1903, and by his first pennant in 1904, he had created the nucleus of a franchise which was to remain the most profitable in the league and in all of major league baseball until the great Yankees teams of the 1920s.

Central to his success was the superb pitching of 'Iron Man' Joe McGinnity and Christy Mathewson. McGinnity topped the 30 mark in 1903 and 1904, but it was Christy Mathewson, acquired by the Giants two years earlier in a trade with Cincinnati for famous pitching great Amos Rusie, one of the titans of the 1890s, who was to supply the key to Giant success until his retirement in 1915.

Even though Mathewson had won 20 games the preceeding season, when McGraw took over stewardship of the Giants in 1902, outgoing manager Horace Fogel was trying to turn him into a first baseman. McGraw, recalling the pitching weakness of his old Oriole clubs and anxious to create a strong pitching staff, put Mathewson back on the mound. Despite the disparities in their personalities and backgrounds, Mathewson and McGraw were to become lifelong friends, and always roomed together on the road.

At a time when most players came from poverty-ridden childhoods, Mathewson, son of a gentleman farmer and a wealthy mother, educated at Keystone Academy and Bucknell (where he was class president and member of the glee club and literary society), supplied a new standard for the baseball idol. Tall, good-looking and literate, a non-drinker who seldom smoked and opposed Sunday baseball (a continuing controversy), he was also a fierce competitor, with uncanny control over the fastball, breaking curve and fadeaway (or screwball), a pitch he pioneered. Both as a player with 373 lifetime wins and as a sportsman he was admired by his peers, and this handsome Adonis was the first baseball player to be held up as an example to young boys. His reputation was so spotless, in fact, that his wife sometimes went out of her way to remind the public that he could swear and had not yet sprouted wings.

Christy Mathewson demonstrates his windup. He became the manager of the Cincinnati club in 1916, staying on until 1918. Unfortunately, his managerial record (.482) did not compare to his pitching record.

Beginning in 1903, with 30 wins, Mathewson won 30 or more games for three straight years – a feat matched by only four other pitchers in the history of the game – and 20 or more for 12 consecutive years. In one stretch of five years he allowed less than 2 earned runs per game each season, and he five times led the league in wins, ERA's, and strikeouts. In 1904, he added 33 wins to McGinnity's 35 as the Giants swept to victory 13 games ahead of the second-place Chicago Cubs, setting a new major-league record of 106 wins. McGraw's jackrabbits also stole a total of 283 bases that year.

Due to a long-standing feud with American League President Johnson, Brush and McGraw refused to meet the American League winner in a 1904 World Series, claiming, 'There is nothing in the constitution or the playing rules of the National League which requires the victorious club to submit its championship honors to a contest with a victorious club in a minor league.' Hoping to prevent further interruptions in the popular postseason playoffs, the National Commission moved over the winter to institutionalize the world championship, and the World Series rapidly captured public interest to become the capstone of the baseball season it remains today.

Far right: Roger Philip 'The Duke of Tralee' Bresnahan, the Hall of Fame (elected in 1945) catcher. His career spanned 17 years, from 1897 to 1915, and he played for Washington, Chicago, New York and St Louis in the National League and Baltimore in the American League. He also managed the Cardinals from 1909 to 1912, but finished in the first division only once – coming in fourth in 1915.
Below: Joe McGinnity warms up.

Mathewson rose to national stardom in the 1905 World Series when he pitched three shutouts against the Philadelphia Athletics (McGinnity pitched one, too) as the Giants took the Series after winning a hard-fought pennant from Pittsburgh. Mathewson won 31 games that season and lost only eight, with a 1.27 ERA. He was to pitch even greater seasons before moving on to manage Cincinnati and become president of the Boston Braves, but lungs weakened by poison gas in World War I interrupted his postwar career time and time again, and he died of tuberculosis in 1925 at the age of 45.

Spurred on by a pitching staff that was exceptional even in an era dominated by tight pitching, the Chicago Cubs took four pennants between 1906 and 1910, coming in second with 104 games in 1909. They set a National League record with an average of 106 wins a season for these five years, and a still-standing major-league record of 116 wins in 1906.

Heading the staff of playing manager Frank Chance's pitching aces was Mordecai 'Three Finger' Brown, who with Mathewson was the outstanding National League pitcher of the century's first decade. A childhood accident with farm machinery had cost Brown half his right index finger and mangled two others, but enabled him to throw a baffling, unnaturally sharp breaking ball. Pitching for the Cubs in 1906, Brown was 26-6, with a 1.04 ERA. Jack Pfeister was 20-8, Ed Reulbach 19-4 and Carl Lundgren 17-6, for a team ERA of 1.76. Chicago's team batting average that year was .262, topping a league with five teams batting under .241. Despite the brutal pitching, Pittsburgh's Honus Wagner hit .339 to take his fourth league batting championship.

The next year, Chicago, winning 107 games, finished 17 games ahead of second-place Pittsburgh. Wagner again took the National League batting championship with a .350 average, the Pirates leading the league with a .254 team average, 11 points above the league average. But it was still a pitcher's game. Aided by an outstanding infield and continued excellent pitching by Brown, Orval Overall, and Reulbach, Chicago recorded a team ERA of 1.73, the lowest in National League history. On 18 May, National League President Pulliam announced that the league was finally out of debt after seven years in the red.

The Chicago club of this dynasty featured the famous infield of Tinker, Evers and Chance, immortalized by columnist Franklin P Adams in a verse which first appeared in a July 1910 edition of the *New York Mail.* Third baseman Harry Steinfeldt, who hit .327 and led the league with 83 RBI's in 1906, should also be mentioned in this memorable infield, which included playing manager Frank Chance on first, Johnny Evers on second and Joe Tinker at shortstop. While the legendary trio was highly efficient, by all accounts they were far from being the era's best infield or its most adept practitioners of the double play. This defensive combination, in fact, only became a familiar play a decade later when the introduction of the lively ball made for more sharply hit balls and faster fielding. More than anything else, the enduring legendary status of this trio illustrates the power of the pen in an age when the game's only medium was the newspaper, and sportswriters could make or break a reputation.

The Cubs took their third straight flag in 1908, but only after a hard-fought battle with the Giants and Pittsburgh that ended in one of baseball's most controversial moments. On 23 September 1908, the Cubs met the Giants at the Polo Grounds for a game which

Above: Johnny Evers (left), the second baseman, and Joe Tinker, the shortstop, of the Chicago Cubs' famous double play combination – Tinker to Evers to (Frank) Chance. Evers – 'The Trojan,' 'The Cat' – played for Chicago for 11 of his 18 years, finishing with a .334 career average. He also managed both Chicago teams. Joseph Bert Tinker's career extended from 1902 to 1916, beginning and ending with the Cubs. Both were elected to the Hall of Fame in 1946.

Far left: Mordecai Peter Centenniel Brown, also known as 'Three Finger' Brown and 'Miner,' began his pitching career with St Louis in 1903. The next year he went to the Cubs, where he stayed until 1912. He then went to Cincinnati, Brooklyn and Chicago of the Federal League, and returned to the Cubs in 1916 – his last year. He was elected to the Hall of Fame in 1949 because of his 239-130 record and his 2.06 ERA.

Above: The Polo Grounds at Coogan's Bluff in New York in 1905.
Right: Frank Chance, the first baseman in Chicago's Tinker to Evers to Chance double play combination. Frank Leroy Chance – 'Husk' or 'The Peerless Leader' – joined the Cubs as an outfielder/catcher in 1898, but by 1903 he was their regular first baseman, and stayed there until 1913, when he joined the Yankees for his last two seasons. From 1905 to 1914, he was the player-manager of his club, winning four pennants and two World Series with the Cubs. He was inducted into the Hall of Fame in 1946 – the same year that his two teammates made it.

could have decided the pennant. With two men out and the score tied 1-1 at the bottom of the ninth, the Giants got men on first and third. Giant shortstop Al Bridwell hit a single to center, and the man on third came home for the winning run. Technically, the man on first, 19-year-old Fred Merkle, should have tagged second before heading for the clubhouse, but he didn't. This was common practice at the time, and Merkle did nothing that any other player wouldn't have done. However, Cub second baseman Johnny Evers got the ball (or *a* ball) and touched second, turning Bridwell's hit into a forceout at second.

That was how umpire Hank O'Day called it. That meant that the run Bridwell hit in was nullified, and the game was still tied and should go into extra innings. But jubilant Giant fans were already swarming the field, certain their team had won, and with darkness descending, umpire O'Day called the game and declared it a tie.

League President Pulliam upheld the umpire's ruling, and the Giants and the Cubs finished the season with identical records. Despite the protests of both clubs, a playoff was scheduled. Three Finger Brown took the game 4-2 from Christy Mathewson, who otherwise had his greatest season with 37 wins and a 1.43 ERA, and the Cubs went on to take the Series from Detroit. Fred Merkle, although stoutly defended by McGraw, lived out the remainder of a fine 16-year career in the majors under a cloud, forever known as 'Bonehead,' hounded by a press which chose to hold him personally responsible for performing according to common practice. President Pulliam's suicide less than a year later was motivated

in part, it was believed, by the criticism he received for upholding the umpires.

1908 marked the high point of the pitchers' dominance, with the hurlers holding the batters to a .239 average, still the lowest in National League history. Honus Wagner, however, managed to take another batting title, hitting .354, and the next year helped his club win 110 games and the pennant to celebrate owner Barney Dreyfuss's new triple-decked steel ballpark, Forbes Field, with a capacity of 25,000. Wagner hit .333 in the World Series, which the Pirates took from the Tigers in seven games.

The Cubs returned to the winner's circle in 1910, 13 games ahead of the Giants, with essentially the same team that had been successful in 1906. Batting averages rose by 12 points over the preceeding year and the hit-and-run play began to replace the sacrifice bunt as a somewhat livelier cork-center baseball patented by A J Reach became available for major-league play. 1910 also saw President Taft toss out the first baseball at the Washington season opener, beginning a practice that developed into a tradition, and of course it was in July of 1910 that Franklin P Adams wrote:

These are the saddest of possible words
– Tinker to Evers to Chance.
Trio of Bear Cubs and fleeter than birds
– Tinker to Evers to Chance.
Thoughtlessly pricking our gonfalon bubble,
Making a Giant hit into a double,
Words that are weighty with nothing but trouble –
– Tinker to Evers to Chance.

Hank O'Day was the Cincinnati manager in 1912 and 1914. Primarily a pitcher, O'Day began his career with Toledo of the American Association in 1884. The next year he was with Pittsburgh of the American Association, then went to Washington of the National League for four years, finishing his career in 1890 pitching for New York.

But McGraw's Giants came back to dominate the league for three years, taking the pennant in 1911, 1912 and 1913. During those years Mathewson's wins totaled 26, 23 and 25; and lefthander Rube Marquard, known as the '$11,000 lemon' after his purchase from Indianapolis in 1908 until he hit his stride, took 24, 26 and 23, including 19 consecutive games in 1912. In the course of taking the 1911 pennant, the Giants stole 347 bases, still the major-league record.

The Giant lineup of those years was generally set with Fred Merkle, Larry Doyle, Art Fletcher and Buck Herzog in the infield; Chief Meyers behind the plate and Red Murray, Fred Snodgrass, Josh Devore and George Burns in the outfield. The team was drilled to perfection in McGraw's system, receptive to his signalled commands. Often a player was bullied by McGraw until he shaped out up responded automatically to a given situation. The way the Giants fired the ball around the bases when they were warming up let the opposition know that McGraw and his team were all business on the ball field.

1911 saw more effects of the cork-center ball, with the Cub's Frank 'Wildfire' Schulte hitting 21 homers to break the previous major-league record of 16. Chief Meyers hit .332 (he hit .358 in 1912, the league record for a catcher) as the National League batting average climbed to .260.

Mathewson, Three Finger Brown, and Brooklyn's Nap Rucker continued to be the league's top pitchers, but only Mathewson had an ERA of less than 2.00 (1.99). The real news in pitching that year came from the Phillies' Grover Cleveland Alexander, who set a still-standing rookie record of 28 wins, 7 shutouts and 227 strikeouts. Alexander was destined to become one of the greatest pitchers of all time, matching Christy Mathewson's National League record win total of 373 games.

Below: Rube Marquard warms up. Richard William Marquard pitched for New York from 1908 to 1915, then went to Brooklyn until 1920, spent 1921 with Cincinnati and finished his career with Boston, retiring in 1925 from the Braves. He was elected to the Hall of Fame in 1971.

1912 featured the incredible year of Chicago's third baseman Heinie Zimmerman. He led the league with 207 hits, including 14 home runs and 42 doubles, for a batting average of .372, but missed the Chalmers Award, that era's equivalent of the Most Valuable Player Award, a Chalmers automobile bestowed by the Chalmers Company. During the four-year life of the award, 1911-1914, its recipients were Wildfire Schulte, Larry Doyle, Jake Daubert and Johnny Evers, who in 1914 was playing for the 'miracle' Boston Braves.

No pennant or World Series race since 1914 ever

passes without some reference to the 'Miracle Braves' of 1914. On 19 July 1914 the Braves were in last place, but after an incredible winning streak, by 10 August they had climbed to second place, 6½ games behind McGraw's Giants. They moved into first place on 2 September, slipped briefly to third, and returned to first on 8 September. After winning 60 of their last 76 games, they took the pennant by 10½ games over the Giants, the first time a club other than the Giants, Cubs or Pirates had taken a National League pennant since 1900.

Braves manager George Stallings announced early in the season, 'I have 16 pitchers, all of them rotten,' but it was Dick Rudolph's 27-10, Bill James's 26-7 and George Tyler's 16-14 hurling that carried the Braves to the title. Walter 'Rabbit' Maranville at shortstop and Johnny Evers at second base supplied excellent

Above: Fred Merkle scores on a close play at the plate. Merkle joined the Giants in 1907 as first baseman, went to Brooklyn in 1916, to Chicago in 1917, and finished up with the Yankees (1925-26). His lifetime batting average was only .273, but he had speed – 271 stolen bases in 16 years, quite good for the time.
Right: Grover Cleveland Alexander – 'Pete.' In his 20-year (1911-1930) career with Philadelphia, Chicago and St Louis, he had a record of 373-208 and was elected to the Hall of Fame in 1938.

Above: The 1914 Boston Braves. At this time, many teams had mascots. There is Boston's – third from left in the bottom row. He must have given them luck, since they won the pennant with a 94-59 record (New York was a distant second – 11½ games back) and went on to shut out the Philadelphia Athletics four games to none in the World Series, outscoring them by a total of 16 runs to six.

infield support. The Philadelphia Athletics were universally expected to put the upstart Braves in their place in the World Series, but instead became the first team to be counted out in four games as the Braves pulled their second major upset of the year. During the Series pitchers James and Rudolph both won two games each, Hank Gowdy batted .545, and Chalmers Award winner Evers, who seemingly willed the Braves to victory, hit .438.

In 1914, with the beginning of the war in Europe, the National League faced a war of its own. The Federal League, boasting such affluent backers as Chicago's James A Gilmore, oil tycoon Harry Sinclair and Brooklyn baking barons the Ward Brothers, began raiding players, and made plans to move from minor to major-league status for the coming season. For its franchises in Chicago, St Louis, Pittsburgh, Kansas City, Brooklyn, Buffalo, Newark and Baltimore, the Federal League purchased such National League stars as Joe Tinker, Three Finger Brown, Howie Camnitz, Claude Hendrix, Ed Reulbach, Tom Seaton – who won 27 games for the Phillies in 1913 – and Lee Magee.

Although the Federal League was never financially successful, it went to plenty of trouble and caused considerable losses. Some estimates for combined league losses run as high as $10 million. Hoping to see something for its efforts anyway, the Federals tried to have the entire structure of organized ball invalidated in court by suing the majors for violating the Sherman Anti-Trust Law. Owner Sinclair applied additional pressure by announcing plans to move his Newark club to New York City, where it would be in direct competition with established major-league clubs.

Judge Kenesaw Mountain Landis, the federal judge who heard the case, took the summer to consider the anti-trust suit, hoping to avoid making a decision, and eventually the National League opted to negotiate. The Federal League agreed to disband, and in return, the National League awarded $400,000 to the Wards, $100,000 to Sinclair, permitted the Federal League's Charles Weigham to buy the Cubs, and arranged for

Far right: Judge Kenesaw Mountain Landis, the commissioner of baseball, throws out the first ball.

buy-backs of National League contract-jumpers, and for the sale of Federal League players. The war, at great cost, was over.

In 1915, with Christy Mathewson pitching 8-14 and about to move on to managing the Cincinnati Reds, Grover Cleveland Alexander became the league's leading pitcher, etching a 31-10 record with twelve shutouts. His 1.22 ERA remained a league record until Bob Gibson broke it in 1968, and was an accomplishment all the more remarkable because half of his games were pitched in the tiny bandbox of Baker Bowl. Alexander was ably abetted in hurling the Phillies to their first National League pennant by outfielder Gavvy Cravath, one of baseball's greatest home run hitters, who tagged 24 homers to break Wildfire Schulte's record of 21. But league batting honors went to Giant second baseman Larry Doyle, with a .320 average, the lowest ever for a title in the league. John McGraw, for the first and only time in his New York managerial career, finished in the cellar, an embarrassment somewhat mitigated by a record which left the Giants only 3½ games behind the fourth-place Cubs.

The Brooklyn Dodgers took the pennant in 1916, becoming the third National League team in a row to earn its first pennant. In those days the Dodgers were known as the Robins, after portly manager Wilbert Robinson, a lovable bumbler and walking sideshow who had played behind the plate on the legendary Orioles teams of the 1890s. Probably the most popular figure in Brooklyn baseball history, 'Uncle Robbie' drew crowds to impressive new Ebbets Field, now in its fourth season, with his clownish antics, but it was his skill in developing pitchers that won him the pennant.

In 1916, Robin hurler Ed Pfeffer won 25 games to lead a pitching staff that included Marquard and Jack Coombs. Slugging power was supplied by Zack Wheat, Jake Daubert and Casey Stengel. Ex-Giants Merkle and Meyers, in addition to Marquard, also played for the Dodgers that year, a fact which added fuel to persisting rumors that the Giants helped their former teammates beat out the Phillies for the pennant by dropping a crucial series to the Robins. At one point during a Robins-Giant game at Ebbets Field, McGraw himself stalked off the field calling his men

A poster advertising the Labor Day doubleheader in Chicago – 4 September 1916. Wrigley Field had not yet been opened, and the Cubs played at Weeghman Park.

'quitters,' and yelled to the press box, 'I'll be no part of this.' An investigation proved inconclusive, and the Robins finished 2½ games ahead of the Phillies. Despite a spectacular 26-game winning streak in September, the Giants finished fourth behind Boston.

Grover Cleveland Alexander posted another extraordinary season with 33 wins, including an all-time record of 16 shutouts, 9 of them in tiny Baker Bowl. Also beginning to be heard from was the Cardinals' Rogers Hornsby, still dividing his time between third base and shortstop, who hit .313 in his first full season.

Two years after dropping such aging stars as Christy Mathewson and rebuilding, McGraw's Giants took the pennant in 1917. Newcomers Ferdie Schupp on the mound and hitters George Burns and Benny Kauff were instrumental in New York's 98 wins, two years after the club had finished at the bottom of the league. Despite his talented youngsters, McGraw lost his fourth consecutive World Series, this time to the White Sox. For delivering an uppercut to the jaw of umpire Bill Byron, however, McGraw received a $500 fine and a 16-day suspension. When he continued the fight by attacking league President Tener and the umpires in the press, he was fined another $1000.

Although the Phillies finished 10 games behind the Giants, Grover Alexander again dominated league pitching with a 30-13 record, his third consecutive 30-game season. Pittsburgh's Honus Wagner retired at the age of 43 with a record of 3430 hits that stood for 45 years.

On 2 May 1917, Fred Toney of the Reds and Jim 'Hippo' Vaughan of the Cubs engaged in the only

Top: An early flag-raising at Ebbets Field. The Dodgers of the period had reason to look glum.
Right: Fred Toney, who pitched for Chicago, Cincinnati, New York and St Louis in a career that went from 1911 to 1923.
Opposite: Charles Dillon 'Casey' Stengel, best-known for his managing feats, during the period when he roamed the outfield for the Giants (1921-23).

James Leslie 'Hippo' Vaughn started pitching for the Yankees in 1908 and went to the Washington Senators in 1912. But with the Cubs from 1913 to 1921 he was almost unstoppable. He ended his career with a 2.49 ERA.

double no-hitter in major-league history. During the first nine innings, each pitcher issued only two bases on balls. In the top of the tenth inning, Vaughan gave up two hits and the Reds scored one run. Toney then retired the Cubs in order, maintaining his no-hitter through the tenth inning.

A few days before the 1917 season began, Congress declared war on the Central Powers of Europe. Hank Gowdy of the Braves was the first major-leaguer to enlist, but it was not until the next season that baseball, classified as a non-essential industry, began to feel the heat. General Enoch Crowder's June 'Work or Fight' order forced all draft age men to choose between the military and essential industries. By the 11 November 1918 Armistice, a total of 103 National Leaguers had entered the service, including Christy Mathewson, Branch Rickey, Casey Stengel, Rabbit Maranville, Rube Benton, Ed Pfeffer, Eppa Rixey, Bill James, Eddie Grant (killed near Verdun) and Grover Cleveland Alexander. At Secretary of War Newton Baker's suggestion, the season was shortened to end on Labor Day, 2 September. As attendance declined, the owners panicked. In 1918 Giant owner Harry Hempstead sold out to Charles Stoneham. Fearing Alexander's conscription, the Phillies had sold him to the Cubs for two players and $60,000 the previous November, a shortsighted move that helped plunge the Phillies into the cellar for years to come.

The war-shortened season was the first in which runner-up clubs were given an incentive to continue playing their best in the final weeks of the season. The practice of allocating a share of the World Series receipts to first division clubs, devised by league President Tener, has continued ever since. The Cubs took the pennant that year, led by Hippo Vaughan's 22 wins.

Under the constant shelling of trench warfare, Grover Cleveland Alexander lost his hearing in one ear and developed epilepsy. Although like many

Baseball continued being the national pastime during World War I. Here soldiers at Camp Gordon, Georgia, play the game in their olive drab uniforms and campaign hats.

Far right: Harold Harris 'Prince Hal' Chase took a long time arriving in the National League. He spent from 1905 to 1913 with the Yankees (managing them in 1910 and 1911), went to the White Sox, spent a year and a half with Buffalo of the Federal League, and then came to the Reds in 1916. He finished his career in 1919 with the Giants, ending with a .291 batting average.
Below: Edd J 'Eddie' Roush began in the outfield with the White Sox in 1913. He then played one year with Indianapolis and one year with Newark in the Federal League, winding up with Cincinnati in 1917. In 1927 he went to the Giants and ended his career back in Cincinnati in 1931. His .323 lifetime batting average helped him into the Hall of Fame in 1962.

players of the era he was a heavy drinker, after the war his drinking increased to epic proportions, largely, it is now supposed, as a mask for his problems. At the time alcoholism was more socially acceptable than epilepsy, and it now seems likely that much of his erratic behavior, attributed to drink, was actually due to his illness. Alexander was never to return to his previous heights of achievement, but it is a tribute to his extraordinary natural ability that he remained an effective pitcher after the war, and three times won at least 21 games in the hit-happy 1920s.

The National League, uncertain what the postwar economy would bring, reduced its playing schedule from 154 to 140 games in 1919, but was pleasantly surprised to find baseball enthusiasm reaching new heights everywhere. In Cincinnati, attendance tripled; in Brooklyn, attendance quadrupled. The Giants saw attendance increase by almost half a million, and the World Series earned almost 50 percent more than the previous all-time high, the half million Series of 1912.

But not all the news was good. During the year developments began which resulted in Giant stars Hal Chase and Heinie Zimmerman and the Cubs' Lee Magee being barred from organized baseball forever, all three trying to induce players to throw games. Disclosures of similar shenanigans shook public faith

in the national pastime, but they were only the warm-up for the famous 'Black Sox Scandal' of 1919.

The Cincinnati Reds, led by slugger Edd Roush, won their first pennant in 1919, finishing 9 games ahead of the second-place Giants, and went on to upset the Chicago White Sox in the World Series, 5-3. (From 1919-21, the World Series was extended to require five wins instead of four.) The White Sox, unquestionably one of the greatest teams of all time, were hands-down favorites to take the Series, and many felt that their performance was suspiciously substandard. A year later it was determined that eight White Sox players had conspired with gamblers to throw the Series.

By then the National Commission, under fire and losing effectiveness for the last five years, had been dissolved, and had been replaced by a single commissioner, Judge Kenesaw Mountain Landis, who was given a seven-year contract at $50,000 annually. Serving until 1944, when he was 78, Landis was given sweeping, dictatorial powers, and charged with cleaning up the game. Nothing else, it was felt, would restore public confidence.

Landis's first major ruling was to banish the eight Chicago players responsible for throwing the 1919 World Series. The eight, who were eventually acquitted by a Chicago grand jury, were Eddie Cicotte, Claude Williams, Chick Gandil, Swede Risberg, Buck Weaver, Joe Jackson, Happy Felsh and Fred McMullin. Landis also barred Chase, Zimmerman and Magee. The message got through to players and fans alike.

With the postwar economy booming and confidence and enthusiasm in the game assured by the presence of Landis and the exploits of Babe Ruth, the beginning of the Roaring Twenties marked a turning point as baseball and the National League entered a period of unprecedented prosperity. New York legalized Sunday baseball in 1920, and rule changes were introduced to handicap pitchers, encourage hitters, and make the game more exciting and popular with fans.

Both leagues outlawed all trick pitches that involved tampering, such as the application of sandpaper, emery, or saliva to the surface of the ball,

President Warren G. Harding throws out the first ball in Washington, DC, to open the 1922 baseball season – 12 April 1922.

although 17 pitchers in the majors who used the spitball as their primary weapon were permitted to continue to do so. In the National League this included Bill Doak, Phil Douglas and Burleigh Grimes, the last legal spitballer, who pitched in the majors until 1934. For the first time since the early days, when batters could call for their pitchers, hitters were favored over pitchers.

But the introduction of the lively ball was probably even more significant. Despite repeated assurances by such National League officials as President Heydler that the only change in the manufacture of the ball was more firmly-bound better quality wool yarn, a baseball officialdom bent on wooing fans after the Black Sox Scandal could not have helped but notice that more home runs and higher-scoring games drew more spectators to the park. From 1918 through 1920, league home run totals climbed from 138 to 261.

In 1921, they shot up to 460; and in 1930, the figure was 892. Officials still claim the ball is the same as it has always been, but it is difficult to reconcile the 1930 National League batting average of .303 (after the 1930 season the ball was made *less* lively) with the knowledge that only six batters in the National League hit above .300 in 1968.

In 1920, spurred on by spitballer Burleigh Grimes's 23 wins and the hitting of veteran Zack Wheat, Wilbert Robinson's Brooklyn Dodgers took their second pennant, finishing seven games ahead of the second-place Giants. McGraw managed to squeeze 20-game seasons from hurlers Jesse Barnes, Art Nehf and Fred Toney as the league returned to the prewar 154-game schedule.

An amazing pitching duel took place on 1 May 1920 between Brooklyn's Leon Cadore and Boston's Joe Oeschger. With both pitchers going all the way, their game was called for darkness at 1-1, but only after 26 complete innings had been pitched. The names of both pitchers in this longest-ever game in baseball history, neither of whom gave up a run after the sixth inning, remain forever fixed in baseball legend.

The Phillies's Cy Williams led the league in home runs with 15 that year (Babe Ruth hit 54, more than any National League team except the Phillies), but the real hitting news in the National League was Rogers Hornsby's .370 batting average. Although modest by his later standards, it was good enough to earn him the first of six consecutive league batting championships. He was to take seven in all. Hornsby's 1920 average of .370 was followed by averages of .397, .401, .384, .424 (still the major-league record) and .403. On

Above: Leon Joseph Cadore pitched for the Dodgers (1915-1923), and ended his career with a lifetime ERA of 3.14.
Right: Joe Oeschger was a mainstay pitcher for several clubs from 1914 to 1925.

the way to earning the league record lifetime batting average of .358, 'The Rajah' led the league twice in homers (his 42 homers and 154 RBI's in 1922 set new league records), four times in doubles, five times in runs scored, four times in RBI's, and nine times in slugging. Hornsby's lifetime slugging percentage of .557 is still a record for the National League.

In 1920, Hornsby led the league not only in batting average, but in slugging, RBI's, doubles and hits. This was also the year in which he was permanently switched to second base, a position he played with excellence. The Rajah was such a fanatic about his hitting that he refused to attend movies or to read much beyond the racing form for fear it might damage his eyes. Without a weakness at the plate and impossible to pitch to, in 1924, when he hit .424, he was walked so often that he got on base more than 50 percent of the time he came to bat.

But if Rogers Hornsby was the greatest all-round hitter in National League history, he was also one of the most arrogant and tactless men in a game not known for refined etiquette. His record of playing for five different teams and managing five different teams is directly attributable to the inability of any owner, manager or player to put up with his 'frankness,' even when he was winning.

In January 1921, the owners of both leagues signed a new National Agreement binding players, umpires, and owners to Commissioner Landis's decisions, and empowering him to levy fines of up to $5000. In baseball matters, the owners even waived their rights to seek justice in civil courts. Should Landis die without a successor being chosen, the President of the United States was to appoint his replacement. Judge Landis again proved he could crack the whip by ordering the Giants's Charles Stoneham and John McGraw to sell their racetrack, club, and casino in Havana or get out of baseball.

McGraw stayed in baseball and completed his current team-building by buying Johnny Rawlings, Emil 'Irish' Meusel and Casey Stengel from the Phillies. The Giants went on to take the pennant, the first of four consecutive flags the club was to take in this decade of hitters, making it the first in major league history to take four consecutive pennants. The unstoppable Giant teams which swept the flags from 1921-1924 featured Frankie Frisch, Art Nehf, Travis Jackson, Dave Bancroft, George Kelly, Ross Youngs, Frank Snyder and Hack Wilson. These were McGraw's greatest teams. Art Nehf, Fred Toney, and the rest of the pitching staff were decent but never great – only Nehf managed a 20-game season during the four

Right: Rogers 'Rajah' Hornsby, was elected to the Hall of Fame in 1942. Primarily a second baseman, he played between 1915 and 1933 for the Cardinals, Giants, Braves, Cubs and the Browns in the American League. He had a lifetime batting average of .358 and managed – from the 1920s to the 1950s – the Cardinals, Braves, Cubs, Browns and the Reds, winning the 1926 World Series with the Cardinals.

Left: Ross Youngs played the outfield for the New York Giants from 1917 to 1926, and was elected to the Hall of Fame in 1972. His career batting average was .322.

Far left: Henry Knight 'Heinie' Groh had a long career at second and third base with the Giants, the Reds and Pittsburgh, and managed Cincinnati in 1918.

Far right: Philips Brooks 'Shufflin' Phil' Douglas near the end of his career. He pitched for the White Sox in 1912, moved to the Reds in 1914, played for the Reds, the Dodgers and the Cubs in 1915, stayed with the Cubs until he went to the Giants in the middle of the 1919 season, and remained there until his retirement in 1922. While his record was a paltry 93-93, he ended up with a 2.80 ERA.
Below: Frankie Frisch practicing his head-first slide. Frank Francis 'The Fordham Flash' Frisch, elected to the Hall of Fame in 1947, had a fabulous career with the Giants (1919-1926) and the Cardinals (1927-1937). This second baseman ended his 19 years with a .316 batting average and 2880 hits. He also managed the Cardinals (1933-38), the Pirates (1940-46) and the Cubs (1949-51), winning the pennant and the World Series with St Louis in 1934.

pennant years – and it was Giant sluggers who gave the club its power. In 1924, Heinie Groh, with an average of .284, had the lowest average in the starting lineup.

Giants Ross Youngs and Frank Frisch particularly stood out for their drive and energy. Youngs, nicknamed 'Pep,' was a favorite of McGraw's, but his brilliant career was cut short by a kidney disease which caused his death in 1927. In McGraw's later years, the only pictures on his office walls were of Ross Youngs and Christy Mathewson.

Frisch, a speedy infielder with even more fire than Youngs, was ranked by many of his contemporaries as the finest National League player of the era. Like Honus Wagner, the versatile and competitive Frisch was always the first pick for any All-Star team. He and his manager respected each other's skill, but Frisch's sharp tongue and intolerance of criticism didn't mix well with McGraw's authoritarian manner, and eventually the two could no longer stand to share the same clubhouse. When McGraw traded Frisch after the 1926 season, it was for none other than Rogers Hornsby, the highest paid National League player, earning $42,000 a year as the playing manager for the Cardinals.

The Giants finished the 1921 season four games ahead of the second-place Pirates. Meeting the Yankees in the Polo Grounds, they lost the first two games, won the second two, lost the fifth to the Yankees, and then took three in a row to clinch the Series. This was the first time a Series winner had lost the first two games, and the first Series played in one park.

With pitchers struggling to adapt to the lively ball,

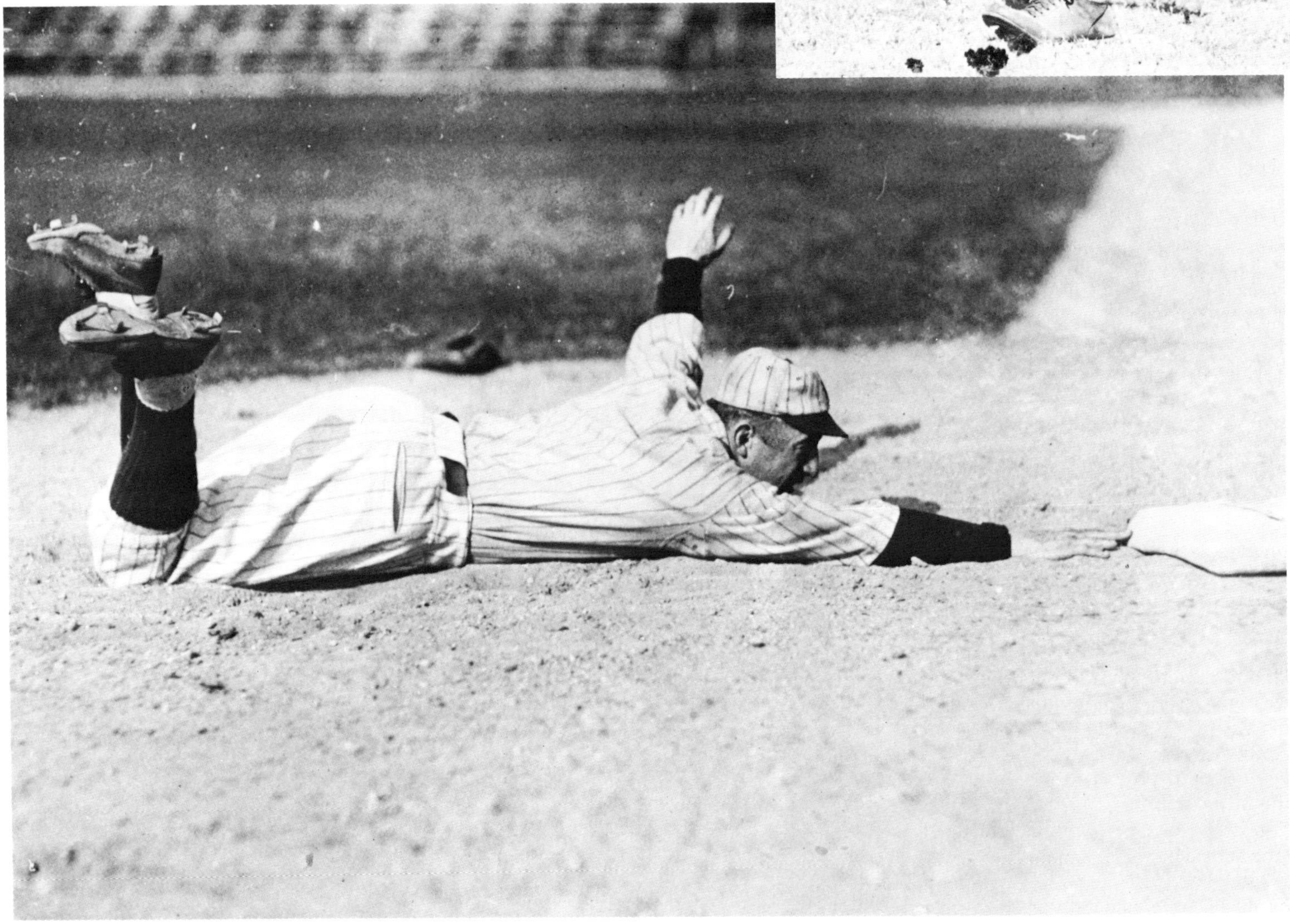

ERA's and batting averages rose steadily. The fans responded to the hitters' game by pushing attendance up throughout the league. In 1927, the Chicago club became the first in National League history to host over one million paying customers. In 1922, the year the Supreme Court ruled that baseball was not subject to Sherman Anti-Trust laws, the league batting average was .292, with the Pirates batting .308 as a team. The Giants finished the season seven games in front of Cincinnati, and once again faced the Yankees in the World Series, which had returned to a best-of-seven match at the suggestion of Commissioner Landis.

The Giants took the Yankees in four games and one tie, but the season was marred by an unfortunate incident involving Giant pitcher Phil Douglas, who wrote a drunken letter to Leslie Mann of the Cardinals in which he offered to 'go fishing' for the rest of the season, for a good price, to help the Cardinals take the pennant. Douglas's offer was undoubtedly in reaction to what must have been an excessively humiliating public chewing out by manager McGraw. He later called Mann and asked him to destroy the letter, but Mann had already shown it to Cardinal manager Branch Rickey, who showed it to Landis, and the Commissioner banished him from the game forever.

The Giants took the 1924 pennant 4½ games ahead of the second-place Reds, but dropped the World Series to the Yankees, 4-2. In 1924 McGraw's men took what was to be his tenth and final flag, finishing 1½ games ahead of Brooklyn, but not without another unfortunate scandal. Before the 27 September game, Giant Jimmy O'Connell offered Phillies shortstop Heinie Sand $500 if he would not 'bear down too hard.' Sand refused the offer, told his manager, and the affair eventually reached Landis.

O'Connell, a promising young outfielder for whose minor league contract the Giants had paid $75,000, testified that he thought all the Giants knew about the bribe offer and that he had only approached Sand because Giant coach Cozy Dolan had told him to. O'Connell particularly implicated Giant stars Frisch, Kelly and Youngs. These three were exonerated, but Dolan's plea of lapse of memory infuriated the Commissioner, who banished O'Connell and the coach from organized ball forever. There was speculation that the whole affair had been an elaborate practical joke played on the gullible O'Connell. The Giants went on to lose the World Series to Washington in the seventh game.

In 1924, the league inaugurated the Most Valuable Player Award. A committee of writers selected Brooklyn pitcher Dazzy Vance, with a 28-6 record, over Rogers Hornsby, who had batted an indelible .424 for the Cardinals. That same year Cardinals first baseman Jim Bottomley established a major league record by driving in 12 runs, with 6 hits, in a single game.

In a decade in which hitters terrorized pitchers, Brooklyn's Dazzy Vance proved it was still possible to strike batters out. The Dodger pitcher, who didn't land permanently in the majors until 1922, when he was 31, led the league in strikeouts from 1922-1928. In his MVP year of 1924 he also led the league in wins, complete games and ERA. His 262 strikeouts in 1922 were achieved in a year in which no other pitcher in the league struck out more than 86, with the exception of spitballing teammate Burleigh Grimes, who fanned 134.

As the National League began its 50th season, the Pirates moved up from their third-place berth in 1924

James Joseph 'Jimmy' O'Connell played for the New York Giants for two years, 1923-24. This outfielder batted .270.

Above: Clarence Arthur 'Dazzy' Vance pitched for 16 years in the majors and was elected to the Hall of Fame in 1955. He started in Pittsburgh in 1915 and went to the Yankees that same year. In 1922 he began his tenure with the Dodgers, leaving for the Cardinals in 1933. He was traded to the Reds in 1934, but returned to the Cardinals that same year. He ended his career with the Dodgers in 1935, with a lifetime 3.24 ERA.
Far right: Harold Joseph 'Pie' Traynor spent his whole career (1920-1937) with the Pittsburgh Pirates. This third baseman had a lifetime batting average of .320 and accumulated 2416 hits.

to take the pennant and end the Giants' four-year reign. The key to their finish 8½ games ahead of McGraw's club was a preseason raid engineered by owner Barney Dreyfuss which brought George Grantham, Vic Aldridge and Al Nichaus to Pittsburgh. Hurler Aldridge won 15 games, and Grantham hit .326 to help compile a team average of .307. Although Johnny Morrison, Emile Yde, Lee Meadows and Ray Kremer also contributed solid pitching, it was Pirate hitting which propelled them to the top.

Pie Traynor, on his way to becoming baseball's all-time third baseman, hit .320; Glenn Wright, the shortstop who made an unassisted triple play that season and formed an airtight left side with Traynor, hit .308; Earl Smith hit .313; Kiki Cuyler hit .357; Max Carey hit .343 and Clyde Barnhart hit .325. In a World Series in which Max Carey hit .458 and Kremer and Aldridge both won two games each, the Pirates finally beat the Senators in the seventh game. On opening day of the Series, Christy Mathewson died of tuberculosis at Saranac Lake.

Rogers Hornsby, batting .403 and taking his second Triple Crown, was selected as 1925's Most Valuable

Until then, most minor-league clubs were independently owned, selling their better players to the big leagues. Rickey's idea was for the Cardinals to buy and run their own farm clubs. Beginning in 1919 with the acquisition of part interest in the Houston club, the Cardinal farm system eventually extended to include 50 teams with more than 800 players under contract. Rickey's eye for talent was legendary, his priority was on speed, and his method proved effective. After the Cardinals paid $10,000 for Jess Haines in 1919, more than 25 years passed before the club purchased another established star. The great St Louis teams of the intervening years were all the products of Rickey's farm system.

The first crop of Rickey's farmers made their mark in 1926, under manager Hornsby. But even in 1943 and 1946, when the Cards took pennants after Rickey was long gone from the organization, the winning teams were still primarily his farm products. By then the farm system had become standard operating procedure for nearly every club in the majors.

Grover Cleveland Alexander, war-scarred and 39, also contributed to the Cardinals' pennant of 1926. After being traded in the middle of the season from

Far left: Hazen Shirley 'Kiki' Cuyler played for Pittsburgh (1921-1927), the Cubs (1928-1935), Cincinnati (1935-1937) and Brooklyn (1938). Elected to the Hall of Fame in 1968, he ended his career with a .321 batting average and 2999 hits.
Below Left: Wesley Branch 'The Mahatma' Rickey did play baseball with the Browns (1905-06) and the Yankees (1907) and back to the Browns (1914) as a catcher and an outfielder, batting .239. But it was as a manager and front office tycoon that he is best remembered. Elected to the Hall of Fame in 1967, this man changed the face of baseball, especially by planning the first farm system for the Cardinals and signing the first black player (Jackie Robinson) to a Dodger major league contract.

Player. In the middle of the season he took over management of the St Louis Cardinals, bringing them in fourth, and in 1926, Hornsby's first and last full season as their manager, the Cardinals took their first modern pennant. Every team in the National League had now won at least one flag.

The last St Louis pennant had been the Brown's win in 1888. Beginning in 1926, the Cardinals were to become a major force in the league, winning nine flags and six World Series over the next two decades. Their greatness during this period was unquestionably the result of the policies of general manager Branch Rickey, one of the finest intellects ever to come into the game and properly known as the father of the farm system, who joined the impoverished Cardinals in 1919 and hit upon a brilliant idea to make his team a contender in a league in which rich clubs could insure their success by outbidding poorer clubs for star players. 'Let's grow our own talent,' he suggested to owner Sam Breadon, 'we can round up promising young prospects and develop them on our own minor-league clubs.'

Below: The great St Louis Cardinal team of 1926 that beat the Yankees four games to three in the World Series. Grover Cleveland Alexander is in the front row, far right.

Far right: Frankie Frisch warms up.
Below: The Waners with the Pirates – Lloyd and Paul (center and right). Lloyd James 'Little Poison' Waner played the outfield for Pittsburgh from 1927 to 1941. In 1941 he went to the Braves and then to the Phillies. In 1945, his last year, he returned to the Pirates. Elected to the Hall of Fame in 1967, he was a lifetime .316 hitter. Paul Glee 'Big Poison' Waner also played the outfield in Pittsburgh, starting in 1926. In 1941 he was traded to Brooklyn and then to Boston. He returned to Brooklyn in 1943, went to the Giants in 1944, and finished his career with the Yankees in 1945. Elected to the Hall of Fame in 1952, he carried a batting average of .333.

the Cubs, who thought he was burnt out, he won nine games. In one of the most dramatic World Series of all times, Alexander, emerging from the bullpen with a legendary hangover in the seventh inning of the seventh game, Cardinals leading 3-2, struck out Tony Lazzeri with bases loaded, and pitched two more hitless innings. He had already won the second and the sixth games. After the Series, winning manager Rogers Hornsby was traded to the Giants for Frank Frisch.

The 1927 pennant went to a Pittsburgh club with a .305 team average. Finishing only 1½ games ahead of the Cardinals, the Pirates featured the hitting of the Waner brothers, Paul and Lloyd, who got more than 5600 hits between them, and so terrorized National League pitchers in the 1920s and 1930s that they became known as Big Poison and Little Poison. In 1927, Paul Waner, in his second season with the Pirates, led the league with a .380 average. Younger brother Lloyd, in his rookie year, hit .355, the two brothers totalling 460 hits toward that year's Pirate pennant.

The Giants, finishing two games behind the Pirates, now featured Hornsby at second base. Hornsby, who hit .361, assumed his duties only after forcing league owners to buy back Cardinal stock he had bought at $45 a share, insisting he be paid $116 a share. Star Giant outfielder Ross Youngs sat out the season with Bright's disease and died on 22 October. The Cardinals were obliterated in four games in the World Series by a Yankee team regarded by many as the best team of all time.

Frustrating McGraw's hopes for an eleventh pennant by two games, the Cardinals, with Frisch on second base, returned to the winner's circle in 1928, clinching the pennant on the next-to-last-day of the season. Chick Hafey, a product of the St Louis farm system and one of the finest National League outfielders ever, hit .337, while teammate Jim Bottomley led the league in RBI's with 136, hitting .325, and tying Chicago's Hack Wilson for home runs with 31. Rogers Hornsby took his seventh and last league title with an average of .387. He was playing for the Braves in 1928. Apparently one season had been all McGraw could stand of the outspoken slugger.

With Babe Ruth hitting .625 and clouting three home runs in one game of the World Series and Lou Gehrig racking up four homers and a .545 Series average, the Cardinals, like the Pirates of the year before, went down before the awesome Yankees in four games. John Heydler, elected league president for another four years, suggested a way to speed up the game and promote interest by substituting a pinch-hitter for the pitcher. The pitcher would stay in the game, but the pinch-hitter would handle his at-bats. In 1973 the idea of the Designated-Hitter was finally adopted by the American League.

Under the stewardship of former minor-league infielder Joe McCarthy, the Cubs beat out the second-place Pirates by 10½ games in 1929, the first of nine pennants for manager McCarthy and the first flag since 1918 for the Cubs. As more and more life was pumped into the ball, batting averages continued to swell and balls flew out of the parks. The Cubs' winning outfield of Kiki Cuyler, Hack Wilson and Riggs

Stephenson batted .360, .345 and .362, respectively. Rogers Hornsby, now on second base for the Cubs, traded the previous November for five players and $200,000, hit 40 homers, 149 RBI's and racked up a .380 average, for which he received his second MVP Award. At the summer meeting the league directors decided to discontinue the award, now in its seventh year.

Philadelphia's Lefty O'Doul took the league title with an average of .398 on a team which averaged .309 overall. His teammate Chuck Klein averaged .356, taking the league home run title with 43. Both Klein's homers and O'Doul's 254 hits were new National League records. While most of the tumbling league records involved slugging, Grover Cleveland Alexander, in the last game he ever won, equalled Christy Mathewson's lifetime mark of 373 wins.

55,980 baseballs were used that year in the National League, topping the previous year's total by 4644, a figure that would have been greater without the new screens erected above the outfield walls at the St Louis and Philadelphia parks. Even so, the National League hit a new record of 754 home runs – an increase of 144 over 1928 – and would have hit more if the umpires hadn't started rubbing the gloss from the balls before the game at mid-season. But the exploits of the sluggers of 1929 was only a prelude to what was to come in 1930.

Left: Chick Hafey stretches for a high one. For 13 years (1924-1937) Hafey played the outfield with the Cardinals and the Reds, carrying a batting average of .317. He was elected to the Hall of Fame in 1971.
Far left: Lefty O'Doul takes a swing. O'Doul played for the Yankees from 1919 to 1922, then for a succession of teams, but ended his career in 1934 with the Yankees, hitting .349.

Hall of Famers Lefty Grove (left) and Dizzy Dean. Robert Moses Grove pitched for the Philadelphia Athletics and the Boston Red Sox between 1925 and 1941. Beginning in 1930, Jay Hanna 'Dizzy' Dean pitched for the Cardinals, the Cubs, and the St Louis Browns.

CHAPTER THREE

The League Takes to the Air

Brooklyn?
Is Brooklyn still in the League?

Bill Terry

In 1930, with the nation in economic crisis, 5.5 million paying customers visited National League ball parks, half a million more than the previous year, setting a new league record. Brooklyn topped the million mark for the first time, and the Cubs set a home attendance record with 1,463,264.

If the National League managed to escape the immediate effects of the Depression, it was probably because the owners, exploiting the fans' enthusiastic reaction to the hitting game, pumped more life into the ball than ever before. As a result, new records were set all season, some of which may never be matched. Six clubs – the Giants, Phillies, Cardinals, Cubs, Dodgers and Pirates – posted team batting averages of over .300. By comparison, in 1968 only six players in the National League hit .300 or better.

Leading the pack in individual hitting was Chicago's stubby, hard-drinking outfielder Lewis 'Hack' Wilson with 190 RBI's – a major-league record – and 56 home runs – a National League record that still stands. Only Hank Greenberg, with 183 RBI's in 1937, has ever remotely approached Hack's 190 RBI's. Wilson was originally with the Giants in 1923, but a clerical error exposed him to the draft, enabling the Cubs to grab him for next to nothing in 1925.

The Giants led the league with a collective average of .319. Giant second baseman Bill Terry, in the midst of ten straight seasons of batting over .300, led the league with 254 hits and a season average of .401. His lifetime average of .341 makes him second in modern National League history only to Rogers Hornsby, and first for left-handed hitters. Terry and Lefty O'Doul, who got 254 hits in 1929, still hold the major-league record for hits. In 1930, Terry became the last National Leaguer to hit .400.

The Phillies, averaging .315 as a team, featured Lefty O'Doul with a .383 average, and Hall of Famer Chuck Klein, who hit .386, including 250 hits, 59 doubles, 40 home runs, 170 RBI's and 158 runs scored. Incredible as it may seem, in this year of the hitter only Klein's doubles were a new record, and his team, with a pitching staff ERA of 6.71, finished a dismal last, 40 games out of first place.

In the National League in 1930, 11 players hit better than .350 and 17 players drove in more than 100 runs. Babe Herman of the Dodgers hit .393 and Fred Lindstrom of the Giants hit .379. With averages of .330-.340 commonplace, ERA's rose correspondingly. The last-place Phillies yielded 7.7 runs per game; Brooklyn, in fourth, had an ERA of 4.03, due largely to the pitching of Dazzy Vance, now 39, who led the

Opposite: Bill Terry of the Giants. William Harold 'Memphis Bill' Terry played first base for New York from 1923 to 1936 with a batting average of .341. He was elected to the Hall of Fame in 1954. Terry managed the club from 1932 to 1941, winning three pennants and the 1933 World Series.

Below: Hack Wilson hits a long fly at Wrigley Field – 1930. Lewis Robert Wilson played the outfield for the Giants (1923-25), the Cubs (1926-31), the Dodgers (1932-34) and the Phillies (1934). In his 12-year career, he batted in 1062 runs and hit .307.

NEW YORK

Above: 'Dizzy' Dean, the young Cardinal super-pitcher.

Left: Johnny Leonard Roosevelt 'Pepper' Martin – 'The Wild Hoss of the Osage' – in the St Louis dugout. Martin played the outfield and third base for the Cardinals for 13 years – 1928 to 1944 – and hit .418 in the three World Series he was in.

league with an ERA of 2.61. His closest competition was New York's Carl Hubbell, with 3.76. The league as a whole averaged an ERA of almost five runs per game.

The Cardinals, featuring eight .300 hitters in their lineup and four more on the bench, finished two games ahead of the Cubs to take the pennant. Once the flag was secure, they broke ground by starting 19-year-old Jerome Dean – also known as Jerome Herman and Jay Hanna – in the last game of the season. Known to the world as Dizzy Dean, the young righthander won his game in nine innings, allowing one run and three hits. The Cardinals dropped the World Series to the Athletics, 4-2.

As the Depression deepened, attendance declined with the nation's financial health. Total baseball receipts of $17 million in 1929 declined steadily to a low of $10.8 in 1933, before climbing slowly to $21.5 million in 1939, followed by a wartime slump, and a new height of $68.1 million in 1948. But during the hard years, baseball provided the public with a chance to at least temporarily forget the harsh realities of its economic winter. At the 1931 World Series, Cardinals *vs* Athletics, President Herbert Hoover's

Members of the St Louis Cardinals Gas House Gang clowning before a game.

presence was greeted with boos, while Cardinal rookie Pepper Martin, following up a .302 rookie year with 5 stolen bases, 12 hits and a .500 Series average, was greeted with tumultuous applause and screams of appreciation.

Johnnie Leonard 'Pepper' Martin, also known as the 'Wild Hoss of the Osage' after the Oklahoma farm country in which he was born, was a product of the Cardinal farm system. An uninhibited natural man who used his chest to slide on or to block hot grounders and for years saved expense money by hopping a freight train south to spring training – both practices giving him his characteristically filthy appearance – Pepper was the perfect antidote for the Depression blues.

He was also the perfect addition to a club which soon came to be known as the 'Gashouse Gang,' one of the best-remembered clubs in league history and the most colorful club since the old Orioles. But even with Pepper spearheading the Cardinals to a 1931 pennant finish 13 games ahead of the Giants and a sensational World Series win, St Louis attendance dipped from 623,960 in 1931 to 290,370 in 1932, bottoming out at 268,404 in 1933. When the Cardinals won the pennant in 1928, they had drawn 778,147 fans.

After the 1930 season, evidently even the owners realized that their formula for success had been mixed a little too rich, and over the winter they squeezed some of the juice out of the ball. Not surprisingly, batting averages declined dramatically in 1931. The league average of .277 for 1931 was 26 points off the preceeding year.

1931 witnessed the closest batting race in history, with the Cardinals' Chick Hafey eventually emerging as league leader with a .3489 average after edging out Bill Terry's 3486 and teammate Jim Bottomley's .3482. Scoring high in the booze league, Hack Wilson hit an unremarkable 13 home runs and 129 fewer RBI's than his record of the previous year. The Cubs led the league with a team average of .289, 30 points less than the Giant's record of 1930. Notable events of the season included the forced retirement of the Dodgers' 'Uncle Robbie,' Wilbert Robinson, manager since 1914, and the refusal of the league directors to reestablish the Most Valuable Player Award. The MVP was taken over by the Baseball Writers Association of America, who awarded it to Frank Frisch.

Beginning a year of surprising managerial moves, in 1932 the Giants' John McGraw followed former Oriole teammate Robinson out of the game, ending one of the longest and most colorful careers in baseball. Strangely enough, only one sportswriter was there to report the event. On 3 June 1932, Tom Meany of the *World Telegram* stopped by the Giant clubhouse looking for a story. A doubleheader with the Phillies had been rained out, and the clubhouse was empty, but he found a notice on the bulletin board announcing that John McGraw had resigned as manager of the Giants and had been succeeded by Bill Terry.

At 59, worn out and ailing – he would die of uremia within two years – McGraw's departure was less of a shock than his choice of Bill Terry to succeed him. Terry was outstanding among a growing number of players who would not put up with McGraw's authoritarian style. The two had barely spoken for years, and most observers felt that brilliant Giant third baseman Fred Lindstrom was McGraw's clear choice, as did Lindstrom, who later asserted he had been lied to. Yet when faced with the task of picking a successor, McGraw rose above personal differences to pick the man he felt was best suited for the job.

Cubs manager Rogers Hornsby was fired with the Cubs in first place on 2 August 1932 after a series of vitriolic policy disputes with club president William Veeck. Charlie Grimm replaced him, and the Cubs went on to take the pennant four games ahead of Pittsburgh, then demonstrated their opinion of Hornsby by not voting him any share in the World Series money.

Below: John McGraw, perhaps the greatest manager in baseball. John Joseph 'Little Napoleon' McGraw played both infield and outfield for Baltimore in the American Association (1891), Baltimore in the National League (1892-99), the Cardinals (1900), Baltimore in the American League (1901-02) and the Giants (1902-06). He hit .344, but is best remembered for his managerial genius. He headed Baltimore in the National League (1899), Baltimore in the American League (1901-02) and the Giants (1902-32), winning nine pennants and three World Series with New York. McGraw was elected to the Hall of Fame in 1937.

Among the notable rookies who came up that year were Brooklyn pitcher Van Lingle Mungo, Chicago second baseman Billy Herman, and Pirate shortstop Arky Vaughan, who was to carve a place for himself as shortstop second only to the great Honus Wagner. The Cardinals, who never rose above fourth place and ended up in a sixth place tie with the Giants, distinguished themselves by adding Joe Medwick and Dizzy Dean to their regular lineup. Called up from Houston at the end of the Texas League season, Medwick batted .349 in 26 games. Dean, pitching 18-15 in his first full season, led the league in strikeouts with 191, as well as in shutouts and innings pitched.

The son of an Arkansas sharecropper, Dizzy Dean, one of baseball's all-time purveyors of joy and a pitcher of uncanny natural ability, succeeded in replacing the fading Babe Ruth as the game's greatest draw. Throughout the Depression his fractured English, homespun personality and amazing antics, both calculated and natural – and unlike many, Dean was no drinker – delighted the American public. He sometimes predicted shutouts and other pitching feats in advance, maintaining that it wasn't bragging if he went out and did it after saying it. On one occasion, after he had pitched a three-hitter in the first game of a doubleheader and his brother Paul pitched a no-hitter in the second game, the Great One remarked, 'If I'd known Paul was going to do that, I'd have pitched a no-hitter too.'

His practical jokes made him undisputed king of the Gashouse Gang, which featured such equally irrepressible personalities as Pepper Martin, short-

– perhaps the best the league has ever seen – was coupled with a control so remarkable that he walked fewer than two men per game in 16 years in the majors.

Chuck Klein of the Phillies was the league's top hitter of 1933, taking the Triple Crown with 28 home runs, 120 RBI's and a batting average of .368. The previous year the Baseball Writers had voted him MVP on the strength of 38 homers, 137 RBI's and a batting average of .348. As a reward, after the 1933 season the Phillies sold him to the Cubs for three players and $65,000. Throughout the decade the Phillies, desperately in need of cash, developed and sold star players.

In the World Series, the Giants beat the Washington Senators, who they had faced at their last Series appearance in 1924, in five games. Mel Ott, the Giant slugger whose 511 home runs were the National League record until Giant Willie Mays broke it, hit two homers and batted .389 for the Series.

Branch Rickey's farm system continued to pay off in 1934 as the Cardinals, managed by Frank Frisch, finished two games ahead of Bill Terry's Giants to take their fifth pennant in nine years. With the fiery Frisch at the helm, the Gashouse Gang (so named when lippy Leo Durocher commented to a sportswriter the year before that the American League would probably call them 'a bunch of gashouse players'), flowered with a spirit achieved by only a handful of clubs in the history of the game. Dizzy Dean pitched his greatest

Left center: Paul Dean (left) and his brother Dizzy – both outstanding pitchers. Paul Lee 'Daffy' Dean played for St Louis from 1934 to 1939 (from 1934 to 1937 the two brothers were the mainstays of the Cardinal pitching staff), then for the Giants and the Browns in the American League. Although he had a 3.75 ERA, he never lived up to the potential he showed during his first two seasons in which he won 19 games each year.

stop Leo Durocher and Joe Medwick. On one afternoon, Dizzy gave three separate interviews to three different sportswriters, claiming a different birthplace in each interview. He later explained that he wanted each writer to have his own story. Dizzy Dean was only one of three or four names he went by anyway.

In their first full season under Bill Terry, the Giants, who finished sixth in 1932, moved into the lead on 10 June 1933 and led all the way, finishing 5 games ahead of the Pirates. Pittsburgh outhit the Giants .285 to .263, but Giant pitching, with Hal Schumacher taking 19, Fred Fitzsimmons 16 and Carl Hubbell 23, made all the difference.

This was the year that Carl Hubbell – henceforth known as 'Meal Ticket' – came into his own, hurling 10 shutouts (including 46 consecutive innings of shutout pitching), and leading the league with a 1.66 ERA, the best in the National League since Alexander's 1.22 in 1915. Hubbell pitched the finest game of his career on 2 July 1933, shutting out the Cardinals 1-0 in 18 innings. In the All-Star game, starting against an American League lineup all of whom became Hall of Famers, Hubbell struck out in order Babe Ruth, Lou Gehrig, Jimmie Foxx, Al Simmons and Joe Cronin, and kept the Americans scoreless for the three innings he pitched under All-Star rules.

In 1933 Hubbell began a string of 5 consecutive years in which he won at least 21 games, averaging 23, with a high of 26 in 1936. Quiet, thoughtful, and publicity-shy, he was in every way the antithesis of his arch-rival Dizzy Dean. Hubbell's notorious screwball

Left: Carl Hubbell warms up. Carl Owen ('King Carl,' 'The Meal Ticket') Hubbell pitched for the Giants from 1928 to 1943, winning 253 games with an earned run average of 2.97. He was elected to the Hall of Fame in 1947.

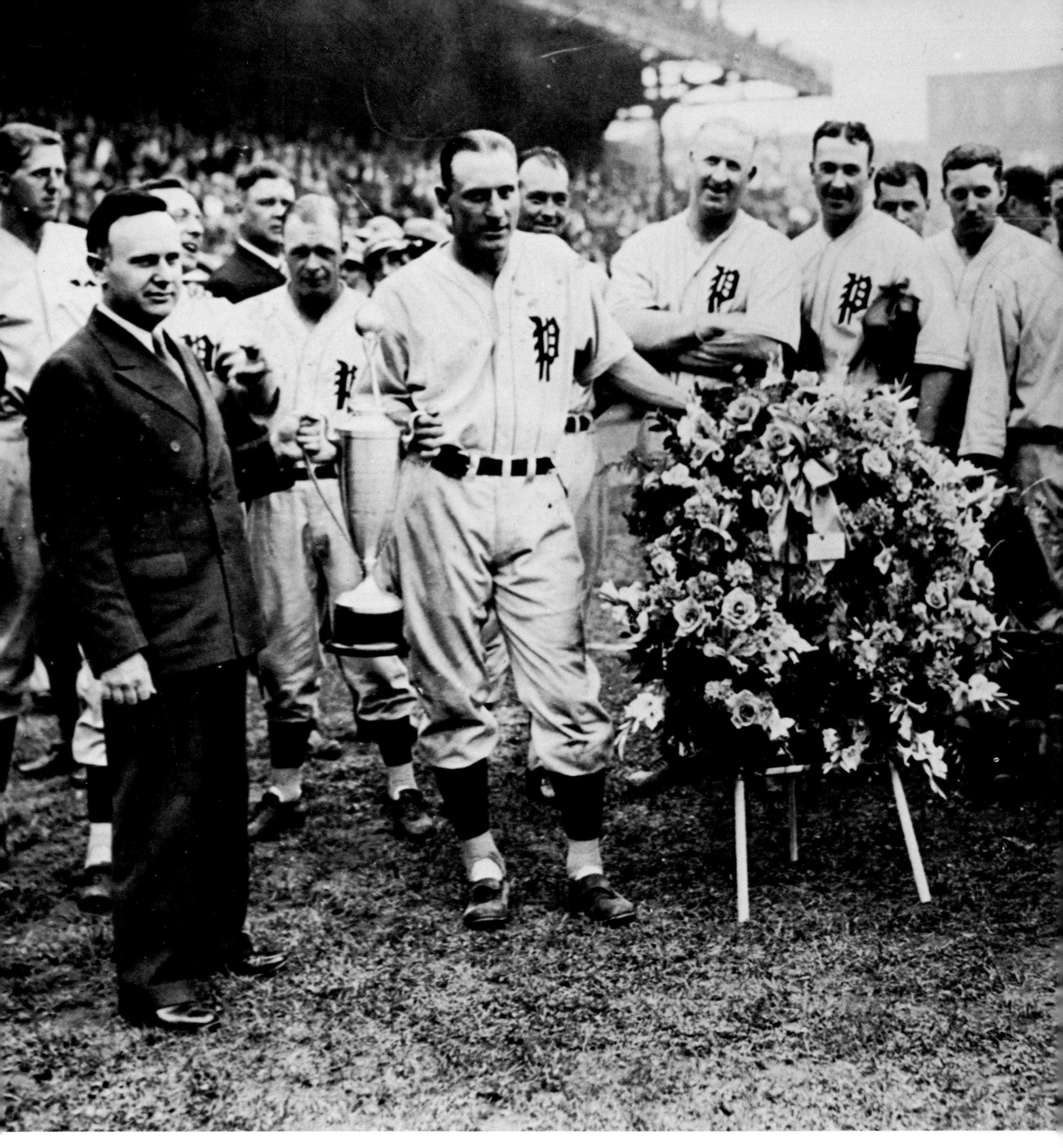

Chuck Klein receiving his 1932 Most Valuable Player trophy. Charles Herbert Klein roamed the outfield for 17 years with the Phillies (1928-33), the Cubs (1934-36), the Phillies again (1936-39), the Pirates (1939) and the Phillies again (1939-44). He hit 300 home runs and carried a .320 batting average.

season, becoming the first National League pitcher to win 30 games since Grover Cleveland Alexander in 1917, and leading the league with 24 complete games, 195 strikeouts and seven shutouts. In true down-to-the-wire Gashouse style, his 30th win and seventh shutout came on the last day of the season, and also clinched the pennant.

At the start of the season, Dizzy had predicted that he and his brother Paul, who came up to the Cardinals through the farm system, would win 45 games. But Paul, quiet and soft-spoken – nicknamed 'Daffy' nevertheless – won 19 games, for a combined total of 49.

Joe 'Ducky' Medwick, on his way to establishing himself as the best National League hitter of the 1930s, backed up his club's pitchers with 106 RBI's and a .319 average. At the World Series, Medwick got into an altercation with Detroit third baseman Marv Owen which resulted in such violent demonstrations of vegetable throwing by the Detroit fans that Commissioner Landis removed him from the game as a safety precaution. The Cardinals won anyway, after Dizzy Dean told the Detroit manager that his starting pitcher on the seventh game would 'never do,' and went on to win by striking out star hitter Hank Greenberg in the bottom of the ninth with two men on and two men out.

This was the year when Giant manager Bill Terry, asked for his pre-season evaluation of various National League clubs, remarked, 'Brooklyn? Is Brooklyn still in the League?' Terry was not given to public wisecracks, and he lived to regret this one. The Dodgers, sometimes known as the 'Daffiness Boys' after a term Westbrook Pegler coined almost a decade earlier, had fallen on hard times indeed, and Terry's quip, because it was so close to home, infuriated the fans.

As fate would have it, with the Giants and the Cardinals tied for first place, the Giants' last two games of the season were against the Dodgers, and the Dodgers, whose fans carried placards with the hated words and greeted Terry with deafening boos every time he made an appearance, won both games. The Cardinals won both of their final games from the last-place Reds, and the Giants were kept from the pennant. McGraw had died on 25 February 1934. Perhaps it was only fitting that the Giants should be disappointed in the year of the passing of their greatest manager by the manager he had chosen to succeed him.

In the 60th year of the National League, baseball tradition was shattered when the Phillies met the Reds at Crosley Field to play the first major-league night game. On 24 May 1935, Franklin D Roosevelt himself pushed a button that turned on 632 lights in a park filled with 20,422 fans, almost ten times the number who would have attended an afternoon contest. Night games are so important to baseball now that it is hard to believe that almost everyone except Cincinnati's dynamic Larry MacPhail opposed them, even though they had already proved successful in the minors. After prolonged negotiations, almost as if to humor MacPhail, each National League team had agreed to play one night game against Cincinnati that season. But once the Depression-hungry clubs evaluated attendance figures at night games, all opposition ceased. Within 13 years, every major-league club except the Cubs had installed lights.

The champion St Louis Cardinals of 1934, who beat the Tigers four games to three in the World Series. Left to right standing – Medwick, Gonzales, Crawford, Whitehead, Mooney, Martin, Vance, P Dean, Frisch, Haines, Hallahan, Durocher, Rothrock, J Dean, Pippen. Left to right seated – Haley, Walker, DeLancy, Orsatti, Carleton, Fullis, Davis, Collins, Wares.

The Hall of Fame has little room for baseball executives, but as front-office men go, the brilliant, irrepressible Larry MacPhail was an undisputed star. In three years with the Reds and five with Brooklyn, he single-handedly pioneered the use of night games as well as of radio, two innovations which changed the face of baseball forever. After taking over the Reds in 1934, his Rickey-like tactics and foresight built the Cincinnati club from a team which hadn't finished better than fourth since 1926 into one which took pennants in 1939 and 1940. After his first year, attendance in Cincinnati doubled.

The challenge he faced in Brooklyn was even greater, but his methods were just as successful. Before MacPhail arrived, the Dodgers had averaged about 500,000 spectators a year. In his first year, they drew 666,000, and in his second, with the club now in third place and their games broadcast on radio, attendance rose to 955,000. Among his many innovations, MacPhail was the first to use motion pictures systematically so that players could study and improve their game.

Babe Ruth came to the Boston Braves in 1935, the year the Braves lost 115 games, the record for the

Far right: Larry MacPhail at the radio microphone.
Below: The first major league night game – Crosley Field, Cincinnati, 24 May 1935.

154-game schedule. Ruth batted only .181 for 28 games before retiring on 2 June, but not before hitting three homers on 25 May at Forbes Field, the 712th, 713th and 714th of his career. He never got another hit.

The Giants and the Cardinals ran a close pennant race that year, the Giants leading most of the way until the Cubs took the lead and the pennant with a historic 21-game winning streak in September. Chicago pitchers Bill Lee and Lon Warneke were both 20-game winners, and second baseman Billy Herman hit .341. Dizzy Dean threw 28-12 for the Cardinals while teammate Joe Medwick accrued a .353 average, but top league batting honors that year went to Pittsburgh's Arky Vaughan. His .385 average remains the highest average ever for a National League shortstop.

The great Casey Stengel contributed an anecdote to the archives after his Dodgers, in a display of exquisite bumbling, ended a four-game winning streak by dropping a doubleheader to the Cubs. As the Brooklyn manager climbed into a Chicago barber chair, he announced, 'A shave please, but don't cut my throat. I may want to do it myself later.'

The Giants came back to take pennants in 1936 and 1937. Outfielder Mel Ott, a quiet man with an unorthodox batting style and a special knack for hitting down the Polo Grounds' short right field line, led the league in homers both years, with 33 and 31, but it was Meal Ticket Carl Hubbell who really smoothed the way.

1936 was Hubbell's greatest year. The great screwballer registered a 26-6 record, and closed out the season with 16 consecutive wins. Voted Most Valuable Player, on his way to a 22-8 record in 1937, Hubbell won eight more games in a row, amassing a total of 24 consecutive wins before he was stopped by the Dodgers on Memorial Day. In 1937, rookie lefthander Cliff Melton helped with the pitching chores by adding another 20 games to the Giants' wins.

Above: Arky Vaughn at the plate. Joseph Floyd Vaughn played shortstop, and later the outfield and third base for the Pirates (1932-41) and the Dodgers (1942-48). His lifetime batting average was .318.

Right: Mel Ott stretches for the ball. 'Master Melvin' Ott played the outfield, second and third base for the Giants from 1926 to 1947. Elected to the Hall of Fame in 1951, he had a .304 lifetime batting average.

Left: Joe Medwick waits his turn at bat. Joseph Michael Medwick – also known as 'Ducky' or 'Muscles' – played the outfield for the Cardinals (1932-40), the Dodgers (1940-43), the Giants (1943-45), the Braves (1945) the Dodgers again (1946) and the Cardinals again (1947-48). Elected to the Hall of Fame in 1968, he carried a lifetime batting average of .324.

On 10 July, Chuck Klein, back with the Phillies after a season with the Cubs, tied the major-league record by hitting four home runs in a single game against Pittsburgh, and a long ball he hit in the second inning which backed Paul Waner against the right field fence almost made it five. After finishing five games ahead of the Cubs and the Cardinals, the Giants lost the Series to the Yankees, 4-2. In the first Hall of Fame election, Honus Wagner and Christy Mathewson were among the first six chosen for the new shrine in Cooperstown, New York.

1937 proved to be Joe Medwick's greatest year. He took the Triple Crown, was voted MVP, and led the league in eight batting categories: average (.374), RBI's (154), home runs (31), runs (111), slugging (.641), at-bats (633), hits (237) and doubles (56). This was the second straight year Medwick led in doubles. The 64 two-baggers he hit in 1936 still stand as a National League record. Cardinal teammate Johnny Mize, another product of the Cardinal farm system, whose lifetime slugging average is second only to Rogers Hornsby's in the National League, turned in a .364 average, hit 25 home runs and 113 RBI's.

In a tragic accident, Cardinal pitcher Dizzy Dean, now 26, sustained an injury that resulted in an incalculable loss to his team and the league. In the third inning of the July 1937 All-Star Game, Dean, who was the starting pitcher for the National League, was hit in the right foot by a line drive off the bat of Cleveland's Earl Averill. The ball broke his toe. Dean returned to action too soon, and in favoring the painful foot he changed his pitching motion, placing an unnatural strain on his arm which eventually ruined it. He managed a 13-10 record that season, but for all practical purposes his career was over. Even so, star

Far right: Johnny Mize hits a long one. John Robert 'The Big Cat' Mize played first base for the Cardinals (1936-41), the Giants (1942-49) and the Yankees (1949-53). In his 15 years he hit 359 home runs and batted .312.

deal-maker Branch Rickey was able to unload him to the Cubs the next spring for $185,000 and three players, including the highly competent righthander Curt Davis.

Bill McKechnie, managing in Boston, produced two rookie pitchers who won 20 games each. Neither Jim Turner nor Lou Fette ever won more than 14 games after that, but McKechnie was named *Sporting News* Major League Manager of the Year for 1937 for his masterful stewardship of a mediocre team. In the World Series, the Giants lost to the Yankees again, Carl Hubbell pitching the Giants' only win, 7-3 in the fourth game.

In 1938, the Phillies, now playing in the Athletics' Shibe Park, were granted permission to play under the lights for the coming season, becoming the third National League club with a night schedule. Cautious

Red Barber, the dean of baseball commentators, who broadcast games for the Dodgers and the Yankees.

Below: Al Lopez when he caught for the Boston Bees. From 1928 to 1947 Alfonso Raymond Lopez played for the Dodgers, the Bees (as the Braves were known for a time), the Pirates and the Cleveland Indians. But he was better known as a manager – of the Indians (1951-56) and the Chicago White Sox (1957-69), where he won one pennant with each club. He was elected to the Hall of Fame in 1977.

as the owners had been about night games, their conservatism was nothing compared to their opposition to and fear of radio broadcasts. While Cincinnati had broadcast some games when MacPhail was with the club, until the very end of the 1930s no club broadcast games on a daily schedule, and the only broadcasts that there had ever been out of New York were of World Series and All-Star games.

But as the 1930s progressed, largely at the prodding of Larry MacPhail, broadcasts on the new but well-entrenched medium of radio gradually became the commonplace thing they are today. Far from hurting attendance, as the owners had every right to fear they would, by the end of the decade it became clear that the enthusiasm generated by announcers such as Red Barber created fans. Newspaper sales gained as listeners bought more papers in order to follow game statistics. The revenue radio broadcast brought was particularly welcome during the Depression. In 1933, Boston earned a modest $5000 from broadcasts. By 1936, Commissioner Landis was able to negotiate $100,000 for World Series broadcasting rights, and the Cardinals, who profited least in the league from radio, were receiving $33,000, while the Giants, who topped the National League in radio revenue, received $100,000 a year for the broadcasts of their games. Altogether, in 1939 National League clubs earned $410,000 in radio money. It is true that major league broadcasts did eventually hurt the minor leagues, but by the time this effect was felt, major league subsidization of the minors was common practice.

1938 will always be remembered as the year that Johnny Vander Meer pitched two no-hitters back-to-back, an unprecedented achievement that remains unequalled. The 23-year-old Cincinnati lefthander, known for speed but also for wildness, was finally brought somewhat under control by Reds manager McKechnie, and on 11 June he pitched a hitless 3-0 victory over the Boston Bees, walking three but allow-

Right: Ebbets Field, 15 June 1938 – Johnny Vander Meer of the Reds beats the Dodgers 6-0 with a no-hitter.

ing no runner to reach second base. With only 20 no-hitters pitched in the league since 1901, Vander Meer's game was a solid achievement.

On 15 June, Cincinnati met the Dodgers at Ebbets Field for Brooklyn's first night game ever. Larry MacPhail, by now running the Dodgers, had arranged pre-game festivities in honor of this historic occasion, including track exhibitions by Olympic champion Jesse Owens and an appearance by Babe Ruth, whom MacPhail had signed as a Dodger coach. Before 38,748 fans, Vander Meer started for the Reds, and although he walked eight men, he kept the Dodgers hitless inning after inning, while the Reds scored four runs in the third. With one out in the ninth, Vander Meer walked three men on 18 pitches, loading the bases, but McKechnie walked out to the mound to calm him down, and Vandy forced Ernie Koy out on a grounder and stopped Leo Durocher with a fly to the outfield, winning his second no-hitter, 6-3.

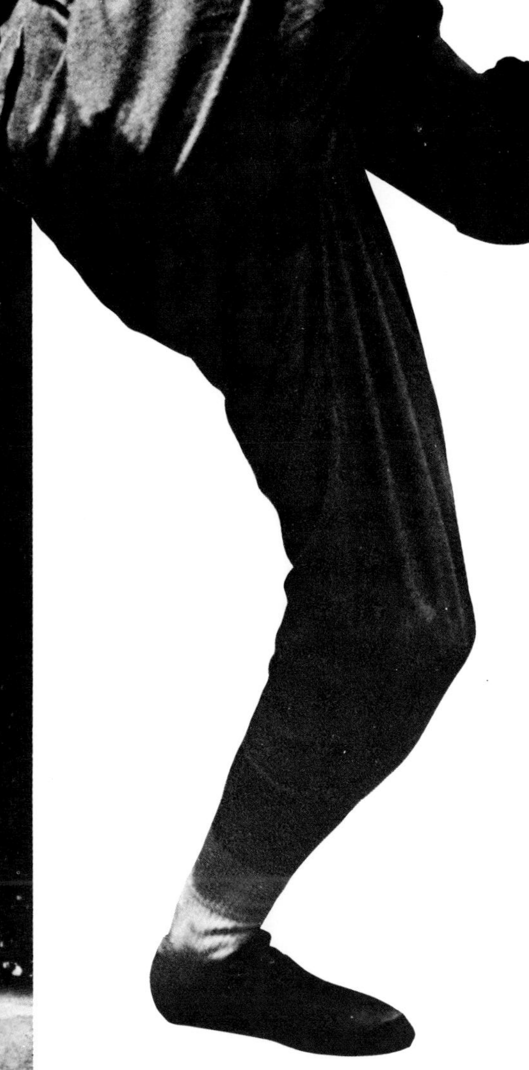

Vander Meer's no-hit streak eventually ended after 21½ innings on 19 June, when Debs Garms singled against him at Boston. With 15 wins for the 1938 season and a 119-121 lifetime total, Vander Meer's record no-hitters, which are apparently destined to stand for some time yet to come, illuminate an otherwise unspectacular career.

A classic pennant race drama that ended in a famous home run took place late in September when the Cubs met the Pirates in Wrigley Field for a three-day series to decide the championship. The Pirates enjoyed a 1½ game lead before leaving for Chicago, but in the opening game the sore-armed Dizzy Dean beat them 2-1. The next day's game was still tied at the bottom of the ninth. With darkness gathering, it seemed likely the game would be called a tie and

Vander Meer warms up. John Samuel Vander Meer, also known as 'The Dutch Master' or 'Double No-Hit,' pitched for the Reds (1937-49), the Cubs (1950) and the Cleveland Indians (1951). He won 119 and lost 121 with a 3.44 earned run average, but his greatest feat was pitching those back-to-back no-hitters.

Far right: Gabby Hartnett – for 20 years the catcher for the Cubs. A .297 hitter with 236 home runs, Hartnett also managed the Cubs from 1938 to 1940. He was elected to the Hall of Fame in 1955.

Below: Bucky Walters warms up. William Henry Walters pitched for the Boston Braves (1931-32), the Boston Red Sox (1933-34), the Phillies (1935-38), the Reds (1938-48) and then went back to the Braves for the 1950 season. He also managed the Reds in 1948 and 1949, coming in seventh both years. He was 198-160 in his career and had an earned run average of 2.79.

replayed as part of a doubleheader the next day. With two out, the Cubs' Gabby Hartnett, manager since July, came up to bat. After two strikes in the fading light he connected on a fast ball from Mace Brown to hit his immortal 'homer in the gloamin',' winning the game. Now half a game up, the Cubs trounced the dispirited Pirates the next day 10-1, to win the pennant again as they had in 1935, 1932 and 1929, on a weird three-year schedule. The Yankees devoured them in the Series, four straight.

Demonstrating the effects of Larry MacPhail's team-building after he was long gone, and aided by the acquisition of Bill Werber from the Athletics, Bill McKechnie's Cincinnati Reds took the pennant in 1939. Their first flag since 1919, this same team, which finished in the cellar in 1937, would take the flag again in 1940. Werber, an honor graduate of Duke University, proved to be the key to tightening up the Cincinnati infield, and the Reds took the lead with a 12-game winning streak in May which included two victories over the second-place Cardinals.

Righthanders Bucky Walters and Paul Derringer threw 27-11 and 25-7 for the Reds that season. Several of his managers had noticed that Walters, who came to the majors as an infielder, sometimes had so much on the ball when he threw to first base that the first baseman had trouble handling it, but he wasn't converted to pitching until 1935 when Phillies manager Jimmie Wilson, a former catcher, talked him into it. Even so, Walters didn't think much of the idea, and made the switch mostly to please his respected manager. Traded to the Reds as a pitcher in 1938, Walters followed his 27 wins in 1939 with 22 in 1940.

First baseman Frank McCormick and catcher Ernie Lombardi supplied Cincinnati's hitting. Starting as a regular in 1938, McCormick led the league in hitting in his first three years, averaging .327, .332 and .309. In 1938, Lombardi, with a .342 average, became the second catcher in major-league history to win a batting title. Big and slow-moving, Lombardi's powerful line drives forced the left side of the infield to move back on the grass when he came to bat, a safe strategy

Left: Ernie Lombardi, the hard-hitting catcher. Ernest Natali Lombardi, also known as 'Schnozz' or 'Bocci,' started with the Dodgers in 1931, went to the Reds from 1932 to 1941, then to the Braves in 1942 and finally to the Giants from 1943 to 1947. His lifetime batting average was .306.

because it took him so long to get to first. Lombardi is remembered for being knocked out in the World Series when Charley 'King Kong' Keller ran into him. Keller was driven in on a single by Joe DiMaggio, who also scored while Lombardi was taking his snooze. The Yankees took the Series from the Reds in four games.

Although the Giants finished in fifth place in 1939, the club set a new record when five of its players hit home runs in one inning of a 17-3 victory over the Reds. The Giant sluggers in the 6 June game were: Harry Danning, Frank Demaree, Burgess Whitehead, Manny Salvo and Joe Moore.

On 12 June, league officials and 10,000 fans celebrated the supposed centennial of baseball at Cooperstown, New York, erroneously believed to be the birthplace of the game.

Commissioner Landis presided over the dedication of the Hall of Fame and Museum, an event which was attended by 10 of the 11 living players so far elected to baseball immortality.

Left: Paul Derringer warms up. Derringer, also known as 'Duke' or 'Oom Paul,' pitched for the Cardinals (1931-33), the Reds (1933-42) and the Cubs (1943-45). The winner of 223 games, he had an ERA of 3.46.

Frank McCormick waits for a throw. Frank Andrew 'Buck' McCormick played first base for the Reds (1934-45), the Phillies (1946-47) and the Boston Braves (1947-48), and had a batting average of .299.

CHAPTER FOUR

Innovation and Upheaval

Nice guys finish last.

Leo Durocher

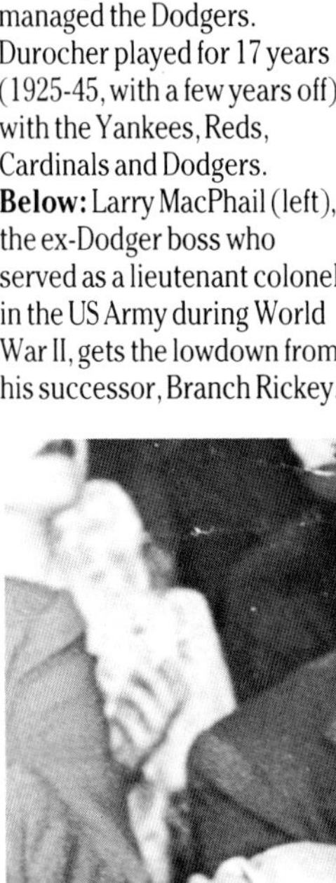

Opposite left: Leo Ernest 'The Lip' Durocher, when he managed the Dodgers. Durocher played for 17 years (1925-45, with a few years off) with the Yankees, Reds, Cardinals and Dodgers.
Below: Larry MacPhail (left), the ex-Dodger boss who served as a lieutenant colonel in the US Army during World War II, gets the lowdown from his successor, Branch Rickey.

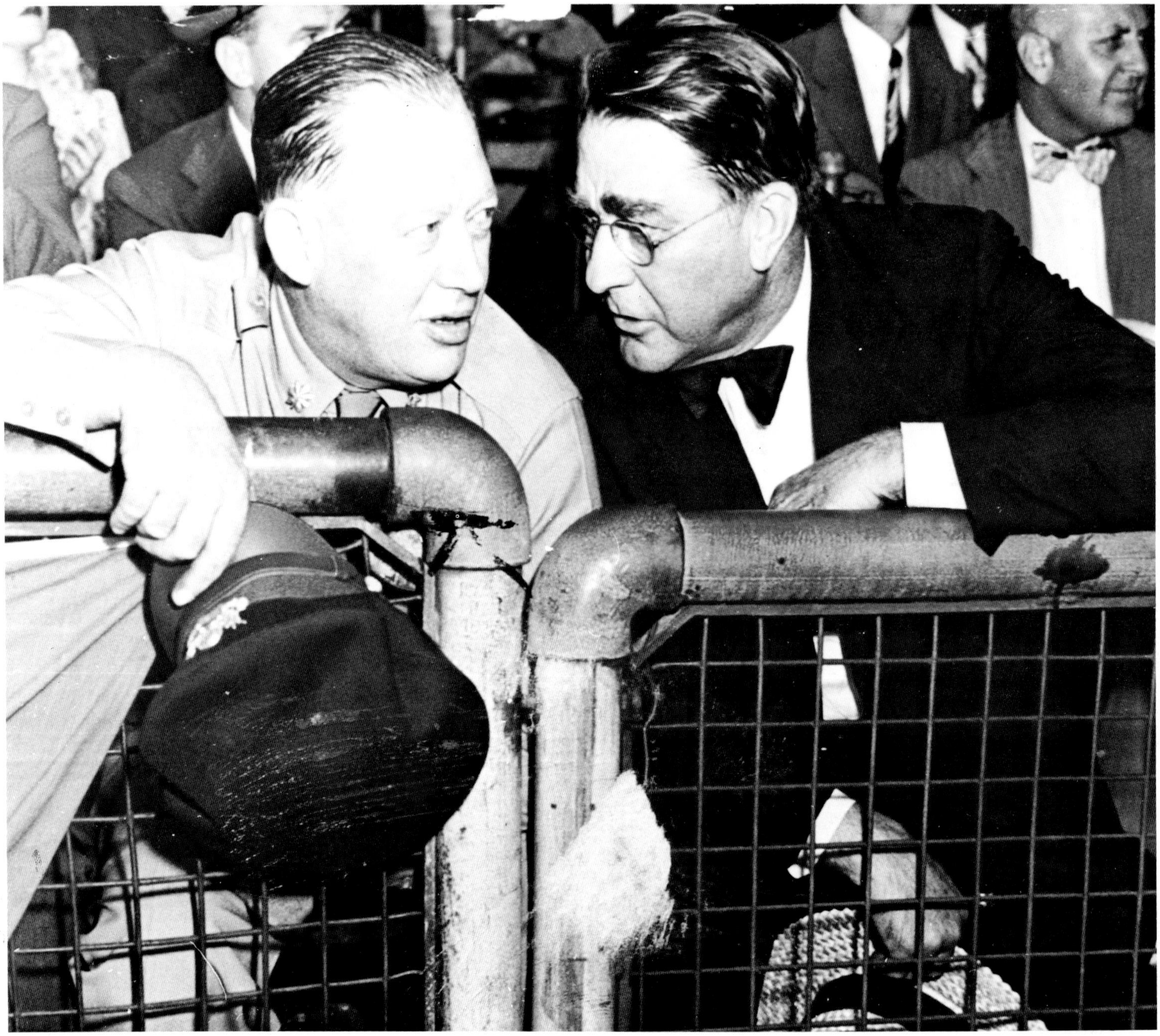

No decade since the 1880s has brought so many changes to baseball and the National League as the 1940s. After climbing steadily out of the pit of the Depression, organized baseball was totally disrupted by America's entry into World War II in December 1941, just at the point when something like normal prosperity had returned to the major leagues. Neither the country, the world nor the game would ever be the same.

Loss of manpower to conscription and wartime travel and materials restrictions were only part of the story. Within the span of a decade, the National League also had to deal with the player-raiding tactics of the Mexican League, the near-organization of a player's union, and the opening of the game to blacks and Hispanics. In the late 1940s, the advent of television and commercial air travel made it possible for clubs to consider new locations and created the potential for the franchise shifts which would soon become a reality. Night games and radio continued to be a growing force in a decade of astounding social and technological change, all contributing to a period of major upheaval for the National League.

The 1940s will always be remembered as a decade dominated in the National League by two great clubs. From 1941 to 1949, the Cardinals and the Dodgers won seven pennants, stepping aside only for Chicago in 1945 and Boston in 1948. In both those years, the Cardinals came in second. St Louis won four pennants during this period, won the World Series three times and finished second five times. Brooklyn won three pennants and finished second three times.

The opening year of the decade went to the Cincinnati Reds, who still displayed the effects of Larry MacPhail's team-building. In a repeat performance of 1939, Reds pitchers Bucky Walters and Paul Derringer both had 20-game years in 1940, Walters winning 22 and Derringer winning 20. Bill McKechnie's star first baseman, powerhouse Frank McCormick, led the league in hits for the third straight year, and was voted Most Valuable Player. The Reds' second straight pennant was marred only by the 3 August suicide of second-string catcher Willard Hershberger, who slashed his throat with a razor in the club's Boston hotel after several days of self-criticism for 'making a bad call.'

The Pirates' Debs Garms, who hit .355, was named league batting champion of 1940, even though he played in only 103 games (358 times at bat). The

Giants, the Cardinals and the Pirates introduced regular night games during the 1940 season, leaving only the Braves and the Cubs yet to join Larry MacPhail's arc-light revolution.

On 19 June, slugger Joe Medwick, who had been purchased by MacPhail for the Dodgers from St Louis one week earlier for $125,000, was traveling in an elevator in the Hotel New Yorker with Dodger manager Leo Durocher and former teammate Cardinal righthander Bob Bowman. Medwick and Durocher took the opportunity to needle Bowman, who was scheduled to start against them in a game that afternoon. As they left the elevator, Bowman's parting words were, 'I'll take care of both of you this afternoon.'

On Medwick's first trip to bat, a fastball from Bowman struck him in the head and rendered him unconscious. The Dodgers grabbed bats and charged the pitcher. As soon as Medwick was safely removed to the hospital, Larry MacPhail called National League President Ford Frick and demanded that Bowman be banned from baseball for life. Frick rejected MacPhail's request, the game went on with Bowman removed, and after about a week Medwick rejoined the Dodgers, but he was never to be the powerhouse hitter he had been for the Cardinals.

Larry MacPhail, who had created pennant winners from a moribund Cincinnati club in 1939 and 1940, signed on as general manager for Brooklyn in 1938, and immediately began rebuilding a Dodgers club which had not won a pennant since 1920. Spending lavishly, he installed lights in Ebbets Field, and in 1939 hired rambunctious Leo Durocher as manager. MacPhail and Durocher formed a powerful, volatile combination that made Brooklyn one of the most exciting and disliked clubs in the league. Battling each other as they battled for pennants, MacPhail fired and rehired Durocher at least once even before his first season as manager began.

Only somewhat daunted by the denting of prize acquisition Joe Medwick, MacPhail proceeded to plug up leaks in a Dodger squad that had come in second to Cincinnati in 1940 by purchasing hurler Kirby Higbe – who won 20 games in 1941 – from the Phillies, catcher Mickey Owen from the Cardinals and Billy Herman from Chicago. Other MacPhail acquisitions included first baseman Dolf Camilli and former American Leaguers pitcher Whitlow Wyatt and outfielder Dixie Walker, 'the Peepul's Cherce.' Wyatt won 22 games in 1941, including seven shutouts, for a 2.34 ERA, his best year ever.

Above: Outfielder Dixie Walker, also known as 'The People's Cherce,' batted a career .306.

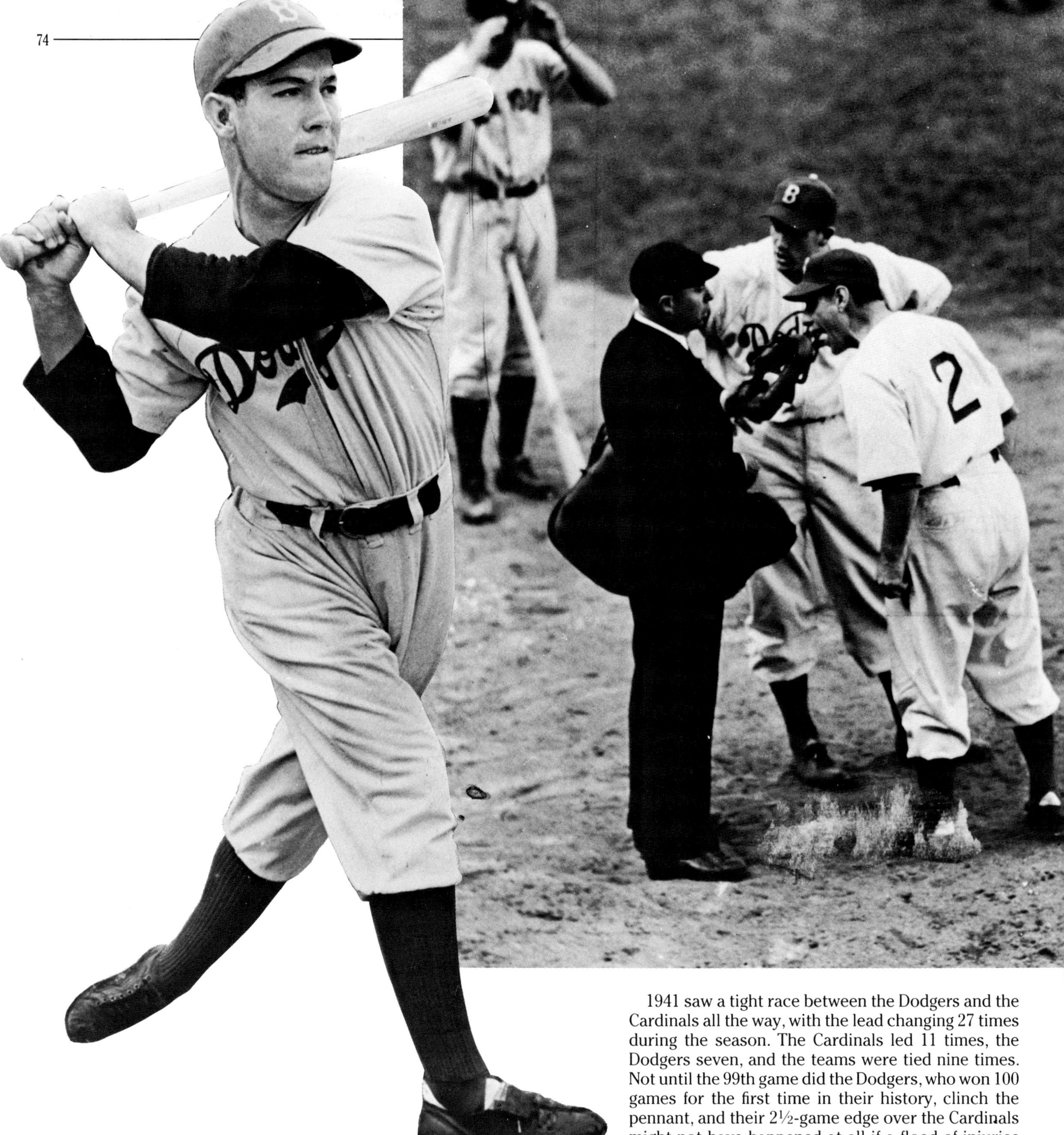

Above: Pete Reiser warms up. Harold Patrick 'Pistol Pete' Reiser played the outfield for the Dodgers (1940-42 and 1946-48), the Braves (1949-50), the Pirates (1951) and the Cleveland Indians (1952), and had a .295 batting average.
Top right: Pitcher John Whitlow 'Whit' Wyatt and manager Leo Durocher of the Dodgers rush in to protest umpire Bill McGowan's call.

Shortstop Pee Wee Reese and centerfielder Pete Reiser were also MacPhail finds. Reese, an excellent shortstop who played for the Dodgers for 16 years, was never a great hitter, but he was a fast, smart player who excelled at all the intangibles, and was usually found at the center of any Dodger rally. 'Pistol Pete' Reiser, a tremendously exciting player and one of the great centerfielders of the National League, hit .343 in his first full season to become, at 22, the youngest player to take the National League batting title. In 1941, Reiser led the league in hitting, slugging, runs, doubles and triples, and came in second, sandwiched between teammates Dolf Camilli and Whit Wyatt, in the balloting for Most Valued Player.

1941 saw a tight race between the Dodgers and the Cardinals all the way, with the lead changing 27 times during the season. The Cardinals led 11 times, the Dodgers seven, and the teams were tied nine times. Not until the 99th game did the Dodgers, who won 100 games for the first time in their history, clinch the pennant, and their 2½-game edge over the Cardinals might not have happened at all if a flood of injuries hadn't sidelined some of St Louis's best players. Experiencing some bad breaks of their own, the Dodgers dropped the World Series to the Yankees, 4-1.

In a game against Pittsburgh on 18 September, Leo Durocher's violent reaction to a call by umpire George Magerkurth caused him to be ejected from the game and fined $150. The next day, in Philadelphia, the Lip ran into Ted Meier of the Associated Press, who questioned him about the previous day's events. Durocher responded by knocking Meier down. Bystanders separated the two, and they parted after shaking hands.

On the occasion of the Dodger victory celebration, which was to be held at Grand Central Terminal,

Durocher was again fired by general manager MacPhail. While the team was returning from New York to Boston, Durocher, fearing some of the players might slip off to avoid the celebration, prevented the train from stopping at 125th Street. Unknown to him, MacPhail had planned to board the train at 125th Street to join his team in its hour of glory. Outraged because the train hadn't stopped, when MacPhail arrived at Grand Central he greeted his manager with, 'You're fired!' but rehired him the next day when he heard the whole story.

Expecting an easy repeat of 1941, the Dodgers built up a 10-game lead by mid-August 1942. By this time every team in the league had become familiar with their beanballs, fists, spikes and mouthy manager. Among the few who felt that the pennant wasn't securely Brooklyn's yet was Larry MacPhail, who invaded the clubhouse one day to caution his team against the Cardinals and warn them that they ought to be 20 games up. MacPhail declined a bet against Dixie Walker, who maintained that the Bums would finish no less than eight games ahead of St Louis.

Unfortunately for the Dodgers, MacPhail's misgivings proved to be correct. The Cardinals put on the greatest stretch run in history, winning 43 of their last 51 games – 34 of their last 40, including 21 of 26 in September – to take the flag from the Dodgers by two games, 106-104.

A heart-breaking injury suffered by Pete Reiser in July contributed to the Dodger defeat. The accident-prone Reiser, considered by many who saw him before this accident to be the greatest natural ball player of all time, was batting .390 when, with characteristic enthusiasm, he ran into an outfield wall chasing a ball in St Louis. Hospitalized with a severe concussion, he returned to the lineup too soon, as was then the practice, and his average dropped to .310 as he finished out the season playing through headaches, dizzy spells and double vision. Although there were flashes of the old Reiser after that – he stole home seven times in 1946 – 'Pistol Pete' was never quite the same.

Be that as it may, the Cardinals of 1942 were quite capable of standing on their own. Twenty-two of their 25-man roster came from the St Louis farm system. Many consider this team, which was to take four pennants in five years, one of the greatest National League teams of all time. Heading the strong pitching staff was Mort Cooper, winning 22 games and the Most Valuable Player Award for a 1.77 ERA and the best year of his career. He was supported by Johnny Beazley, with 21 wins in 1942, Ernie White, Howie Pollett and Max Lanier, all recording a team ERA of 2.55. Marty Marion played peerless shortstop, and Mort Cooper's brother Walker played behind the plate. Enos Slaughter and Terry Moore in the outfield were joined by a rookie named Stan Musial.

Stanislaus Musial had started in the minors as a pitcher, but a shoulder injury forced him to concentrate on hitting. Brought up to the Cardinals at the end of 1941, he hit .426 in 12 games, and in his first full season averaged .315. Modest, likeable, and one of the most popular players in National League history, beginning with his rookie year he batted well over .300 for 16 consecutive seasons, totally dominating league hitting for more than a decade. His popularity was such that it transcended the usual team loyalties – it was hypercritical Brooklyn fans admiring his style at Ebbets Field who first called him 'Stan the Man.'

The Man hit his stride in 1943, when as Most Valuable Player he led the league in hitting (.357), hits

Left: Stanley Frank 'Stan the Man' Musial was a star in the outfield and at first base for the Cardinals from 1941 to 1963 (with service time off in 1945). He had 3630 hits, 475 home runs and a batting average of .331. He was elected to the Hall of Fame in 1969.

Right: Walker Cooper was a star catcher for 18 years with the Cardinals (1940-45), the Giants (1946-49), the Reds (1949-50), the Boston (later the Milwaukee) Braves (1950-53), the Pirates (1954), the Cubs (1954-55) and the Cardinals again (1956-57).

(220), doubles (48), triples (20), total bases (347) and slugging (.562); and came in second in runs with 108. His best season wasn't until 1948, but in 1962, in his 42nd year, he still managed to hit .330, just one point below his lifetime average. In the 22 years of his career, Stan Musial won seven batting titles and led the league six times in hits, eight times in doubles, five times in triples and six times in slugging. A strong defensive outfielder and an excellent base runner, Stan the Man remained accessible and considerate to fans and writers even as he rose to world fame, and was a truly loved ballplayer. When he retired, the city of St Louis honored him by commissioning a statue of the slugger and placing it outside the stadium.

Despite the Cardinals' great stretch drive of 1942, few people were prepared to believe that they had a chance against the Yankees, a club that had won its last eight World Series contests, and which in fact hadn't lost since the Cardinals beat them in 1926. In the first game, the Yankees were leading 7-0, but with two outs in the ninth inning, the Cardinals scored four

Right: Rip Sewell demonstrates his 'eephus' pitch to catcher Al Lopez. Truett Banks 'Rip' Sewell was famous for this blooper pitch when he played for the Tigers (1932) and the Pirates (1938-49). He won 143 games in his 13-year career, and carried an earned run average of 3.48.
Below: Elmer Riddle pitched for the Reds (1939-47) and the Pirates (1948-49).

runs. They lost the game but, according to announcer Dizzy Dean, that was 'just the shot in the arm our boys needed.' The Cardinals swept the next four games of the Series, rounding out their incredible year of 1942 with a resounding defeat of the Yankees.

By the beginning of the 1942 season, American participation in the war was in full swing, and 161 National League players were already serving in the armed forces. After the end of the 1942 season, Larry MacPhail left the Dodgers to accept a commission as lieutenant colonel in the Service of Supply, and was replaced by Branch Rickey, who signed on for a five-year contract. Most of the superstars of the 1930s were off to war by the end of 1943. More than 1000 major leaguers – a 60 percent turnover of personnel – would don military uniforms by 1944.

Only a few good players remained. Stan Musial's children exempted him from the draft until 1945, when he entered the Navy, but by then the major leagues, filled with 4-F's, overage players, youngsters and a handful of Latin-Americans, were no longer playing major-league ball. In 1944, Cincinnati, with two infield positions held down by epileptics, sent fifteen-year-old Joe Nuxhall to the mound. The Waner brothers (Paul collected his 3000th hit in 1942), Debs Garms and Pepper Martin were among the elderly who returned to the diamond during what is often charitably referred to as the caretaking era.

Lack of talent was compounded by transportation restrictions – temporarily ending spring training in the South – low salaries in an inflated wartime economy, and shortages of equipment and food. Everyone knew that this was not really baseball, but the fans gave no sign of deserting the game. Although attendance slumped considerably in 1942-1943, it picked up rapidly in 1944-1945, topping all records since 1930 and giving hope for the postwar future. During the war every major-league team except the Yankees stepped up radio broadcasting, a factor which probably increased interest in the game, and in 1944, American League attendance topped the 5 million mark for the first time since 1940. The World Series of 1945, which one sportswriter characterized as a test to see which wartime 'team' could lose first, set a new record for attendance and profit.

During the war years baseball was classified as a non-essential industry but, contrary to official treatment in World War I, the game was encouraged and even exhorted to continue as a morale builder and a diversion. Early in 1942, in response to a letter from Commissioner Landis, President Roosevelt wrote his famous 'green light' letter, lauding baseball for its contribution to sustaining national morale, and urging the game to 'Carry on to the fullest extent consistent with the primary purpose of winning the war.' In 1943, Manpower Commissioner Paul V McNutt even permitted ballplayers to leave essential winter factory jobs to play ball.

Among the many players who entered the service in 1943 were Pee Wee Reese and Pete Reiser of the Dodgers and John Beazley and Terry Moore of the

Above: A big league reunion is held by three former baseball players at a camp in the Pacific. Left is Marine PFC James 'Big Jim' Bivin, a former Phillies pitcher. Center is Army Lieutenant John Thomas 'Long Tom' Winsett, a former outfielder for the Red Sox, Cardinals and Dodgers. Right is Marine Corporal Calvin Leavell 'Preacher' Dorsett, a former pitcher with the Indians.

Top: While soldiers of two units are relaxing with a game of baseball in Luxembourg during World War II, a detonation charge is set off in the background – a reminder of the grim business of war.

Above: Outfielder Bill Nicholson in batting practice. In his 16 years with the Cubs and Phillies (1939-53), William Beck 'Swish' Nicholson hit 235 home runs, batted in 948 runs and had an average of .268.
Opposite: Phil Cavaretta played first base and outfield for the Cubs (1934-53) and the White Sox (1954-55). He had a .293 batting average.
Below: Left to right – Will Harridge, Judge Kenesaw Mountain Landis and Ford Frick – the professional baseball hierarchy.

Cardinals. Even though the Cards lost many of their regulars, because of their extensive farm system they were able to come up with more competent replacements than any other National League team. Mort Cooper was still on hand, and Stan Musial didn't enter the Navy until 1945. It was small wonder that St Louis swept to easy victories in 1943 and 1944, taking three flags in a row.

Musial batted .357 to lead the league in his 1943 MVP year, and hit a respectable .347 in 1944. The Yankees took their revenge on the Cardinals for 1942 by taking the 1943 World Series in five games, but the Cards came back to take the Series from the Browns in six games in 1944, in the first World Series played entirely west of the Mississippi. Redbird second baseman Emil Verban batted .421 for the Series, reportedly out of anger at the Browns for seating his wife behind a post for three of the games.

Chalking up his third 20-game season in a row, Mort Cooper won 22 games for the Cardinals in 1944. Ted Wilks, released by the Army because of a stomach ulcer, was 17-4, and George Munger won 11 of 14 games before his induction in July. The Most Valuable Player Award stayed in St Louis for the second straight year, going to 'Mr Shortstop' Marty Marion. In the outstanding pitching achievement of the year, Boston righthander Jim Tobin pitched two no-hitters, blanking the Dodgers, 2-0 on 27 April, and the Phillies, 7-0 on 22 June.

Baseball's first Commissioner, Kenesaw Mountain Landis, died on 25 November 1944, five days after his 78th birthday, after 44 years of service. On 24 April 1945, club owners of both leagues elected gung-ho 'Ah love baseball' Albert Benjamin 'Happy' Chandler to replace him. The former governor and United States Senator from Kentucky was signed to a seven-year contract at $50,000 a year.

In 1945, the Cubs, spearheaded by first baseman Phil Cavarretta, finished three games ahead of second-place St Louis to take the last pennant they would win for decades. Stan Musial's absence in the Navy helped, but Cavarretta turned in a respectable .355 average to take the MVP Award and the league batting championship, and righthander Hank Borowy, acquired by the Cubs at the end of July from the Yankees, was 11-2 for the Bruins, becoming the only pitcher ever to win 20 games while dividing a season between two leagues.

The real batting achievement of the 1945 season went to Boston outfielder Tommy Holmes, who established a new National League record for hitting safely in 37 consecutive games. During his streak, which lasted from 6 June through 8 July, he batted .423, although his season average of .352 fell three points short of league-leading MVP Cavarretta.

The war was over. Even before the end of the pennant races, some regular players managed to slip out of the military and back into baseball uniform. Perhaps it was public jubilation at the successful conclusion of the wars in Europe and the Pacific that brought record numbers of fans to the World Series – the Cubs lost to the Tigers in seven – or perhaps it was anticipation of the return of the big-name heroes that drew the public to the parks. Baseball had more than weathered the war, and with profits and attendance finally rising above Depression and wartime lows, everyone looked forward to the coming season.

Having waited patiently for the right moment, Branch Rickey chose this happy time of rising expectations and social upheaval to break baseball's color line by signing three black players for the Dodgers. Pitchers Ray Partlow and John Wright, of the Newark Eagles, went to Three Rivers, Quebec. Shortstop Jackie Robinson, who had played with the Kansas City Monarchs, was signed on 28 August 1945 and sent to the Dodger's top farm club in Montreal, in the International League. Jackie Robinson, one of the most exciting players of his era, was destined to be the first black to play major-league ball in the 20th century.

Excluded from National League baseball in the 1880s by an unwritten but ironclad 'gentlemen's agreement,' blacks had formed their own leagues, and could boast players the equal of any in the majors. Exhibition games between blacks and white major leaguers left no doubt about the quality of black talent. Dizzy Dean once remarked, 'I have played against a Negro All-Star team that was so good, we

didn't think we had an even chance against them.' But despite antidiscrimination laws, baseball remained steadfastly segregated.

In 1943, when Bill Veeck, Jr proposed to purchase the limping Phillies and build the club up with black players, including the legendary pitcher Satchel Paige, he was warned off by Commissioner Landis and League President Ford Frick, and the club was sold elsewhere for less than he had offered. At about the same time, under similar pressure, Pittsburgh Pirate President William Benswanger called off tryouts for

Dixie Walker, the Dodger outfielder, takes batting practice.

Roy Campanella, Sam Hughes and Dave Barnhill. In 1901, when John J McGraw, then managing the Orioles, tried to sneak black second baseman Charlie Grant onto his team by passing him off as a full-blooded Cherokee, Chicago White Sox President Charlie Comiskey – who had seen Grant play with the Chicago Columbia Eagles in the black leagues – made sure it didn't happen. When Jackie Robinson arrived in Montreal 44 years later, the manager of the Dodger farm team asked Branch Rickey, 'Do you really think a nigger's a human being?'

Rickey's motives in choosing Jackie Robinson as a test case for the 1947 season were mixed, and will probably remain forever obscure. Certainly Robin-

Jack Roosevelt Robinson at the plate. Jackie was the courageous player who broke the color barrier in baseball, playing both the infield and the outfield in his ten-year career with the Brooklyn Dodgers (1947-56). He was voted Rookie of the Year in 1947, Most Valuable Player in 1949, elected to the Hall of Fame in 1962 and had a lifetime .311 batting average.

son, a college graduate and a superior infielder, was the right man, capable of enduring the ordeal he was about to go through. But whatever Rickey's moral imperative, no one doubts that he was driven at least as strongly by his legendary fondness of the dollar. Black players represented a vast, untapped reservoir of major-league talent, and Rickey was convinced that the Dodgers would get an edge on other teams if they were the first to sign blacks. He was evidently correct, as the Dodgers became the dominant team in the league for a decade following Robinson's debut, and the National League gained a supremacy over the American League that still holds today. The Yankees didn't play a black until eight years after the Dodgers, the White Sox not until 12 years after Robinson's breakthrough.

When Jackie Robinson came up to the Dodgers in 1947 he faced years of vicious insults at every level. The Dodgers themselves talked of circulating a petition asking that Robinson not be brought up. Dixie Walker asked to be and was traded. The Phillies, and manager Ben Chapman in particular, were warned by Ford Frick to curb their abuse. The Dodgers were for a time obliged to move spring training out of the American South to Cuba.

Fortunately, Robinson proved to be a superstar ballplayer and a man with enough restraint to integrate the league. Other blacks followed after he broke

Sal Maglie warms up. Salvatore Anthony 'The Barber' Maglie pitched for ten years in the majors, with time off for the Mexican League. He started with the Giants (1945, 1950-55), went to the Cleveland Indians (1955-56), then to the Dodgers (1956-57), then to the Yankees (1957-58) and finally to the Cardinals (1958). He had a phenomenal 119-62 record with a 3.15 ERA.

the ice, until by the 1960s more than 100 black players had joined the majors. In 1967, 23 blacks in the National League and 17 blacks in the American League accounted for well over half of the base hits made that year. A recent study has shown that black pitchers have consistently better averages than white pitchers, and black batters generally hit harder and have higher averages than do whites, but the most profitable endorsements and peripheral rewards still go primarily to whites.

In 1946, with the nation just beginning to adjust to a peacetime economy, National League club owners faced two separate but related precedent-setting challenges. In the spring, Mexican millionaire Jorge Pascual and his four brothers, attempting to create a Mexican League to compete with the American majors, began luring away top American players by offering them princely salaries. Pascual succeeded in enticing away some excellent players, many of whom were dissatisfied with the domestic pay scale. The Giants lost seven players to the Mexican League: pitchers Sal Maglie and relief star Ace Adams, Harry Feldman, Adrian Zabala, Roy Zimmerman, George Hausman and Danny Gardella. The Cardinals lost their star pitcher, Max Lanier, as well as pitcher Fred Martin and infielder Lou Klein. The Dodgers lost outfielder Luis Olmo and their regular catcher, Mickey Owen. Just back from a year in the Navy, Stan Musial considered a $65,000 advance against a five-year offer of $130,000, but opted to remain with the Cardinals.

American owners, with the blessings of Commissioner Chandler, outlawed the Mexican League and blacklisted any jumping players, vowing they would be barred from organized baseball for five years if they ever returned. As it turned out, the Mexican League proved to be a makeshift affair, and most of the jumpers were quickly disenchanted. Mickey Owen, the first of the returnees, came back to the States in August. But both American players and the Mexican Government were infuriated by the blacklisting and the declaration of illegality.

When Danny Gardella, who jumped to the Mexican League from the Giants, took the matter of his blacklisting to the courts, baseball executives, who knew their legal position was weak, rescinded the blacklists and issued amnesties to all fugitive players. No players were ever barred from returning to the American majors for much more than three years. Gardella was also paid an out-of-court settlement to drop his suit in 1949. Baseball men were beginning to understand that their regulations – such as the 'gentlemen's agreement' barring blacks – were subject to some limitations, and even to federal court jurisdiction if they involved international matters or matters of personal rights.

Far right: Baseball Commissioner A B 'Happy' Chandler (former governor of Kentucky) throws out the first ball at the World Series in 1947.

In the spring of 1946, at the same time that major strikes were taking place throughout the United States, onetime examiner for the National Labor Relations Board, Harvard lawyer Robert Murphy, formed the American Baseball Guild to represent players against owners. On 7 June, under Murphy's direction, the Pirates came very close to striking against Pittsburgh owner Bill Benswanger. Players across the league were remarkably united in their grievances, and the owners realized that they were not in a strong position, especially with the Mexican League checkbook ready to snap up players who were tired of waiting for things to get better.

Commissioner Chandler, hoping to outflank the formation of a serious players' union, invited the players, who were dissatisfied with their lack of financial security, to send delegates to discuss their grievances. In September the owners granted a number of concessions to the players, really a sort of players 'magna charta,' which included a $5000 minimum salary, limit of salary cuts to 25 percent per year, a pension fund bolstered by club payments, shorter spring training, free medical benefits and an allowance for spring training – $25 per week – known ever since as 'Murphy Money.' Player organization was stopped short of full unionization, but the incident led in time to the formation of the powerful Major League Baseball Players' Association.

In 1946, as if picking up where they left off, the Dodgers and the Cardinals ran a tight and exciting pennant race. At the end of the season the clubs were tied 96-58, necessitating the first pennant play-off in major-league history. The Cardinals took the first two of the best two-out-of-three series and went on to even greater glory by defeating the heavily-favored Red Sox in the World Series, 4-3. Leo Durocher, managing the Dodgers, enunciated the famous 'Nice guys finish last' in the dugout before a game at the Polo Grounds on 5 July. He was referring to famous nice guy 'McGraw's Little Boy' Mel Ott, who was managing the Giants.

Stan Musial helped his team to the pennant with a league-leading .365 average, and also led the league in doubles, triples, hits, runs, slugging and total bases. Pittsburgh's Ralph Kiner led the league in homers, with 23. The 23-year-old rookie outfielder, hitting high and far, would continue to tie or lead the league in home runs for his first seven seasons. Also in 1946, the Braves became the seventh National League team to install arc-lights, leaving the Cubs as the last holdouts (as they remain to this day).

During the spring training exhibition season of 1947 in Havana, Leo Durocher climaxed a series of run-ins with baseball's top executives when he heckled his former boss Larry MacPhail, now with the Yankees, who was apparently entertaining two well-known gamblers in a private box behind the Yankee dugout. Quipped Durocher, who had been accused of gambling on more than one occasion, 'Are there two sets of rules, one for managers, and one for owners?'

MacPhail, who was already involved in an acrimonious dispute with Dodger general manager Branch Rickey which featured public name-calling, did not take kindly to Durocher's remarks. Durocher further entered the fray by telling the *Brooklyn Eagle*

Far left: Ralph McPherran Kiner, who hit 369 in his 10 years in the majors, with the Pirates (1946-53), the Cubs (1953-54) and the Indians (1954). This outfielder led the league seven times in home run production and had a .256 average; he also batted .429 in the only World Series he appeared in. A Hall of Famer, he is now an announcer for the New York Mets.

Below: Bert Shotten (left) greets Mel Ott. Burton Edwin 'Barney' Shotten had had a so-so career as a player, playing the outfield for the Browns, the Senators and the Cardinals from 1909 to 1923, but he came into his own as a manager with Philadelphia (1928-33), Cincinnati (1934) and Brooklyn (1947-50). In his four years at Brooklyn, he won two pennants and one World Series. Ott was the manager of the Giants in 1947 and 1948.

that MacPhail had offered him the management of the Yankees. McPhail retorted that the reverse was true, that Durocher had solicited the job from him, and filed a bill of particulars with Commissioner Chandler accusing Durocher of 'conduct detrimental to baseball.'

After a couple of hearings, Commissioner Chandler, who seemed to harbor a particular dislike for Durocher, suspended the Lip from baseball for one year. The Yankees and the Dodgers were both fined $2000 each for dragging baseball's good name though the mud, and old-timer Burt Shotton was called out of semi-retirement to replace Durocher for the year.

At the very height of the commotion – Durocher was suspended about one week before the opening of the season – the Dodgers announced that they had purchased Jackie Robinson's contract from Montreal. Major-league baseball was now officially integrated.

Robinson's rookie season was greeted with a flood of racial incidents, ranging from abuse by some of his teammates to serious tension in many cities. The Cardinals threatened to strike rather than appear on the same field with a black man. League President Ford Frick responded immediately and forcefully, vowing to suspend any player who struck. 'I do not care if half the league strikes. Those who do it will encounter quick retribution. All will be suspended and I do not care if it wrecks the National League for five years. This is the United States of America and one citizen has as much right to play as another.'

There was no strike. Robinson, despite a hellish reception, managed to play better than competent ball, batting .297 and stealing 29 bases. Named Rookie of the Year, his performance undoubtedly helped his team take the pennant, and he became the mainstay of a Dodgers club that was to win six pennants in the next ten years.

Above: Ewell 'The Whip' Blackwell, described as a 'buggy whip with ears,' winds up. Blackwell pitched for the Reds (1942-52), the Yankees (1952-53) and Kansas City (1955). His best year was 1947, when he won 22 and lost eight.

Right: Ford Frick, the president of the National League.

Pitching for fifth-place Cincinnati, righthander Ewell Blackwell had a 22-8 season that included 16 wins in a row, and came close to duplicating teammate Johnny Vander Meer's double no-hitters. After no-hitting the Braves on 18 June, Blackwell had only two outs to go to win a second consecutive no-hitter when Eddie Stanky of the Dodgers grounded a single through his legs. Curiously, the Dodgers and the Braves were the same two clubs Vander Meer won his back-to-back no-hitters from. Asked what he was thinking while he watched his teammate from the dugout, Vander Meer replied that if Blackwell did it, 'I wanted to be the first one out there to shake his hand.'

In his second year, Ralph Kiner hit 51 home runs for his last-place Pittsburgh team to tie Johnny Mize of the Giants for the 1947 league title. Mize and Kiner became the second and third players in National League history, after Hack Wilson, to hit more than 50 home runs in one year. The fourth-place Giants, with big guns Mize hitting 51 homers, Willard Marshal 36, Walker Cooper 35 and Bobby Thomson 29, set a new team home run record with 221.

Postwar baseball had entered a lucrative period. The National League became the first league to pass the 10 million attendance mark, with 10,388,470 paying spectators attending National League games in 1947.

Leo Durocher returned to the Dodgers in 1948, but only for half a season. Giant owner Horace Stoneham, who was tired of likeable but ineffectual manager Mel Ott, and Branch Richey, who had apparently had enough of lippy Leo and his squabbles with his players, arranged one of the most shocking managerial shifts in baseball history. Stoneham, who went to Rickey to ask for his approval to approach Burt Shotton to replace Ott, found himself being offered Durocher instead. He accepted the offer, Leo agreed, and the Lip took up his new duties on 16 July. Branch Rickey called Burt Shotton back to manage the Dodgers, and Mel Ott accepted a position in the Giant front office as assistant to farm director Carl Hubbell.

For the first time in 34 years, the Boston Braves, an unremarkable team except for their pitchers, won a pennant, finishing 6½ games in front of the Cardinals. Righthander Johnny Sain won 24 games and lefthander Warren Spahn won 15, the duo's exploits inspiring the doggeral verse, 'Spahn and Sain/Then pray for rain.' They each won a game in the World Series, but the Braves lost to the Indians, 6-2.

Stan Musial won another Most Valuable Player

Above: Willard Warren Marshall played the outfield for the Giants, the Boston Braves, the Reds and the White Sox from 1942-55, carrying a .274 batting average.

Far left: Hall of Famer Warren Edward Spahn pitched for the Braves from 1942 to 1964 – first in Boston and then in Milwaukee – before spending 1965 with the Giants. He won 363 games and had an ERA of 3.09.

Right: First baseman 'Eddie' Waitkus played for the Cubs, Phillies and Orioles from 1941 to 1955. He carried a .285 batting average.

Opposite: Hall of Famer Roy Campanella caught for the Dodgers (1948-57), hit 242 home runs and batted in 856 runs.
Below: Elwin Charles 'Preacher' Roe pitched for the Cardinals, the Pirates and the Dodgers.

Award in 1948, in what was his best year and the finest all-round year of any National League hitter since the war. The Man led the league in eight offensive categories, and came just one run short of tying for the league home run lead of 40, which was again shared by Ralph Kiner and Johnny Mize.

In his third year in the league, Jackie Robinson, now at second base, was voted the National League's Most Valuable Player by a wide margin. Robinson, in his best year ever, led the league with a .342 batting average, scored 122 runs and drove in 124. His league-leading 37 stolen bases was a sum greater than the team totals of the Cardinals, Phillies, Braves and Reds.

Eddie Waitkus of the Phillies was batting .306 when, shortly after midnight on 15 July 1949 at the Edgewater Beach Hotel in Chicago, he received a note requesting his immediate presence from Ruth Ann Steinhagen, also a guest at the hotel. When he reached her room, young Miss Steinhagen shot him in the chest with a .22-caliber rifle bullet. Waitkus eventually recovered, but played no more that season. Miss Steinhagen, who had previously consulted a psychiatrist about her secret, uncontrollable crush on the ballplayer and had been told that it was nothing to worry about, was committed for psychiatric therapy.

Leo Durocher, backed up by Giant coaches Fred Fitzsimmons and Frank Frisch, was exonerated at a hearing before Commissioner Chandler of the charge of slugging a fan on 28 April after a game at the Polo Grounds. As a result of the episode, however, Giant owner Horace Stoneham instituted a policy of keeping all spectators off the playing field until all uniformed personnel of both teams reached their clubhouses.

National League players who had been barred for jumping to the Mexican League were permitted to return to play this year (Max Lanier and Fred Martin dropped a \$2,500,000 damage suit and Danny Gardella withdrew his \$500,000 suit), and Mrs Ernie Bonham received the first death benefits of the player pension fund. Hurler Ernie Bonham died on 15 September following abdominal surgery. His widow received \$90 a month for ten years.

Fired by Jackie Robinson's stellar year, the Dodgers took the 1949 pennant. In what was to become the tension-filled trademark style of this exciting club, they clinched the flag in the tenth inning of the last game of the season, edging out the Cardinals by one game.

With other clubs still reluctant to sign blacks, the Dodgers had their pick of the finest black talent, and made choices that helped keep them on top for years. 1949 saw Roy Campanella and Don Newcombe play their first full seasons with the Dodgers. Largely because of Robinson's success, the Giants signed their first two blacks in 1949, Hank Thompson, who had played with the St Louis Browns in 1947, and Monte Irvin, from the Newark Eagles. Both first went to the Giants' Jersey City team.

The Dodgers almost signed Larry Doby, but Branch Rickey, learning that Bill Veeck wanted to sign him for Cleveland to integrate the American League, let the young power-hitter go, to further 'the cause,' as he put it. The pennant-winning 1949 Dodger club dropped the Series to the Yankees (their 12th Series win), but this team, put together by Branch Rickey, which in addition to its great black players included Pee Wee Reese, Gil Hodges, Billy Cox, Carl Furillo and Duke Snider, went on to dominate the 1950s as few clubs have ever dominated any decade.

C B S
TELEVISION
W M G M
DIAL
1050

James Lamar 'Dusty' Rhodes played the outfield for the Giants from 1952 to 1959.

CHAPTER FIVE

Dodger Dynasty

Home run hitters drive Cadillacs, singles hitters drive Fords.

Ralph Kiner

Opposite: Gilbert Raymond 'Gil' Hodges had a long career with the Dodgers (1943, 1947-61) before playing first base with the Mets (1962-63). He hit 370 home runs and batted .273. Hodges managed the Senators from 1963 to 1967 and the Mets from 1968 to 1971, bringing them their only World Series championship.
Opposite inset: Edwin Donald 'Duke' Snider, also called 'The Silver Fox,' played outfield for the Dodgers (1947-62), the Mets (1963) and the Giants (1964). His batting average was .297 and he hit 407 home runs.
Below: Carl Anthony Furrillo, also known as 'Skoonj' or 'The Reading Rifle,' played the outfield for the Dodgers (1946-60). Hitting .299, he batted in 1058 runs.

The team Branch Rickey built in Brooklyn after he took over from Larry MacPhail in 1942 was not only the greatest of his incredible career, but arguably the greatest National League team of all time. In the ten-year period 1947-1956, the Dodgers won six pennants and came in tight second three times. Only in 1948, when they came in third, 7½ games behind Boston, were they really out of the race. If the Dodgers had ended the seasons of 1946, 1950 and 1951 with winning rather than losing games, they would have won nine pennants in 11 years, including five in a row. If they had won 19 more games in the 11-year stretch 1946-1956, they could have won 11 pennants in 11 years.

The Dodger lineup that formed the guts of the 1949 pennant-winners remained essentially intact for the next decade, with Reese the only holdover from MacPhail's 1941 champions. He and Campanella, Snider, Hodges and Furillo remained in the lineup and at their positions until the Dodger move to Los Angeles in 1958. Third baseman Billy Cox left the Dodgers in 1954, and after Jim 'Junior' Gilliam arrived to take over second base in 1953, Jackie Robinson alternated between third base and the outfield for his remaining four years with the club.

The trio of Snider, Hodges and Campanella had five seasons in which they hit over 100 homers combined, and Robinson and Reese were the league's best base stealers. Defensively, Furillo, Cox, Snider, Reese, Robinson, Hodges and Campanella were all at one time or another considered the best in the league at their positions. The only weakness in the club – and probably the reason they didn't win every pennant of their era – was lack of depth in their pitching staff. The only pitchers with any sustained success were Don Newcombe, who won 20 games three times and 17 or more five times, and Carl Erskine, who won at least 11 games for six straight seasons. Preacher Roe and Clem Labine had brief flashes of excellence, but otherwise, in marked contrast to the stability of the team as a whole, inconsistent hurlers, some with moments of great brilliance, came and went.

At the beginning of the 1950s, the club was young, and it could hit and run and throw. As the century reached its mid-point and the National League

FIRST IN
NEWS
CIRCULATION
ADVERTISING
The Washington Post
MINNESOTA
WASHINGTON
BALL
AT BAT

entered the last quarter of its first 100 years, the team that Rickey built showed its stuff by taking five of the 1950s pennants, coming in second three times and finishing out of the first division only once in the decade.

The 1950 pennant went to the Phillies. Nicknamed the 'Whiz Kids' for their spirited play and their youth – their average age was only 26 – the first Phillies pennant in 35 years climaxed seven years of rebuilding by owner Robert Carpenter, a heavy investor in the postwar bonus boom that saw half a dozen young players collect over $50,000 each. The Phillies' first flag win since 1915 was spearheaded by a pitching staff which featured Robin Roberts, their first 20-game winner since 1917; Curt Simmons, who won 17 games before being inducted into the Army; and relief ace Jim Konstanty, whose 16 wins in 74 relief appearances earned him the Most Valuable Player Award, the first time the award ever went to a relief pitcher.

With 11 games remaining in the season, the Phillies were seven games up, but injuries to two starting pitchers and Curt Simmons's September induction precipitated a decline which cost the club eight of their next ten games. As fate would have it, the Phillies, only one game ahead, faced the Dodgers at Ebbets Field on 1 October.

Manager Eddie Sawyer chose Robin Roberts to save the pennant from Brooklyn's Don Newcombe. For Roberts, now in his third National League season, this was the third start in five days. He held Newcombe to a 1-1 standoff until the bottom of the ninth inning, when the Dodgers put men on first and second with none out. Duke Snider singled to center, and center fielder Richie Ashburn, who with the rest of the Phillies had been expecting a bunt, managed to scoop up the ball and throw Cal Abrams out at the plate.

Carl Furillo fouled out and Gil Hodges was retired on a fly ball. In the top of the tenth inning, Dick Sisler, son of first base immortal George Sisler, hit a three-run homer to save the day. His father, now the Dodgers' chief scout, was there to see his son help Robin Roberts to the first of six consecutive 20-games seasons.

On 31 August, Dodger first baseman Gil Hodges hit four home runs in the course of a 19-3 victory over the Braves at Ebbets Field to become the fourth National Leaguer, the sixth major-leaguer, and the first National Leaguer in the 20th century to hit four homers in a game. On 13 September, Giant pitcher Sal Maglie was only four outs away from breaking Carl

Opposite: Carl Daniel Erskine, pitcher for the Dodgers (1948-59).
Opposite inset: Hall of Famer Robert Evan Roberts pitched from 1948 to 1966, winning 286 games.
Below right: Outfielder Don Richie 'Whitey' Ashburn played for the Phillies, Cubs and Giants from 1948 to 1962.
Below left: Donald 'Newk' Newcombe pitched for the Dodgers, Reds and Cleveland.

Opposite: Willie Howard 'Say Hey' Mays played for the Giants (1951-52, 1954-72) and the Mets (1972-73). Elected to the Hall of Fame in 1979, he hit .302, stole 338 bases, and had 3283 hits and 660 home runs.

Hubbell's record of 46 and 1/3 consecutive scoreless innings when Pittsburgh's Gus Bell shattered his streak with a home run over the Polo Grounds' right field wall. Other 1950 business as usual included a 21-game year for Warren Spahn, another batting title for Stan Musial, and another home run title for Ralph Kiner.

In 1950 Grover Cleveland Alexander, who in 1915 pitched the Phillies to their only other pennant, died in St Paul, Nebraska in a room he rented out of his $150-a-month pension. Branch Rickey sold his interest in the Dodgers to Walter O'Malley and became general manager of the Pirates, Ford Frick was awarded another four years as National League president and major-league club owners, reflecting a growing distaste for the dictatorial style originated by Commissioner Landis, voted not to extend Commissioner Chandler's contract.

On 27 February 1951, the National League observed its 75th anniversary with a magnificent celebration at the Broadway Central Hotel, formerly known as the Grand Central Hotel, the place of the league's birth. A telegram from President Truman was read in which the chief executive called baseball 'our national sport' and made the following observation:

> The founders of the National League and the fans of that era never dreamed the game would achieve such popularity or there would be such inventions as radio and television to carry it to millions of Americans all over the world.

As the 1951 season began, what looked like an easy walk to the pennant for the Dodgers turned into a race that ended in one of the National League's most dramatic playoffs. The Dodgers took the lead on 13 May, while the Giants lost 11 of their first 12 games, and by mid-August, with a comfortable 13½ game lead on the second-place Giants, the Dodgers were apparently invulnerable. But then something happened.

Below: Alvin Ralph 'Blackie' Dark played the infield, mostly shortstop, for the Braves (1946-49), the Giants (1950-56), the Cardinals (1956-58), the Cubs (1958-60) and the Braves (1960), batting .289. He also managed the Giants (1961-64), the Royals (1966-67), the Indians (1968-71), the A's (1974-75) and the Padres (1977), winning two pennants and one World Series.

Leo Durocher, who took over the Giants in 1948, had been rebuilding a team he had inherited which featured a lot of power but not much running speed. Big Guns Mize, Cooper, Marshall and Sid Gordon were gone by 1951, and a crucial trade with the Braves had brought the Giants Alvin Dark and Eddy Stanky. Durocher was able to begin 1951 with Monte Irvin on first, Stanky at second, Dark at shortstop and Henry Thompson or Bobby Thomson at third. Bobby Thomson, Whitey Lockman and Don Mueller covered the outfield, with Lockman and Irvin switching places early in the season. Sal Maglie, who returned from the Mexican League in 1950 to win 18 games, headed a strong pitching staff which included Larry Jansen, Jim Hearn, lefty Dave Koslo and sinkerball doctor George Spencer.

Late in May, Durocher brought up a 20-year-old center fielder from the Giants' Minneapolis farm club named Willie Mays. In Leo's own words, Mays 'could do the five things you have to do to be a superstar: hit, hit with power, run, throw and field. And he had that other magic ingredient that turns a superstar into a super superstar. He lit up the room when he came in. He was a joy to be around.'

Not everyone would agree that Mays was a joy to be around, particularly sportswriters and the fans he often treated with disdain, but no one has ever questioned that the Giants' center fielder was one of the most spectacular players of all time, and ranks with Honus Wagner among the very best players in National League history. From his first season as Rookie of the Year, with a modest .274 average and 20 home runs, Willie Mays demonstrated that he was born to hit home runs, make incredible catches, incredible throws and run out from under his hat with incredible flashes of speed and a sensational style that inspired the Giants to overcome insurmountable odds to take the pennant.

Mays was to compile a record ranking him in the National League all-time top five in hits, home runs, runs, RBI's, slugging and extra base hits, but by those who saw him he will probably best be remembered for a fielding style and a base-running flair that made impossible plays look easy and easy plays look exciting. In one four-year stretch he stole 136 bases, leading the league each year. In six seasons he stole at least 20 bases and hit at least 20 home runs, and in two others he stole at least 30 bases and hit at least 30 home runs, a feat equalled by only one other player in National League history, Bobby Banks, who played with Mays in San Francisco and learned from him.

A player who could do everything, offensively as well as defensively, Mays had six seasons in which he hit more than 40 home runs and two in which he hit more than 50 home runs, and he could also hit for average, leading the league with .345 in 1954 and reaching his personal peak of .347 in 1958. Just how important he was to the Giants' success was demonstrated dramatically when he disappeared into the service after the beginning of the 1952 season.

It was only after Mays' appearance in 1951 that Durocher's Giants began to make the most historic dash toward a pennant since the run of the Miracle Boston Braves in 1914. Starting on 12 August, the Giants won 16 consecutive games until, by 9 September (with the Dodgers losing 9 out of 18), they were only 5½ games behind. Then the Giants won 16 of their last 20 (while the Dodgers lost 11) to force the pennant race into a playoff.

GIANTS

Jim Hearn took the opening game for the Giants, 3-1, and Clem Labine took the second for the Dodgers, 10-0. The Dodgers were leading in the deciding game 4-1 when, in the bottom of the ninth, the Giants launched a rally. Alvin Dark singled, Don Mueller singled and Monte Irvin pop-fouled out. Then Whitey Lockman doubled, driving Dark home and putting the tying runs on second and third. Brooklyn's Don Newcombe was replaced by righthander Ralph Branca, who faced Giant Bobby Thomson.

So far in the game Thomson had distinguished himself by getting caught in a rundown after heading to second without realizing that Lockman was already there. Thomson let Branca's first strike go by, but sent the second one into the left field stands to clear the bases and give the Giants the pennant with 'the home run heard round the world,' etching into baseball legend one of the most dramatic climaxes in National League history.

It is interesting to note that an estimated three million family television sets were turned to the dramatic playoffs between the Dodgers and the Giants, and a few million others viewed it from bars and lounges. By 1951, television was an important force in American sports, and the income to baseball from telecasts was soon to be a major factor in the first National League franchise shifts in over 50 years. Profits to baseball from telecasts had risen steadily since television was introduced in the late 1940s, and amounted to $27.5 million in 1966.

On 20 September, Ford Frick was elected to succeed Happy Chandler as baseball commissioner, and one week later Warren Giles, general manager of the Reds, was elected president of the National League, to succeed Frick.

The Dodgers came back strong to take pennants in 1952 and 1953. The Giants actually took the lead early in 1952, but after Willie Mays was inducted into the Army on 29 May, they lost eight of their next ten games, and never recovered. Don Newcombe of the Dodgers was also inducted, a loss somewhat mitigated by the arrival of rookie righthander relief pitcher Joe Black, whose 15-4 season included 15 saves. Brooklyn unveiled its own rookie, Hoyt Wilhelm, who continued to throw his impossible knuckle ball for 21 years through 1070 games in the majors, retiring in 1972 at the age of 49.

On the way to the 1952 pennant, the Dodgers set a modern major-league record when they scored 15 runs in the first inning of a game against the Reds. Twenty-one Dodgers went to the plate in that inning, with 19 in a row reaching base safely. On 19 June, Carl Erskine held the Cubs hitless for a 5-0 win. By walking opposing pitcher Willard Ramsdell in the third inning, Erskine just missed becoming the first pitcher in 30 years to pitch a perfect game during the regular season.

The Dodgers faced the Yankees in the World Series, taking the first, third and fifth games, but losing their sixth consecutive Series clash. Notable in failure was Gil Hodges, with 32 homers and 102 RBI's for the season, who went hitless in 21 Series at-bats. In his first season as league president, Warren Giles set something of a record by fining Leo Durocher three times, all for clashes with umpires.

1953 marked the first National League franchise shift in 53 years. Only five years before, the Boston Braves had attracted 1,455,439 fans in a pennant winning season, but with total attendance for 1952 at only 281,000 and losses of $600,000, on 18 March 1953 owner Lou Perini announced the transfer of the

Opposite: Bobby Thomson takes his cuts. Robert Brown 'The Staten Island Scot' Thomson batted .270 and hit 264 home runs in his 15-year career. He played mainly the outfield for the Giants and for several other teams in the fifties, but he is best known for the home run that won the pennant for the Giants in 1951.

Left: Jackie Robinson reaches third base on a steal as a chagrined Gill McDougald stands helplessly by in the 1952 World Series between the Dodgers and the Yankees.
Below: Hoyt Wilhelm winds up. James Hoyt Wilhelm lasted a phenomenal 21 years in the majors (1952-72), pitching for nine teams. He won 143 games with his 2.52 earned run average.

Boston Braves to Milwaukee, citing sagging attendance and apathy on the part of the fans.

The move to Milwaukee paid off magnificently. The first 13 home games at Milwaukee showed an attendance total of 302,667, more than for all of 1952, and the Braves' 1,826,397 season attendance total marked a new National League record. 2,131,388 people paid to watch the Braves in 1954, and by 1957, with the Braves taking the first of two back-to-back pennants, attendance at Milwaukee topped 2 million for the fourth straight season, setting a new league record of 2,215,404. The thinking of club owners whose teams were struggling at the gate began to undergo some changes.

The Braves responded to their enthusiastic reception in Milwaukee in 1953 by moving from seventh to second place. Warren Spahn threw 23-7 for a 2.10 ERA year, the lowest of a career in which he 13 times won 20 or more games, while 21-year-old third baseman Eddie Mathews hit 47 homers to lead the league and end the seven-year reign of Ralph Kiner, who moved to the Cubs on 4 June. Kiner was also bested by Cincinnati's Ted Kluszewski and Brooklyn's Duke Snider and Roy Campanella, who took his second MVP.

From 13 May, the Braves were first or second in the pennant race. On 25 May, Braves righthander Max Surkant established a modern record by striking out eight consecutive batters. Lew Burdette won 15 games in the first of ten consecutive seasons in which he would win at least 10 games, Bill Bruton won the first of three consecutive stolen base titles and Joe Adcock hit 18 home runs.

Above: Edwin Lee 'Eddie' Mathews played third base for the Braves in Boston and Milwaukee (1952-65) and then went with them to Atlanta (1966). He went to Houston in 1967 and then switched to the American League and played for the Tigers (1967-68), hitting 512 home runs with a .271 batting average.
Right: Lew Burdette warms up. Selva Lewis Burdette pitched for the Yankees (1950), the Braves (1951-63 both in Boston and Milwaukee), the Cardinals (1963-64), the Cubs (1964-65), the Phillies (1965) and the Angels (1966-67). He won 203 games with a 3.66 ERA and in World Series play he was 4 and 2.

Only a Brooklyn club considered among the most powerful if not the most powerful in the history of the franchise was able to stop the rejuvenated Braves, but after taking the pennant by a whopping 13 games, the Bums once again lost to the Yankees in the World Series. Carl Erskine distinguished himself by striking out 14 Yankees in the third game, setting a new record, and Gil Hodges redeemed himself for his 1952 world championship performance by hitting .364 for the Series.

Charlie Dressen, who had managed the Dodgers to their last two pennants, found himself out of a job less than a week after the Series. When he formulated his demand for a three-year contract in terms of an ultimatum, the Dodgers, who preferred one-year contracts for managers, let him go, and owner O'Malley brought up Walter Alston from the Montreal (International League) farm club. Alston was unable to bring home the pennant in 1954, but he eventually helped the Dodgers to nine pennants, and signed 23 one-year contracts, ending his career with the Dodgers in Los Angeles.

Willie Mays came out of the Army stronger than when he went in, and it was a Giant team reinvigorated by his return that came out on top in 1954. Mays's batting average of .345 led the league, and he hit 41 home runs and 110 RBI's, with the usual spectacular fielding, for a 1954 Most Valuable Player Award performance that propelled his club to a finish five games ahead of the second-place Dodgers.

Johnny Antonelli, whom the Giants had acquired from the Braves in a trade for 1951 pennant hero Bobby Thomson, turned in a 21-7 season with a league-leading ERA for his new team. Don Mueller's average was second only to teammate Willie Mays'. In other hitting events of 1954, Stan Musial established a new major-league record when he hit five home runs in a doubleheader against the Giants on 2 May in St Louis, and Milwaukee's Joe Adcock hit four homers in one game against Brooklyn to equal the modern record. On 23 April, Milwaukee rookie Henry Aaron hit his first home run. Little attention was given to the homer he hit off Cardinal Vic Raschi, but it was the first of an amazing career which saw Aaron gain the all-time home run championship.

The Cleveland Indians, who set a new American League record with 111 wins, were highly favored to take the Series from the Giants, many thought in four games. But it was the Giants who swept the Series from the Indians, led by an incredible performance by James Lamar 'Dusty' Rhodes, whom Durocher had tried to trade at the beginning of the season, calling him the worst fielder he had ever seen.

Willie Mays lit up the first game with a spectacular catch that many regard as the most famous in World Series history. In the eighth inning, with the score tied at 2-2, two men on and none out, Mays caught Vic Wertz's 440-foot drive over his shoulder and returned it to the infield so fast that neither base runner could advance, squelching what had seemed a certain triple. In the tenth inning, with two Giants on, Dusty Rhodes was called in to pinch hit and produced a home run to win the game.

Rhodes hit a single driving in Mays in the fifth inning of the second game, and another homer driving in another run in the seventh inning. In the third game, a Rhodes single in the third inning drove in two runs. In his first four Series at-bats, Series MVP Rhodes got four hits – including two homers – and knocked in a total of seven runs.

This was the first National League Series win since 1946, and the first National League Series sweep since the Miracle Braves of 1914. The initial tendency to think of it as a fluke due to Rhodes's performance gave way over the passing years to the realization that the National League had now become baseball's power center. With the American League still proceeding cautiously in the signing of black players, most outstanding young black players chose to sign on with National League clubs, which they also

Joseph Wilbur Adcock played outfield and first base for 17 years in the majors – with the Reds (1950-52), the Braves (1953-62), the Indians (1963), the Dodgers (1964) and the Angels (1965-66). He hit 336 homers and had a .277 batting average. He also managed Cleveland in 1967, coming in eighth.

Right: Roy Campanella takes his swings.
Opposite: The Dodgers greet Roy Campanella as he returns to the dugout after one of his 242 home runs.
Below: Pee Wee Reese of the Dodgers forces Willie Mays of the Giants in the first half of a double play. Harold Henry 'The Little Colonel' Reese played shortstop for the Dodgers from 1941 to 1958, with three years off for military service during World War II. His lifetime batting average was .269. Mays hit .302 with 660 home runs in his 22-year Hall of Fame baseball career.

preferred for the opportunity to play alongside players such as Willie Mays and Jackie Robinson. Largely as a result of this trend, the National League eventually gained a dominance over the American League that is still unquestioned a quarter of a century later.

The Dodgers won 22 of their first 24 games in 1955, opening up a 9½-game lead by the end of the season's first month. Clinching the flag on 8 September, the earliest date in National League history, they never dropped out of first place, and finished 13½ games ahead of the second-place Braves. Don Newcombe had a 20-5 season and Roy Campanella joined baseball's elite few who have won three Most Valuable Player Awards. Featuring Gil Hodges, Carl Furillo, Jackie Robinson, Pee Wee Reese and RBI leader Duke Snider, the Dodgers as a team hit 201 home runs.

Best of all, the Bums won the World Series. After losing every one of their first seven contests, including five to the Yankees, in 1955 the Dodgers won what was to be their first and last World Series as the Brooklyn Dodgers. The deciding seventh game featured a famous play by Sandy Amoros in the bottom of the sixth when, with two on, Yogi Berra sliced a line drive down the left field line. Amoros managed to catch it with a sprint that carried him into the railings, but recovered quickly enough to relay the ball to

Dodgers
Dodger
Dodger
16
39

Right: Ted Kluszewski is welcomed at the plate after his 14th home run of the 1955 season by (left to right) Wally Post, Wes Westrum and the batboy. Theodore Bernard 'Klu' Kluszewski played first base for the Reds (1947-57), the Pirates (1958-59), the Cubs (1959-60) and the Dodgers (1961). He had a lifetime batting average of .298 and hit 279 home runs. **Below:** The young Henry Aaron.

Reese, who doubled up on McDougald at first. The Yankee's rally was over, and they never came close again.

Representing National League power this year was Mays with 51 homers, Kluszewski with 47, Ernie Banks with 44 and Mathews with 41. Henry Aaron had his first big year with 27 homers, 106 RBI's and a .314 average. Pittsburgh's 20-year-old Roberto Clemente, whom the Dodgers had mistakenly exposed to the draft, and who was eventually to take his place alongside Pirate greats Honus Wagner and Ralph Kiner, debuted with a modest .225.

At the annual winter meeting, National League directors voted 6 to 2 to make compulsory the wearing of protective headgear by all players when batting. Leo Durocher resigned as manager of the Giants at the end of the season to take an executive position with the National Broadcasting Company.

The Dodgers, who played seven 'home' games, one with each league rival, in Jersey City, New Jersey in 1956, as they would in 1957, sparking speculation that they would soon depart from Brooklyn permanently, took the pennant again in 1956, but only after taking the race down to the last day of the season, for the fourth time in eight years. Don Newcombe won his 27th and last victory of the regular season against the Pirates in the last game of the season to give the Dodgers the game they needed to secure the pennant from the Braves. For his performance that season, Newk was voted the first Cy Young Award, which was inaugurated at the suggestion of Commissioner Frick to recognize pitching excellence in the majors, and was also named Most Valuable Player.

The Milwaukee Braves, with annual attendance continuing above the 2 million mark, had now become serious contenders. Warren Spahn, Lew Burdette and Bob Buhl led the strong pitching staff, with Mathews, Adcock and Aaron supplying the power. Henry Aaron, by now as strong an all-round player as Willie Mays, if lacking his flamboyance, took his first batting title in 1956 with a .328 average.

Cincinnati, which the Dodgers eliminated only in the last days of the pennant race, tied the Giants' major-league home run club total record of 221, 20-year-old Frank Robinson hitting 38 home runs to take the Rookie of the Year Award with the only unanimous vote since the award's inception. Robinson's 38 homers tied the 1930 record for a rookie set by Wally Berger, and added to the established power of Reds' sluggers Kluszewski, Wally Post, Gus Bell and Ed Bailey.

The Dodgers lost the World Series to the Yankees in seven games in 1956, but not before Yankee hurler Don Larsen retired 27 Brooklyn batters in a row in the fifth game, the only perfect game in World Series history. In other landmark events, Pittsburgh first baseman Dale Long hit home runs in eight consecutive games – baseball's greatest consecutive-game home run streak – before Don Newcome stopped him

Frank Robinson when he played for Cincinnati. Robinson played, usually as an outfielder, for the Reds (1956-65), The Orioles (1966-71), the Dodgers (1972), the Angels (1973-74) and the Indians (1974-76). Hitting .294, he also belted 586 home runs. When he became the manager of the Indians in 1975, he was the first black man to manage in the major leagues. This Hall of Famer was voted the Most Valuable Player in the National League in 1961 and the Most Valuable Player in the American League in 1966.

Dale Long connects for a home run at Forbes Field in Pittsburgh. The catcher is Roy Campanella of the Dodgers and the umpire is Lee Ballafant. Richard Dale Long, with his .267 batting average, bounced around quite a bit in his 10-year career. He played first base for the Pirates (1951), the Browns (1951), the Pirates again (1955-57), the Cubs (1957-59), the Giants (1960), the Yankees (1960), the Senators (1961-62) and the Yankees again (1962-63).

on 29 May. On 1 October, the Major League Baseball Players' Association was formally organized in New York.

The Braves, losing the pennant by one game in 1956, bounced back hard in 1957 to take the flag, finishing eight games ahead of the second-place Cardinals while setting a new National League attendance record of 2,215,404. The best a somewhat aging Dodger team could do was third, the first time in nine years the Bums fell below first or second. Warren Spahn pitched his eighth 20-game year, and was ably assisted by Braves Lew Burdette and Bob Buhl, a specialist at beating the Dodgers. Henry Aaron hit 44 home runs and 132 RBI's with a season average of .322, and took the MVP.

The Braves crowned their pennant by beating the Yankees in the World Series, which for the third consecutive year went to seven games. Lew Burdette won three of those for the Braves, two of them shutouts, and Aaron polished his MVP crown by hitting .393 for the Series.

The Cardinals' Stan Musial, now 36, took his seventh and last National League batting title with a .351 average. This was the fifth time The Man topped .350, a feat equalled in the National League only by Wagner, Hornsby and Paul Waner. Jackie Robinson, who broke the color line with the Dodgers ten years earlier, retired before the start of the season rather than be traded to the Giants.

But the real news of the 1957 season was the announcement that the Giants and the Dodgers were moving to the West Coast. Startling as the Braves' move to Milwaukee had been, their move had kept the National League east of the Mississippi, where it had always been. Milwaukee had even hosted a National League club in 1878.

Until the early 1950s, organized baseball was really only practical in the cities clustered in the East and Midwest, where travel by train was neither overly

expensive nor time-consuming. But air travel and income from radio and television made franchise shifts possible to clubs which faced declining attendance in antiquated ball parks in deteriorating urban settings. The Braves' spectacular success – in 1957 they led the league in attendance – convinced beleaguered club owners that greener pastures did indeed exist.

The Giants, in New York since 1883, announced on 19 August 1957 that they had decided to play their last game at the Polo Grounds on 29 September and move to San Francisco. The reasons for moving out of their outmoded ball park were classic, particularly with respect to attendance, which had fallen from 1,155,067 in their 1954 championship year to 629,179 in 1956. When President Horace Stoneham was asked if he felt bad about taking the Giants away from the kids of New York, he replied, 'I feel bad about the kids, but I haven't seen too many of their fathers lately.'

On 8 October the Brooklyn Dodgers confirmed years of persistent rumors by announcing that they too had decided to move west, to Los Angeles. Brooklyn had no problems with attendance, although Ebbets Field had become impossible, but owner O'Malley was fascinated by the prospect of the profits to be reaped by planting his team in one of the

Fans chase their Giants into the clubhouse after the game of 30 September 1957 as the Pirates trot up the steps at left. This was the Giants' last appearance at the Polo Grounds before their move to San Francisco.

nation's most affluent, rapidly growing metropolitan areas. It was O'Malley, in fact, who finally convinced Giant owner Stoneham to move west, partly out of fear that the league might not approve a single franchise shift to the West Coast.

The New York clubs' dreams of riches panned out in 1958 with the Dodgers hosting 1,845,566 fans at the Los Angeles Memorial Coliseum, almost 40,000 more than their best at Ebbets Field, and the Giants drawing 1,272,625 at the much smaller Seals Stadium. On 18 April, Los Angeles set a new single-day attendance mark for the league when 78,672 fans came to see the Dodgers play the Giants in the first major-league game ever played on the West Coast.

Despite the cheers of their new fans, the Dodgers fell to seventh place in 1958, only two games out of the cellar, due in part to a pre-season automobile accident which left their three-time MVP Hall of Famer star catcher Roy Campanella permanently paralyzed. The Giants fell to third, 12 games behind the league-leading Braves, although Willie Mays hit his best-ever .347 and Rookie of the Year first baseman Orlando Cepeda hit .312. Ernie Banks of Chicago hit 47 home runs to set a record for shortstop and win the MVP Award.

Three of 1958's 20-game winners – Warren Spahn, Lew Burdette, and Bob Friend of Pittsburgh – were with the pennant-repeating Braves, who finished 8 games ahead of the second-place Pirates. After taking a 3-1 lead, the Braves dropped the World Series to the Yankees.

The main event on the diamond in 1959 was the pitching of 12 perfect innings by Pittsburgh's Harvey

Opposite: Ernie Banks. Ernest 'Mr Cub' Banks played shortstop and first base for the Cubs from 1953 to 1971 and was elected to the Hall of Fame in 1977. Batting .274 and hitting 512 home runs, he was the first man ever to be named the MVP in the National League in two successive years (1958-59).

Below: Orlando Manuel 'The Baby Bull' or 'Cha-Cha' Cepeda played for a number of teams from 1958 to 1974. He hit 379 home runs and carried a .297 batting average.

Haddix. For most of his 14-year career an unremarkable pitcher, on 29 May the 34-year-old southpaw established a major-league record by retiring the first 36 Braves he faced. These included Aaron, Mathews and Adcock, on a Milwaukee team that was undoubtedly the hardest-hitting in the league.

Harvey saw his first man reach base when third baseman Don Hoak made a bad throw after fielding a grounder hit by Felix Mantilla in the bottom of the 13th. Mathews sacrificed Mantilla to second, Aaron was purposely walked, and Adcock, whom Haddix had already struck out twice, hit a home run just over the right-center field fence. Confused base-running by the Braves voided two runs, but Haddix lost baseball's best pitched game, 1-0.

The 1959 pennant race was a three-way fight between the Dodgers, the Braves and the Giants, with the Giants leading by two games into the final week. As the Giants slipped, the Braves and the Dodgers added steam, ending the season tied, and forcing the third pennant playoff in National League history.

The Dodgers, in their third playoff appearance, won the first game in Milwaukee and wrapped up the best two-out-of-three in the next game in Los Angeles with a heroic three-run rally in the bottom of the ninth, and another in the bottom of the 12th. Their dramatic comeback from seventh to first place in the second year of their move west was rewarded by record-breaking crowds at their three home games in a World Series they won from the White Sox in six games. The Series games at the Los Angeles Coliseum drew 92,394, 92,650 and finally 92,796, the largest crowds in World Series history, topping the 86,288 mark set at Cleveland in 1948.

Both Warren Spahn and Lew Burdette again won 20 games for the Braves, and Henry Aaron took the league batting title with .355, his highest average ever. For Spahn, now 38, this was his tenth 20-game year. Chicago's Ernie Banks became the first in league history to take the MVP two years running, and Giant Willie McCovey, batting .354, Rookie of the Year.

Events on the playing field in 1959 were to a considerable extent overshadowed by the attempt of Branch Rickey's Continental League to become the third major league, and by Congressional hearings into the laws governing professional baseball. The failure of Congress to pass a bill sponsored by Senator Estes Kefauver of Tennessee effectively killed Rickey's idea on the drawing board, but in its failure sowed the seeds for the first expansion of the major leagues in 60 years. The American League would increase to ten clubs in 1961, and the National League, bowing to public demand, would expand to accommodate America's growing love of baseball in 1962.

Right: Willie McCovey takes a swing. Willie Lee 'Stretch' McCovey played most of his career at first base for the Giants and was a prodigious home run hitter who was voted Most Valuable Player in the National League in 1969.

Opposite: Harvey 'The Kitten' Haddix pitched for 14 years in the big leagues with the Cardinals (1952-56), the Phillies (1956-57), the Pirates (1959-63) and the Orioles (1964-65), winning 136 games with a 3.63 earned run average. He also stood 2-0 in World Series play.

Hall of Famer Sandy Koufax on the mound. Sanford Koufax spent all his ten years in the majors pitching for the Dodgers.

CHAPTER SIX

The Unpredictable Decade

I didn't think our pitchers were all that good!

Hank Bauer, Manager of the Orioles, 1966

The 1960s have come to stand as one of the most unsettling and divisive decades in the history of America, and in some ways professional major league baseball did reflect at least some of the dynamism of the period. By the end of the 1950s, for instance, television was already having an impact on the development of major league baseball. For one thing, television was creating a new and more widespread public for major league baseball – a public that lived far beyond traditional population centers that had supported baseball teams. As millions of Americans in the Far West and the South began to enjoy the games on television, they began to wish they might have a team closer to home to support. A new group of entrepreneurs also began to consider owning a baseball club; it was a potentially profitable enterprise, and beyond that a major league club was for both the owner and the home town a matter of prestige and just plain fun.

The failure of the Continental League only brought the issue of more teams for more cities to a head. So it was that in 1962 the National League – following the lead taken by the American League in 1961 – added two new teams: the New York Mets and the Houston Colt 45s. (It would be 1965 before the Houston team would exchange this rather awkward name for the Astros.) This same year – and for the same reason that the American League had done so in 1961 when it added two teams – the National league increased the number of games played for a full season from 154 to 162.

Then, in 1969 – the same year, as it happened, that Bowie Kuhn took over as the new Commissioner of Baseball – both leagues expanded to 12 teams. The new National League teams were the San Diego Padres and the Montreal Expos – the first major league club outside the United States, and further testimony to the spread of baseball's public. In expanding to 12 teams, each league also split itself into two six-team divisions, Eastern and Western. At the time, some 'purists' complained that this was a thinly disguised move to four leagues, but very quickly the new teams became identified with their respective leagues. Although the standings on any given day called attention to the divisions, most fans retained a strong sense of identity with either their favorite National or American league.

Far right: Bowie Kuhn, the commissioner of baseball at the time.
Opposite: Robert 'Hoot' Gibson, who pitched for the Cardinals from 1959 to 1975. He won 251 games with a 2.91 ERA, striking out 3117. Bob Gibson is in the Hall of Fame, won the Cy Young Award as best pitcher in 1968 and 1970 and was voted the National League's Most Valuable Player in 1968.
Below: Stan Musial is greeted by his Cardinal teammates as he returns to the dugout after getting hit number 3431 against the Dodgers – Chavez Ravine, 19 May 1962.

For the National League, this expansion to 12 teams proved to be the limit: the National League would not follow the lead of the American League, which expanded to 14 teams in 1977. Likewise, the shifting of teams from city to city that continued in the American League well into the 1970s ended in 1966 for the National League when the Milwaukee Braves moved to Atlanta. With this move, the National League remained 'in place' at least into the 1980s if not for all time. But the National League could not become too smug about its traditionalism: after all, it had been the Boston Braves' move to Milwaukee in 1953 that had begun the whole post-war shifting of clubs – and the Braves only moved from Milwaukee because they had experienced a loss in attendance.

There would be other developments in the 1960s that, if not necessarily linked to the dynamism of society at large, did seem to suggest that organized baseball was at least trying to keep up with the times. In 1969, for instance, the major leagues adopted two changes in the rules of the game because there were fears that pitchers had been gaining so much control over the hitters that the sport would lose fans. Whether this was a concern generated by the rising prominence of television was debatable: true fans, it has been said, can enjoy a tight pitchers' duel on any given day at the ballpark as much as a slugfest, while on the small screen a slugfest undoubtedly seems more exciting.

Cardinal

The argument that the pitchers were becoming too dominant, in any case, seemed somewhat questionable in the decade that would witness assaults on several of the major all-time records by hitters. It would be in 1961 that Roger Maris hit 61 home runs, while Henry Aaron and several others continued to hit home runs at such a pace that a number of players would break into the charmed circle of 3000 lifetime hits and 500 home runs. True, Sandy Koufax, Bob Gibson, Denny McLain and some other pitchers would set some amazing records. But any decade that began with a World Series that had the Pirates defeating the Yankees and ended with a Series that saw the Mets defeating the Orioles had no cause to fear that baseball was becoming too predictable.

Below: Richard Morrow 'Dick' Groat played shortstop for 14 years in the National League with Pittsburgh (1952-62), St Louis (1963-65), Philadelphia (1966-67) and San Francisco (1967). Voted Most Valuable Player in the National League in 1960, he had a lifetime batting average of .286.

When the 1960 season began, no one would have picked the Pittsburgh Pirates to win in the National League. The Milwaukee Braves seemed to be the team

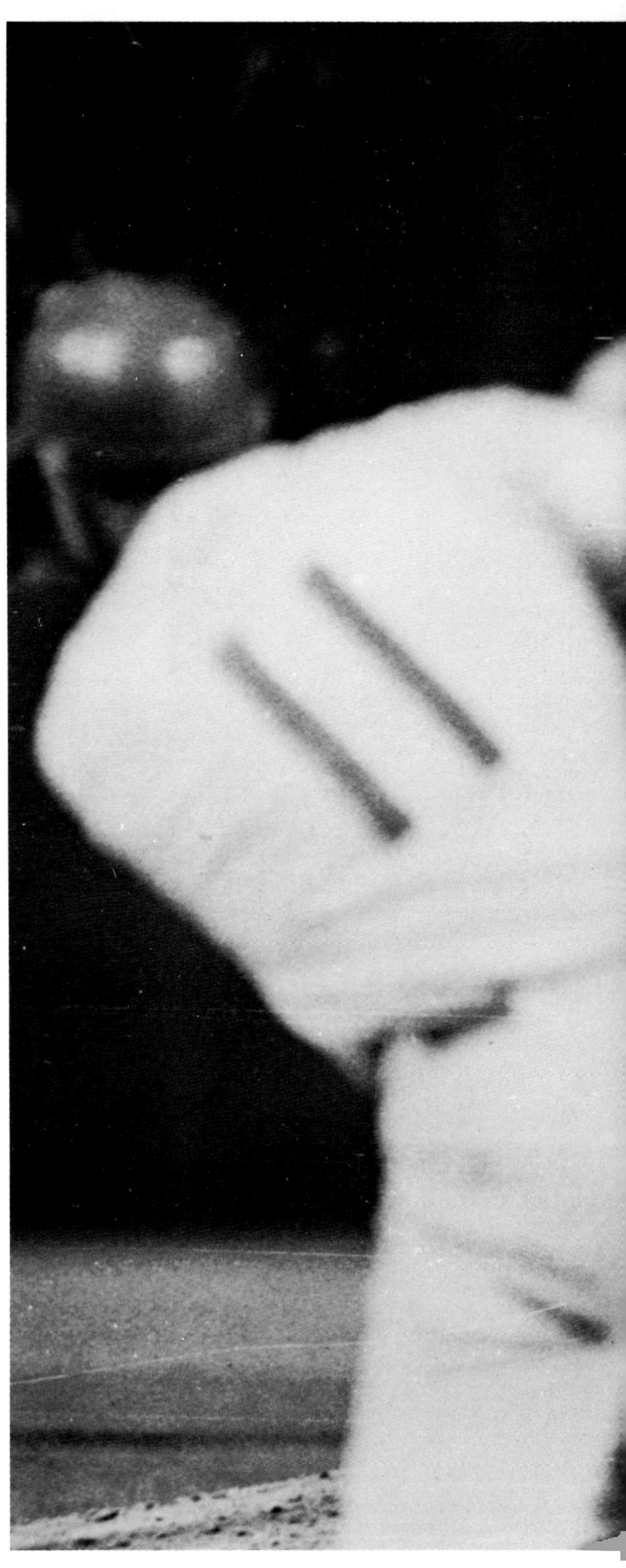

to beat, what with Warren Spahn pitching himself and Eddie Mathews and Hank Aaron hitting themselves into the record books. Or there were those perennial threats, the Dodgers, fresh from their 1959 World Series win over the Chicago White Sox. The Dodgers had Wally Moon and Maury Wills and the league's leading strikeout pitcher, Don Drysdale; they also had a still promising pitcher, Sandy Koufax, who by the end of the season, with only an 8-13 record, would have given signs of something special; Koufax struck out 197 and he led the league in fewest hits per nine innings. But the best the Dodgers could do in 1960 was fourth place.

The Pirates, meanwhile, neither on paper nor on

the field were a team of superstars. But Roberto Clemente hit .314 and shortstop Dick Groat came through with a .325 to take the league batting title (and the Most Valuable Player award); for pitchers, Pittsburgh had Vernon Law, who won 20 while losing nine; Bob Friend, who won 18; Wilmer 'Vinegar Bend' Mizell, just purchased from the Cardinals, who won 13; and Elroy Face for relief. And under the savvy management of Danny Murtaugh, the Pirates took first place, leaving the Braves seven games behind.

The Yankees who took the American League that year were hardly the powerhouse of other years, but they had Mickey Mantle, Roger Maris and Bill Skowron, and Whitey Ford for pitching. Furthermore, the Yankees were a team used to taking the World Series while the Pirates hadn't appeared in one since 1927 – when the Yankees, in fact, wiped them out in four straight. So most people probably would have picked the Yankees for 1960. And indeed, looking only at the stats, the Yankees seem to have cleaned up: the Yankees set new Series records with 55 runs scored (*vs* only 27 for the Pirates), 91 hits, including 27 extra-base hits, and a .338 team batting average (*vs* .256 for the Pirates). Yet with some well-timed hits, and some tight pitching by Vernon Law and Elroy Face, the Pirates forced the Series into the seventh game on 13 October. The starting pitchers, Bob Turley for the Yankees and Vernon Law for the

Above: Donald Scott 'Big D' Drysdale pitched for the Dodgers for 14 years (1956-69), both in Brooklyn and Los Angeles. He won 209 games with a 2.95 earned run average and a strikeout record of 2486. This Hall of Famer won the Cy Young Award in 1962.

Above: Maury Wills steals another base against the Giants. Shortstop Wills, the MVP in the National League in 1962, had 2134 career hits, carried a .281 batting average, and stole 586 bases (104 of them in the 1962 season).
Right: Vernon Sanders 'Deacon' Law pitched for the Pirates (1950-67). His ERA was 3.77 and he beat the Yankees twice in the 1960 World Series.

Pirates, were soon knocked out and the game seesawed back and forth until it went into the ninth inning, where the Yankees tied it up, 9-9. In the bottom of the ninth, Ralph Terry was by then pitching for the Yankees; Bill Mazeroski, the Pirates second baseman, connected with Terry's second pitch and sent it over the ivy-covered left-field wall of Forbes Field to climax one of the most exciting Series in memory.

The 1961 season turned out to be memorable in another way – with its various records set. Of course the one that dominated everyone's attention was the race by Mantle and Maris to at least tie Babe Ruth's major league record of 60 homers in a season (1927); as everyone knows, Maris broke that record with his 61st homer on the last game of the 162-game season. Meanwhile, over in the National League, some other records were being set in 1961. The Phillies, alas, lost 23 games in a row between 29 July and 20 August – the longest losing streak in modern major-league baseball. Willie Mays hit four homers on 30 April. Warren Spahn, pitching for the Milwaukee Braves, got his second no-hitter on 28 April and his 300th win on 11 August (only the third in the National League, after Mathewson and Alexander). Maury Wills, the Dodger shortstop, stole 50 bases – the best in the league since 1923.

In the National League's pennant race, it was between the Dodgers and the Cincinnati Reds. The Dodgers had strong pitching from Don Drysdale, Johnny Podres and Stan Williams, but the most amazing performance was that of Sandy Koufax: he found his control this year and pitched 269 strikeouts, walking only 96, in 256 innings to gain an 18-13 record. But

Left: Frank Robinson when he played for the Dodgers.

the Reds had not only pitching – Joey Jay (21 wins) and Jim O'Toole (19 wins) – but also solid hitting from Vada Pinson (.343) and Frank Robinson (.323). No one gave the Reds much chance, though, in the Series, where the Yankees were regarded as one of the most powerful teams since their 1927 team with Ruth and

Below: Bill Mazeroski being greeted at home plate after his magnificent clutch home run in the 1960 World Series. William Stanley 'Maz' Mazeroski played second base for the Pirates from 1956 to 1972, batting .260.

Gehrig. And indeed, the Reds were knocked out, four games to one, although more by Yankee pitching than the expected powerhitting. There are some seasons that just have to be accepted and 1961 was such a one for the National League.

The 1962 season, however, proved more eventful. To begin with, the League added two new teams – as the American League had done in 1961 – so there was now a National League team back in New York, the Mets, while Houston had its first team, the Colt .45s – which would be renamed the Astros in 1965. Under their manager, Casey Stengel, who had been dropped by the Yankees in 1960, the Mets won the hearts of many fans but also lost many games – 120, in fact, out of 162, the most games ever lost by a modern major league team. The season also witnessed some other more inspiring records. Stan Musial, on 19 May, got his 3431st hit, taking over first place (from Honus Wagner) in the National League. And Maury Wills overtook and tied Ty Cobb's 47-year-old record of 96 stolen bases in 156 games (Detroit had played two extra games because of ties that year) and then went on to steal 104, then a major-league record.

Wills' base stealing feats helped to spark the Dodgers team, which also included such standout performances as Tommy Davis' .346 batting average and 153 RBI's and Don Drysdale's 25-9 record. Sandy Koufax tied his own (1959) and Bob Feller's (1938) record of 18 strikeouts in nine innings but a circulation problem in his pitching hand kept him out of action in the last half of the season. The result was that the Dodgers ended up on the last day in a tie for first place with their arch enemies, the Giants. These Giants had a total of 204 home runs, thanks to players like Mays, McCovey, Alou and Cepeda. In the playoff – the fourth in National League history, all of which the Dodgers had been involved in – the first two games were split. The Dodgers went into the ninth inning with a 4-2 lead, but before three Dodger pitchers could retire the Giants, they had taken the lead, 6-4. And that was it for the Dodgers of 1962.

Now the Giants turned around to face another

Opposite: Maury Wills demonstrates his batting stance. After his playing career was over he became a baseball broadcaster.
Below: Casey Stengel when he was manager of the rag-tag New York Mets – 'Can't anybody here play this game?'

LA

Above left: Ron Perranoski warms up. Perranoski pitched for 13 years in the big leagues (1961-73) – with the Dodgers, Twins, Tigers and Angels – maintaining a 2.79 ERA.
Above right: Stan Musial of the Cardinals comes into second base as a very young Pete Rose of the Reds looks on. This was Rose's first year in the majors (1963), and he won the Rookie of the Year Award.

traditional rival – the New York Yankees: it would be the seventh Series these teams had played, although the previous six had been subway affairs. The teams seemed about evenly matched: the Yankees had Whitey Ford and Ralph Terry – but the Giants had Juan Marichal and Jack Sanford; the Yankees had Mantle and Maris, but the Giants had Willie Mays and Orlando Cepeda. And right through the first six games, the teams did indeed stay even. In the seventh game, at Candlestick Park, Terry faced Sanford, and going into the ninth inning the only score was a run by the Yankees in the fifth inning. In the bottom of the ninth, with two out and Felipe Alou on third, Willie McCovey came to bat, and you can be sure that everyone watching the game was talking about Mazeroski's homer of 1960. McCovey took Terry's pitch and lined it toward right field – but this time second baseman Bobby Richardson caught the ball. The Yankees had won, 1-0, and were the World Champions for the second year in a row.

But baseball is the classic 'Wait till next year!' sport, and never was this truer than in 1963. For one, the Dodgers came back from their humiliating defeat by the Giants at the end of 1962 and took the National League pennant. The Giants, despite the fine pitching of Marichal (25-8), simply couldn't stand up to the Dodgers and the Cardinals this year. Neither could the Milwaukee Braves, despite another fine season by

the 42-year-old Warren Spahn: his 23-7 record was his 13th (if last) 20-game season. And in the end, the Cardinals couldn't hold off the Dodgers. The Dodgers had a couple of power hitters in Frank Howard and Tommy Davis, but mostly they relied on the fast and clever base running by Maury Wills, Willie Davis and Jim Gilliam. In addition to another solid season from Don Drysdale and Johnny Podres and fine relief from Ron Perranoski, the Dodgers got an extraordinary season from Sandy Koufax: a 25-5 record, an earned run average of only 1.88, 306 strikeouts (almost one per inning), and 11 shutouts.

And this year the Dodgers got another chance to avenge themselves on the Yankees. In the first game, Koufax struck out 15 Yankees (breaking Carl Erskine's Series record of 14, set in 1953, on the exact same date), and in the second game Podres, with some help from Perranoski in the bottom of the ninth, beat the Yankees 4-1. In the third game, Jim Bouton gave up only four hits and one run, but that was good enough for Drysdale to win 1-0 on only three hits. In the fourth game, it was Koufax against Ford again, and the game remained tied, 1-1, going into the seventh inning; then Yankee first baseman Joe Pepitone missed a throw (he blamed it on the wall of white shirted fans he was facing!) and the Dodgers had a man on third; a deep outfield fly allowed him to score, and even with only two fair hits, this was enough to give the Dodgers the game, 2-1, and the Series.

The 1963 season was also notable for National League fans as it was the last for Stan Musial as a player. His final hit of the season came on 29 September, and as number 3630 it would stand as the league record for many years. Watching Musial that day was the Cincinnati Red's rookie second baseman, 21-year-old Pete Rose, who would have reason to remember the occasion.

And the Phillies would long remember the 1964 season. They had come breezing into the last two weeks of the season with what seemed like a safe 6½-game lead. Then, beginning on 20 September, they lost 10 straight games. Well, teams had gone into tailspins before – the Phillies themselves had done so in 1950, losing seven of their last nine, but they had just managed to pull out in first place. But in 1964, while the Phillies went cold, the Cardinals went hot: they won eight in a row – and by the last day, the Cardinals had taken the pennant with a one-game lead.

Juan Marichal – one of the toughest pitchers of all time. Juan Antonio Sanchez 'Manito' or 'The Dominican Dandy' Marichal pitched for the Giants (1960-73), the Red Sox (1974) and the Dodgers (1975). His record was 243-142 and he had a fine 2.89 earned run average with 2303 strikeouts and 52 shutouts, which got him elected to the Hall of Fame.

Right: Jim Bunning delivers a pitch. Bunning pitched for the Tigers, Phillies, Pirates and Dodgers from 1955 to 1971, winning 224 games with 3.27. **Opposite:** Lou Brock comes to bat. This Hall of Fame outfielder played for the Cubs and Cardinals. Eight times he led the league in stolen bases (118 in 1974) while hitting .292. **Below:** The fleet Curt Flood played mostly outfield for the Reds, Cardinals, and Senators, batting .293.

Actually, the 1964 season yielded several memorable occaions for the National League. One was on 21 June, when Jim Bunning of these same Phillies pitched a perfect game against the New York Mets – the first perfect game in the National League in modern baseball. And only a few weeks before, the Mets had been involved in another memorable game: on the night of May 31, the Mets played the Giants in a doubleheader, and as expected, the Giants took the first, 5-3; but the second game went on and on – 23 innings, in fact, until the Giants won that, too, 8-6 – and the fans had been treated, if that's the word, to nine hours 52 minutes of baseball, a modern record. Everyone over a certain age who was in New York City that night can recall how the whole town buzzed with a mixture of incredulity and amusement as the game went on into the early hours of the morning.

But the Cardinals were no laughing matter that year. They had solid hitters in Dick Groat, formerly with the Pirates, Ken Boyer, Bill White, Tim McCarver and Curt Flood; they also had acquired a new outfielder in a swap with the Cubs, a Lou Brock, who could run – and steal – as well as hit. And they had a fastball pitcher and hardball player in Bob Gibson. Still, the Yankees, with their fifth straight American League pennant, had to be the favorites. And with Mickey Mantle hitting record-breaking home runs, it did seem that the Yankees were going to overpower

Above: Nolan Ryan, the master of the strikeouts. Lynn Nolan Ryan of the Houston Astros began his career in 1966 with the Mets, who traded him to the California Angels in 1972. His earned run average is usually just above 3.00 and he has led the league in strikeouts numerous times – most notably his 383 in 1973.

the Cardinals. But the Cardinals never gave up and they took the Yankees into a seventh game. Gibson pitched and gave up homers to Mantle, Clete Boyer and Phil Linz, but his teammates gave him a couple runs more to spare, and the Cardinals won the Series, 7-5.

But in 1965, the Cardinals couldn't hold their own against the two traditional rivals, the Dodgers and Giants; both teams got hot in September – amazingly so, with the Dodgers winning 13 in a row and the Giants winning 14 in a row. Willie Mays hit 52 home runs, but this wasn't enough to win the pennant, for the Dodgers moved into the lead under their superb pitching and ended up in the first place by two games. Don Drysdale had a 23-12 record while Koufax had 26-8 – between them they struck out almost 600 opponents. Koufax had some other amazing stats, including 382 strikeouts, a new major league record that would hold until Nolan Ryan struck out 383 in 1973; and Koufax joined that most exclusive of all major league clubs when he pitched a perfect game against the Cubs on 9 September. (The Cubs pitcher, Bob Hendley, gave up only one hit, so the Cubs lost only by 1-0.)

So it was that the Dodgers once again found themselves in a World Series – for the 12th time, in fact – but facing a team that was in it for the first time, the Minnesota Twins (although these Twins were actually old Washington Senators). The Twins had made their way into the Series with such heavy hitters as Harmon Killebrew, Bob Allison, Don Minchner and Tony Oliva. The Dodgers, however, had fewer home runs than any other major league time in 1965, but relied instead on putting together steady base hits and smart baserunning: Maury Wills, for instance, batted only .286 but he stole 94 bases. And then, to be sure, there were Koufax and Drysdale. When the Series opened, it looked as though the Twins' big bats were going to prove stronger than the big arms: the Twins beat Drysdale in the opener, 8-2, and then knocked Koufax off the mound in the second and went on to win, 5-1. Back at Los Angeles, the Dodgers rebounded and with a combination of hitting, pitching and baserunning, they swept all three games there. The Twins took the sixth game, so the Series once more went into the seventh game. But here is where the Dodgers' depth paid off. Minnesota pitched Jim Kaat, good, but not a match for Koufax at his best: Koufax gave up only three hits and kept the Twins from ever reaching home, shutting them down, 2-0, and giving Walt Alston his fourth World Championship.

Once in a while major league baseball needs a seaon with no particular fireworks or spectacular surprises, and 1966 was such a season. It was a time of foundation-laying, of consolidation. The Mets, for instance, brought up a 19-year-old fastball pitcher, Nolan Ryan, while the Chicago Cubs acquired a promising young pitcher named Ferguson Jenkins from the Phillies. Meanwhile, the Cincinnati Reds had let their ace batter, Frank Robinson, go because he was asking more money than they thought he was worth: he jumped the league and went over to the Baltimore Orioles, who soon discovered he was worth every penny. The Los Angeles Dodgers made no such mistake, though, when their ace pitchers, Sandy Koufax and Don Drysdale, both held out for what was then regarded as Big Money – over $100,000 – and got it.

The National League race was fairly tight, right up to the end. The Pirates looked like they might take it,

Far right: Ferguson Arthur 'Fergie' Jenkins pitched for the Phillies, the Cubs, the Rangers and the Red Sox. Perhaps his best year was 1969, when he played for Chicago. He struck out 273 and had a 21-15 won-lost record. He won the Cy Young Award in 1971.

what with such hitters as Matty Alou – whose .342 was the league's high – and Willie Stargell, Donn Clendenon and Roberto Clemente (whose all-round play made him the most valuable player) but the team lacked pitchers. The Braves had just settled in Atlanta this year, after 13 years in Milwaukee, but despite Hank Aaron's continuing home run production, the Braves could do no better than fifth place. And the Giants, despite the fine pitching of Juan Marichel (25-6) and Gaylord Perry (21-8) could do no better than second place, 1½ games behind the Dodgers.

Yes, the Dodgers did it again, although not with much to spare. Drysdale had an off year with 13-6, but Koufax had a brilliant season, with a 27-9 record and an ERA of 1.73. Claude Osteen, Ron Perranoski and rookie Don Sutton also pitched in, while the batting and fielding of such as Maury Wills, Willie Davis, Lou Johnson, Jim Lefebvre and Tommy Davis gave them the winning edge. The Dodgers went into the World Series the favorites over the American League winner, the Baltimore Orioles. But the Orioles' pitching staff – Dave McNally, Jim Palmer, young Wally Bunker and aging Moe Drabowsky – shut down the Dodgers (the last 33 innings the Dodgers went scoreless) and took the Series in four straight. It was not only an ignominious end to the season, it was the end of an era for the Dodgers. Tommy Davis and Maury Wills would be traded away that winter, while Sandy

Above: Johnny Podres delivers a fastball. John Joseph Podres played for the Dodgers, both in Brooklyn and Los Angeles (1953-66), the Tigers (1966-67) and the Padres (1969). He won 148 games and had an earned run average of 3.67.

Above: A young Tom Seaver on the mound. George Thomas Seaver pitched for the Mets from 1967 to 1977, when he was let go to the Reds and then the Mets again and then, through an apparent front office error, he was claimed by the White Sox. Voted Rookie of the Year in 1967, he has won the Cy Young Award three times.

Koufax, who had long been bothered by painful arthritis in his left elbow, announced he was retiring. He was only 31, and in his last five seasons he had a 111-34 record, but the doctors had warned him he would suffer permanent injury if he continued. Many students of the game would claim that Koufax would go down as one of the great left-handed pitchers of modern baseball.

The 1966 season had been one in which the predictable had happened during the regular season, what with the Dodgers winning the National League; the 1967 season was full of surprises, what with the St Louis Cardinals coming back from a sixth-place finish in 1966 to take both the National League pennant and the World Series. How this came about is the stuff of baseball history. To begin with, the Dodgers of 1966 were virtually wiped out by a series of retirements and trades; although the rest of the league was not unhappy to be liberated from Koufax's control – the league's batting average rose from .249 in 1966 to .256 in 1967 – the Dodgers finished in eighth place.

Meanwhile, some other National League teams

were on the rise. The Chicago Cubs had their hot young pitcher, Ferguson Jenkins, acquired from the Phillies in 1966; Jenkins gave the Cubs the first of his seven 20-game seasons in 1967. The Mets had their own promising young pitcher, one George Thomas Seaver, who had been picked out of a hat the year before. Seaver had been signed to a $50,000 bonus contract by the Braves, but because he had signed before his class, at the University of Southern California, had graduated, a violation of organized baseball's agreement, Seaver had been declared a free agent; the commissioner's way of resolving this was to have the teams that wanted to negotiate with Seaver place their names in a hat; the New York Mets won the draw, and after one year in the Mets' farm system, Tom Seaver came up to New York and pitched 16 victories in this first season, 1967 (and became Rookie of the Year).

Left: The handsome and articulate Sandy Koufax tried his hand at baseball broadcasting.
Below: Orlando Cepeda takes a hefty swing.

Hall of Famer Red Schoendienst ready to throw. Primarily a second baseman, Schoendienst played for the Cardinals, the Giants and the Braves. He then managed the Cardinals from 1965 to 1976, winning two pennants and one World Series. He batted .289 during his career, getting 2449 hits.

But none of this was enough to stop the Cardinals. They had made their own wily deals, having acquired Orlando Cepeda, the first baseman, from the San Francisco Giants, and Roger Maris, the Yankee who had been unhappy in the glare of publicity ever since he had hit his record-breaking 61 home runs in 1961. By 15 July, the Cardinals had a lead of four games, when in that day's game against the Pirates, the Cardinals' star pitcher, Bob Gibson, had his right leg fractured by a line drive by Roberto Clemente. That seemed to mark the end of the Cardinals, but their former relief pitcher, Nelson Briles, replaced Gibson in the starting rotation, and Briles and the rest of the team did so well – Cepeda hit .325 and drove 111 runs – that they took the pennant almost two weeks before the season ended, leaving San Francisco 10½ games behind by the end.

Bob Gibson had returned to active duty in September and was in fine form by the time the World Series came round. And if the Cardinals were somewhat surprised to find themselves there, their opponents, the Boston Red Sox, were even more astonished to be playing in the Series. To counter Gibson, the Red Sox had Jim Lonborg, but he had been forced to pitch the final game of the season, when Boston clinched the pennant, so he could not pitch the opener. Gibson won that with a six-hitter, then pitched the Cardinals to their third win in the fourth game with a five-hit shutout. The showdown came in the seventh game, but Gibson had had three days of rest, Lonborg only two; Gibson pitched a three-hitter and the Cardinals got to Lonborg and won the game 7-2. The Cardinals also owed a lot to Lou Brock's hitting and base-running – he set a series record by stealing seven bases.

The Cardinals' triumph in 1967 also represented a repeat and final performance for one of the great duets of National League history – that of Red Schoendienst and Stan Musial. For ten years, from 1946 through 1955, these two were virtually inseparable from the Cardinals and from each other. Schoendienst had become the manager of the Cardinals in 1964, and Musial had become the club's general manager in 1966, and their World Championship in 1967 was a fitting climax to their years of collaboration. In December 1967, Musial resigned from the Cardinals and retired permanently from organized baseball to devote himself to his business interests.

But the Cardinals by no means retired and in 1968 they came right back and took the National League pennant for the second year in a row, with the San Francisco Giants in second place (for the fourth consecutive year), nine games behind. But that does not begin to tell the story that made the 1968 season so distinctive, that made it come to be known as 'The Year of the Pitcher.' One of the most extraordinary feats was that of the American League's Detroit Tiger, Denny McLain; his 31-6 record made him the first major leaguer to win 30 games since Dizzy Dean had done so in 1934. But the Cardinals' Bob Gibson achieved his own series of feats that are equally astounding: his earned run average was 1.12, the lowest in major league history (breaking the National League record of 1.22, set by Grover Cleveland Alexander in 1915, and the major league mark of 1.14, set by Walter Johnson in 1913); Gibson also won 15 games in a row, and pitched 13 shutouts; no wonder that Gibson won both the league's Most Valuable Player award and the Cy Young award.

But the whole season was dominated by outstanding pitching. Don Drysdale of the Los Angeles Dodgers pitched six consecutive shutouts (breaking Doc White's 64-year-old major league record) that included 58⅔ scoreless innings in a row (which broke Walter Johnson's record of 56, set in 1913). Juan Marichal of the San Francisco Giants had a 26-9 record that would have gained him far more recognition in any other season – but this always seemed to be Marichal's fate, to be eclipsed by more spectacular pitchers while he was steadily piling up a superb career. The Mets' Tom Seaver won 16 for his second year in a row. Altogether, there were 185 shutouts pitched in the National League alone – a record for any league's season – while the league's batting average was held to .243. Yet Pete Rose of the Cincinnati Reds hit .335 and got 210 hits, while Willie Mays raised his home runs total to 587, putting him in second place behind Babe Ruth.

The Cardinals confronted the Detroit Tigers in the World Series in what was assumed would be a duel between Gibson and McClain. In the first game, Gibson had 17 strikeouts, a World Series record, gave up five hits, and the Cardinals won 4-0. McLain was driven from the game in the fifth inning. But in the second game, the Tigers produced an unexpected winner in Mickey Lolich, who gave up six hits as the Tigers won, 8-1. The Cards took the next two games – Gibson taking the fourth, his seventh straight series win, a major league record – but Lolich led the Tigers to a victory in the fifth game, and McLain returned to form in the sixth game, with the Tigers winning 13-1. So in the end, the season came down once again to one game, and it was Lolich against Gibson this time. The score was 0-0 in the seventh inning, when Gibson gave up two singles and then Northrup hit what should have been a routine out; instead, the usually flawless Curt Flood misjudged it and two runs scored; the Tigers went on to win the game, 4-1, and become the World Champions. Lou Brock of the Cardinals, however, hit .464 and stole seven bases, and tied seven series records for batting and baserunning.

So concerned were the powers-that-be that the pitchers were shutting down the action – and thus driving away the fans – that the rules committee of

Pete Rose questions a call. Peter Edward 'Charlie Hustle' Rose began his career in Cincinnati in 1963, where he was named Rookie of the Year. He moved to Philadelphia in 1979, then to Montreal and finally made a triumphant return to the Reds as player-manager in 1984. In 1985 he set the record for the most career hits of anyone in baseball – breaking Ty Cobb's record of 4191.

Mets

organized baseball voted in two major changes after the 1968 season ended. The height of the pitching mound was lowered from 15 inches to 10 inches – to strip pitchers of some of their 'superiority' – and the strike zone was reduced (from its longstanding shoulders-to-knee) down to the armpit to top of the knee. Whether such changes would seriously affect the game was argued intensely at first, but they soon seemed to become just two more factors among many variables, in a sport that often seemed to depend on unpredictables and incalculables as much as pitchers' statistics.

And never was this more so than in the 1969 season. When the season began, the biggest topic of speculation was the expanded 12-team leagues with two divisions, Eastern and Western. The pressure to add more teams had been building for some time, and the final plans were agreed upon at the end of the 1968 season. The National League added the San Diego Padres and the Montreal Expos and then divided itself as follows: The Eastern Division, with Chicago Cubs, Montreal Expos, New York Mets, Philadelphia Phillies, Pittsburgh Pirates and St Louis Cardinals; and the Western Division, with the Atlanta Braves, Cincinnati Reds, Houston Astros, Los Angeles Dodgers, San Diego Padres, and San Francisco Giants. Each league held to the 162-games with schedules that had a team playing all of the other 11 teams but more of their games against those in their division; there would be playoffs between the divisional winners to decide the pennant winner and World Series representative.

And so the 1969 season began with this new format, and even though each of the new clubs was allowed to draft 30 players from the rosters of the other 10 teams in their league, it was accepted that these expansion teams had little chance against the older, established teams. Why, one only had to look at the New York Mets, one of the expansion teams of 1962; in its seven years in the league, the team had never finished above ninth place, and their very name had become synonymous with amateurish, bumbling play. Yet the individual Mets certainly didn't regard themselves as any less professional or hard-playing than any other major leaguers; yes, they made their share of errors (and perhaps a few extraordinary bloopers) but they hung in there, year after year. Now, in 1969, they had as manager Gil Hodges, once a first baseman for the Brooklyn Dodgers, a man who knew how to get the most out of his young players. For these Mets were young: 21 of them were between 21 and 28 years old. And they were not especially strong in the hitting department: they ended up with a team batting average of .241, eighth in the league, and eight other teams in the league outscored the Mets. But the Mets got the hit when they needed it. In one game, Steve Carlton of the Cardinals struck out 19 Mets, but they went on to win 4-3 because Ron Swoboda hit two two-run homers.

Above: Ron Swoboda of the Mets. Ronald Allan 'Rocky' Swoboda was a journeyman outfielder for the Mets (1965–70), the Expos (1971) and the Yankees (1971–73), hitting a mere .242 and hitting 73 home runs. But he will be remembered for his work in 1969, when his miraculous catches and .467 batting average in the World Series helped so much to win the championship for New York. He later became a creditable sports commentator on television.

Opposite: The great Gil Hodges. Gilbert Raymond Hodges had managed the Senators from 1963 to 1967 and took over the lackluster Mets from 1968 to 1971. He inherited a last-place ball club and worked a miracle, leading them to the World Series championship in just two years.

Above: Philip Henry Niekro began pitching for the Braves in 1964, when they were still in Milwaukee. He now pitches for the Yankees and registered his win number 300 in 1985 at the age of 46 – the oldest pitcher to reach that level – and it was a shutout, which made him the oldest pitcher to pitch a no-run game.
Far right: Tug McGraw and Jerry Koosman share a sandwich. Frank Edwin McGraw played for the Mets and the Phillies and Jerome Martin Koosman was also a Met. These were two of the stalwarts who, along with Tom Seaver, starred in the pitching lineup for the Miracle Mets of 1969.
Opposite top: Jerry Koosman in 1968.

What the Mets did draw on was some exceptional pitching, especially by Tom Seaver, whose 25-7 record was the best in the majors. Jerry Koosman ran up a 17-9 record, while Tug McGraw in relief saved 12 and won 9. Mostly, though, the Mets of 1969 drew on some uncalculable spirit, some energy. The Chicago Cubs were leading the Eastern Division almost all season and were outhitting and outscoring the Mets; by 13 August, the Mets were 9½ games behind the Cubs and most smart money would have declared the Mets out for another season. But something happened. By 10 September, the Mets had sneaked into the lead; Seaver and Koosman pitched 19 victories in August and September; the Mets won 38 of their last 49 games; meanwhile, the Cubs collapsed, and when the season ended, they were in second place, 8 games behind the Miraculous Mets.

But now there were two divisions, and the Mets had to go into the league playoffs against the Western Division winner, the Atlanta Braves. The Braves had hit their way to the top against a lot of strong competition and were favored to take the Mets handily: after all, these Braves had Hank Aaron, with his 44 home runs, and Phil Niekro with his 23 wins. And the Braves did get to the Mets' pitchers. But the Mets got to the Braves pitchers even more so – 37 hits, in fact, as the Mets took the playoff in three straight, 9-5, 11-6, 7-4.

Still, many people felt, a playoff series was one thing – the World Series against the experienced Baltimore Orioles was something else. And when the Orioles took the first game, 4-1, with Tom Seaver losing to Mike Cuellar, reason seemed to have returned to the game. But Jerry Koosman gave up only two hits in the second game, and the Mets won 2-1. Then Gary Gentry and Nolan Ryan combined to lead the Mets to a 5-0 victory. In the fourth game, the Mets went into the 10th inning with the score 1-1; Jerry Grote got a double when Buford misplayed a simple fly ball, Weis was given a walk, J C Martin bunted toward the mound and the Orioles' pitcher Pete Richert threw to first but hit Martin on the wrist and the ball bounced away – allowing a winning run to score. Replay photos showed that Martin had in fact run illegally into foul territory, but it was not caught by the umpires in the field, so now the Mets had three victories. In the fifth game, the Orioles were leading 3-0 when the Mets Cleon Jones came up in the sixth

inning; when the umpire failed to agree that he had been hit on the foot by one pitch, Jones proved it by showing that there was shoe polish on the ball; he then scored when Clendenon hit a homer; in the seventh inning, Al Weis hit another homer and the game was tied. In the eighth inning, the Mets got two doubles, but Baltimore made two throwing errors and the Mets took the lead, 5-3. It held – and the Mets were the World Champions.

The New York Mets fans were not the only Americans to become almost delirious with this incredible climax to the season. The whole country had become somewhere between intrigued and obsessed by this 'team of destiny.' And this in a summer that saw the first human beings walk on the moon. It was no coincidence that the National League set a new attendance record this year, 15,094,946, although this was undoubtedly due also to the expansion to 12 teams. And although the new rules designed to curb pitchers did indeed produce 17 .300 hitters (versus only six of them in 1968), 15 pitchers won 20 or more games – the most such in 40 years. So much for the calculations of rules committees as major league baseball prepared to embark on the 1970s.

Manager Sparky Anderson argues with an umpire. George Lee Anderson first managed Cincinnati, where he won five pennants and two World Series, and then Detroit, where he won one pennant and one World Series. Between these two

CHAPTER SEVEN

Untraditional Seventies

. . . baseball is a business in every sense of the word. It is part of the entertainment industry.

Business Week

The 1960s are perceived as a decade of turmoil in American society in general, and to the extent that organized baseball also experienced such changes as the expansion of the numbers of teams and numerous franchise shifts, the National League also went through some turmoil of its own. But in many respects, the 1970s proved to be a more tumultuous decade for the major leagues – indeed, almost a decade of revolution. No one can ever prove these things, but to the extent that baseball is so deeply enmeshed in American society, perhaps it was no coincidence that a decade that included the collapse of the war in Vietnam and the debacle known as Watergate should also see baseball players going out on their first strike and challenging the 'reserve clause,' long regarded as the very foundation of organized baseball. After all, if American Presidents traditionally throw out the baseball that opens the season and there were three different presidents in the 30 months between August 1974 and January 1977 – is it any wonder that baseball players were confused?

Quite seriously, the 1970s were in many ways distinguished by a general breakdown in respect for traditions and authority. This had begun in the 1960s in society at large, and baseball, as one of the more traditional institutions, was a bit tardy in accepting this new spirit. But when it came to baseball in the 1970s, it came in many forms. Jim Bouton's *Ball Four*, the first 'let-it-all-hang-out' book by a contemporary major leaguer, might be regarded as a signal of the change, and the players of the 1970s carried on this new spirit of rebelliousness in such ways as allowing their hair to flourish and their tempers to flare. We shall examine the challenge to and eventual defeat of the reserve clause in the proper years, but perhaps the most immediate impact on baseball's loyal fans was the sight of the newly 'liberated' players scurrying around to whichever team would pay the biggest salary.

At the same time, the 1970s can hardly be dismissed as the decade when the players went for the Big Bucks. They also went for the Big Records – and came through: several of the most indomitable records of modern baseball would be wiped out in the 1970s – homeruns, season and career stolen bases, career runs batted in, season strikeouts, season games pitched. And many fans would point out that most of these records were being re-set by National League players – a National League, furthermore, that was increasingly dominating the All-Star Games and a

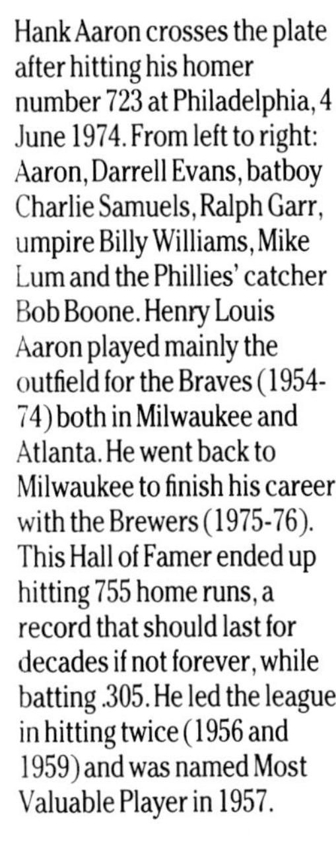

Hank Aaron crosses the plate after hitting his homer number 723 at Philadelphia, 4 June 1974. From left to right: Aaron, Darrell Evans, batboy Charlie Samuels, Ralph Garr, umpire Billy Williams, Mike Lum and the Phillies' catcher Bob Boone. Henry Louis Aaron played mainly the outfield for the Braves (1954-74) both in Milwaukee and Atlanta. He went back to Milwaukee to finish his career with the Brewers (1975-76). This Hall of Famer ended up hitting 755 home runs, a record that should last for decades if not forever, while batting .305. He led the league in hitting twice (1956 and 1959) and was named Most Valuable Player in 1957.

National League that rejected the American League's adoption of arguably the most revolutionary change in modern organized baseball – the designated hitter. Purists – and these may or may not be synonymous with National League fans – might argue that any league to adopt such a device only deserved to take second place in the record books.

This decade of turmoil and change, then, was launched on 16 January 1970, when Curt Flood, a 32-year-old outfielder, filed a suit against organized baseball's so-called reserve clause. Curt Flood had played 12 years for the St Louis Cardinals and had been recognized as one of the leading players in the league; even his employers had recognized this by paying him $90,000 for the 1969 season – one of the highest salaries in both leagues. But when that season ended, Flood was traded by the Cardinals to the Philadelphia Phillies – a transaction that for decades

Cincinnati manager Sparky Anderson (#10) and catcher Johnny Bench dispute an umpire's call while pitcher Pat Zachry (left) seems disinterested.

Above: Curt Flood, who began the fight to eliminate the reserve clause.

Opposite top: 'Tom Terrific' Seaver when he was a young Met.

Opposite bottom: Roberto Clemente gets his 3000th hit – 30 September 1972. Roberto Walker 'Bob' Clemente played the outfield for Pittsburgh from 1955 to 1972, hitting .317 and belting 240 homers. He died in a plane crash in 1972 while taking supplies for the relief of Nicaraguan earthquake victims, and the five-year waiting period for election to the Hall of Fame was waived as he was elected the following year. He was named the league's Most Valuable Player in 1966, the World Series' Most Valuable Player in 1971 and won the National League batting championship in 1961, 1964 and 1965.

had been taking place in organized baseball and that had been both formally enforced by the United States Supreme Court and tacitly endorsed by generations of traded players. But now here was Curt Flood charging that the reserve clause was 'a contract for perpetual service' and that he did not want to go on being treated as 'property ... a chattel ... a slave for a team against his will.'

What was this 'reserve clause' that could prompt such charged language? Actually, it was a series of clauses or terms that were part of the standard contract of every player in professional baseball. Under these terms, a player was legally bound to a team until he was sold or traded to another team, which in turn owned this player. Oh, a team might release a player and thus free him to sign on with another of his choice – but most players were never released until their playing days were about over. And if a player didn't like a team that held him under contract, the only thing he could do was to quit professional baseball.

It does indeed sound suspiciously like a form of slavery or at the very least like a restraint of trade that had come to be struck down by American antitrust laws and rulings. Yet without ever actually ruling on the reserve clause itself, the Supreme Court, since its first landmark decision in 1922 and in several decisions in the 1950s, had held that organized baseball was not subject to the antitrust laws that governed the conduct of business in America. In fact, it was a form of tribute to baseball's special standing in American life that exempted it from such antitrust laws, for this same Supreme Court often ruled that other organized sports – hockey, boxing, professional football, for instance – did fall under the antitrust laws. Such a tribute, however, was little consolation to players who saw their salaries and movements dictated by the owners, who in turn argued that the reserve clause was the only thing that prevented the richest teams from buying all the better players – and thus upsetting the balance that allowed so many teams to remain competitive over the years.

But Curt Flood, backed by the Major League Baseball Players Association, challenged that assumption in 1970 in the United State District Court in New York City. (One of Flood's lawyers was Arthur J Goldberg, a former associate justice of the Supreme Court.) The District Court soon ruled that it could not overturn the decisions of the Supreme Court regarding baseball; Flood appealed this decision to the US Circuit Court of Appeals, which upheld the District Court; Flood then appealed to the Supreme Court itself. It would be 1972 before the Supreme Court ruled that since baseball remained exempt from antitrust laws, the reserve clause was legal; however, the majority opinion went on to call this exemption an 'aberration' and called on Congress to reconsider the special status accorded organized baseball – since even its most devoted fans could hardly deny that it had become a business. (Whether it was Big or Show would be a question that would emerge in the late 70s and early 80s.)

Curt Flood, meanwhile, sat out the 1970 season – a considerable sacrifice for a player of his salary level. In November of that year, however, assured that it would not prejudice his suit still being appealed, he signed with the Washington Senators when they acquired his contract in a trade with the Phillies. (Yes, it included the reserve clause.) So in the immediate sense, baseball began the 1970s as usual. But the first strike of change had been thrown.

(After starting the 1971 season with the Senators, Flood abruptly retired – and went off to the Spanish island of Majorca to operate a bar. His explanation was that he could not deal with the glare of publicity focused on him. Although he returned to California in 1976 and worked for a few years as a sportscaster, Flood never profited from the overthrow of the reserve clause and the large salaries this led to in later years.)

When the season began, the New York Mets and all their fans were still euphoric over the incredible miracle of their 1969 triumph, but the team could not maintain that elevation. Yet on 22 April, it looked as though Tom Seaver was going to be able single-handedly to carry the Mets to new heights: on that day, he struck out 19 batters of the San Diego Padres, thus tying Steve Carlton's record, and set a new record by striking out 10 (the last of the 19) in a row. But other Met stars of the 1969 season such as Jerry Koosman and Cleon Jones couldn't repeat, and even Seaver, although 16-5 on 1 August, fell to a 2-7 record during the closing weeks. The Mets finished third in the Eastern Division, only one game behind Chicago but six behind the division winner, Pittsburgh. The Pirates won with a re-hired manager, Danny Murtaugh, and with the help of an old standby, Roberto Clemente, who hit .353.

In the Western Division, it was almost no contest: the Reds left the second-place Dodgers 14½ games behind. They, too, had a new manager, George 'Sparky' Anderson – at 36, the youngest then in the major leagues. They also had a spectacular 22-year-old catcher, Johnny Bench, who among his other distinctions was of part Amerindian descent; not only did his sharp reflexes behind the plate give his team an edge, but his power at the plate led to 45 home runs and 148 runs batted in; both performances combined to win him the league's Most Valuable Player award. But no one player or manager wins 102 games in a season: Cincinnati blasted away the opposition with four .300 hitters: Tony Perez (.317), Pete Rose (.316), Bobby Tolan (.316), and Bernie Carbo (.306).

Cincinnati's Jim Merritt (20-12) was one of four 20-game winners in the National League; the others were Bob Gibson (23-7) of St Louis, Gaylord Perry (23-13) of San Francisco, and Ferguson Jenkins (22-16) of Chicago. No records there, but batters were assaulting all kinds of records. Hank Aaron became the 9th man in major league history to get 3000 hits, and Willy Mays was right behind him as the 10th; Ernie Banks of the Cubs became the 9th man to hit 500 home runs.

The Big Red Machine of Cincinnati went rolling

along through the National League play-offs, defeating the Pirates in three straight games – although the scores (3-0 in 10 innings, 3-1, 3-2) reveal that the Pirates were hardly a pushover. But then, although the National League had won the All-Star game, 5-4 (in 12 innings), for the league's eighth straight victory, the Baltimore Orioles took Cincinnati in the World Series, 4-1. Only Lee May's three-run homer in the eighth inning of the fourth game kept the Orioles from a clean sweep.

As the 1971 season began, many picked the Cincinnati Reds to repeat in their Western Division, but their power hitters didn't produce and they finished only fourth. The division winners, instead, were the San Francisco Giants (even though they had traded George Foster to the Reds – a trade they would come to regret as the years passed). At one point, the Giants enjoyed a 10½ game lead, but as they came into the final game of the season they were leading only by one game – and that over their opponent in the game, the Los Angeles Dodgers. What had gone wrong? Well, Willie Mays, for one, was 40 and had bursitis in his shoulder, while Willie McCovey, the most powerful Giants slugger, had arthritis in his right knee and a torn cartilage in his left knee. But the Giants right fielder Bobby Bonds hit 33 home runs and in that final game the Giants came through and beat the Dodgers.

In the Eastern Division, the Pittsburgh Pirates repeated their victory, this time leaving the St Louis

Above: Richard Anthony 'Richie' or 'Dick' Allen hits a long one. In his career with the Phillies, the Cardinals, the Dodgers, the White Sox and the A's (1963-77) he hit 351 home runs.
Left: Sparky Anderson.
Opposite: Johnny Bench of the Cincinnati Reds. Johnny Lee Bench started with the Reds in 1967 and played his whole career in Cincinnati. An all-time great catcher, he was voted the league's Most Valuable Player in 1970 and 1972 and was the World Series' Most Valuable Player in 1976.

Right: Willie Stargell hits a long one. Wilver Dornel 'Pops' Stargell played his entire career with the Pirates, playing the outfield and first base. He started in 1962, and was named the Most Valuable Player in the National League in 1979, when he was 39 years old. That was also the year that he was named the Most Valuable Player in the World Series.

Bottom: Pete Rose in another head-first slide – this time against the Cubs – as teammate Tony Perez cheers him on. In this case he defied one of his own rules: 'I don't recommend the head-first slide for sliding into home plate. One time I tried it and cut up my face on the catcher's shin guards.'

Cardinals seven games behind. The Pirates may not have had any superstars, but they had a team of solid players such as Al Oliver, Dave Cash, Rob Robertson, and Manny Sanguillen (who would go on to become a great catcher); they had Willie Stargell who got hot and hit 48 home runs to lead the league (and the majors); and in Roberto Clemente, in right field and hitting .341, they had a player who was on the verge of finally being recognized as one of the game's best all-round players.

Certainly the Pirates did not win on pitching. The pitching stars in 1971 played elsewhere. Tom Seaver of the Mets not only had a record of 20-10 but the lowest earned-run average in the majors – 1.76. Meanwhile, Ferguson Jenkins (24-13) pitched his fifth consecutive 20-game season and also racked up the astonishing stat of only 37 walks in 327 innings. Hank Aaron hit 47 home runs and raised his total to 639 – a career high trailing only Willie Mays' 646 and Ruth's seemingly impregnable 714. But with Aaron still going strong, that 714 no longer looked quite so remote.

In the National League play-offs, the Giants beat the Pirates in the first game, 5-4, but led by Bob Robertson's four home runs, the Pirates swept the next three, 9-4, 2-1, 9-5. Even so, the Pirates went into the World Series against the Orioles as the underdogs. After all, hadn't Baltimore wiped out the Big Red Machine in the 1970 series, won the last 11 games of their regular season, and then taken the Oakland A's in three straight? And when the Series opened in Baltimore and the Orioles took the first two games, 5-3 and 11-3, even the most loyal Pirates fans must have had a sinking feeling. But then the Pirates

mounted a boarding party – and behind the superb pitching of Steve Blass, Bruce Kison and Nelson Briles, and the strong hitting of Roberto Clemente, Pittsburgh took the next three, 5-1, 4-3, and 4-0. The fourth game, incidentally, was the first night game in the history of the World Series.

Back in Baltimore, the Orioles took the sixth game, 3-2, but only on Brooks Robinson's sacrifice fly in the 10th inning. And then, in one of those cliffhangers that give the World Series such a special role in Americans' memories, Steve Blass held the Orioles to four hits and the Pirates took the final game, 2-1, and became the World Champions. Once again, it was a team effort, but the whole country now had had a chance to see just what a consummate player Clemente was: he hit .414 in the series, his 12 hits falling just one short of the record in a Series but like his fielding, coming exactly where and when needed to keep his team ahead.

The 1972 season began somewhat inauspiciously during the training-exhibition weeks as the players in both major leagues were demanding that the club owners contribute more to the medical and pension

Above: Roberto Clemente scores while playing for Los Cangrejeros in the Puerto Rican Winter League.
Far left: Steve Blass of the Pirates. Stephen Robert Blass pitched for Pittsburgh from 1964 to 1974. Striking out 896 batters, he won 103 and lost 76 with an earned run average of 3.63. His 1971 World Series record was two wins and no losses.

Above: Joe Morgan takes a cut. Joseph Leonard Morgan has played with several teams during his career, which began in Houston in 1963. He won back-to-back Most Valuable Player Awards in 1975 and 1976, when he was with the Cincinnati Reds. **Opposite:** Steve Carlton lets one go. Stephen Norman 'Lefty' Carlton pitched for the Cardinals and the Phillies. His ERA is usually around 3.00 and in 1972 he struck out 310 batters. He won the Cy Young Award in 1972, 1977 and 1980.

funds. Finally the players went out on a strike for 10 days – the first general strike in the history of organized baseball. The strike ended on 13 April, but 86 regular season games had already been missed; it was decided not to try to make them up, so various teams in the majors ended up playing different numbers of games. It was only one of many indications that the traditional immutability of major league baseball was beginning to bend to the realities of modern life. Imagine the players of 50 years earlier striking for medical benefits and salaries of over $100,000 a year. And although the Supreme Court ruled this same spring that the reserve clause was legal and that Curt Flood's contract still held, there were portents of the future in the Court's urging of Congress to reconsider baseball's exemption from antitrust legislation.

But once on the field, the players gave the fans another exciting season. In the Eastern Division, the Pirates won for the third consecutive year, leaving the Cubs 11 games behind in second place. The Pirates succeeded with a combination of hitting and pitching, and once again Clemente came through, hitting .312 for the season; on the last day of the season, he got his 3000th hit, the 11th player in the history of baseball till then to achieve this. In the Western Division, Cincinnati's Big Red Machine – powered by Johnny Bench's 40 home runs and 125 runs batted in – took first place, leaving Houston 10½ games behind. The talk of the season, though, was Manager Sparky Anderson's habit of quickly removing his pitchers as soon as they got into a bit of trouble: only 25 Cincinnati pitchers survived complete games, while Sparky gained a new nickname, 'Captain Hook.' The Reds then went on to beat the Pirates in the league play-offs, but it took them all five games and a wild pitch by the Pirates Bob Moose in the bottom of the ninth inning of the final game.

The World Series pitted the Reds against the Oakland A's and it went into seven games before Oakland won that, 3-2, and became the champions. Except for the A's' Gene Tenace's four homers, equaling a record shared by Babe Ruth and Lou Gehrig, the series was dominated by the pitchers: the Reds' combined batting performance was held to .208, the A's to .207 and six of the seven games were decided by one run (a record). But the most spectacular pitching of the entire season was that of Steve Carlton, who had been traded away by the Cardinals to the Phillies; while posting a 27-10 record, he completed 30 of 41 starts, struck out 310, and ended with an earned run average

on those terms by the National League – here, as so often, the somewhat more conservative of the leagues. (Although it might be pointed out that it would be National League players who would take the lead in setting aside the reserve clause....) In the immediate sense, the designated hitter rule did what its proponents promised: the American League scored more runs and raised its over-all batting average (and it also saw the American League setting a new attendance record for the league). So successful was it, in fact, that the American League adopted the designated hitter permanently at the end of the 1973 season. (And it was agreed that World Series would be played with the designated hitter allowed only in alternate years.)

The 'miracle' of the 1973 season was a re-run of the 1969 season by the Mets. On 30 August, the Mets were in last place in the Eastern Division. Then, fired up by their star relief pitcher, Tug McGraw, with his cry of 'Ya gotta believe!' the Mets won 20 of their last 28 games and came rolling into the last day of the season needing to win at least one game of a doubleheader against Chicago to keep St Louis and Pittsburgh from tying with them for first place. The Mets took the first game – taking their division lead with a win-lost percentage of only .509 (the lowest of any pennant winner in baseball history). In fact, the Mets had been outscored by every team they played except one and their team batting average of .246 left them in 9th place in the National League. The Mets best pitcher was Tom Seaver, but his record was only 19-10 (and the Mets had traded another young pitcher, Nolan Ryan, to the California Angels – where his 383 strikeouts broke by one the modern major-league record that Sandy Koufax set in 1965).

In the Western Division, the Cincinnati Reds made their own fairly spectacular 'charge': at one point 11 games behind the Dodgers, they overtook them and then left them 3½ games in second place. Led by Pete Rose (.338, 230 hits), Tony Perez (.314, 27 homers), Joe Morgan (.290, 26 homers) and Johnny Bench (25 homers), the Big Red Machine once again seemed invincible. But in the National League play-offs, the

Above: Tug McGraw after he was traded by the New York Mets to the Philadelphia Phillies.

of only 1.98. And all this for a team that finished in last place.

A year that began with the death of the Mets manager, Gil Hodges, in spring training, and then saw the death of Hodges' old Brooklyn teammate, Jackie Robinson – always to be respected for pioneering the way for black players in the major leagues – ended on a truly tragic note. Roberto Clemente was in Puerto Rico, his homeland, when an earthquake devastated Managua, Nicaragua; on 31 December, he joined others on a DC-7 that was to fly supplies from San Juan to the earthquake victims; barely airborne, the plane crashed into the sea, taking Clemente to his death. Among the bitter ironies was that Clemente had never liked all the flying that went with modern major league schedules; and a player who had often gone unrecognized in his long career was given the ultimate recognition when the Hall of Fame waived its traditional five-year rule in 1973 and voted him immediately into baseball's shrine.

The 1973 season seemed to be one of those that come along every few years – a season full of oddities. It began with one of the most revolutionary changes in the basic rules of baseball since the modern game was organized: the adoption of the designated hitter by the American League. Although announced as merely a three-year experiment, it was rejected even

Far right: Tony Perez. Atanasio Rigal Perez began his career with the Reds in 1964, then went to Montreal in 1977.

Mets caught them off-guard and behind the pitching of Seaver, Koosman and Matlack, the Mets beat the Reds in five games. One of the less admirable episodes in the season came in the third game when both teams rushed onto the field after Pete Rose of the Reds got into a fight with Bud Harrelson of the Mets – and then the Mets fans threw so many objects at Rose that Sparky Anderson refused to continue playing until manager Yogi Berra and some of his players went out and calmed down their fans.

The Mets' dream of repeating their 1969 miracle, however, was not to be, as the Oakland A's defeated them, 4 games to 3. But the World Series this year was somewhat overshadowed by Hank Aaron's pursuit of Babe Ruth's career record of 714 homeruns: when the season ended, Aaron had hit 40, bringing his total to 713. (His fellow Braves, Darrell Evans and Dave Johnson had hit 41 and 43, respectively – the first time that any major league club could boast of three 40-homer men in a season.) It was obvious that Ruth's record was going to fall in 1974.

So obvious, in fact, that when the 1974 season began, the owners of the Atlanta Braves decided they would order Aaron to sit out the first three games, which the Braves were scheduled to play in Cincinnati, so that Aaron would most likely break the record at his home field. An understandable desire, but Bowie Kuhn, commissioner of baseball, overruled

Pete Rose playing third base.

the Braves. And so it was that when Hank Aaron came to bat for the first time in the opening game on 4 April, on his first swing he hit his 714th home run. Then, on 8 April, playing before 53,000 in the Atlanta stadium (and a television audience estimated at 35,000,000) Aaron hit the record-breaking 715th home run (off the Dodgers' Al Downing). Aaron had come in for an incredible amount of pressure – and abuse – for taking over Babe Ruth's record, but he himself was gracious after his moment of triumph: 'It's the Cadillac of baseball records. But Babe Ruth will still be regarded as the greatest home run hitter who ever lived.' That may be true for a certain generation, but the recordbooks will long show that Henry Aaron has hit the most home runs.

The 1974 season was distinguished by two other new records. One still stands: Mike Marshall, who only the year before, while pitching for Montreal, had appeared in 92 games, set a new record by appearing in 106 games for the Los Angeles Dodgers. The other record would eventually be broken, but at the time it seemed monumental: Lou Brock of the Cardinals broke Maury Wills 1962 record of 104 stolen bases in a season by stealing 118. On the one hand, it was not a surprise, as Brock had led the National League in stolen bases for seven of the last eight years; what was amazing was that Brock was 35 and seemed to have reached his peak during the 1960s as a power hitter.

The regular season of 1974 provided no special excitement. In the Eastern Division, the Pirates managed to squeeze by St Louis by 1½ games, mostly due to the heavy hitting of Richie Hebner, Willie Stargell, Al Oliver and Richie Zisk. (The Pirates' best pitcher, Jerry Reuss, only had 16 wins.) In the Western Division, the Dodgers led from the first week, and ended up four games ahead of the Reds. Along with Andy Messersmith's 20 wins – and Mike Marshall's 106 appearances at the mound – the Dodgers could count on a superbly coordinated infield: Steve Garvey at first, Davey Lopes at second, Bill Russell at shortstop and Ron Cey at third – they would play together through 1981. In the National League playoffs, the Dodgers took the Pirates in four games, with Don Sutton winning two of these by holding the Pirates to

Below: Lou Brock of the St Louis Cardinals breaks for second in an attempted steal against the Pittsburgh Pirates.

Left: Willie Mays, then with the New York Mets, argues with umpire Augie Donatelli during the 1973 World Series.

Above: Mike Marshall delivers one to the plate. Michael Grant Marshall, a relief pitcher for the Tigers, the Astros, the Expos, the Dodgers, the Braves, the Rangers and the Twins, began his career in 1967. He won the Cy Young Award in 1974 while he was with the Dodgers.
Right: Dave McNally on the mound. David Arthur McNally pitched for the Baltimore Orioles (1962-74) and the Montreal Expos (1975), winning 184 games and losing 119 with a 3.24 earned run average.

seven hits. In the World Series, however, the Dodgers lost out to the Oakland A's, four games to one – despite the A's strange uniforms, moustaches, and antics: as Dodgers Manager Walt Alston put it, 'They play the game the way it should be played.'

The 1975 baseball season is memorable primarily for its post-season activities – both on and off the playing field. For the regular season produced few surprises. In the Eastern Division, the Pittsburgh Pirates took their fifth title in six years, leaving the Phillies 6½ games behind. And in the Western Division, the Cincinnati Reds won 108 games – the third highest total ever, and the best record since Pittsburgh won 110 in 1909 – and left the Dodgers 20 games behind in second place. They achieved this awesome feat with some heavy hitting and by Manager Sparky Anderson's clever – and frequent – use of relief pitchers (none of his pitchers won over 15

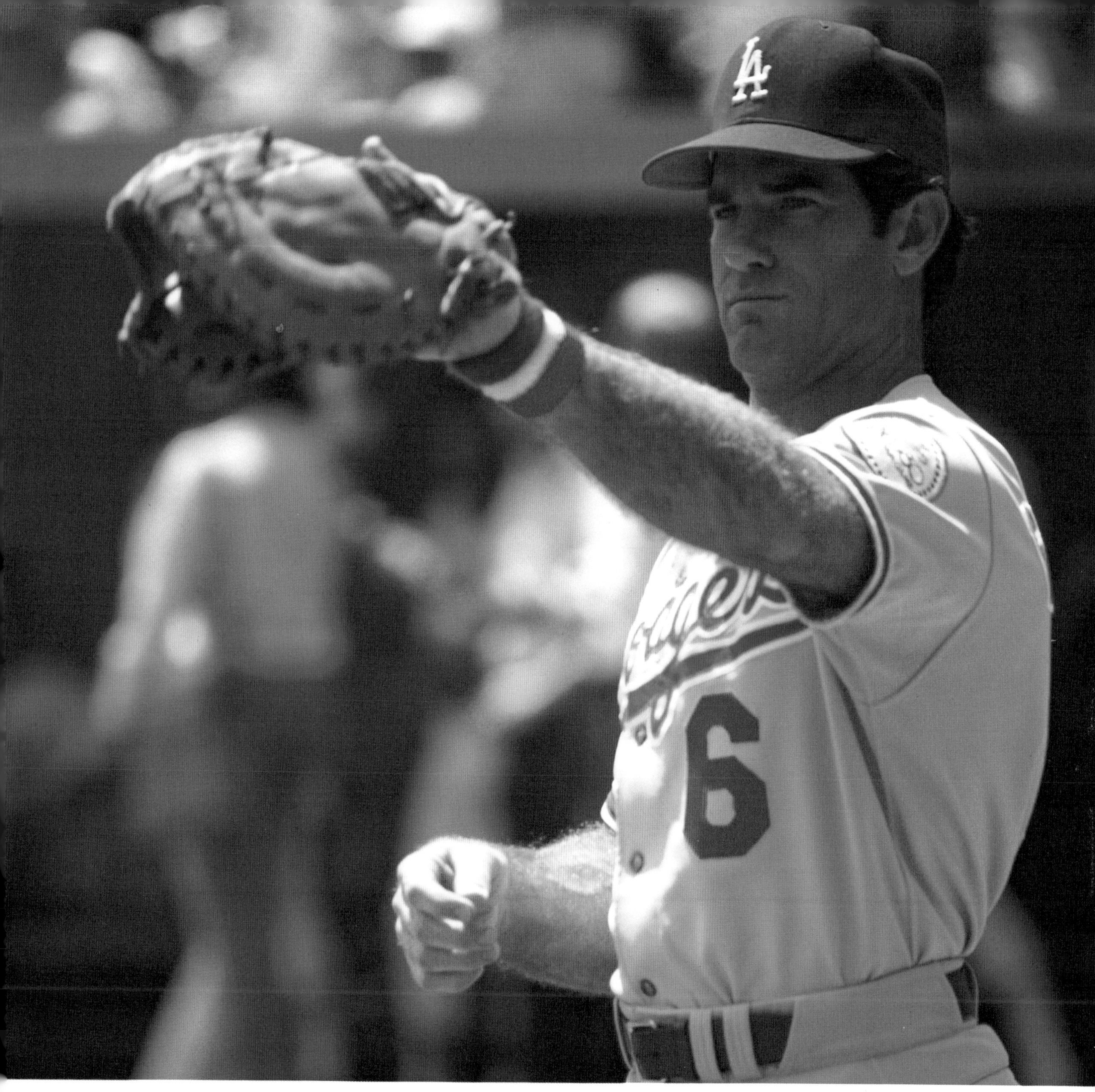

Steve Garvey at first base. Steve Patrick Garvey played primarily first base for the Los Angeles Dodgers, beginning in 1969. He was later traded to the San Diego Padres. He usually bats around .300 and was the National League Player of the Year in 1974.

games). The Big Red Machine then went rolling over the Pirates in the playoffs in three straight games.

Considering that the American League champions were the Boston Red Sox, who surprised everyone by beating out the Oakland A's, the Reds looked like a shoe-in for the Series. True, Boston had a hot young rookie, Fred Lynn – their other hot rookie, Jim Rice, missed the last of the season due to a broken hand – but even Boston's Lynn and Yastrzemski seemed outclassed by the Reds' Joe Morgan, Pete Rose, Johnny Bench and Tony Perez. Yet the Red Sox took the Reds to the seventh game, which the Reds won in the 9th inning on Morgan's single. The sixth game had taken over four hours to play, going into 12 innings and ending at 12:33 AM. And the third game provided one of those incidents that true fans would always argue over: Ed Armbrister of the Reds bunted in the 10th inning, and then failed to move away fast enough, so that Fisk, the Sox catcher, bumped into him; Fisk's resultant bad throw allowed a Red to get to third and Armbrister to get to second; the Reds then scored and won 6-5.

But even this controversy was overshadowed by what happened on 23 December 1975. Andy Messersmith of the Los Angeles Dodgers and Dave McNally of the Montreal Expos had chosen to play the 1975 season without signing contracts – and they argued that therefore they were now 'free agents,' able to sign with any team they chose to negotiate with. The owners naturally disputed this, for it effectively did away with the reserve clause. It was essentially a re-run of Curt Flood's challenge of 1970, but this time the players tried an end run – not treating it as a fundamental legal issue but merely a contractual dispute. So the issue went not into the courts but into arbitration, and in December the arbitrator, Peter M

Right: Andy Messersmith. John Alexander Messersmith pitched in both the National and the American Leagues, beginning with the Angels in 1968. His earned run average was usually below 3.00.

Seitz, ruled that Messersmith and McNally were indeed free agents – that a player's contract cannot be renewed indefinitely by the original owner until the player is traded, sold, released or retires.

Thus in one neat blow was organized baseball's hallowed keystone, the reserve clause, struck down. Not immediately, though, for the owners contended that the arbitrator's ruling was limited to only Messersmith and McNally. The owners then decided to have the decision set aside by the courts, after all, and since there was no resolution of the dispute by 1 March 1976, when spring training was to begin, the owners simply refused to open the camps. On 17 March, though, when there were signs of compromise, Commissioner Bowie Kuhn ordered that spring training begin immediately. And on the eve of the All-Star Game, 12 July, the players and owners finally announced they had agreed on a new basic contract. After five years in the major leagues, a player could demand to be traded; if he was not, he could become a free agent. Then, after six years in the majors, a player could become a free agent; however, he could negotiate only with a maximum of 13 clubs (including his present one) that had acquired the right to bargain in this re-entry draft.

At once the cry went up – and not only from the owners themselves – that this would be the end of true competition within the major leagues: the few very rich owners and clubs would always be able to buy up the best free agents and the teams would be divided among 'the haves and the have-nots.' And at first it did appear this way. Andy Messersmith, fittingly enough, seems to have become the first major league 'millionaire' now that he was free to leave the Dodgers and sign with the Atlanta Braves in April 1976. And when the first free-agent draft was held on 4 November 1976, numerous players did sign contracts for large sums of money. But it did not lead immediately to any drastic split between the richer and the poorer clubs, nor could anyone prove that a roster of millionaires guaranteed a pennant. There would always be the unpredictable element in baseball – the rookies who came out of nowhere to spark a team, the 'over-the-hill' veterans who produced some grand final efforts, and above all the inexplicable team spirit – perhaps best shown by the Mets of 1969 – that defied all the bookmakers and bookkeepers.

Above: Mike Schmidt takes a cut. Michael Jack Schmidt has played third base for the Philadelphia Phillies since he broke into baseball in 1972. A prodigious long-ball hitter, he won back-to-back Most Valuable Player Awards in 1980 and 1981.

Far left: Tony Perez (#24) about to shake Pete Rose's hand after Rose scored a game-winning run for the Reds against the Phillies.

The 1976 season itself produced no particular surprises. Once again the Cincinnati Reds swept the Western Division, winning 102 games and leaving the Dodgers 10 games behind; with a team batting average of .280, the highest in the majors, five of their eight regulars batted over .300; the Reds also led defensively, with the highest fielding percentage and the fewest errors. In the Eastern Division, the Phillies beat out Pittsburgh, but even with Mike Schmidt, Greg Luzinski, Garry Maddox and 20-game winner Steve Carlton, the Phillies fell in three straight to the Reds in the playoffs. There was no stopping the Big Red Machine after that, and they wiped out the Yankees four straight in the World Series, thus becoming the first National League team to repeat as World Champions since the New York Giants had done so in 1922.

The 1976 season, in fact, was memorable less for what happened on the field than what occurred around the negotiating table. But for the National League, it was also memorable for the retirement of two of its longtime stars. Walter Alston, after 23 years as manager of the Dodgers, retired. And Henry Aaron, also winding up his 23rd year as a major leaguer, retired at age 42; his 755 home runs now stood as a record that seemed unassailable as Ruth's 714 once did, while Aaron's 3771 lifetime hits at the time left him second only to Ty Cobb. It was hard not to think of it as the end of an era.

But if Alston was gone from the Dodgers, the Dodgers were not gone from the National League. In 1977, they came charging back under their rookie manager, Tom Lasorda, and won the Western Division, leaving the Reds the same 10 games behind that the Dodgers had been in 1976. Both teams seemed loaded with talent, in fact. The Dodgers had a 20-game winner in Tommy John, while four of their players – Garvey, Ron Cey, Reggie Smith and Dusty Baker – hit 30 or more homers. Meantime, the Reds had Tom Seaver (who had asked to be traded from the Mets because of a contract dispute) and a one-man powerhouse in George Foster, who hit 25 home runs and batted in 149 runs. (Voted the league's Most Valuable Player, he was the fifth Red in the last six years to be so honored.)

In the Eastern Division, the Chicago Cubs led in the early part of the season, but they faded and the Phillies won the title again, with Pittsburgh five games behind. Steve Carlton came through with a 23-10 season, while Mike Schmidt hit 40 homers and Greg Luzinski hit 39. In the pennant playoffs, however, the Phillies fell to the Dodgers in four games. In the Series, the Dodgers in turn fell to the Yankees, four games to

Tommy LaSorda, the Dodger manager. Thomas Charles LaSorda pitched for just three years in the majors – for Brooklyn (1954-55) and Kansas City (1956) – winning no games and losing four with his 6.48 earned run average. But it was as a manager that his genius became evident. Beginning the job in Los Angeles in 1976, he has won five Western Division Championships, three National League pennants and one World Series.

Right: George Foster at the plate. George Arthur Foster, whose career in the outfield began in San Francisco in 1969, has played with Cincinnati and New York in the National League. He twice was the league's home run leader (1977 and 1978, while at Cincinnati) and in 1977 was the Most Valuable Player in the National League.
Opposite: Tom Seaver when he played for the Cincinnati Reds.

CINCINNATI
41

two – or perhaps it would be more exact to say the Dodgers fell to Reggie Jackson, who set records of five home runs and 10 runs scored for a Series, three successive home runs and four runs scored in a single game.

But an even more fundamental record of major league baseball fell in 1977, when on 29 August Lou Brock of the St Louis Cardinals stole his 893rd base, breaking Ty Cobb's lifetime record of 892. Attendance records were being set, too, as Los Angeles set an all-time major league record for one club, with 2,900,000 fans at its 79 home games. And the 26 major league teams – the American League had added two more teams this year – boasted 38,700,000 spectators, a 24 percent increase over 1976, the previous record year. Any fear that the 'desertions' by free agents in pursuit of the Top Dollar might turn off the fans was proving groundless.

The 1978 season seemed in many ways a re-run of the 1977 season. In the Western Division of the

Below: Lou Brock of the St Louis Cardinals avoids the tag at home.

Right: Lou Brock at the plate.

National League, the Dodgers beat out the Reds again, but only after the Reds collapsed after 6 August, losing 15 of their next 21 games, and the Dodgers went on to win 22 of their last 37 games. The Dodgers achieved their victory without any particular superstars – only Steve Garvey took a lead in statistics, with his 202 hits – but some good pitching by Tommy John, Burt Hooton and Don Sutton, plus Tom Lasorda's savvy managing did the trick. In the Eastern Division, the Phillies and Pittsburgh battled it out again, with the Phillies taking their third consecutive title in the division. In the playoffs, the Dodgers were leading two games to one, when in the tenth inning of the fourth game, the Phillies Garry Maddox, usually the most surehanded of players, dropped a flyball and the Dodgers took the game and that series.

The Dodgers went into the World Series against the Yankees again, but this time they were favored – in part because the Yankees were coming out of a sea-

son in which good playing was overshadowed by bad conduct. When the Dodgers took the first two games, it appeared that the Good Guys would win – but then the Yankees went on to take the next four and become the first team ever to lose the first two of the World Series and come back to win it in six. All Ron Cey of the Dodgers could say was, 'They had better pitching, defense and hitting. What else is there?'

1978 was the year, though, that one of the National League's long favorite players began to claim everyone's serious attention. On 14 June, Pete Rose of the Reds began a hitting streak that first broke the modern National League record of 37, by Tommy Holmes in 1945, and then went on to hit safely in 44 games, tying the all-time National League record set by Wee Willie Keeler in 1897. And on 5 May, Rose had become the 13th player in major-league history to get 3000 hits in a career. At the end of the season, though, Rose surprised everyone, and disappointed some of his special Cincinnati fans, by signing a four-year contract (for $3,200,000) with the Phillies. The Reds had already fired their manager, Sparky Anderson, and it looked as though the Cincinnati dynasty had come to an end.

But the Reds held in there for the 1979 season, and with solid performances by George Foster, Johnny Bench, Dave Concepcion and Tom Seaver, they led the Western Division, with Houston 1½ games behind. Meanwhile, over in the Eastern Division, the Phillies – despite Rose's .331 batting average and his tenth season with over 200 hits – could only come in fourth. The winner in the East was Pittsburgh, and it was confirmation that team effort still counted at least as much as astronomical salaries, as welcome as they might be for the individual recipients. Willie Stargell, now 39 and fondly known as 'Pops,' came up with 32 home runs (and won himself a tie for the Most Valuable Player, with Keith Hernandez of St Louis); Omar Moreno stole 77 bases and Kent Tekulve, Enrique Romo and Grant Jackson appeared as relief pitchers in a total of 250 games. The Pirates then went on to defeat the Reds in the league playoffs in three straight games.

The World Series was a fitting climax to the decade of extremes and upsets. For one thing, many of the games were played in the rain and cold, with players' fingers really numb on occasion. The Orioles represented the American League and soon moved into the lead with three games to one for the Pirates. But in the last three games, the Pirates held the Orioles to only 17 hits and two runs; Stargell was the inspiration, making four hits, including two home runs, in the last game. The Pirates had done the near-impossible (for in fact, three other teams had previously done it) winning the World Series after being down three games to one.

Several individual National League players stood out in 1979. Lou Brock of the Cardinals got his 3000th hit, the 14th player in major league history to do so. J Rodney Richards of the Houston Astros struck out 313, a new league record for righthanders. And in one of the most unusual situations, two brothers – Phil Niekro (21-20) of the Atlanta Braves and Joe Niekro (21-11) of the Houston Astros – led the National League in victories. And with a new all-time regular season attendance record of 43,548,450 (eight teams bettered 2,000,000 at home), it seemed that major league baseball, for all the vicissitudes of the 1970s, was in a strong position to take on the challenging decade of the 1980s.

Opposite: Some of the 'Bleacher Bums' in the friendly confines of Wrigley Field in Chicago – the oldest ball park in the National League – which boasts no lights and natural grass.

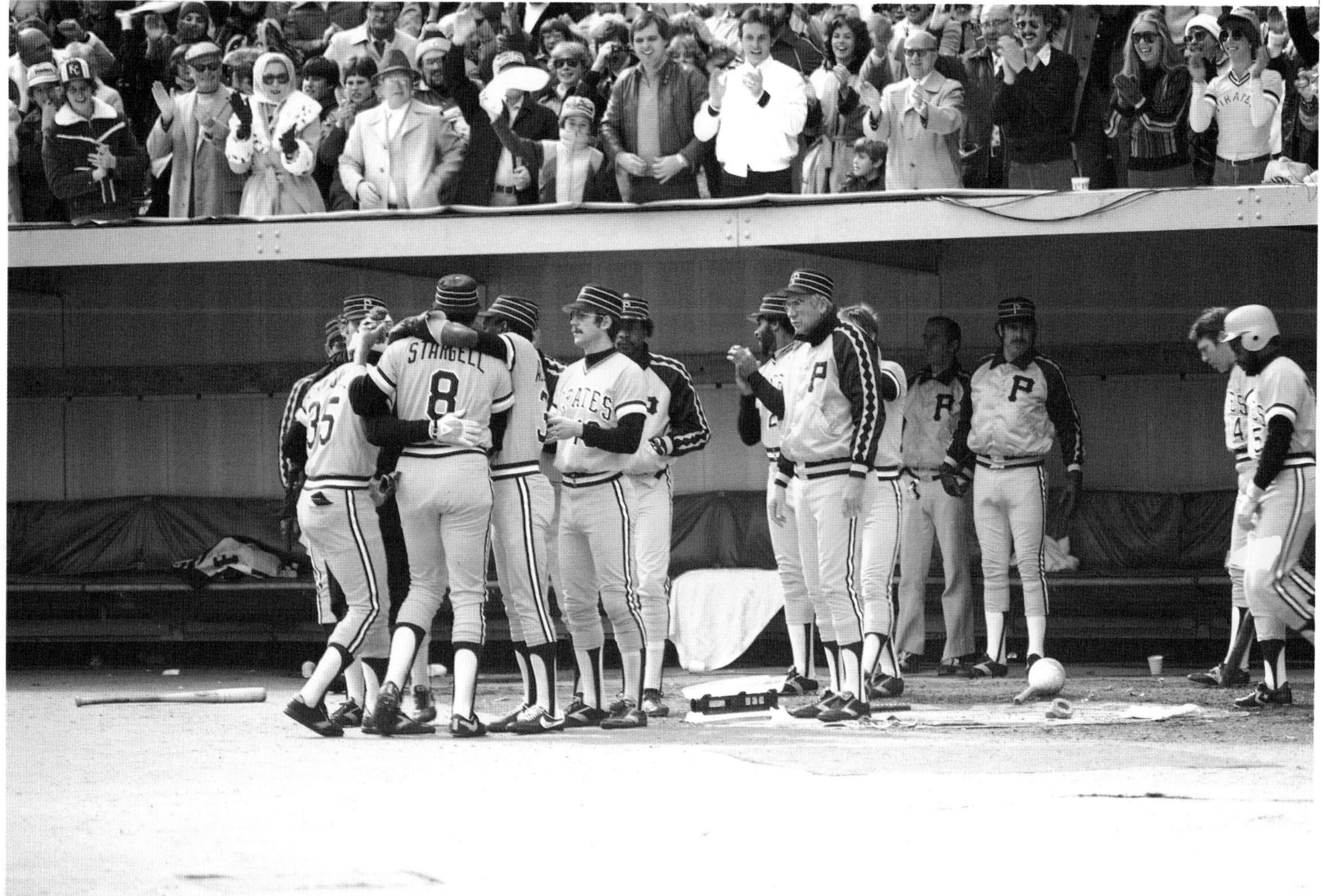

Below: The Pittsburgh Pirates leave the dugout to hug Willie Stargell after he scores against the Baltimore Orioles in the 1979 World Series.

CHAPTER EIGHT
The Decade Past and Present

The game gave me a great feeling.

Pete Rose on the Opening Day game, 1985

It would take several decades before major league baseball of the 1980s could be seen in true perspective. But if other decades might be characterized as those of the Big Bats or the Big Strikeouts, then viewed close up, the 1980s seemed to be the decade of the Big Bucks and the Big Strikes. The era of the Big Bucks, of course, really began with the effective discarding of the reserve clause in 1976 and the resultant boom in the free-agent market. Between 1978 and 1981, for instance, 43 players received contracts worth over a million dollars to each; the then summit was attained by Dave Winfield in November 1980 when he signed a ten-year contract with the New York Yankees worth a reported $13,000,000 (with a cost-of-living clause that could make it worth at least $20,000,000). And not only were the free agents and superstars of the game enjoying this boom; all players were riding the wave, as the average salary of all major-league players advanced from $50,000 in 1976 to $200,000 in 1981.

Opposite: Joe Morgan at the plate when he was with the Houston Astros (1963-71). **Below:** Cesar Cedeño at bat as a Houston Astro. He later went to the Reds and then the Cardinals.

The Big Strike followed directly in the wake of the Big Bucks, because the owners decided in 1980 that they would try to gain some adantage from the free-agent boom. The owners demanded that any club that lost a player because of the free agent move must get a player from the club that signed the free agent. The players, through their formal Players' Association, naturally objected; they staged a walkout during the final week of spring training and threatened to go on strike on 23 May 1980 if there was no agreement with the owners; minutes before the deadline, the club owners and the Players' Association agreed to set up a player-management committee to study the issue of free agency and proper payment; if agreement was not reached by 31 January 1981, each side in the dispute could take whatever action it was prepared to support.

So the disagreement was temporarily sidetracked and the 1980 season proceeded. And proceed it did right up to the last day – plus one, for the Western

Astros

GARVEY
6
P
14

Division of the National League. This was the year that another so-called expansion team made its challenge against a tough veteran team – the Houston Astros, that is, in existence only since 1962, found itself fighting for the division lead against the Los Angeles Dodgers. Houston had lost out in 1979 by only 1½ games to Cincinnati, and they still had a couple of ace pitchers in Joe Niekro and J R Richard, but Richard suffered a stroke in July. Still, going into their last three games, the Astros had a three-game lead – except that their opponent in these last games was the Los Angeles Dodgers. The Dodgers took all three, so there had to be a single game playoff to determine the division winner. Joe Niekro won it for the Astros, who then had to face the Eastern Division winner, the Philadelphia Phillies. The Phillies were loaded with talent – having acquired Pete Rose in 1979, and with Mike Schmidt hitting 48 home runs and Steve Carlton winning 24 games – but even so they did not tie up the Eastern Division title until the next-to-last game of the season, and then only beating off Montreal with Schmidt's home run.

The National League playoff for the pennant proved to be one of the most exciting and exacting in recent memory. It went into the fifth game – with four games going into extra innings – but experience finally provided the edge and the Phillies took the fifth game. It was only the third time in their long history that the Phillies had made it into a World Series, and in their first, in 1915, they had lost to the Red Sox, four games to one, while in 1950 they had been swept away in four straight games by the Yankees. But 1980 proved to be the Phillies' year. They met the Kansas City Royals and defeated them four games to two. Mike Schmidt was voted the Most Valuable Player of the Series, with his .381 batting average, two of the Phillies' three homers, and team-leading seven runs batted in.

One of the most memorable games of the 1980 season was that pitched by Jerry Reuss of the Los Angeles Dodgers against the San Francisco Giants, on 28 June. In the first inning, Dodger shortstop Bill Russell made a slight throwing error and Jack Clark got to first base. But he was the only Giant to get to first base: Reuss then retired the next 25 batters in a row and thus missed a perfect game by that one error.

The 1981 season began under a cloud, for the Players' Association and the owners had still not resolved their differences over the issues of free agents. The owners had come up with what they regarded as a compromise: for every 'premium' player who left a club as a free agent, that club was to be given a professional replacement by the club that

Left: Mike Schmidt at third base for the Philadelphia Phillies. Schmidt led the league in home runs seven times – 1974, 1975, 1976, 1980, 1982, 1983 and 1984 and was the runs batted in leader in 1980, 1981, and 1984.

Opposite: Steve Garvey avoids catcher Ed Ott's tag in a game between the Dodgers and the Pirates.

Above: Tim Raines of the Montreal Expos at bat. Raines is a consistent .300 hitter.

Far right: Determination shows on the face of Dodger pitcher Fernando Valenzuela. Valenzuela won the Cy Young Award in 1981 as well as the Rookie of the Year Award that same year.

signed the free agent. A 'premium player' was to be so designated by a complicated formula involving his statistics in relation to other players of his position. The players saw this as still restricting the negotiating rights of players and although they began the season they made it clear that they were prepared to strike.

But this did not stop the players from giving their best as the season commenced. There were close races going in all four divisions of the major leagues, attendance was setting new records and there were a couple of sensational rookies in Tim Raines of the Montreal Expos and Fernando Valenzuela of the Dodgers. Valenzuela, in fact, became a national celebrity. Only 20 years old and from Mexico – he spoke very little English – he had pitched in relief in 1980 but now this lefthander was literally unbeatable: by 14 May he had an 8-0 record, five of those shutouts. Baseball was the talk of the nation.

And then suddenly there was no baseball to talk about: on 12 June, exactly as they had warned they might, the players went on strike. It went on for 50 days – the longest strike in the history of organized sports – and before it ended and play resumed, 714 games were cancelled. The terms of the settlement, which were agreed to on 31 July, were fairly com-

34

plicated, but they represented a compromise: teams losing 'premium' free agents would receive compensation from a pool of players that drew on all clubs rather than just from the signing club, and the teams that lost players through the pool would be compensated from a fund maintained by all the clubs. In effect, by dispersing the cost and impact, the owners would be more inclined to compete for the free agents.

That took care of the legal technicalities – but what about the game and its fans? Some people were so disgusted at what they regarded as a violation of a sacred rite that they vowed never to attend another major league game. Others simply turned to minor league games. (In the end, everyone seems to have returned to the fold.) But in an attempt to introduce a new race into the split season, the club owners got Commissioner Bowie Kuhn to establish a 'second season.' The four teams leading their divisions when the strike began would meet their respective division winners from the second half. Everyone had alternative plans or objections to this one, but one obvious flaw was the possibility that a team might have the best total record for the year but still not have led in either half (the two halves not actually involving the same number of games).

Below: Steve Rogers on the mound for the Montreal Expos. Stephen Douglas Rogers has had an earned run average of about 3.00 since coming to the Expos in 1973.

And that is exactly what happened. In the Western Division, the Cincinnati Reds had the best total record, 62 wins and 42 losses, but it came in second – by only ½ game! – to the Dodgers in the first part of the season; then in the second part of the season, the Reds were beaten out by the Houston Astros. And in the Eastern Division, the St Louis Cardinals also had the best over-all record – 59 wins and 43 losses – but the Phillies beat them out in the first half and the Expos took the second half – again, with the Cardinals only ½ game out.

Then began what seemed like an endless series of playoffs. The Dodgers beat the Houston Astros three games to two, but only after losing the first two; the Expos defeated the Phillies also three games to two, but they did it the other way – winning the first two, dropping the next two, and then taking the fifth. Then came the playoff for the league pennant, and most people once again picked the experienced Dodgers to eliminate the young expansion team, the Expos. They did, but it took five hard games to do so. Valenzuela lost the second game and Jerry Reuss lost the third game, so the Dodgers needed to win the last two. They evened the series in a 7-1 win with Burt Hooton giving up only five hits in 7½ innings. The fifth game was rained out but rescheduled for the next day. Ray Burris pitched for the Expos and Valenzuela pitched for the Dodgers, and going into the ninth inning it was a 1-1 tie. By then, Steve Rogers had relieved Burris, and with two out he threw a sinker that Rick Monday hit over the centerfield fence; the Dodgers held off the Expos and won the game and pennant, 2-1.

The Dodgers then went on to meet the New York Yankees for the 11th time in a World Series – the Yankees having won eight of the previous. And when the Yankees took the first two games, it looked like they were going to continue their dominance. Only one other team in Series history had come back to take the next four – and that team had been the Yankees, when they did so against the Dodgers in 1978. But this year was to be different, as the Dodgers took the next four games, winning their first Series since 1965. It was a true team effort, too, so that for the first time in Series history three players shared the most valuable player award – the Dodgers' Ron Cey, Steve Yeager and Pedro Guerrero.

The 1981 season, although overwhelmed by the Big Strike, did in fact witness several records in the National League. Nolan Ryan, pitching for the Astros against the Dodgers on 26 September, got his fifth career no-hitter, a major league record (he had been sharing the record of four with Sandy Koufax). Tom Seaver of the Cincinnati Reds got his 3000th strikeout in a game against the Cardinals on 18 April and took over fifth place on the all-time strikeout list; then on 29 April, Steve Carlton got his 3000th strikeout in a game against the Montreal Expos, and he took over sixth place on the all-time list. Both Seaver and Carl-

ton would continue their climb up the list in the years that followed.

Another National League player who was making his own assault on the record books was Pete Rose, and on 10 August 1981 he got his 3361st hit, thus moving ahead of Stan Musial's National League record – set in 1963, in a game where Rose had been present. Rose got his record-breaking hit against these same Cardinals, and was now free to take on the all-time major league record of total hits, Ty Cobb's 4191.

The 1982 season might be characterized as the roller-coaster season for the two principal headliners of major league baseball that year – Bowie Kuhn and the Atlanta Braves. For Bowie Kuhn, after 14 years as Commissioner of Baseball, it was out-again, in-again, as some of the owners organized a move to oust him; they finally succeeded in November (although even then he was asked to stay on until a successor could be chosen). It was primarily National League club owners, spearheaded by Nelson Doubleday, principal owner of the New York Mets, who opposed Kuhn on a mixture of personal style and economic motives.

In some respects the Atlanta Braves came out of 1982 no better than Bowie Kuhn. They started off the season in April with an incredible 13 straight wins –

Above: Pete Rose while he played for the Montreal Expos.
Left: Nolan Ryan pitching for the Houston Astros.

setting a new National League record – not losing their first game until the Reds defeated them on 22 April. By the end of July, the Braves seemed uncatchable: the Padres were nine games behind, the Dodgers 10. But then in August the Braves went into a tailspin and the Dodgers and Giants came alive. Because the Dodgers beat the Braves in two series in August, by the end of the month Los Angeles had taken over first place.

How had it happened? It was one of those mysteries that make baseball continually exciting. There was no single factor. Fernando Valenzuela, who had begun the season by threatening to sit it out because of a contract dispute, ended up getting the pay he felt he deserved and then was having a less than spectacular season. True, the Dodgers had Steve Garvey, 'Mr. Clean,' who became only the fifth major leaguer to play in 1000 consecutive games. But the Braves had Dale Murphy – eventually named Most Valuable Player of the league – and hard-hitting Bob Horner. In any case, when the final weekend of the season came around, the Braves had managed to sneak back into first place, but only by one game over the Dodgers and the Giants; in one of those flukes of scheduling, the Dodgers and Giants were to play a three-game series at the end, so one of them was clearly going to be knocked out of the running. The Dodgers beat the Giants in the first two, so the Giants were out. Meanwhile, the Braves were facing the Padres that last weekend in a three-game series, and the Braves also took their first two. This meant that on the last day, the Braves needed either a win or a Dodgers loss to clinch the Western Division. The Braves lost to the Padres, but Joe Morgan of the Giants hit a three-run homer to lead his team over the Dodgers. So the Braves that had seemed unbeatable in April just sneaked into first place in October.

In the Eastern Division there was a less dramatic race. The Reds, usually a major threat, were having a poor season, as were the Pirates; each team had a once-great star who was in decline – Tom Seaver for the Reds, Willie Stargell for the Pirates. (Stargell, in fact, announced that this was his last season, come what may.) But Montreal seemed strong, with the likes of Al Oliver, Gary Carter and Andre Dawson. And the Phillies were back in there, with two veterans leading the way: Pete Rose was still hitting, getting his 3771st hit on 21 June and thus tying Hank Aaron's record for second place in the majors; and Steve Carlton was to be the only 20-game winner in the

Opposite: Dale Murphy of the Atlanta Braves. Dale Bryan Murphy broke into the Atlanta lineup in 1976 as a catcher/first baseman. In 1983 he led the league in runs batted in, and won back-to-back Most Valuable Player Awards in 1982 and 1983.
Below left: Bob Horner at the plate. James Robert Horner broke in with the Braves in 1978, playing the outfield.
Below right: Dodger pitcher Fernando Valenzuela warms up.

Opposite: Gary Carter at the plate. Gary Edmund Carter came up to the Montreal Expos in 1974 as a catcher/outfielder and hit .407 that year. He then switched to catching. Traded to the Mets for the 1985 season, he immediately became a team leader.

Below: Bruce Sutter, the ace relief pitcher, while he was with the St Louis Cardinals. Breaking in with the Cubs in 1976, he immediately established himself as one of the best firemen of all time. Howard Bruce Sutter won the Cy Young Award with the Cubs in 1979. A rare honor for a relief pitcher.

National League, his 23-11 record gaining him his fourth Cy Young Award (the first pitcher to win that many).

But in the end it was the St Louis Cardinals that took first place, and with no particular stars. The team's total home runs came to only 67 – the lowest for any major league team that year – while one of their pitchers, Jim Kaat, was playing for his 24th straight major league season, a record. But they stole bases – 200 altogether – and got the timely hits, and they beat out Montreal and the Phillies. And then to spoil the Cinderella ending that the Braves were counting on, the Cardinals defeated them in three straight games to take the National League pennant. In the World Series, the Cardinals faced the Milwaukee Brewers, and in a hard-fought slugging duel that went to seven games – with a total of 40 runs for the Cardinals and 33 for the Brewers – the Cardinals came out as World Champions, thanks to some fine pitching by Joaquin Andujar and superb playing by Darrel Porter (named the most valuable player for the Series).

Above: A get-together with former Dodger great Pee Wee Reese (left), Baseball Commissioner Bowie Kuhn (center) and Dodger manager Tommy LaSorda.

The season of 1983 was one of the type that seems to be increasingly more frequent: namely, a year when the action off the diamond threatened to overshadow the game on the field. The whole year, for instance, was marked by the on-going controversy over the dismissal of Bowie Kuhn, as he and some of his supporters made last-ditch efforts to renew his contract; in the end, they failed, but it seemed almost immaterial as he was retained as the interim Commissioner until his successor could be found – and Kuhn went right on exercising to the full all the powers of the Commissioner. In particular, drug and alcohol abuse had now burst onto the scene as a major problem with more and more players, and Kuhn was both praised and attacked for the firm stand – including heavy fines and suspensions – he took against the players whose problems with drugs or alcohol became public.

Right: Andre Dawson, another speedster for the Montreal Expos. He came up at the end of the 1976 season and made Rookie of the Year in 1978.

Another sign of the times was the signing of an agreement in April by which NBC and ABC guaranteed the 26 major league clubs over $1,000,000,000 over six years for telecast rights to games. Since this meant that each team would be guaranteed an average of over $6,000,000 each season even if not one single spectator showed up, it seemed to change the nature of a team's relations with its fans, and taken in conjunction with such developments as Warner Communications' purchase of 48 percent interest in the Pittsburgh Pirates, it seemed to foreshadow a day when baseball games were little more than TV 'productions,' part of some larger entertainment industry. Yet the fact was that by the end of the 1983 season, the 26 major league clubs had once again set a new record for total attendance – 44,587,874 fans had left their TV screens to go out to the ballpark. So perhaps the reports of baseball's demise were a bit premature, after all.

The season itself produced few surprises, although a number of records and all-time stars did figure prominently. In the National League's Eastern Division, the Phillies had first place all for themselves by 28 September, thanks to the performances of such future Hall-of-Famers as Steve Carlton, Joe Morgan

Left: Pete Rose in the on-deck circle.
Far left: Rose takes a cut while playing with Philadelphia.

and Mike Schmidt. Steve Carlton became only the 16th pitcher in modern baseball to win 300 major league games, while he and Nolan Ryan of the Astros raced neck-and-neck throughout the year to see who would take the all-time lead for strikeouts. Walter Johnson's record of 3508 had been compiled between 1907-27 and it was Nolan Ryan who broke it first, in April; by June, Carlton had overtaken Ryan with his own 3526 strikeouts; the race between these two would go on through 1985.

Another record-breaker was Pete Rose, still with the Phillies and still hot on the trail of several records, including his most coveted, the major-league career hits total; another record race he was forced to abandon was the consecutive games played, when he was benched after playing 745 (leaving him in 10th place for the major leagues). And when the Phillies would offer him a contract only as a part-time player at the end of the season, Rose rejected it, and moved on to start 1984 with the Expos. Meanwhile, Steve Garvey would end his streak of consecutive games played at 1207 on 29 July, when he dislocated his left thumb; it left him in first place in the National League (if considerably behind Lou Gehrig's major league record of 2130).

CARLTON
32

There was little surprise in the Western Division, either, where the Dodgers took first place. And when the Phillies beat the Dodgers in three out of four games to take the National League pennant, they found themselves facing the Baltimore Orioles in what was a rarity in contemporary baseball – a 'railroad series.' (That is, in an era when teams usually have to jet back and forth to maintain schedules, here were two cities conveniently linked by railroads.) In the end, this didn't help the Phillies, as their stars such as Mike Schmidt fell into a batting slump and the Orioles took the Series, four games to one.

The 1983 season would be remembered for several other highpoints. Bob Forsch of the St Louis Cardinals pitched the second no-hitter of his career. At the end of the season, Johnny Bench retired, as did Gaylord Perry. Jim Kaat, the 44-year-old Cardinals pitcher, was placed on waivers, which no one picked up; this left Phil Niekro, also at 44, the oldest player in major league baseball, but when he was released by the Braves – after 19 seasons – he was signed up by the Yankees (and was still going strong in 1985).

Finally and most flattering to the National League was a poll taken by *The New York Times* of all active major league players. They voted Steve Carlton of the Phillies as the best pitcher active, Andre Dawson of the Expos as the best all-round ball player and Whitey Herzog as the best manager. So even though the National League lost the All-Star game this year – for the first time in many years – the Nationals could still take pride in their standing in the eyes of all players.

The 1984 season was a 'tale of two cities.' For one, Detroit of the American League, it was 'the best of times.' For the other it was . . . well, if not 'the worst of

Opposite: Steve Carlton, whose Phillies took the pennant in 1983, led the league in strikeouts that year with 275.

Below: Dennis Eckersley pitching for the Chicago Cubs. Dennis Lee Eckersley played for the Indians (1975-77), the Red Sox (1978-83) and then the Cubs. He immediately became a valued member of the starting rotation with the Cubs, with a 10-8 record and a 3.03 earned run average in 1984.

Above: Jodie Davis, the Chicago Cub catcher.
Right: Leon Durham, the Cub first baseman, rounds the bases after hitting a home run. 'Bull' Durham's best year was 1984, when he hit 23 home runs and drove in 96 while batting .279.

Opposite: Ryne Sandberg (top) of the Cubs, although almost taken out of the play by the runner, makes the throw to first to complete a double play. Sandberg hit .314 in 1984, while leading the Cubs, with his hitting and fielding, to the National League East title, becoming the league's Most Valuable Player.

times,' it was certainly a hard year to swallow. That city was the home of a certain National League club that had gone 39 years without getting into any post-season play. Yes, the Cubs of Chicago. And thereby hangs the tale.

As the season was just beginning, *The New York Times* sportswriters picked the Expos to take the Eastern Division and the Dodgers to take the Western Division. So when the Cubs found themselves in an unfamiliar first place in May, they along with the rest of the country were pleasantly surprised. Not that the Cubs didn't have the talent: when the season was over, in fact, Ryne Sandberg of the Cubs was named the most valuable player in the National League, Rick Sutcliffe got the Cy Young award for the league's best pitching and the Cubs' manager, Jim Frey, was voted National League manager of the year.

But there were other teams with plenty of talent, too. The Mets, for instance, had signed Keith Hernandez from the Cardinals and Ray Knight from the Astros; in addition, they had the Rookie of the Year 1983, Daryl Strawberry. Above all, they turned up with an unexpected sensation in Dwight Gooden, who ended up with a 17-9 record but with 251 strikeouts, broke Seaver's old record of 13 games with 10 or more

strikeouts and won Rookie of the Year for his league. One player they did not have was Tom Seaver: at the end of 1982, they had signed him on from Cincinnati, but then, in a monumental blooper, they forgot to add his name to those players to be protected from the free-agent compensation pool – and the Chicago White Sox claimed him in January 1984. Seaver eventually came to terms with the White Sox, as he was determined to keep pitching.

But although the Mets seemed hot at times, they slipped and as the season drew into the final weeks, pennant fever swept Chicago. So confident, in fact, was Chicago that it would win the pennant that an unanticipated controversy arose. The Cubs' home park, Wrigley Field, was the only major league field never to have installed lights for night games, and since the TV networks expect to show at least the midweek Series games at night, there was pressure on the Cubs to install temporary lights at least. But the traditionalists won out: despite all the arguments, the Cubs were not going to play any Series games in Wrigley Field at night.

In fact, the Cubs did not get to play any World Series games in any field nor at any time of day. Oh, they won the Eastern Division by 24 September, their first championship of any kind since 1945. But the San Diego Padres had won the Western Division, and they were no respecters of tradition. The Cubs wiped the Padres out in the first game, 13-0, setting several Series records (including five home runs), and then the Cubs won the second, 4-2. Chicago – indeed, most of the country – could begin to write the headlines proclaiming the Second City Number One. But the next three games were played in San Diego – and the Padres took them, one, two and three.

Opposite far left: Dwight 'Dr K' Gooden, the phenomenal strikeout artist of the New York Mets.

Above: Thirteen sequence shots showing the smooth delivery of the Great Gooden.
Below: A vendor selling souvenirs in Chicago's Wrigley Field.

So ended the best and worst of years for Chicago. But the whole country had enjoyed the Cubs' race while it lasted. And in the end, the Padres had no chance against the Detroit Tigers, who had led the American League from the first day, wiped out the Oakland A's three straight to take the league pennant, and set down the Padres, four games to one. But the National League had some other memorable occasions for 1984. Pete Rose broke the National league record for career doubles (726) and attained one of his career 'plateaus' – 4097 hits, putting him in second place (behind Ty Cobb's 4191) for all-time major leaguers. And when he left the Expos to return to Cincinnati, where his notable career began, and became a playing-manager, it seemed definite that Rose would go on playing until he took over first place sometime in 1985.

The 1985 season took up pretty much where the 1984 season left off. There was much talk of Pete Rose's virtually certain overtaking of Ty Cobb's long-standing record; indeed, it was predicted that Rose would do so sometime late in August, and when Rose

Opposite: Darryl Strawberry, the young Met outfielder. Strawberry came up to the Mets in 1983 and won the Rookie of the Year Award, primarily for his hitting.
Below: Rick Sutcliffe, the star of the Cub pitching staff, who came to the Cubs early in the 1984 season, and won 16 while losing only one, earning the Cy Young Award.

14
Winston America's Best.
4192
375

AT BAT
AVG
BALL
STRIKE
OUT
Major
PADRES
REDS
Coca-Cola
375

Previous spread: Pete Rose stands in a crowd at first base in Riverfront Stadium, Cincinnati, after breaking Ty Cobb's record of 4191 career hits. In the inset, Rose salutes the fans on that momentous day.

opened the season with two hits it appeared that he was well on his way. In the end, he tied Cobb on 8 September and then took the lead on 11 September. The other hot topic of the first part of the season was the threatened strike by the players; they did strike on 6 and 7 August, but were back on the field by 8 August (and missed games were made up later).

In other respects the 1985 season had an air of familiarity. The professional sports writers were picking the Cubs and Padres to repeat as winners in their respective Eastern and Western divisions, but with a major difference: the Cubs were being picked to overcome their jinx and defeat the Padres in the playoffs to go on to the World Series. But in fact, by the midseason All-Star break on 14 July, the Cardinals were in first place in the Eastern Division, with the Mets two and a half games behind (and the Cubs seven and a half games down); while in the Western Division, the Padres trailed the Dodgers by half a game. As the season rolled into September, those four

Left: Vince Coleman readies himself to steal second. Speedster Coleman won Rookie of the Year in 1985, and batted lead-off for the National League championship team, the St Louis Cardinals.

Above right: Keith Hernandez broke in with St Louis as a first baseman in 1974. After being traded to the Mets he became a team leader, hitting .311 with 15 home runs in 1984. He was voted the league's Most Valuable Player in a tie with Willie Stargell in 1979.

teams held those same positions – with the gaps only wider.

The 1985 season saw a number of notable records in addition to Pete Rose's. Nolan Ryan, now with the Houston Astros, increased his lead as the all-time strikeout leader by ending the year with 4083. Dwight Gooden, the sensational pitcher for the Mets – already known as 'Doctor K' became the youngest pitcher, at age 20, to gain 20 victories.

And when the 1985 season ended, there were the Cardinals in first place in the Eastern Division and the Dodgers in first place in the Western Division, proving that sports writers could occasionally be wrong. The Cardinals confronted the American League's pennant-winning Kansas City Royals in the World Series, which went to seven games until the Royals emerged as World Champions.

In 1986 the New York Mets finally achieved the success that had eluded them for the previous two seasons, and with a vengeance. Winning 108 games and clinching the division on 17 September, the Mets displayed both talent and tenacity. Although the Cardinals had taken an early lead, by 23 April the Mets had moved into first place for good; by the mid-season All-Star game, the Mets had a commanding 13-game lead over the Montreal Expos.

In the West a changing of the guard occurred as the Houston Astros, a team picked to finish low in its division, rose to the top. The San Francisco Giants, a team which had finished in the basement in 1985, and the rising star of the Cincinnati Reds, were Houston's challengers, but the Astros would hold them off under Hal Lanier, in his first season as a major league manager.

So the playoffs began with the Astros confronting the Mets. Both were observing their twenty-fifth year (having been expansion teams of 1962) but the resemblence seemed to end there – the Mets, on paper at least, looking far the stronger. Not only did they boast those 108 wins, they had outscored their opponents by 181 runs, while the Astros had outscored theirs by only 71. Houston did have some solid pitching, not only from all-time great, Nolan Ryan, but from the underrated Mike Scott, plus Bob Knepper, Jim Deshaies and relievers Dave Smith and Charlie Kerfeld. For hitting, the Astros could count on Kevin Bass, Davey Lopes, Glen Davis and Jose Cruz. But the Mets could more than match these, with strong pitching from Dwight Gooden, Ron Darling, Sid Fernandez and Bob Ojeda, and with Roger McDowell and Jesse Orosco standing by for relief. And for hitting, the Mets could count on Keith Hernandez, Darryl Strawberry, Gary Carter, Lenny Dykstra and Ray Knight. The consensus was that, as good as the Astros were, the Mets were better.

But the playoffs were no pushover. The Astros took the first game, in fact, 1-0, thanks to Mike Scott's masterful pitching, but the Mets quickly came back to take the second, 5-1. The Series moved to Shea Stadium, where the Mets won again, thanks to Lenny Dykstra's ninth-inning homer. But in the fourth game, Mike Scott led the Astros to another win, 3-1. In the fifth and sixth games, the Mets were able to summon up all their superior reserves, but they had to work for their wins – 12 innings in the fifth, while the sixth was an exciting 16-inning epic that the Mets won 7-6, to take the pennant.

The Mets went into the World Series against the Red Sox as the favorite (except throughout New England) and everyone was unsettled when the Boston team took the first two games in Shea Stadium. Up in Fenway Park, however, the Mets also ran counter to the odds and took the next two. The teams went back to Shea with the Red Sox having won three of the five games. And when in the sixth game the Red Sox came into the ninth inning with a 2-0 lead, it looked like the Mighty Mets were about to concede the championship to the Amazin' Red Sox. But a combination of poor pitching and bad fielding on the part of Boston, plus scratch hitting and baserunning by the Mets, allowed the Mets to tie the game in the bottom of the ninth inning. The Red Sox got two more runs in the top of the tenth, but the Mets came back in the bottom to score three themselves and take the game. Play resumed after a day's postponement due to rain, which allowed Boston to start Bruce Hurst, who had already beaten the Mets in two games. The Mets soon found themselves behind, 3-0, but they caught up, then went ahead on Ray Knight's homer, and added four more runs to win the game 8-5, and the Series. So the Mets came through, and their championship was all the sweeter for having had to come from behind.

Individual National Leaguers could also look back on the 1986 season with considerable satisfaction. Bob Horner of the Atlanta Braves, for one, became only the eleventh player in modern major-league baseball to hit four homers in one game (on 6 July). Steve Carlton, although he was dropped by the Phillies early in the season, signed on with the San Francisco Giants but then retired near the end of the season – his 4,040 strikeouts putting him in second place for career strikeouts (behind Nolan Ryan's 4,277 through 1986), while 323 victories put him squarely in tenth place among all of modern baseball's pitchers. One of the biggest news items of the season was the appointment of the recently retired president of Yale University, A Bartlett Giamatti, as new president of the National League – a sign, it might be said, of the special role that baseball has come to play in American society.

Above: The 1986 National League Cy Young Award winner Mike Scott.

The National League began its 1987 season under not one cloud but three. To begin with, there was the charge of collusion on the part of all major-league club owners. For at least the last three years, it was alleged, they had in one way or another been conspiring to stop bidding for free agents in an effort to force players to settle for smaller salaries. The charge was placed in arbitration. On 21 September 1987 it was ruled that the owners had been engaged in some sort of collusion. But aside from the question of what would now be done to right this wrong, it was hard to prove if this had had any identifiable impact on team standings. Some of the free agents simply returned to their former teams – Tim Raines, for instance – but others were so angry that their owners hadn't bid for them that they jumped to other teams for considerably lower salaries (Ray Knight to the Orioles, for instance, and Andre Dawson to the Cubs). Bob Horner of the Braves was so angry that he went all the way to Japan, where he became something of a cult figure.

Then there was the charge of racism that came about primarily through the actions of a National League executive. Al Campanis of the Los Angeles Dodgers' front office went on national TV in April as part of the observation of the 40th anniversary of Jackie Robinson's having joined the Dodgers – but Campanis ended up making some incredible remarks about blacks lacking the proper capacity to hold management or administrative positions. Before the dust settled Campanis was fired by the Dodgers, but ironically he had succeeded in calling attention to a glaring flaw in the structure of organized baseball: Blacks (and Hispanics) were not being allowed to hold any significant posts except as players. The resolution of this deep-seated problem lies many years in the future but at least it is now out in the open.

The third problem was one that had been around for a while and also was not going to go away soon: drugs. It was thrown into the spotlight at the very start of the season by the discovery that Dwight Gooden, the Mets' young superstar pitcher, had come up positive in a test for cocaine. Gooden went into a drug clinic immediately, but the message was clear: A lot of ballplayers were probably still using drugs and the problem – like those of money and racism – was not going to be solved in one season.

Even with the loss of Gooden for the first weeks, the Mets were generally conceded to have a chance of taking at least the pennant after their 1986 championship. But the Mets' pitchers and hitters never quite put it all together. Hitting home runs was not the problem: The Mets' Howard Johnson was hitting so many that he was one of several players accused of using 'corked' (that is, doctored) bats, but in fact it was never proven. In any case, the Mets never even dominated their own division. The St Louis Cardinals, instead, took over first place and gradually made it clear they were going all the way. The Cardinals lacked the power hitters and the super pitchers of other teams, but they played a scrappy base-running game, and by the time the Mets came up against the Cardinals on the last weekend of the season the Cardinals had clinched the division title. The Montreal Expos, meanwhile, surprised many by also staying up there with the Mets until the end.

In the Western Division the Cincinnati Reds were singled out by many as the team to watch. Sure

Left: Formerly of the World Champion New York Mets, Ray Knight joined the Baltimore Orioles for the 1987 season.

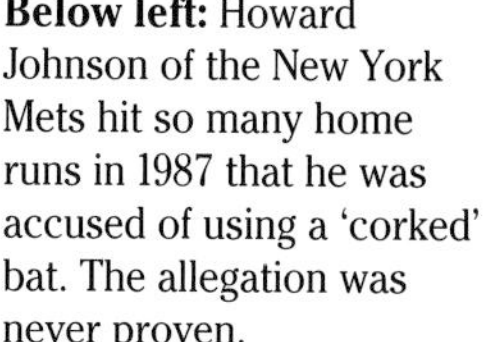

Below left: Howard Johnson of the New York Mets hit so many home runs in 1987 that he was accused of using a 'corked' bat. The allegation was never proven.

Above: Tim Raines became a free agent in 1987, but wound up rejoining his old team, the Montreal Expos.

Mets

enough, the Reds raced out of the starting gate with an 18-8 record. Pete Rose, their manager, chose not to activate himself at the outset, stating that he'd wait to see what the team's needs were later in the season. In the end, he never did activate himself, so for now Rose remains unofficially retired (and his 4256 hits remain the all-time record). Perhaps Rose should have taken a more active role, because something happened to the Reds: on 7 August they were leading the San Francisco Giants by five games; over the next 19 days the Reds went 5-15, while the Giants went 15-5, and on 26 August their situations were reversed. The Reds never could recover, and the Giants ended up with the Western Division title.

Going into the playoffs the Giants were considered the underdogs. True, they had several strong players – Will Clark, Candy Maldonado, Jeffrey Leonard, Kevin Mitchell, Jose Uribe, along with solid pitchers like Mike Krukow, Rick Reuschel and Dave Dravecky. But many felt they were no match for the more experienced Cardinals – Ozzie Smith, Willie McGee, Vince Coleman, Tony Pena and pitchers such as John Tudor, Danny Cox and Todd Worrell. But the Giants went out in front and had a 3-2 game advantage. It took all the talents the Cardinals could muster to even the series in the sixth game with a 1-0 score and then go on to take the seventh game and the pennant.

In the World Series the Cardinals faced the Minnesota Twins, and although the Cardinals were certainly the more experienced team, they were going to be without the injured Jack Clark, one of their heaviest hitters, while another, Terry Pendleton, would not be able to play at full strength. When the Twins took the first two games it looked like the Cardinals' brand of scrappy hitting and running might not be a match for the big bats of the Twins. Then the Cardinals came back and took the next three games in St Louis. But the Twins were able to do what no other team had ever done in the 31 years that the Series had gone to seven games – win all their home games. Even though many observers felt the Metrodome gave the Twins a special advantage (with its distracting lighting, high-decibel acoustics and general artificiality), all agreed that the Cardinals had fought to the finish, even if they were beaten for the World Championship.

As for individual records during the National League's 1987 season, who should end up with the most home runs – 49 – but Andre Dawson, the same Dawson who had left the Expos in disgust to play with the Cubs for a reduced salary. Dawson also had the most RBIs (137) for the majors. Tony Gwynne of the Padres had the best batting average, .369, for both leagues, and Vince Coleman's 107 stolen bases far and away led both leagues. As it happened, no National League pitcher won 20 games, but veteran Nolan Ryan ended up with the best earned run average (2.76) and most strikeouts (270). The league's MVP was Andre Dawson, while Steve Bedrosian won the Cy Young award. One of the more remarkable performances of the season was that of San Diego's rookie catcher, Benito Santiago, who hit safely in 34 games.

And so the National League continued as it had since its year of organization, 1876, providing thrills and surprises – yes, and occasional disappointments. True, there were some major problems threatening major league baseball: the cases of drug and alcohol abuse; the skyrocketing salaries that were leading some club owners to claim they were on the verge of bankruptcy; increasingly more open conflicts between players and owners. But major league baseball had a new commissioner, Peter Ueberroth, who had

Above: Speedy Ozzie Smith was one of the stars of the 1987 St Louis Cardinals, winners of the National League pennant.
Right: Pete Rose, manager of the Cincinnati Reds, chose not to activate himself in 1987 and was sorely missed by his team. After a strong start, the Reds ended up seeing the San Francisco Giants take the Western Division title.

Opposite: Mets' ace pitcher Dwight Gooden tested positive for cocaine early in the 1987 season and had to go into a drug rehabilitation clinic for a month.

Above: Nolan Ryan of the Houston Astros had the best ERA (2.76) and most strikeouts (270) of any pitcher in the National League in 1987.
Right: World Series action: the St Louis Cardinals versus the Minnesota Twins. The Twins took the Series, four games to three.
Bottom: Another stolen base for Vince Coleman of the St Louis Cardinals. His 1987 total of 107 stolen bases was the best by far in both leagues.

taken over on 1 October 1984, after his dazzling success as president of the Los Angeles Olympic Organizing Committee, and Ueberroth gave every indication of providing strong yet fair leadership.

Before the 1988 National League season began most experts predicted that the New York Mets would walk away with the National League pennant and face the Yankees in a Subway Series. A month later the Pirates and the Dodgers led their respective divisions, but by the All-Star break the Mets had indeed captured first place in the East and looked like they intended to keep it. Sparked by a great season from hurler Orel Hershiser, in the National League West the Dodgers finished on top of a division they had dominated from the get-go.

Considerable controversy was generated prior to the season when major league baseball announced its intention to strictly enforce the balk rule. Balk calls due to closer scrutiny of the pitchers' 'set' position

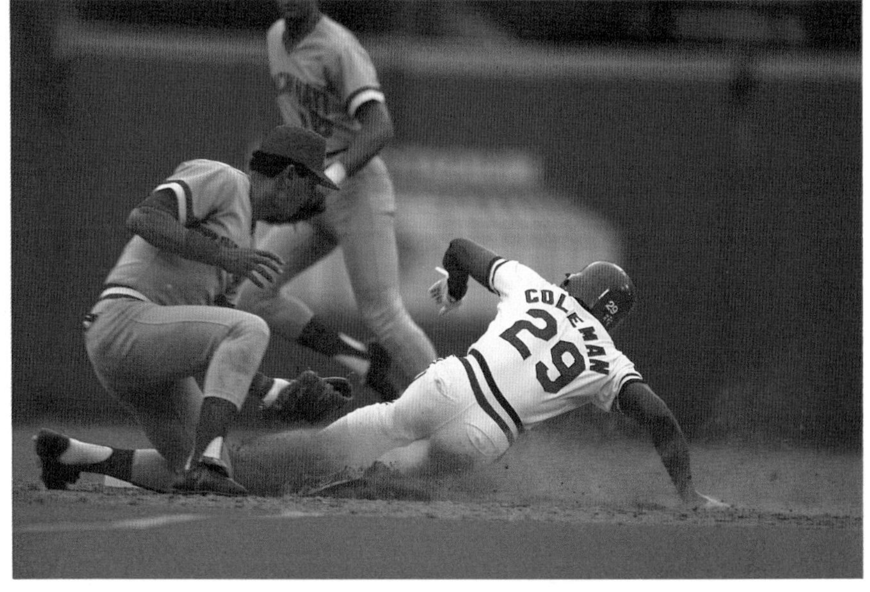

rose 160 percent during the season, quickly wiping out the combined-league season record of 356. But the dire effects on the outcomes of games due to strict enforcement of the balk rule that some had predicted never materialized, and the issue gradually faded from the sports pages.

Meanwhile home runs dropped 29 percent from 1987's record-setting pace. Team batting averages and ERAs also declined, leading some to wonder if the ball had been made less lively. Despite some convincing statistical evidence to the contrary, the consensus was that improved pitching accounted for the drops. Other rule changes empowered umpires to choose between warning and expulsion when a pitcher threw intentionally at a batter; and catchers were required to wear helmets when fielding their positions.

Behind stingy pitching and booming bats – Darryl Strawberry led the league with 39 home runs – the Mets clinched the Eastern Division title, only to be stopped by the Dodgers in a seven-game championship series. The Dodgers' Orel Hershiser, who had smoked through the regular season with 23 wins, 8 shutouts and a record 59 scoreless innings, took two games from the Mets, including a five-hit shutout, with some able assistance from slugging MVP teammate Kirk Gibson. In addition to receiving the Cy Young Award, Hershiser was voted both league champion-

Right: Dodger ace Orel Hershiser had a banner year in 1988. The Cy Young Award winner also garnered NLCS and World Series MVP honors.

ship MVP and World Series MVP for his part in a classic Dodger performance that saw Tommy Lasorda's bums drop the highly favored Oakland Athletics in five games.

In July arbitrator George Nicolau found the owners guilty in the second collusion case the players brought against them for their conspiracy not to sign free agents (in 1986-87). A. Bartlett Giamatti, who had resigned the presidency of Yale to become president of the National League at the end of the 1986 season, was chosen to succeed Peter Ueberroth as commissioner of baseball. And in 1988 Chicago's Wrigley Field, the last holdout in the majors, finally installed lights and hosted its first night game.

The 1989 season saw some major upheavals in the National League. At the beginning of spring training, former Cincinnati superstar, player-manager, and current manager Pete Rose was summoned to the commissioner's office to answer allegations of gambling. Despite Rose's repeated denials and challenges to Commissioner Giamatti's right to judge his case, the special counsel appointed by Giamatti concluded that Rose had indeed bet on baseball and on the Reds, and Giamatti suspended Rose from involvement with organized baseball for life.

Eight days later, on 1 September, Giamatti, age 51, who had served less than five months as commissioner, died of a heart attack. He was succeeded by his hand-picked Deputy Commissioner Fay Vincent. Bill White, a former Golden Glove National League player and Yankee broadcaster, became the first black league president and the highest ranking black sports official in American history when he filled the National League presidency that Giamatti had vacated when he ascended to the commissionership on 1 April. In May, superstar Mike Schmidt hung up his glove with a tearful good-bye.

The pundits picked the Mets to top the National League East, but to the pleased surprise of many, the Chicago Cubs soon took over first place and hung onto it. Out West, San Francisco fended off threats from the Padres and the Astros to take the Western

Above left: Baseball Commissioner A. Bartlett Giamatti died suddenly and unexpectedly in September 1989, after serving less than five months in office.
Above: Fay Vincent succeeded Giamatti as baseball commissioner in 1989.

Division. Despite a strong pitching staff, the Cubs were unable to silence the bats of Giants Kevin Mitchell, Will Clark and Matt Williams, and the Giants took the pennant from the Cubs in five games. League MVP Mitchell logged 47 home runs, 125 RBIs, and a .635 slugging average; playoff MVP Clark batted a blistering .333 with 196 hits, 104 runs, and 111 RBIs.

San Francisco met Oakland in a 'BART' (Bay Area Rapid Transit) Subway Series dedicated to – and nicknamed after – the recently deceased 'Bart' Giamatti. In the first two games the Giants fell to the pitching of Dave Stewart and Mike Moore. Then on 17 October, at Candlestick Park, just 26 minutes before the start of the third game, the Bay Area was hit by a major earthquake that killed 63. Observed Giant centerfielder Brett Butler, 'At the start I realized what a privilege it was to be in the Series. Now, I realize what a privilege it is to be alive.' Ten days later the Series resumed. Oakland's pitchers of the first two games repeated their magic, and the Giants fell in four.

After a 32-day lockout by the owners during spring training, the 1990 National League season got underway with Lou Piniella at the helm of a Cincinnati team still smarting from the loss of Pete Rose. Once again the Mets were heavily favored for divisional and pennant honors, but the Pittsburgh Pirates, behind the slugging of Barry Bonds and Bobby Bonilla, who combined for 65 home runs and 235 RBIs, and the pitching of a no-name bullpen headed by Doug Drabek and Zane Smith, sewed up the division in a three-game sweep of the Mets in September. Drabek, with 22 regular season wins, took the Cy Young Award. MVP Bonds batted .301, slugged .565 with 33 homers and 114 RBIs, and scored 104 runs. At 40 round-trippers, Cub Ryne Sandberg became the first second baseman to lead the league in homers since Rogers Hornsby.

Lou Piniella's reinvigorated Reds, with his Nasty Boys leading the bullpen, topped the Western Division

Opposite top: The lights are switched on for the first night game at Chicago's Wrigley Field on 8 August 1988.

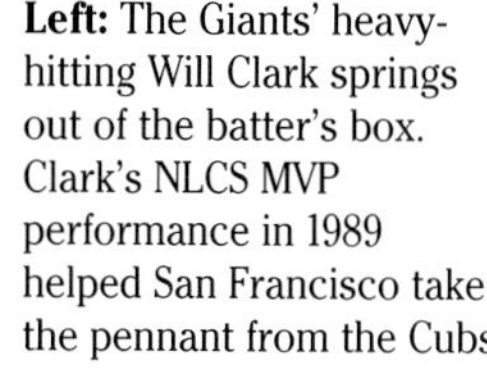

Left: The Giants' heavy-hitting Will Clark springs out of the batter's box. Clark's NLCS MVP performance in 1989 helped San Francisco take the pennant from the Cubs.

Right: The scene at Candlestick Park moments after an earthquake interrupted the start of the 1989 World Series' game there. The Bayside World Series between the Oakland Athletics and the San Francisco Giants was resumed after an 11-day hiatus.

Below: Pittsburgh's Doug Drabek, winner of the 1990 Cy Young Award, also helped his Pirates win their division in 1991.

five games ahead of the Dodgers, then fulfilled the promise they had been unable to realize during the preceding years by stopping the Cubs in the playoff in six games. In a decisive Series upset, Cincinnati swept the defending Athletics. The Reds' Billy Hatcher set an all-time Series batting average record of .750, while Cincinnati's batters averaged .317 overall and slugged .472 for the four games. Series MVP Jose Rijo won two of the games by following the Reds' strategy of pitching fastballs inside, which seemed to unnerve Oakland's sluggers.

As the National League entered the last decade of the 20th century, the age-old struggle between players and owners closed another chapter when the players' third collusion grievance against the owners for conspiring against free-agency was decided in their favor. The owners agreed to pay the Players Association a total settlement of $280 million. The contract negotiations that precipitated the spring lockout ended with a new Basic Agreement that raised a player's minimum salary from $68,000 to $100,000, and prescribed triple damages for any future owner collusion concerning free agents. Pete Rose was sentenced to five months in federal prison and fined $50,000 for tax evasion.

The 1991 season got underway with a pre-season umpire strike that ended hours before the first game. The real news, however, was in the National League West, acknowledged the toughest division in the majors, where the upstart Atlanta Braves snatched the division championship from the Dodgers on the second-to-last day of the season. While their fans waved thousands of foam-rubber tomahawks in the 'tomahawk chop' and sang an eerie 'war chant,' the Miracle Braves, who lagged nine and a half games behind the Dodgers at the All-Star break, put together an eight-game end-of-season winning streak that was all the more remarkable because they had finished last in the previous three seasons. Atlanta's dramatic turnaround was sparked by sluggers Ron Gant and

MVP Terry Pendleton, who totaled 54 home runs between them; by 20-game winner Tom Glavine; and by young pitching phenomenon Steve Avery and hurlers Charlie Leibrandt and John Smoltz. David Cone of the Mets, in the last regular game of the year, matched the league record of 19 strikeouts and tied the season's major league strikeout record of 241 in his tenth career shutout.

Once again the drug issue came to the fore when the Braves' star outfielder, Otis Nixon, batting .297 and leading the league with 72 steals, tested positive for cocaine and was suspended for 60 days late in the season. But his absence didn't stop the Braves from snatching the pennant from the Pittsburgh Pirates in a seven-game playoff that featured two brilliant shutouts by series MVP Avery, one by teammate Smoltz, and a new NLCS record of seven steals by Ron Gant. Pittsburgh's second pennant disappointment in as many years paved the way for the Braves to meet the

Minnesota Twins in the World Series – Atlanta's first ever Series appearance. The Twins and the Braves shared honors as the first teams to go from last to first in the 22 years of division play.

In one of the most thrilling World Series in memory, the Braves battled the favored Twins through seven games. Five games were decided by one run, four in the last at-bat, four in the last inning, and three reached extra innings. Atlanta won all three home games, Minnesota all four of theirs. In the seventh game, the Twins scored the game's only run in the bottom of the tenth. It was baseball at its best, a Series that not only went the limit, but went into legend. Atlanta's Lonnie Smith hit home runs in three consecutive games, and teammate Mark Lemke turned in the kind of surprising virtuoso performance that postseason play is known for. Off the field, the old Negro Leagues were honored in a special ceremony in Cooperstown, and National League President Bill White spoke out forcefully when the new Colorado Rockies franchise filled six upper-level executive positions without even interviewing a black or Latino candidate despite promises to do so.

But regardless of the changes and tensions in the National League and in the country for which ball playing has long been the national pastime and obsession, the Senior Circuit continued to provide a unique continuity of joy and promise of future glory. To balance every earthquake and fallen idol, a new achievement and rising star was born; for every Pete Rose and Otis Nixon, a Ron Gant and Steve Avery emerged to stand the test of time and perhaps join the hallowed ranks of Christy Mathewson, Honus Wagner, Stan Musial, Jackie Robinson, Willie Mays, Roberto Clemente, Orel Hershiser, and Hank Aaron. This much is certain: as long as there is a United States there will be baseball, and as long as there is baseball, the National League will continue to set the pace.

Above left: In 1991 the Braves' Ron Gant set a new NLCS record for steals, with seven, as Atlanta downed Pittsburgh in seven games.
Above: Atlanta's David Justice connects for a home run against the Twins' Scott Erickson in game three of the 1991 World Series.

Part Two

THE AMERICAN LEAGUE

CHAPTER ONE

The Beginnings of the American League

"Never get Mr. Cobb angry."

– Connie Mack's advice to his team

While the history of baseball reaches well back into the nineteenth century, and the National League takes the honors as the older of the two leagues, professional baseball as we know it today began with the formation of the American League in 1901. It was then that two competing leagues were solidly in place for the first time, and that grand American institution, the World Series, became as much the mark of autumn as the turning of the leaves.

There had been a number of attempts in the nineteenth century to create a second baseball league, but the National League succeeded in fighting them off and maintaining its monopoly over what was rapidly becoming the country's most popular sport. It was the drive and the dreams of two men, player-turned-sportswriter Byron Banford Johnson and first baseman-manager Charles Albert Comiskey, that brought the American League into existence. They were the ones who built the new league into a powerhouse that not only broke the National League's grip on baseball but also dominated the game for decades to come.

'Ban' Johnson, a native of Norwalk, Ohio, had played ball at Marietta and Oberlin Colleges. An injury kept him from making a career as a player, so instead he became a sportswriter for the Cincinnati *Commercial-Gazette.* Comiskey came from Chicago. Like Johnson, he played ball in college – at St Mary's in Kansas, where he was captain of the freshman baseball team. Before long, he was playing professionally for St Louis, but when owner Chris van der Ahe sold off the best of the roster, Comiskey moved to the Cincinnati Reds team. There he became Ban Johnson's drinking and cardplaying partner, and in 1892 the two began to put together the dream of a second major league.

By the time Comiskey and Johnson joined forces, success and monopoly had already begun to soften the powerful National League. Grown to an unwieldy 12 teams, it had antagonized its players with rough treatment in the Brotherhood strike of 1890. While it had weathered a series of gambling scandals and the threat of competition from such attempts at second leagues as the American Association, the Union Association and the Players League, it had not done much to clean up the game itself.

In those days baseball had a reputation as a rough-and-ready sport. Players baited the umpires as well as opposing players, and foul language was commonplace. Fistfights often broke out, and intentional spiking was not unheard of. It was not exactly an environment thought to be fit for ladies of the Victorian era. Johnson and Comiskey agreed on the need to end the rowdiness, to discourage the sale of liquor in ball parks, to stop the use of profanity, to instill respect for umpires and to encourage women's attendance. Part of their dream was a new image for the game.

Below: Byron Bancroft Johnson, the founder of the American League, poses with Albert Reach. As president of the Western League, Ban Johnson had worked to clean up the reputation of America's pastime, and he used the same determination in his fight for a second major league.

Right (inset): 'The Old Roman' Charles Comiskey, former player and manager, worked with Ban Johnson to establish the American League, becoming owner of the Chicago franchise and building Comiskey Park.

While Johnson and Comiskey may have been fast friends in the early days, Ban had developed a strong dislike for Comiskey's boss, clothing manufacturer John Brush, the owner of the Cincinnati Reds. Ban raked Brush over the coals regularly in his columns, accusing him of stinginess, among other things. In a stroke of inspiration, Comiskey persuaded team owners in the new, minor Western League, who were eager for reform, to tap his drinking buddy Ban as their new leader. Comiskey may even have enlisted Brush's help by suggesting that getting Ban out of Cincinnati would make life a lot more pleasant for the Reds' owner. In any event, Johnson came back from the Western League's convention in 1894 as the league's new President.

Comiskey himself left Cincinnati for Sioux City, Iowa, at the end of the 1894 season, and then moved that club to St Paul. Johnston started work immediately to upgrade the Western League, which was made up of Indianapolis, Kansas City, Milwaukee, Minneapolis, Toledo, Grand Rapids, Detroit and Sioux City. Within two years, he had built its reputation as the strongest of the minor leagues. Although he was already prediciting that the Western League would make it on its own, Johnson recognized that he would have to expand eastward if he were to lose the label of a regional organization. He wanted a Chicago base for his friend Comiskey, but the Chicago National League team's manager Jim Hart was dead set against competition, so Ban bided his time.

Although he might later come to be called one of the greatest organizers and executives in the history of the game, Ban Johnson was hardly the first or only one to see that the time was ripe to get a second major league going. While Johnson maneuvered to make his league strong enough to qualify as a major league, attempts were afoot to revive the old American Association, and the still monopolistic National League initially worried more about that effort. Started in 1882 as a counter to the 'rich man's league,' the American Association had lasted only until 1890, when competition with the Players League during the Brotherhood War did it in. Then in 1899 a group of those associated with the defunct American Association, including Chris van de Ahe and Taylor Spink, met in Chicago. Intent on resurrecting the American Association, they elected former Chicago White Stockings (now the Cubs) Manager Cap Anson as their president and set about the business of trying to find financial backing, players and ball parks. Johnson was offered the chance to join forces, but turned it down, opting to stay on his own.

Above: As president of the American League until 1927, Ban Johnson ruled both capably and shrewdly, contributing to baseball's growing popularity during that time.

Struggling to keep its monopoly going, the National League pared itself down to eight clubs in 1900. The teams in Louisville, Cleveland, Washington and Baltimore were sold to the league and their franchises were allowed to be abandoned. Ban struck while the iron was hot. In October of 1899, the Western League officially had changed its name to the American League in order to develop a more national image. With financial backing from coal magnate Charles Somers, Johnson now moved his Grand Rapids franchise to Cleveland. The next step, a crucial one, was Chicago.

The American Association's Cap Anson had already come up empty-handed there, but Ban's steamroller tactics prevailed. He promised Chicago National League's general manager Jim Hart that he would abide by the National Agreement, which tied players to their current club through options, and agreed to pay for improvements already made by the National League's Cleveland club before its demise. He was also said to have given Hart options on some of the new American League's players. In return, Hart allowed Johnson to sct up a ball club on Chicago's South Side, figuring that the smell of the stockyards would keep fans from patronizing it. In 1900 Chicago native Comiskey gladly packed up his team in St Paul and moved back to the Windy City.

Left: Clark Calvin 'The Old Fox' Griffith, when he was a pitcher for the Chicago National League team. Elected to the Hall of Fame in 1946, Clark Griffith pitched for both leagues and several teams from 1891 to 1914, and managed from 1901 to 1920. As a pitcher he had a winning percentage of .649 and a 3.31 ERA.

Although Hart had stipulated in the agreement that the American League team was not to identify itself as a Chicago club, the canny Comiskey named his team the White Sox – clearly evoking the earlier Chicago National League team, the White Stockings. The White Sox soon established themselves with the Chicago fans and not too many years later – 1910, to be exact – when the team acquired a magnificent new playing field, Comiskey Park, replete with steel and concrete grandstands faced with brick, it could boast probably the grandest baseball stadium of its day.

In the meantime, the first year of the new century, 1900, saw players in the National League less than happy and ready to organize. Because of this, they were to help move Ban that much closer to establishing his dream of a major league. In June, the National League players met in New York and formed the Protective Association of Professional Baseball players. They presented a list of demands to the National League management and got a cold shoulder. Johnson, however, was quick to see an opportunity presenting itself, and agreed to everything the players asked. Then when the National Agreement expired, Ban purposely did not renew. The explanation he gave National League President Nick Young was that attempts to revive the old American Association were causing a threat to organized baseball and that he had already made clear his intention to establish clubs in the East. Under such circumstances, it was no longer appropriate to honor draft protection arrangements.

Johnson even agreed to confer with representatives from the National League over his moves into eastern territories, but the National League, instead of supporting Ban, chose to ignore the offer of compromise. The battle lines were drawn. The Nationals then let it be known that they would look favorably on American Association efforts to establish eastern clubs, and awarded Kansas City and Minneapolis to a new minor Western League in an attempt to create direct competition with American League teams.

Right: Al Reach, who played both infield and outfield for the original Philadelphia Athletics, became the Philadelphia National League club president, but viewed the establishment of a second major league in a positive light.
Below: Pitcher Rube Waddell's glove, photographed in 1902. Hall of Famer George Edward Waddell began his pitching career in 1897 and played his finest years for the Philadelphia Athletics (1902-1907), ending his fabulous career in 1910. His 2.16 ERA ranks sixth in the all-time records, and he led the American League in strikeouts for six consecutive seasons. A colorful personality with a passion for fishing, drinking and chasing firetrucks, this awe-inspiring lefthander died of tuberculosis at the age of 37.

A key figure in the jockeying for power between the National and American Leagues was Albert J Reach, one-time player and business partner to influential National League owner and sporting goods manufacturer Albert G Spalding. Reach was President of the Philadelphia National League club, but he was also sympathetic to establishment of a successful second major league, viewing it as something that would benefit the game as a whole. In the battle for an American League Chicago club, it was Reach who acted as mediator. He didn't resist when Johnson moved onto his turf in Philadelphia, and in fact was to

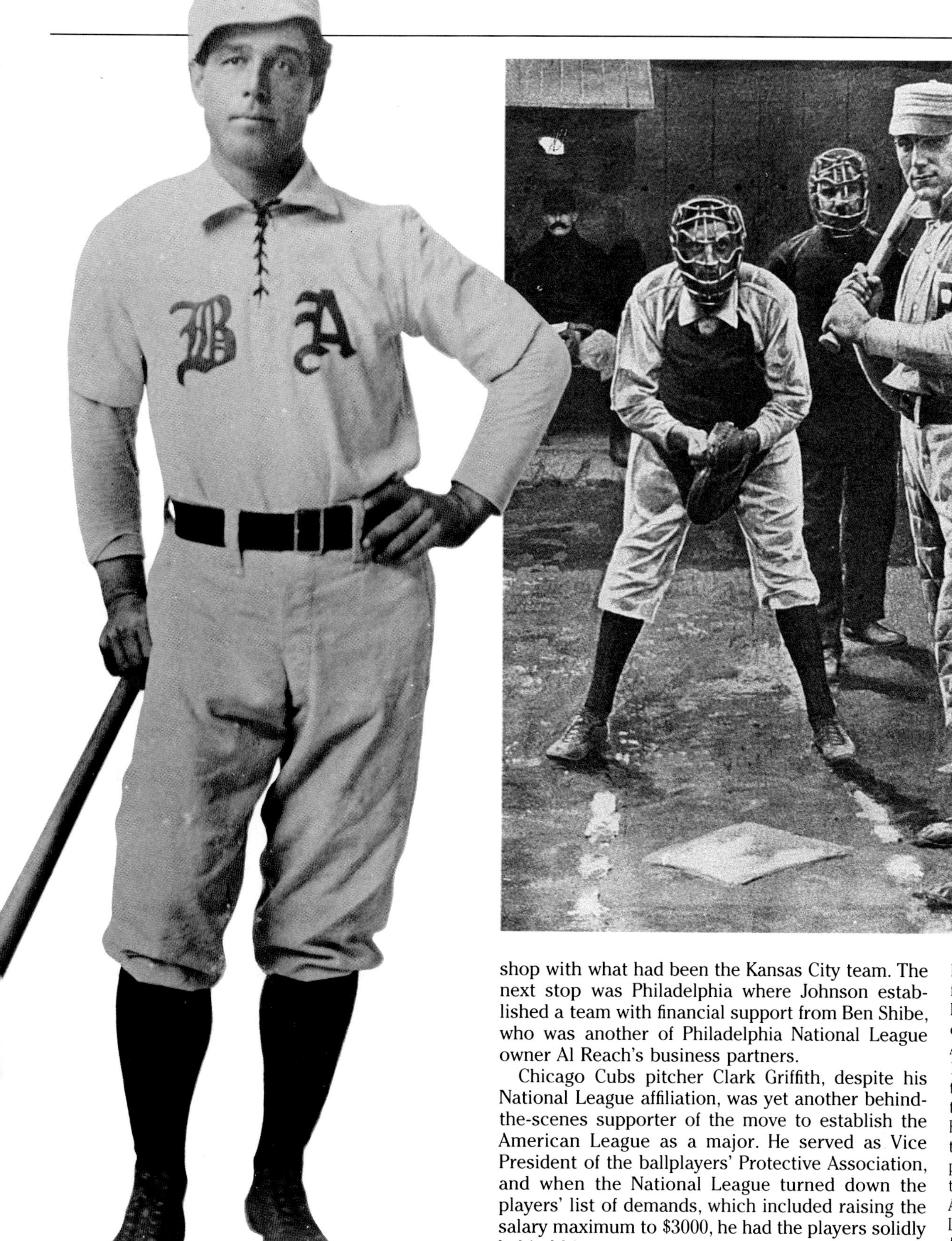

provide the official baseball for the American League, as his partner Spalding had done for the National League. Johnson's response to the National League's assignment of the Kansas City and Minneapolis franchises to minor league clubs was to pull his teams out of those towns and head East.

He moved into Baltimore and Washington first. Feisty John G McGraw, who had been with the National League in Baltimore and then cast his lot with the attempt to revive the American Association, was hired to head the new American League's Baltimore team. In Washington, Jimmy Manning set up shop with what had been the Kansas City team. The next stop was Philadelphia where Johnson established a team with financial support from Ben Shibe, who was another of Philadelphia National League owner Al Reach's business partners.

Chicago Cubs pitcher Clark Griffith, despite his National League affiliation, was yet another behind-the-scenes supporter of the move to establish the American League as a major. He served as Vice President of the ballplayers' Protective Association, and when the National League turned down the players' list of demands, which included raising the salary maximum to $3000, he had the players solidly behind him.

Some 30 National League players joined American League teams before the start of the 1901 season. They deserted National League teams in droves, lured by higher salaries and the promise of better treatment. In addition to John McGraw came pitchers Cy Young and Joe McGinnity, and Napoleon Lajoie and Jimmy Collins. By the time the dust settled, 111 of the American League's 182 players came from their arch-rivals. The only National League club that remained intact in the face of American League raids was Pittsburgh. Johnson had steered clear of stealing players from Barney Dreyfuss's team because he was hoping to persuade him to join the American League.

The historic decision by American League owners to give their clubs major league status came at a

Left: Jimmy Collins, one of four players from Boston's National League team to cross over to Boston's American League team in 1901, played and managed the team to greatness, winning the first World Series in 1903. Holding the fourth-place all-time record for single-season put-outs, Collins was elected to the Hall of Fame in 1945. **Above:** Hall of Famer Nap Lajoie in a Philadelphia Athletics uniform, up at bat in the Polo Grounds. Second baseman Lajoie, who crossed over to the American League in 1901, played for the A's until the middle of 1902, then played for Cleveland from 1903 to 1914. He ended his career back with the A's in 1916, with a .339 batting average and four batting titles under his belt.

Rube Waddell warms up before a game.

meeting in Chicago in January of 1901. The first game took place on 24 April 1901, at Comiskey Park in Chicago between the White Sox and the Cleveland Bronchos (subsequently known as the Blues, Naps, Molly McGuires and Indians). The Sox beat Cleveland 8 to 2. While the birthing had been accomplished, the battles between the new major league and the Nationals were far from over.

Still building up the strength of his new major league, Ban was ready to move into Boston next. He preempted an attempt on the part of the not-yet-dead American Association to field a team there by sending Connie Mack north to find property, using Somer's money, after Mack had organized the Philadelphia club, and moving the league's Buffalo team there. Now the American League lineup was almost complete: in the West were Cleveland, Chicago, Milwaukee and Detroit; in the East were Baltimore, Washington, Philadelphia and Boston. With two changes over the next two years, the league would crystallize into the form it was to keep for the next 50 years.

With clubs in three National League cities, Chicago, Philadelphia and Boston, the American League now posed a serious threat to the Nationals. The National League decided to take legal action in an attempt to stop the Johnson juggernaut. Lawyers for the owners of the Philadelphia Phillies argued that celebrated former Phillies second baseman Napoleon Lajoie, who had signed with the Athletics, should not be allowed to play ball for that American League Philadelphia team. The legality of the reserve option was upheld by Pennsylvania's Supreme Court, which ordered Lajoie back to the Phillies. Connie Mack's answer was to sell Nap Lajoie and three other ex-Phillies players to Cleveland, where they were outside the Pennsylvania court's jurisdiction. When Cleveland played Philadelphia, Nap and the other ex-Phillies stayed home.

Comiskey's White Sox won the pennant that year, behind a 24-7 season by right-hander/manager Clark Griffith, who had crossed over from the Cubs. The stench of the stockyards was obviously not strong enough to keep the Sox from outdrawing their arch-rivals that year. Nap was the top hitter for the season. The Rhode Island-born athlete had been offered almost $6000 by Connie Mack to switch from the Phillies to the Athletics, and he took the Triple Crown with 14 home runs, 125 runs batted in and a .422 batting average.

Another of the all-time greats, Denton True Young, playing for the Boston American League club, was the top pitcher. Nicknamed 'Cy,' an abbreviation for Cyclone in honor of his fastball, he gave the Boston Somersets (known as such until 1905, when they became the Puritans for a brief two years and the Red Sox ever after) a 33-10 record. He pitched five shutouts, had a 1.62 ERA, and walked only 37 batters in 371 innings – a one in ten average. Yet Boston still finished four games behind the Chicago White Sox. At 34, Young already had 285 out of the 511 wins he would take before he retired in 1911.

By 1902, the National League saw that its strategy was falling flat. They decided to scrap the National Agreement themselves, and try to fight fire with fire by raiding American League teams. Their most notable success was in Baltimore, where manager John McGraw was on the ropes with Johnson over umpire baiting. In July of 1902 Ban suspended McGraw indefinitely. McGraw, in cahoots with Johnson's arch-enemy from his sportswriting days, John Brush, got hold of the majority of stock in the Orioles and sold it to New York Giants owner Andrew Freedman. McGraw took four Baltimore players with him to the Giants, for whom he became manager, and sent two others to Cincinnati. McGraw always claimed that he had been released from the American League team in exchange for $7000 in advances to players for which he had never been reimbursed, but charges and countercharges flew back and forth.

Johnson put Wilbert Robinson in charge of his Baltimore teammates and patched together a club with players from other American League teams and the minors. Baltimore finished last that year, but at least the team scraped by. At the end of the season, Johnson got ready to move it to New York. Milwaukee got shifted to St Louis in 1902 because it was the largest midwestern city outside of Chicago which didn't ban Sunday baseball, and the American League lineup was set for half a century.

One measure of the American League's success in 1902 was the fact that it outdrew the Nationals in Boston, Chicago, Philadelphia and St Louis for a total of 2.2 million fans, compared to the Nationals' 1.7 million. Six American League teams showed a profit that year. Connie Mack took the first of his nine pennants when the Philadelphia Athletics, aided by leftie Rube Waddell, topped the St Louis Browns by five games. (Stone-faced Eddie Plank was the other leftie who helped pitch the Philadelphia Athletics to 83 wins to take the 1902 pennant.) What made the American League such a hit? It was, no doubt, Ban Johnson's call for 'clean baseball and more 25-cent seats.'

By winter, the National League, beset by internal as well as external problems, sent up the white flag. The ensuing peace talks, held at the St Nicholas Hotel in Cincinnati in January 1903, were a clear victory for the American League. The Nationals asked for a merger, but settled for recognition of the American League as a major league, respect for reserve clauses by both leagues, permission for the American League to keep most of its pirated players and the green light for an American League team in New York, as long as no attempt was made to move into Pittsburgh. A three-member National Baseball Commission, comprised of the presidents of the two major leagues and a third member chosen by them, was set up to act as arbiter between clubs and between clubs and players. August Hermann, the new owner of the Reds, was tapped, along with Johnson and Harry Pulliam, who had served as Secretary of the Pittsburgh Club before being elected to lead the National League. The Commission stayed in place until the appointment of a Baseball Commissioner in 1920 after the Black Sox scandal.

Despite the National League's peace talk concessions in allowing the American League to place a team in New York in 1903 – the Highlanders – establishment of a team there was hardly a piece of cake. New York was part of the turf for Johnson's nemesis John Brush, and Brush was determined to make life difficult for Ban by pulling strings to see that any site he picked for a ball field in New York had streets run through it or was declared a public park. Whenever Johnson began to close in on a likely spot, Brush got wind of it and got in touch with Andrew Freedman, who put the word out to his Tammany Hall cronies. Finally the Highlanders found a vacant field in upper Manhattan (where Columbia Presbyterian Hospital now stands) and managed to put a fence around it before anyone could interfere. Because of this unorthodox approach, it is alleged, among the team's

Hall of Famer Eddie Plank pitched for the Philadelphia A's from 1901 to 1914, finishing with a career ERA of 2.34 and a .630 winning percentage.

Above: An overflowing crowd of Boston Somersets (later Red Sox) fans cheer their team to victory in the 1903 World Series. This first of the modern World Series championships between the two major leagues was played at Old Huntington Avenue Grounds against the Pittsburgh Pirates. Boston won five games to three.
Right: William Henry 'Big Bill' Dinneen won three out of the four games he pitched for Boston in the 1903 World Series, including two shutouts. Dinneen had four 20-plus game-winning years, ended his 12-year career with a 3.01 ERA and later became a famous umpire.

early nicknames were 'The Porchclimbers' and 'The Burglars.'

The St Nicholas peace pact had left the establishment of a World Series up to the individual clubs, and the 1903 season saw the first World Series between the two majors. In the National League, Barney Dreyfuss's Pittsburgh Pirates took their third pennant in a row and challenged the American League Boston team, managed by third baseman Jimmy Collins. With Cy Young still heading up his pitching staff, Collins felt confident that the American League was the stronger of the two majors, and that Boston could beat Pittsburgh. The series came close to being aborted when the Boston team, under contract to play only up to 30 September, threatened to strike if they didn't get all the Boston gate receipts. Owner Henry J Killilea nipped the rebellion in the bud by offering the players extra money for playing.

Pittsburgh owner Dreyfuss and Boston owner Killilea agreed that their teams should play up to nine games in the World Series. The winner had to take five, with the first three to be played in Boston, four in Pittsburgh, and then two more, if necessary, in Boston. New players, those who signed after 31 August, could not play. Hampered by injuries and other problems, Pittsburgh still managed to take the first game, 7-3. Boston took the next one, but dropped a second on its home turf before moving to Pittsburgh and losing a third. Then Boston broke through for good, winning 11-2 in the fifth game and following that with three more wins – two of them shutouts – to clinch the first World Series. Killilea's stinginess, however, resulted in the Pittsburgh players making more from the Series than the winners in Boston, and he was forced out the next season.

There would be no World Series in 1904, thanks to National League owner John Brush and manager John McGraw, who refused to give their archenemy Ban Johnson the satisfaction of matching the pennant-winning New York Giants against the American League entry. At the time Brush and McGraw made the decision, it looked as if the American League winner was going to be the New York Highlanders, a team Brush particularly despised and derisively called the Invaders. The American League pennant race for 1904 had the Boston Somersets and the New York Highlanders – not to become the Yankees until 1913 – neck and neck for much of the season. Their five-game closing series was the decisive factor, and after an initial win by New York, Boston took the next three, with Cy Young posting a 26-16 pitching record, backed up by Bill Dineen's 23-14 and Jesse Tannehill's 21-11.

Left: Hall of Famer Joseph John 'Little Napoleon' McGraw played baseball for 16 years (1891-1906) – only one and a half years of which were spent in the American League. Primarily a third baseman, McGraw was also a talented but tough-minded manager. After a short stint as the Baltimore Orioles' manager, McGraw became a thorn in Ban Johnson's side, moving back to the National League and refusing as New York Giants manager to participate in the 1904 World Series.

college graduates, a less-than-usual occurrence in those early days of the game. Mathewson's pitching for the Giants flattened the Athletics, 9-0, in the third game of the Series, and they took the next two, 1-0 and 2-0. It was a World Series without home runs. The Giants batted .209 and the Athletics .161. A gong had even been installed next to Broad Street Station in Philadelphia, which was to ring out doubles, triples and home runs. It was rung a total of only five times. The National League was riding high again, but only temporarily.

That year was the debut for an 18-year-old Georgia rookie named Tyrus Raymond Cobb. Playing in his first season as an outfielder for the Detroit Tigers, he batted a modest .240. But in the next 23 years, Ty Cobb almost never batted under .300 and finished with a lifetime average of .367. Not any easy man to get long with, Cobb was thought to carry the psychic wounds caused by his father's death at the hands of Ty's mother. Rumor had it that the senior Cobb, suspecting his wife of infidelity, had announced that he would be gone overnight, but then had tried to sneak into the house under cover of night to confront her and her lover. Mrs Cobb, mistaking him for an intruder, allegedly shot her husband dead. Whatever

Below: Elected to the Hall of Fame in 1953, pitcher Chief Bender was crucial to the success of Connie Mack's Philadelphia A's, with his .621 winning percentage and his 2.45 career ERA.

Although Johnson had protested McGraw and Brush's rejection of a World Series, saying that the 'refusal to play would be a violation of our agreement and a sign of weakness in the National League,' in fact the St Nicholas peace pact did not stipulate that there must be a World Series. Recanting after the Boston team ended up winning the American League pennant, Brush announced he would be willing to meet an American League team in 1905. It was Brush, in fact, who established the rules governing World Series play, rules which are in force to this day. The nine-game series was scrapped for a four-out-of-seven format and mandatory participation. Receipts for the first four games were to go to the players, 10 percent to the National Commission, and the rest to the managements of the two competing clubs.

Brush got his chance to play the American League, since the Giants did win the National League pennant in 1905. Connie Mack's Philadelphia Athletics had taken the American League title, led by pitchers George 'Rube' Waddell with 26 wins, Eddie Plank and Albert 'Chief' Bender, a Chippewa Indian.

The World Series that year was a pitcher's dream, with all five games shutouts. Unlike today's power baseball, the emphasis then was on pitching discipline and place hitting. Christy Mathewson won for the Giants their first game, allowing just four hits. Waddell, ever the prankster, had injured his arm supposedly chasing after a teammate wearing an out-of-season straw hat, and was out of the running for Philadelphia. Chief Bender evened the score for Philadelphia with a second 3-0 game, again allowing four hits. A crowd of nearly 25,000 then filled New York's Polo Grounds to watch the next battle of the pitchers. Both Mathewson and Eddie Plank were

Right: Lefthander Guy Harris 'Doc' White moved to the American League in 1903 and pitched for the Chicago White Sox from 1903 to 1913. Turning in a 1.52 ERA in 1906, he formed part of Comiskey's tough pitching core, who beat their Chicago National League counterparts in the World Series that year, four games to two.

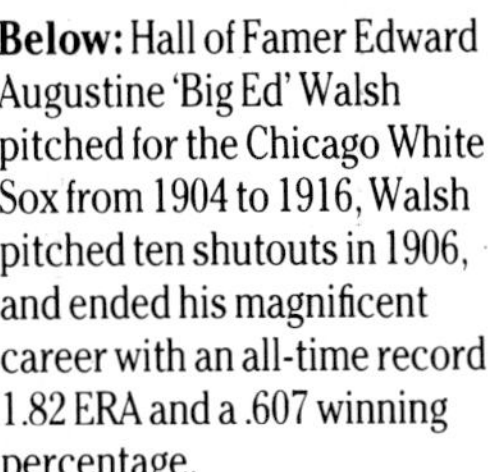

Below: Hall of Famer Edward Augustine 'Big Ed' Walsh pitched for the Chicago White Sox from 1904 to 1916. Walsh pitched ten shutouts in 1906, and ended his magnificent career with an all-time record 1.82 ERA and a .607 winning percentage.

Ty Cobb, a legend in his own time, played outfield for the Detroit Tigers for 22 years during his 24-year career. His .367 batting average, 4191 career hits and 2244 runs speak for themselves.

the reasons, Ty Cobb was a cold and arrogant man who used his spikes like lethal weapons on his way around the bases. His speed, along with his bunting and place hitting talents, made him, however, one of baseball's greatest and most revered players.

In 1906 Chicago's two teams faced each other in the World Series. Comiskey's White Sox, who had been dubbed the hitless wonders with a .228 average – the lowest in the league – stole the American League pennant from New York and Cleveland, and all odds were on the Cubs to take the Series. Instead, the White Sox won four games out of six behind the pitching of spitball specialist Ed Walsh. Much of the credit went to the substitute shortstop George Rohe, who over-reached himself, giving the Sox winning triples in the first and third games, then adding five hits in the last two games and leading the White Sox to victory.

The 1907 season brought three more baseball greats to the American League and helped keep the newer league on top for decades to come. From Humboldt, Kansas, came right-handed pitcher Walter Perry Johnson. The story of Johnson's rise to baseball fame has it that Johnson never served any apprenticeship in the minors. He was supposedly discovered when he was pitching semi-pro baseball in Idaho by a traveling salesman who contacted the Washington Senators. When a Washington scout saw his fastball, he signed Johnson on the spot. Good-natured and easygoing, Johnson couldn't have been more different than Ty Cobb, who once said of him, 'That busher throws the fastest pitch I've ever seen.' Fearful of maiming players with the deadly speed of his pitches, he refused to throw at batters and Cobb exploited Johnson's gentleness by often crowding the plate when he came up to bat. Unfortunately for Johnson, who was known as 'The Big Train,' the Senators spent most of their time at the bottom of the League, and the pitcher who many have called the fastest in the game didn't get a chance to perform in the World Series until 1924.

Another one of the American League greats who began his career in 1907 was second baseman Eddie Collins. Columbia University educated, Collins racked up a .333 lifetime batting average as a left-handed hitter for the Athletics. During the 25 years he played, Collins took the honors as the top fielder nine times, stole 743 bases, and had 3311 hits. He surpassed even Nap Lajoie in infield skills.

The third great American League player to enter the game in 1907 was a 19-year-old Texan, Tristram Speaker, who played center field for Boston. 'Tris' was known for his seemingly shallow outfield positioning which allowed him to make a record-breaking four unassisted double plays during his career. Nicknamed 'Spoke' and 'The Gray Eagle' (because of his prematurely gray hair), Speaker stayed in Boston until 1916, when he was traded to the Cleveland Indians. His lifetime hitting total of 3515 included a record 793 doubles, and his lifetime batting average was .344.

With the rising star of Ty Cobb to guide them, the Detroit Tigers dominated the American League for three seasons, from 1907 to 1909. Hitting .350, Ty took

Above: Tris Speaker hits a line drive up the middle. Hall of Famer Tristram E Speaker turned in nine dazzling years as a Boston outfielder, then played for Cleveland from 1916 to 1926. Speaker's outstanding speed, throwing arm and batting achievements made him one of the best all-around players of all time. His record of 793 doubles still stands today.

Left: Walter Perry 'The Big Train' Johnson pitched for the Washington Senators from 1907 to 1927. A big man with incredible talent and a placid temperament, Johnson won 416 games with 3508 strikeouts and a career ERA of 2.17. He was elected to the Hall of Fame in 1936.

Hall of Famer Addie Joss pitched for Cleveland for nine years (1902-10), achieving a 1.88 career ERA. In 1908, when Cleveland and the White Sox were embroiled in a pennant race, he pitched a perfect game, turning in a league-leading 1.16 ERA that year.

the first three of his nine batting titles, leading in hits and runs batted in from 1907 to 1909. Strong pitching from Wild Bill Donovan, George Mullin, Ed Killian, Ed Willett and Ed Summers helped the Tigers edge out the Philadelphia Athletics by one and a half games for the pennant in 1907. The White Sox were in third place. Chicago's National League team faced the Tigers for the Series that year.

In the first game the two teams fought to a 3-3 standstill when the game was called on account of darkness. Then Detroit became the first team not to win a single World Series game after the Cubs took four straight, 3-1, 5-1, 6-1 and 2-0. Cobb hit an anemic .200, but the Tigers' real Achilles heel was the catching of Charlie 'Boss' Schmidt.

One of the quirks of the 1907 World Series was the fact that Tiger player representative Herman 'Germany' Schaefer asked the Baseball Commission in a pre-series meeting what its policy would be on sharing gate receipts if one of the first four games were to be a tie. The Commission deliberated and ruled that in the event of a tie, the players would have a share in the first five games. Then the first game ended in a 3-3 tie, and many cynics wondered if the game had been rigged. The Commission ordered an investigation, but no skullduggery was uncovered. In the meantime, the Commission rescinded its five-game decision and proclaimed that from then on, players would share in the receipts from only the first four games.

In 1908 the American League pennant race was a cliff-hanger. It was almost a three-way tie among the Tigers, the Indians and the White Sox, with Cleveland just a half game behind at the season's end, and Chicago one and a half games back. Although the Tigers ended up with the pennant, a battle between the Indians and the White Sox early in October became a well-remembered pitching duel. Chicago's pitcher Ed Walsh, with 40 wins under his belt and a 1.42 ERA, was matched against Cleveland's Addie Joss, who would probably have become one of the finest pitchers in baseball if he hadn't died at age 30 from meningitis. Joss's pitching was perfect in that game; he retired 27 batters in order, winning the historic game for Cleveland.

The Tigers faced the Cubs again for the World Series. With Manager Frank Chance, 'The Peerless Leader,' at first base, Johnny Evers on second, and Joe Tinker playing shortstop, the Cubs proved unbeatable. Newspaper columnist Franklin P Adams had put it into verse:

> These are the saddest of possible words –
> Tinker to Evers to Chance.
> Trio of Bear Cubs and fleeter than birds –
> Tinker to Evers to Chance.
>
> Thoughtlessly pricking our gonfalon bubble,
> Making a Giant hit into a double,
> Words that are weighty with nothing but trouble,
> Tinker to Evers to Chance.

Even with a .368 batting average, Ty Cobb couldn't outplay the Cubs. He got seven hits and stole two bases, but the Tigers won only one game and were shut out in the last two.

Some said the World Series that year was an anti-climax after an incident in a Cubs-Giants game that would long be known as 'Merkle's boner.' The Giants' Fred Merkle came up in the bottom of the ninth, with the scored tied at 1-1, two men out and a Giant on first. Merkle's single moved his teammate to third; then another Giant singled and as Merkle moved toward second, he saw his man from third cross the plate with the apparent winning run. As many would later insist was an accepted custom, Merkle didn't bother touching second but ran for the clubhouse. Cub second baseman Johnny Evers called for the ball, but it was alleged that the Giants' Joe McGinnity saw what was about to happen so he intercepted it and threw it into the stands. Evers, however, got another ball,

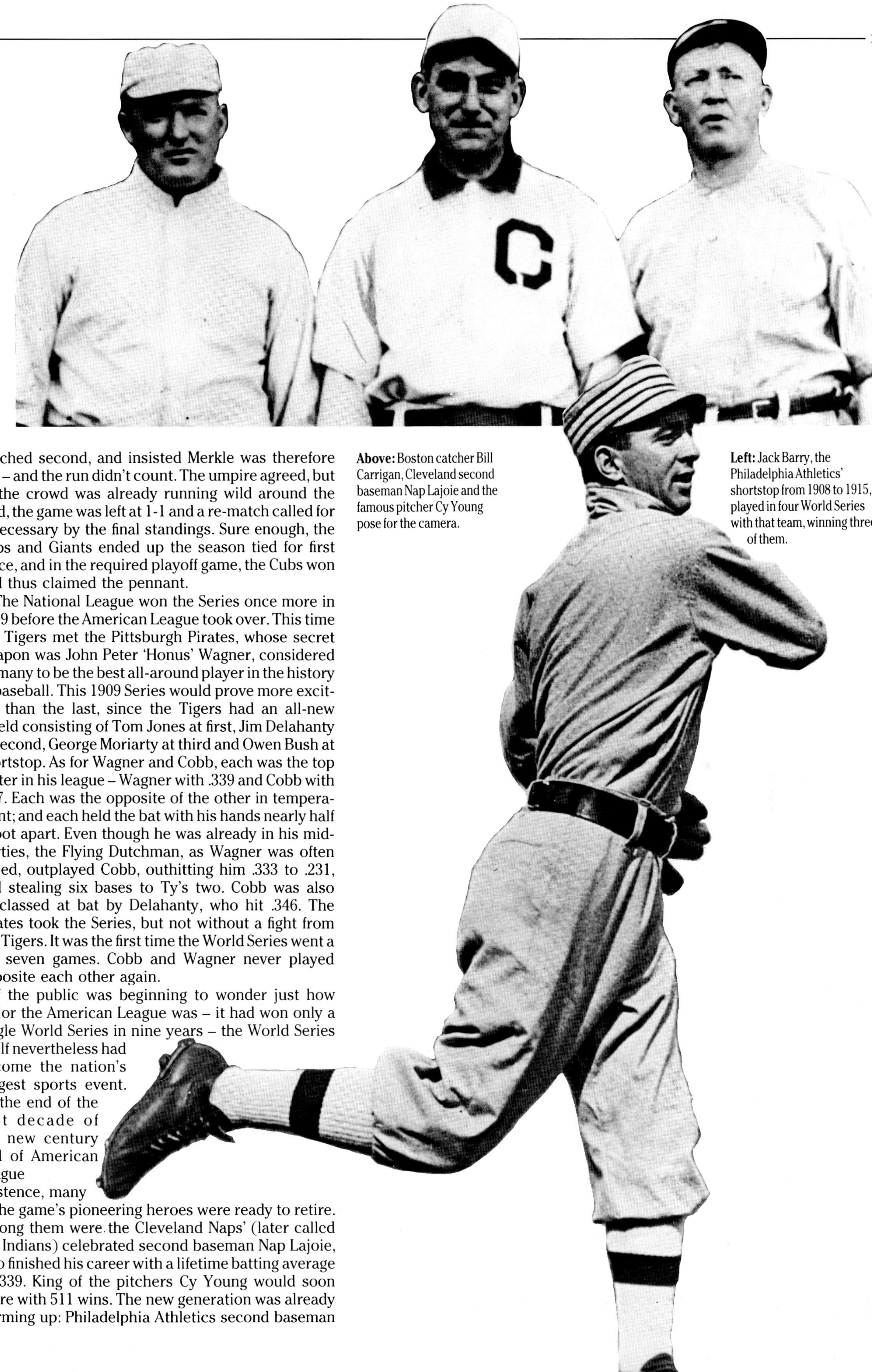

touched second, and insisted Merkle was therefore out – and the run didn't count. The umpire agreed, but as the crowd was already running wild around the field, the game was left at 1-1 and a re-match called for if necessary by the final standings. Sure enough, the Cubs and Giants ended up the season tied for first place, and in the required playoff game, the Cubs won and thus claimed the pennant.

The National League won the Series once more in 1909 before the American League took over. This time the Tigers met the Pittsburgh Pirates, whose secret weapon was John Peter 'Honus' Wagner, considered by many to be the best all-around player in the history of baseball. This 1909 Series would prove more exciting than the last, since the Tigers had an all-new infield consisting of Tom Jones at first, Jim Delahanty at second, George Moriarty at third and Owen Bush at shortstop. As for Wagner and Cobb, each was the top batter in his league – Wagner with .339 and Cobb with .377. Each was the opposite of the other in temperament; and each held the bat with his hands nearly half a foot apart. Even though he was already in his mid-thirties, the Flying Dutchman, as Wagner was often called, outplayed Cobb, outhitting him .333 to .231, and stealing six bases to Ty's two. Cobb was also outclassed at bat by Delahanty, who hit .346. The Pirates took the Series, but not without a fight from the Tigers. It was the first time the World Series went a full seven games. Cobb and Wagner never played opposite each other again.

If the public was beginning to wonder just how major the American League was – it had won only a single World Series in nine years – the World Series itself nevertheless had become the nation's biggest sports event. By the end of the first decade of the new century and of American League existence, many of the game's pioneering heroes were ready to retire. Among them were the Cleveland Naps' (later called the Indians) celebrated second baseman Nap Lajoie, who finished his career with a lifetime batting average of .339. King of the pitchers Cy Young would soon retire with 511 wins. The new generation was already warming up: Philadelphia Athletics second baseman

Above: Boston catcher Bill Carrigan, Cleveland second baseman Nap Lajoie and the famous pitcher Cy Young pose for the camera.

Left: Jack Barry, the Philadelphia Athletics' shortstop from 1908 to 1915, played in four World Series with that team, winning three of them.

Eddie Collins, Boston center fielder Tris Speaker, and Washington pitcher Walter Johnson.

Connie Mack's Philadelphia Athletics were the cream of the American League in 1910. In addition to Eddie Collins and veteran first baseman Harry Davis, Mack had a stable of promising new players, especially with Jack Barry at shortstop and Frank Baker at third base. They came to be known as Connie's $100,000 infield – an estimate of their worth at the time. Veteran pitchers Jack Coombs and Chief Bender gave the Athletics a win-loss record of 54-14.

Second-place New York was 14 and a half games behind the pennant-winners, and Detroit came behind them in third, despite Ty Cobb's title-winning .385 average. Already one of the most disliked of players, Cobb was the target of an attempt on the part of the St Louis Browns to throw Nap Lajoie the title as the season's top hitter. When Ban Johnson heard about the goings-on, he kicked the participants, Browns' manager Jack O'Connor and coach Harry Howell, out of the American League for life. Despite the attempted manipulation, Cobb beat out Lajoie by a hundredth of a point. In the World Series, the Athletics steamrolled the National League's Cubs four games to one. It was the first in a winning streak that would see them win the American League pennant four out of the next five years.

The Athletics took the Series with Collins, who had broken his leg, on the sidelines. Heinrich 'Heinie' Zimmerman replaced him. For the first time since 1906, the Athletics (with Chief Bender and Jack Coombs pitching) won the opening game of the Series, 4-1. It was superb hitting that clinched the Series, with the A's batting .316 overall, a record that held until 1960.

Mack's Philadelphia team repeated in 1911, the year Frank Baker earned his title as Home Run Baker. Although the A's didn't move into first place for the pennant until late in the season, they still topped the Tigers by 13 and a half games. Ty Cobb had his best hitting season yet, with .420, and he and Sam Crawford racked up 465 hits. That still wasn't enough to stop Connie Mack's wonder team, though.

An American League star for Cleveland who premiered that season was 'Shoeless' Joe Jackson, said to be illiterate. The South Carolinian had a .408 batting average for the Naps with 233 hits, 45 doubles and 19 triples. The rookie was known as the greatest natural hitter who ever lived.

The Athletics met McGraw's New York Giants in the 1911 World Series. Baker hit two home runs in two days during the second and third games, convincing New York's catcher Chief Meyers that the American League team must have some mysterious access to the Giants' signals. While Home Run Baker's overall record of 100 home runs does not seem spectacular by today's standards, the game was different then. It was the era of the 'dead' ball, and while the cork-centered ball had just been introduced, the emphasis was on place hitting, bunting and base stealing. Judged by the standards of the times, Baker's record of nine homeruns that year was indeed outstanding.

In 1912 it was a Boston Red Sox player who won the kudos. Fenway Park was opened that year, and Smokey Joe Wood, a 22-year-old pitcher, gave the Sox a 34-5 season to mark the occasion. He struck out 258 batters, pitched 10 shutouts and batted .290 to boot. Washington's Walter Johnson was close behind with a 32-12 record, 303 strikeouts and a 1.39 ERA. He also posted a record-breaking 16 consecutive wins.

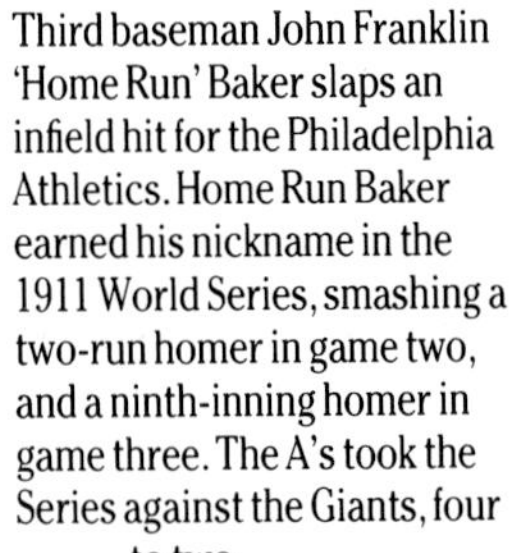

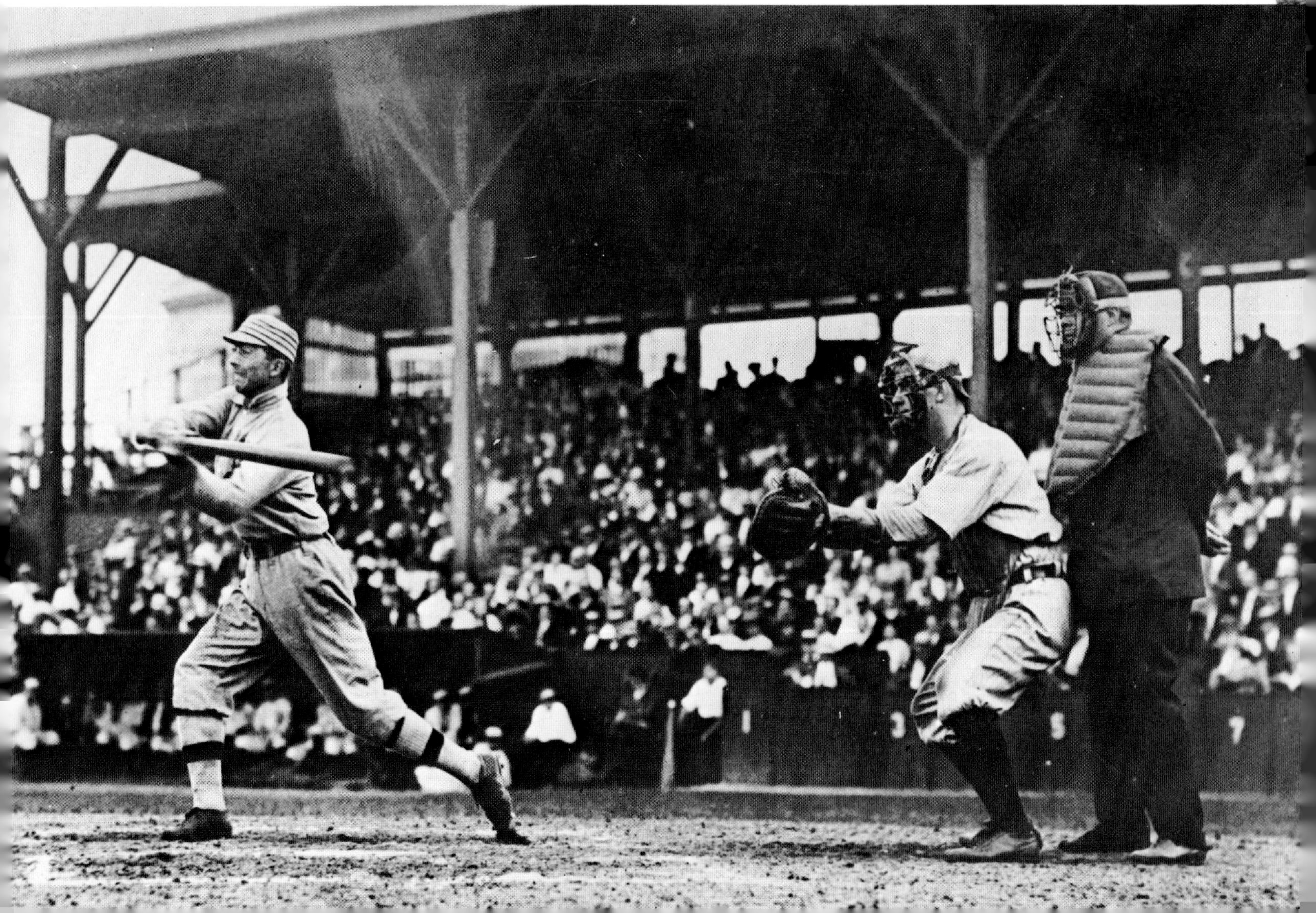

Third baseman John Franklin 'Home Run' Baker slaps an infield hit for the Philadelphia Athletics. Home Run Baker earned his nickname in the 1911 World Series, smashing a two-run homer in game two, and a ninth-inning homer in game three. The A's took the Series against the Giants, four to two.

The two American League pitchers got to face each other on 12 September 1912, with fans overflowing Boston's new ball park. The game ended 1-0 in Boston's favor when the Sox scored in the sixth inning on consecutive doubles by Tris Speaker and George 'Duffy' Lewis. With George 'Duffy' Lewis in left field, Speaker playing center, and Harry Hooper covering right, the Sox's outfield was as solid as its pitching. They went on that year to win the pennant, and Washington finished second ahead of the Philadelphia Athletics, despite Connie Mack's claim that they were the best team he'd ever managed.

The World Series that year has been characterized as sloppy but excitingly close, with the Boston Red Sox competing against the New York Giants. When the seventh game of the Series had to be called for darkness at a tie, an eighth game became necessary. The final game went ten inning. Pitchers Christy Mathewson (New York) and Hugh Bedient (Boston) battled till the seventh innings, when Bedient was replaced by Joe Wood. The score was 1-1 at the end of nine innings. The Giants scored another run in the tenth, but when the Red Sox came to bat, the Giants' center fielder committed the celebrated error called 'Snodgrass's $30,000 Muff' by dropping an easy fly

Above: Ty Cobb and Nap Lajoie are each awarded a '30' motorcar by Hugh Chalmers in a ceremony witnessed by 20,000 spectators. Although Cobb beat out Lajoie for the 1910 batting championship by a fraction of a point, the two players received equal awards.

Left: Two Hall of Fame managers, Connie Mack of the Philadelphia Athletics and Clark Griffith of the Washington Senators, shake hands.

Above: Boston Red Sox pitcher Smokey Joe Wood and New York Giants pitcher Jeff Tesreau shake hands before the first game of the 1912 World Series. Wood won this contest for Boston, striking out 11 batters, and Boston went on to win the Series four games to three.

ball. The Sox racked up two runs to win by a final score of 3-2. Before the game was over, the Giants had chalked up 16 errors and the Sox, 14 for the Series.

The 1913 season saw Smokey Joe Wood, the Red Sox's brightest star the year before, vanish from the firmament almost as quickly as he had appeared when he injured his arm during spring training. Washington's legendary pitcher Walter Johnson had his best season in 1913. He pitched 36-7 and topped the league in wins, in ERA's with 1.09, in strikeouts with 243 and in shutouts with 12. For more than a month, early in the season, he kept all batters at bay and allowed no runs at all, pitching 55 and two thirds scoreless innings. It took Don Drysdale to top that record in 1968.

Despite Johnson's brilliance, Washington finished six and a half games behind the Athletics, in second place. Ty Cobb took his seventh batting crown in a row at .390, and Shoeless Joe Jackson was right behind him with a .373.

Connie Mack's A's were matched against McGraw's Giants in the World Series that year, and the A's had an easy win, 4-1. Mack's infield had added Stuffy McInnis at first base, along with Eddie Collins, Jack Barry and Frank Baker. Injuries kept the Giants from operating at full strength. The Giants' Mathewson, who had pitched in eleven World Series games and won five, of which four were shutouts, went down in defeat in what was to be his last World Series performance.

1914 launched the Great War in Europe and the battle against the Federal League in American baseball. More a spoiler than a serious threat, the Federal League didn't have much success in wooing players, and within two years it was just a memory. It's possible, however, that because of the Federal League, the Philadelphia A's lost the Series that year. With Connie Mack's $100,000 infield in full swing, the A's won the pennant with ease. The second-place Red Sox were eight and a half games behind them, but they picked up a 19-year-old rookie – in a deal with the Baltimore Orioles for three players – who was

Right: John Phalen 'Stuffy' McInnis played first base for the Philadelphia A's as part of Connie Mack's $100,000 infield. During his nine years with the A's (1909-17), Stuffy McInnis maintained a .304 batting average.

New York Highlanders' manager William Edward 'Wild Bill' Donovan and Washington Senators' manager Clark Griffith shake hands before a game. Also known as 'The Old Fox,' Griffith managed a first-place team only once during his 20-year career, although his 1491 wins places him tenth on the all-time list.

destined to become one of baseball's greatest players. His name was George Herman Ruth, soon to be nicknamed 'Babe,' and that first season he batted .200, with one double.

The Tigers' powerhouse Ty Cobb took the honors again with .368, and the Senators' pitcher Walter Johnson had a 25-18 season, something of a high-low record. Even winning their fourth pennant in five years, the A's stood on the brink of disaster. Chief Bender and Eddie Plank had succumbed to the blandishments of the Federal League and were playing their last season for Connie Mack. Morale was low and what should have been an easy win in the World Series turned into a rout.

They faced the Boston Braves, who had earned the nickname 'Miracle Braves' for their spectacular rise from the bottom of the National League to first place. Spurred to victory by manager George Tweedy Stallings, the Braves were on a roll. Stallings used two sets of outfielders, one for right-handed pitchers and one for left-handers. Chief Bender lost the opener to the Miracle Braves, 7-1, and never pitched for the A's again. The rest of the games were close, but the Braves took them one after another, 1-0, 5-4 and 3-1. With his .545 batting average, Braves player Hank Gowdy became the first to hit over .500 in the World Series, while Home Run Baker led the A's with .250.

As if that defeat were not enough, Connie Mack then sold off the team's best players and sent the Athletics to last place in the league. Eddie Collins went to the White Sox, Jack Barry and Herb Pennock to the Red Sox and Bob Shawkey to the Yankees. Frank Baker retired, and Jack Coombs was released. It took many years for the team to recover.

The Red Sox replaced the Athletics as the American League's leading team for the next few years, taking three pennants from 1915 to 1918. Particularly strong was the Boston team's pitching. The outfield, featuring Tris Speaker at center, Duffy Lewis at left and Harry Hooper at right, was a defensive powerhouse. In 1915, Babe Ruth played his first full season in the majors, batting .315 and hitting four home runs.

The Phillies were the National League entry against Boston in the World Series that year. It was the

Above: The formidable pitching staff of the 1917 Boston Red Sox. From left to right: Ernie Shore, Dutch Leonard, George Foster and Babe Ruth.
Below: Detroit Tigers Ty Cobb (left) and Sam Crawford (right) talk with Chicago's Shoeless Joe Jackson.
Opposite: Hall of Fame catcher Ray Schalk played for the White Sox (1912-28).

Phillies' first shot at the Series and their last pennant until 1950. The magic ingredient that took them to the World Series in 1915 was right-handed pitcher Grover Cleveland Alexander. He had won 31 games that season, 12 of which were shutouts. The Phillies took the first game in the Series, but even Alexander couldn't stop Boston, and the Red Sox cinched the rest – all with a 2-1 score. It was Babe Ruth's World Series debut. He played his first World Series game at Baker Bowl, the Phillies' home park, where 21 years later he played his last major league game.

Once the Federal League threw in the towel, players' salaries, which had risen to stave off the contenders, took a nosedive. Players who refused to cooperate found themselves traded, like Tris Speaker, who ended up in Cleveland. Even without Speaker, though, the Red Sox won the pennant again in 1916. Pitching was the key, with Babe Ruth turning into the league's top left-hander. Winning 23 games, he helped bring a speedy defeat to the Brooklyn Dodgers, who opposed the Red Sox in the 1916 World Series.

The next year brought a pause in the Red Sox sweep, as the White Sox took the pennant. The White Sox had a strong infield, pitching on a par with the Red

Sox, and Shoeless Joe Jackson in the outfield. The highlight of the World Series between the White Sox and the Giants was one disastrous inning that cost the Giants the Series.

Chicago won the opening game, 2-1, after a standoff in which each pitcher gave up seven hits and struck out two batters. With five runs in the fourth, the Sox racked up their second win, 7-2. Then the Giants rallied and won 2-0 in the third game and 5-0 in the fourth. The two teams went neck and neck through the seventh inning of the fifth game, with the score tied at 5-5, until the Sox pulled ahead to win 8-5.

The Giants' infamous blunders came during the fourth inning of the sixth game. White Sox player Eddie Collins sent a grounder to Heinie Zimmerman, but Zimmerman's throw missed first base and so Collins was able to get to second. Shoeless Joe Jackson then hit an easy fly into right field – but the Giant Dave Robertson dropped it. Now Collins was on third, and when Happy Felsch's hit was caught by the pitcher, Collins was caught between third and home. Collins got past the Giant catcher while Zimmerman had the ball and since no one had bothered to back up at home plate, Collins beat Zimmerman there. The White Sox won the game, 4-2.

America's entry into the War in 1918 made it questionable whether there would even be a World Series that year. The pennant went back to the Red Sox, despite the continued strength of Chicago. The leagues had orders to end play by Labor Day because of the war; then a 15-day grace period was allowed so the Red Sox could play the Cubs in the World Series. Although Red Sox manager Ed Barrows had begun to use Ruth increasingly in the field in order to take advantage of his hitting talent in more games, Ruth pitched two games of the Series, winning the first 1-0, and the fourth, 3-2. The star of the series, though, was George Whiteman, an aging outfielder from Toronto whom the Red Sox had picked up in midseason. His fielding and hitting helped the Sox in all six games. In the series-winning game his hit gave the Red Sox the winning run in their 2-1 victory, and his spectacular catch in the eighth inning stopped a Cub rally dead. The next year Whiteman was back playing in Toronto.

The year 1919 stands out in baseball history, but not for good reasons. It was the year of the White Sox scandal. Babe Ruth spent the season in the outfield, setting a new home run record of 29 and a new batting record of .657. Despite the Babe's brilliant play, the Red Sox finished fifth and the pennant went to the White Sox. Comiskey's team had a reputation for being outstanding – when they wanted to be. The problem was gambling, and they threw the 1919 Series to Cincinnati, earning the ignominious title for themselves of the Black Sox.

Eight players were involved in the scandal: outfielder 'Shoeless' Joe Jackson, third baseman George 'Buck' Weaver, first baseman Arnold 'Chick' Gandil, shortstop Charles 'Swede' Risberg, pitchers Eddie Cicotte and Claude 'Lefty' Williams, center fielder Oscar 'Happy' Felsch and utility infielder Fred McMullin. Eddie Collins was one of those who remained untainted. The Sox had been said to be split into cliques for some time, and the split was along the lines of who was crooked and who was straight. Weaver, it was argued by some, was guilty only by association, having sat in on the negotiation over the fix, but having decided not to participate in it.

The ringleaders were Cicotte, Gandil and Williams, who approached the gamblers (including the notorious Arnold Rothstein) in New York at midseason to

Above: The 1919 Chicago White Sox team, eight players of which threw the World Series in a gambling scandal that shook America's faith in the integrity of their national pastime.

Right: Judge Kenesaw Mountain Landis, named the first Commissioner of Baseball in 1920, served until 1944 and was known for his autocratic and tough-minded ways.

set the stakes. The players were promised $100,000, most of which they were never to see. It must have seemed like a lot of money in those days, when a player was doing well if he earned $6000. Comiskey contributed to the trouble in the sense that he was notoriously tight, paying the lowest salaries in either major league.

Betting odds before the Series began went from 3-1 in favor of the White Sox to 8-5 in favor of Cincinnati, a sure clue to the shenanigans going on. The pre-established high sign was for the White Sox pitcher to hit the first batter in the first game. Eddie Cicotte performed on cue, and Cincinnati won, 9-1.

Claude Williams walked three batters in a single inning in the second game, an unheard of feat for him, and the Reds won again, this time 4-2. When Comiskey got wind of what was going on, he passed the word to John Heydler, president of the National League, who informed Ban Johnson. Johnson, who by now had fallen out with Comiskey in a personal feud, dismissed it as 'the yelp of a beaten cur.'

The Sox won the third game, 3-0, possibly because the gamblers were reneging on their promise to pay the players $10,000 of the $100,000 total after each game. Two errors by Cicotte gave the Reds a 2-0 win in the fourth game, and they won again, 5-0, in the fifth. The Commission had temporarily lengthened the Series to a best of nine that year, so the Reds needed one more win to take the Series.

Cicotte talked Manager Kid Gleason into letting him pitch again, and the Sox won 4-1. Then Claude Williams lost to the Reds, 10-5, and the Series was over. It broke all records in receipts and attendance, and the Reds were the first to earn more than $5000 in a series. Nothing was said publicly about the fix until the following September, but rumors flew fast and furious. Boxer Abe Attell confessed to being involved in the deal and named the eight players. The *Chicago Tribune* called for a grand jury investigation.

When confronted by Gleason and Comiskey, Cicotte broke down. He, Jackson and Williams gave the details of how the games were rigged to a grand jury, and Comiskey suspended all eight. As Shoeless Joe Jackson was leaving the courthouse after the grand jury hearing, a small boy supposedly came up to him with tears in his eyes, and as the legend has it, cried, 'Say it ain't so, Joe.' Criminal indictments followed, but by then the players' written confessions had disappeared, and they all were acquitted. According to the letter of the law, they could have been reinstated.

The three-man National Commission was replaced

that year, however, by a single Commissioner of Baseball. Judge Kenesaw Mountain Landis, named for a Civil War battle, took quick and decisive action: 'Regardless of the verdict of juries, no player that throws a game, no player that entertains proposals or promises to throw a game, no player that sits in conference with a bunch of crooks and gamblers where the ways and means of throwing games are discussed, and does not promptly tell his club about it, will ever again play professional baseball.'

The 'Black Sox' scandal seriously undermined the confidence of many in the game that had become the national pastime, but Landis's firm handling of the scandal helped mitigate the disgrace. Some felt some of the players deserved a pardon. Buck Weaver never shared in the ill-gained profits, and played .324 ball in the Series. Ten thousand fans signed a petition calling for his reinstatement, but Judge Landis sternly turned a cold shoulder.

Shoeless Joe Jackson got no fix money either and averaged .375 for the Series, the best in both leagues, but he was never allowed back in baseball. In fact when word got back to Judge Landis that Jackson had been hired to coach a class D minor league team, he ordered him fired. It took the legendary Babe Ruth to wipe the slate clean in the roaring twenties and make the crowds forget about the dirty deeds their heroes in Chicago had done.

'Shoeless' Joe Jackson (left) and Oscar 'Happy' Felsch were both suspended from baseball forever by Commissioner Landis for their involvement in the Black Sox scandal.

George Herman Ruth – Babe Ruth – whose name is synonymous with the game of baseball, is considered by many to be the greatest player of all time.

CHAPTER TWO

The House that Ruth Built

"... they fixed up a ball that if you don't
miss it entirely it will clear the fence."

–Ring Lardner

Through his dramatic commissionership, Judge Landis provided a symbol that reassured the public of baseball's honesty and integrity, and made it a respected and admired sport. As the new decade began, a rising interest in baseball was further enhanced by the advent of the lively ball, by rule changes that encouraged hitters, by post-World War I affluence, and above all by Babe Ruth, whose rising popularity and playing style revolutionized the game. All these elements combined to usher in an age of unprecedented prosperity for the American League.

During the twenties, the fast and colorful new game of home run baseball emerged to draw crowds in increasing numbers and set the style for years to come. The American League, after two decades of struggling to survive league wars, scandal and its own magnates, at last achieved an element of stability and maturity. The greatest stars the league had ever known – Ty Cobb, Tris Speaker, Walter Johnson, Eddie Collins, Lou Gehrig, Lefty Grove, Babe Ruth, George Sisler, Harry Heilmann, Jimmie Foxx, Al Simmons, Goose Goslin – were assembled as the new power game competed successfully in the unrestrained, fast-moving, action-oriented postwar society.

Beginning with President Taft, who originated the custom of throwing out the first ball on opening day, presidents continued to preside over key games, and baseball regained its status as the national sport. As if to prove that the revitalized game could keep American League fans from turning to other sports and the lure of such stars of the twenties as Red Grange, Jack Dempsey, Gene Tunney, Walter Hagan and Bill Tilden, in 1920 American League attendance jumped by one and a half million as American League fans, supposedly disillusioned by the Black Sox scandal, stormed the gates. In 1920 the American League became the first to top the five million mark.

Crucial to the creation of the more popular, more exciting game was the elimination of trick pitches. In February 1920, both leagues outlawed all tampering with the ball, banning the application of sandpaper, emery, licorice, mud and particularly spit to the baseball's surface, although 17 pitchers in the major leagues who used the spitball as their primary weapon were permitted to continue to do so. In the American League this included five-time 20-game winner Cleveland Indian Stanley Coveleski, Red Faber of the White Sox and Jack Quinn, who pitched for several teams from 1909 to 1933. For the first time since the early days, when batters could call for their pitches, hitters had the edge over pitchers.

On 16 August 1920 popular Cleveland shortstop Ray Chapman was hit on the head by an inside fastball thrown by Yankee pitcher Carl Mays at a Yankee-Cleveland game. Chapman collapsed at the plate and died the next day from the effects of a blow that put a three-and-one-half-inch fracture in his skull. After his death, which remains the only fatality in major league

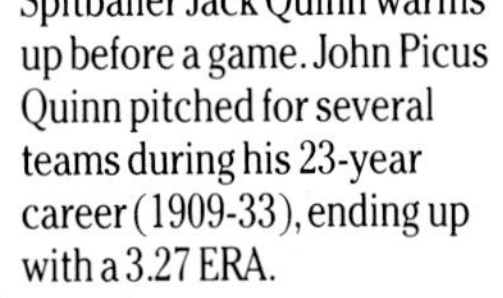

Spitballer Jack Quinn warms up before a game. John Picus Quinn pitched for several teams during his 23-year career (1909-33), ending up with a 3.27 ERA.

baseball history, precaution was taken to reduce the danger of a batter getting beaned by substituting a new ball whenever the ball in play became even slightly scuffed or soiled. A pitched ball with rough spots or scrapes is more affected by air currents than a smooth one, and can sail unpredictably. This use of new balls protected the batter, but even further handicapped the pitcher, who found it more difficult to put stuff on a smooth, tightly-covered ball. On the other hand, a new white ball is more visible, more predictable in flight, easier to hit, and goes farther and faster when it is hit.

But the introduction of the lively ball was probably even more significant. Despite repeated assurances by baseball officials and manufacturers that the only change in the manufacture of the ball was a better quality wool yarn (made available from Australia after the war), which was more tightly wound on improved machinery, a baseball officialdom obsessed with wooing back fans after the Black Sox scandal could not have helped but notice that more home runs and higher scoring games drew more spectators to the park. Undoubtedly Babe Ruth was the catalyst in this great revolution, just as surely as his bat was the lever that changed the game.

Left: Spitballer Stan Coveleski pitched brilliantly for the Cleveland Indians from 1916 to 1924, achieving the 20-game mark four times during those years. He was elected to the Hall of Fame in 1969.

Below: Henry Louis Gehrig poses in his Columbia University baseball uniform. Lou Gehrig played his entire 17-year career for the New York Yankees (1923-39).

'Gorgeous George' Sisler played first base for the St Louis Browns from 1915 to 1927, then played briefly for Washington before ending his career on Boston's National League team. In 1922 his .420 batting average, with 246 hits, 134 runs and 51 stolen bases earned him the league MVP title.

In 1919 Ruth broke all existing records by hitting 29 home runs for the Boston Red Sox. The Red Sox were a mediocre team, finishing the season in a tie for fifth place, but large crowds came out to see Ruth wherever he appeared in the league. The lesson was not lost on the baseball owners. As Ring Lardner so eloquently put it:

> . . . the master minds that controls baseball says to themselfs that if it is home runs that the public wants to see, why leave us give them home runs, so they fixed up a ball that if you don't miss it entirely it will clear the fence, and the result is that ball players which used to specialize in hump back liners to the pitcher is now amongst our leading sluggers.

By the 1920 season, with trick pitches outlawed and the ball juiced up, the stage was set for the change in the game. The substitution of new balls whenever the one in play was even slightly soiled ran up the curtain, and players and fans performed beautifully. In 1920, Babe Ruth, by then with the New York Yankees, hit 54 homers, and Yankee attendance of 1919 doubled, setting a league record of 1,289, 422 which stood until the Yanks themselves broke it in 1946.

It was a new game. Combined major-league batting averages for 1920 were almost 30 points higher than in 1915. By 1925, they were 45 points higher. In 1915, nine batters in the majors hit above .300; in 1927, 35 major-leaguers hit over .300. Although only four batters hit .400 between 1901 and 1920, from 1920 through 1930, eight batters hit .400 – twice as many in

Left: Heinie Groh of the New York Giants puts Cleveland Indian Tris Speaker out at third during a spring training game in Lakeland, Florida.

Elmer Smith played outfield for Cleveland from 1914 to 1921, with a short stint for Washington in 1916 and 1917. His moment in the sun occurred on 10 October 1920, when he smashed the first World Series grand slam ever.

half the time – including in the American League's Ty Cobb, Harry Heilmann and George Sisler (twice).

Major leaguers hit 384 home runs in 1915. In 1920 they hit 631, in 1925 they hit 1167 and in 1930 they hit 1565, four times the number of homers hit in 1915. In 1930 the ball was hotter than ever. Twenty major-leaguers hit above .350 and nine teams averaged above .300, with American League teams averaging better than five runs per game each. Repeated official assertions that the ball was the same as it had always been are difficult to reconcile with the all-time record National League 1930 average of .303 (after the 1930 season the ball was made *less* lively) and the knowledge that only six batters in the National League hit above .300 in 1968.

Somewhat overshadowed by the breaking Black Sox scandal, a Cleveland team powered by playing manager Tris Speaker's .388 average and pitcher Jim Bagby's 31 victories took the pennant in 1920. It was a tight three-cornered race with the Yankees and the White Sox, the Indians finishing two games ahead of a White Sox team that saw most of its regular players suspended as the season progressed. Only three games separated the three clubs at the close of the season.

Hitting .303 as a team, the 1920 Indians were the first club in the century to have three men hit 100 RBI's. Two Indian pitchers besides Bagby had 20-game years, and their sluggers led the league in runs scored as Cleveland took its first pennant after 20 years of struggles and near misses. Their two-game finish over Chicago suggests that they might not have taken the pennant without the demise of the White Sox, but the Indians themselves had had to scramble to find a replacement for star shortstop Ray Chapman after he was killed at the plate by Carl Mays's pitched ball.

Cleveland faced the Brooklyn Dodgers in a precedent-setting World Series. In the fifth game, with the teams tied at two games each, the Indians' outfielder Elmer Smith hit the first grand-slam Series homer, the Indians' Jim Bagby hit the first Series homer by a pitcher, and the Indians recorded the first unassisted Series triple play, made by second baseman Bill Wambsganss (who in the next year set the still-standing record of seven consecutive extra-base hits). The Dodgers were so demoralized by that fifth game that they remained scoreless from then on, and Cleveland took the Series, 5-2

1920 was in every way a year of shocks and superlatives. Babe Ruth hit a record 54 homers and slugged an all-time record .847. The White Sox became the first team in history to have four 20-game winning pitchers. It was also the first year that the Brown's George Sisler hit above .400, leading the league with .407. But above all, it was the year that Babe Ruth came to the Yankees. Not without coincidence, New York won six out of the next ten pennants. The arrival of the Babe signalled the beginning of a Yankee dynasty that would take 29 pennants and 20 World Series championships in the next 44 years.

Waite Charles 'Schoolboy' Hoyt pitched for a number of teams during his 21-year career, turning in ten solid years for the Yankees from 1921 to 1930. During that time he pitched in five World Series, winning six games and losing three. He was elected to the Hall of Fame in 1969.

The players who formed the backbone of the Yankees' first winning teams came almost entirely from the Boston Red Sox. Boston owner Harry Frazee, who liked to invest in Broadway productions, frequently found himself in need of cash, and found a ready buyer for his star players in wealthy Yankee owner and brewery tycoon Jacob Ruppert. The first of the purchases which eventually became known as the 'Rape of the Red Sox' and resulted in the 'Dead Sox' began in July 1919 with New York's acquisition of fastballer Carl Mays for two players and $40,000. In December 1919, Boston was shocked to learn that its best player, Babe Ruth, had been sold to New York for $125,000 and a loan to Frazee of $300,000 (for which Fenway Park was mortgaged as security).

Over the next four years, this startling deal was followed by a steady flow of players from Boston to New York as Frazee gradually liquidated his loan. By 1923, Boston had given the Yankees Mays and Ruth, catcher Wally Schang, shortstop Everett Scott, third baseman Joe Dugan and pitchers Herb Pennock, Waite Hoyt, Joe Bush and Sam Jones. In 1920 the Yankees also acquired Bob Meusel. Red Sox field manager Edward G Barrow came to the Yankees from Boston late in 1920, filling the vacancy left by the death of business manager Harry Sparrow. Joining forces with shrewd, diminutive field manager Miller Huggins and Ruppert's bucks, general manager Barrow deserves much of the credit for New York's era of success. Not surprisingly, the Red Sox spent eight of the next nine years in last place.

The Yankees finished three games out of first place in 1920, but Babe Ruth batted .376, hit more home runs than any American League team had ever hit (54), racked up the all-time record .847 slugging average and batted in 137 runs. Unschooled, uncouth, lovable, and incredibly talented, George Herman Ruth by this performance did more to revive interest in baseball than Commissioner Landis or anyone else inside or outside baseball, and made it the game we know today.

No athlete in this country has ever achieved greater reknown. Trying to write about Ruth, Arthur Daley of *The New York Times* once remarked, is like trying to paint a landscape on a postage stamp. His popularity was such that he packed the house almost anywhere he appeared. When the Yankees played an exhibition game in March 1921 in Lake Charles, Louisiana, the town declared a holiday, banks and businesses closed, and townsfolk who couldn't get in the park climbed trees and telegraph poles to watch the game.

Ruth's slugging accomplishments are so great that his skill as a pitcher is sometimes overlooked. Red Sox manager Ed Barrow switched him permanently to the outfield in 1919 in order to take advantage of his batting in every game, but until that time he compiled a record as a pitcher which leads many to believe that if he had stayed with pitching he would have established himself as the best left-hander in American League history.

In 1915, his first full season on the mound, Ruth won 18 and lost 8. In 1916 he was 23-12, and led the league with a 1.75 ERA with nine shutouts. In 1917 he was 24-13, and in both 1916 and 1917 he allowed only about 6.5 hits per nine innings. At age 22, Ruth had recorded two 20-game years and a total of 67 major-league victories, a win total Lefty Grove didn't reach until he was 28. He was considered in some quarters the best pitcher in the league.

Ruth won six out of eight pitching contests with the great Walter Johnson in his brief career as a hurler, three by 1-0 scores. He never lost a World Series game. His record of 29 and two-thirds scoreless Series innings stood until it was broken by New York's Whitey Ford in 1961. After he was removed from the mound, Babe Ruth, quite likely the greatest all-around player in baseball history, continued to be an alert and aggressive base-runner and a skillful outfielder with surprising grace.

But it is of course for his hitting that he will always be best-remembered. The Big Guy's 54 home runs in 1920 were twice what anyone else had ever hit, and more than any other team except the Yankees. His personal magnetism and swaggering style made even his strikeouts memorable, but all statistics fall short of revealing how he dominated the era, how he outdistanced his contemporaries, and how much more incredible his exploits were in the context of his times than they seem now.

In 1921, probably his best all-around season, he broke the home run record for the third straight year with 59, totalled 204 hits, and achieved an .846 slugging percentage, a .378 batting average, 170 RBI's, 177 runs scored and 144 walks. In 1927, when he set a home run record that stood for 34 years, his 60 homers represented 13.7 percent of all the home runs hit in the American League that season, and again surpassed the individual totals of most major-league teams.

Throughout his long career the Babe hit a home run every 11.7 times at bat. He was the first to hit 30 home runs, the first to hit 40, the first to hit 50, and the first to hit 60. Before Ruth, the career home run record was 136. He surpassed this record in 1921, and his lifetime total of 714 was more than twice that of anyone else.

Ruth averaged 50 home runs a season for six years (1926-1931) and 47 homers a season for twelve years (1920-1931). The Sultan of Swat was one of those rare power hitters who also hit for average. His lifetime

Bottom: A contemporary cartoon illustrates the effect Babe Ruth's extraordinary hitting had on gate receipts.

During his six years as a left-handed hurler for the Boston Red Sox, Babe Ruth's diverse talents were evident in his won-lost record of 89-46 and his 23- and 24-win seasons, and his simultaneous batting average of .309.

Copyright by the Press Publishing Company (New York World), 1927

THE GREAT TURNSTILE WHIRLER

—Cassel in the New York World.

Above: Ty Cobb at bat in 1922. He hit .401 that year, scoring 99 runs and driving in 99 to account for about 23 percent of the Tigers' runs.

average of .342 has been surpassed by only a handful of players. In eloquent testimony to his home-run-hitting threat, Ruth also holds the lifetime record for being walked.

As surely as his style revolutionized baseball and made it the foremost spectator sport of the twenties, Ruth also changed the way the game was paid. Perhaps no one sums up Ruth's influence on salaries better than Yankee pitching great Waite Hoyt: 'Wives of baseball players, when they teach their children their prayers, should instruct them to say: "God bless Mommy, God bless Daddy, God bless Babe Ruth! Babe has upped daddy's paycheck by 15 to 45 percent!"'

The Babe was receiving $10,000 a year from the Red Sox in 1919. This doubled when he came up to the Yankees in 1920, and tripled the next year. In 1922 he signed a five-year contract for $52,000 a year, an astounding and precedent-setting amount. In 1927-1929 he got $70,000, and in 1930 he hit $80,000. The story goes that in 1930 the Bambino was asking for more money than President Hoover was getting. Confronted with this statistic, Ruth replied, 'I had a better year than he did.' Baseball salaries, like the game, would never be the same again.

1920 also saw the flowering of American League slugging great George Sisler, ace first baseman for the St Louis Browns. Like Ruth, Sisler had begun his career in baseball as a left-handed pitcher, although with much less success. Sisler hit a league-leading .407 in 1920, the same year he achieved the still-standing major-league single-season record of 257 hits. Sisler also drove in 122 runs, scored 136 and stole 42 bases.

Right: After 12 years with the Boston Red Sox, Harry Hooper played right field for the Chicago White Sox from 1921 to 1925. Although he batted a blazing .325 in 1921, his team came in seventh.

After slumping to .371 in 1921, Sisler reached his season peak with .420 in 1922. A persisting eye ailment prevented him from sustaining these heights – he missed the entire 1923 season – but he hit respectably after his return, compiling a classy .340 lifetime average. Sisler's 1922 mark left Ty Cobb, with .401, in second place. Although Cobb kept playing until 1928, hitting .323 in his last season, Babe and the home run hitters made his kind of strategic game a thing of the past.

Most of the outrageous slugging in the new hitters' game took place in the American League. Outstanding American League sluggers of the era also included Al Simmons of Philadelphia; Heinie Manush, who played for several teams and registered a .330 lifetime average; Hall of Famers Sam Rice and Goose Goslin of Washington; and Charley Gehringer, the 'Mechanical Man,' who had a .320 lifetime average while playing second base for Detroit with flawless mechanical efficiency.

Harry Heilmann of the Tigers, tutored by playing manager Ty Cobb, took the league honors with a .394 average in 1921. An otherwise undistinguished player, Heilmann took league batting titles in the first four odd years of the twenties – trading off with Sisler, Ruth and Manush – and never fell below .346 during those years. But it was Babe Ruth, in what remains the single greatest offensive season in major-league history, who really held the magic wand in 1921. That season he hit 16 triples and 44 doubles, had 170 RBI's, scored 177 runs and averaged .378. With a slugging percentage of .846, Ruth set a new home run record for the third year in a row with 59.

Faced with this slugging onslaught, pitchers' ERA's ballooned correspondingly. Detroit as a team hit the still-standing American League record average of .316 in 1921, topping four clubs that batted over .300. But despite the still-standing league record of 1724 hits churned out by Heilmann and the Tigers, Detroit, cursed with dismal pitching, finished the year in sixth place.

Propelled by Ruth's 59 homers and a league-leading team total of 134, the Yankees took the first of three consecutive pennants in 1921. While the team was blessed with great sluggers, the first three flags of the dawning New York dynasty owed much to the pitchers the Yanks harvested from the Boston Red Sox. In 1921, Carl Mays won 27 games for the Yankees, and young Waite Hoyt took 19.

In January 1921 the owners of both leagues signed a new National Agreement which bound players, umpires and owners to Commissioner Landis's decisions, and empowered him to levy fines of up to $5000. In baseball matters, the owners even waived their rights to seek justice in civil courts. In the eventuality that the commissioner should die before a successor had been chosen, the president of the United States was designated to appoint his successor. Landis immediately demonstrated that he was worthy of the authority vested in him by ordering the owner and the manager of the New York Giants to sell their gambling-related enterprises in Cuba or get out of baseball.

Yankee slugging at the plate enabled the Yankees to take the pennant again in 1922. The season saw a tight race between the Yankees and the St Louis

Below left: Hall of Famer Harry Edwin 'Slug' Heilmann takes a few swings. Harry Heilmann played right field and first base for the Detroit Tigers from 1914 to 1929, winning the batting title in 1921 with 237 hits, 139 RBI's and a .394 batting average.

Below: Right-hander Urban James Shocker loosens up before a game. Urban Shocker pitched for the St Louis Browns from 1918 to 1924, turning in four 20-game seasons during that time. In 1921 he won 27 games and lost only 12, striking out 132 batters.

Above: Bob Shawkey pitched for the Yankees from 1916 to 1927, compiling a won-lost record of 164-124. He pitched in four World Series for the Yankees, including the controversial game on 5 October 1922, which was called for darkness.

Browns. Spearheaded by George Sisler's MVP year, in which he led the league with a .420 average and also set a league record by getting hits in 41 consecutive games, the Browns finished only one game behind New York. Once again the Yankees owed much to pitchers acquired from the Red Sox. Joe Bush won 26 games and Waite Hoyt won 19.

Babe Ruth, limited to 110 games because of repeated suspensions caused by protracted squabbles with umpires (he threw sand in one umpire's face) hit only 35 homers, and failed to take the home run title for the first time in five years, 1922's honors going to St Louis' Ken Williams. This was one of only two years in the 14-year span between 1918 and 1931 in which Babe Ruth did not win or tie the home run title. But his lesson was apparently learned, and he steered clear of serious quarrels with umpires for the rest of his career.

The Yankees were again frustrated in the Series, however, suffering their second straight defeat at the hands of the New York Giants. The 1922 loss was even more devastating than the previous year's, with the Yankees managing only one tie in five games. The great Babe Ruth hit .118 for the Series, collecting one single and one double in 17 times at bat. After the Series was over, half-owner Colonel T L Huston was so disgusted that he called for the dismissal of manager Huggins, a move which widened the rift between Huston and co-owner Jacob Ruppert, resulting in Huston selling out to Ruppert over the winter.

With the Yankee team and manager now receiving the undivided support of success-oriented Ruppert,

Right: The flags are flying and people are gathering outside Yankee Stadium on opening day – 18 April 1923.

Opposite top: Hall of Famer Herbert Jefferis Pennock moved from the Red Sox in 1923 and pitched for the Yankees for 11 years. He won all five of the Series games he pitched, and played his last year in 1934 back with Boston, ending his career with a won-lost record of 241-162.

the New York club skated to their third straight pennant in 1923, finishing a remarkable 16 games ahead of second-place Detroit. Former Red Sox pitchers Joe Bush and Herb Pennock won 19 games each, and Sox transplants Sam Jones and Waite Hoyt won 21 and 17 respectively. Seven of the 13 Yankee front-line players in 1923 were former Red Sox. Of the formidable New York pitching staff of Mays, Hoyt, Jones, Bush, Pennock and Shawkey – known to sportswriters as the 'Six-Star Final' – all were former Red Sox except Shawkey. Former Red Sox pitcher George Pipgras was now waiting in the Yankee wings.

Babe Ruth had a good year in 1923, hitting his best-ever average of .393, although league honors went to Detroit's Harry Heilmann, with .403. In a year in which nobody else even broke 100, Babe set the league record for bases on balls, with 170 walks. Most appropriately of all, he hit a game-winning home run on opening day at the Yankees' new Yankee Stadium.

New York was baseball's biggest market, and Yankee Stadium was the biggest, most modern park in baseball. Before the 65,000-plus seat landmark was opened in 1923, the Yankees had used the Polo Grounds as their home field, renting from the Giants. The new park, built largely from the proceeds of Ruth's success, was also largely built to order for Babe Ruth. Although 'Ruth Field' was ultimately rejected in favor of 'Yankee Stadium,' the right field bleachers in 'The House that Ruth Built' soon became

known as 'Ruthville.' As a left-handed batter, most of the Babe's hits went to right field, and Yankee management insured that there would be an ample number of Ruthian round trips by locating the right field bleachers only 296 feet from home plate, behind a fence only 43 inches high. Constructing ballparks to benefit hitters was not an uncommon practice in this era. The arrangement and seating capacity of Yankee Stadium insured that the American League in general and the Yankees in particular would gain an edge on attendance and profits for some time to come.

Babe Ruth redeemed himself for his Series showing of the previous year as his team chalked up their first world championship ever in 1923, defeating the Giants 4-2 in their third straight Series in as many years with that club. Babe's .368 Series average included three homers – two in a row in the second game – a triple, a double and three singles – as well as eight walks. Former Red Sox hurlers Pennock and Bush accounted for three victories, and Shawkey took the fourth. Bob Meusel set a Series record by driving in eight runs. Babe Ruth's slugging and the excitement of the home run game – each team hit five homers – continued to pay off at the box office, where all attendance and financial records were broken. The Yankee share of $6143.49 was not topped until 1935.

The Washington Senators took their first pennant in 1924, preventing the Yankees from winning four pennants in a row by a two-game margin. Their victory made them the third American League club to take their first pennant in the twenties, and left St Louis as the only club in the league yet to take a league championship.

Below: Walter Johnson with Captain Edith Ivings of the Salvation Army. The great pitcher's gentle and unassuming nature is as legendary as his exploits on the mound.

Below right: Left fielder Charles Jamieson played for Cleveland from 1919 to 1932. In 1923 he smashed 222 hits, with a .345 batting average.

The well-balanced and determined Washington team featured hurler Walter Johnson, now 36, again demonstrating why he was called the greatest pitcher in American League history by compiling a 23-7 record in his 18th year with the Senators. Johnson also led the league in strikeouts, shutouts and ERA's. Firpo Marberry broke all relief records with 15 saves. 'The Boy Wonder' – playing manager Stanley 'Bucky' Harris – 27, who with Peckinpaugh led the league in double plays, spurred his team on to victory with a spirit so tough even Ty Cobb thought twice about sliding into second base. Herold 'Muddy' Ruel, a Yankee castoff who reached the Senators via Boston, provided excellent catching.

For once, Johnson received solid support from his hitters. Goose Goslin hit .344 to lead the league in RBI's (the first Senator ever to do so), Sam Rice came back with .344 and Joe Judge hit .324. The Senators' victory was greeted with an emotional reaction that was extraordinary even for the twenties, including a cup and a special commendation from President Coolidge, in part because it enabled Walter Johnson to compete in a World Series for the first time in his magnificent career.

President and Mrs Coolidge attended three of the games played in Washington in what turned out to be

Left: Second baseman Bucky Harris played for the Washington Senators for ten years, ending his career with Detroit in 1931. In the 1924 World Series, he batted .333 and slammed two home runs to help the Tigers win the title. He was elected to the Hall of Fame in 1975.

Below: Hall of Famer Leon Allen 'Goose' Goslin spent most of his 18-year career with the Senators, but played for the St Louis Browns and the Tigers as well. His superb batting helped bring the Senators to four league pennants, beginning with their first ever in 1924, in which Goslin hit three home runs.

Above: During the ten years that outfielder Robert William 'Long Bob' Meusel played for the New York Yankees (1920-1929), he played in six World Series.

the most exciting World Series in years. The hard-fought contest between the Senators and the Giants was not settled until the 12th inning of the seventh game. Sir Walter lost the two games he started, but performed heroically in the seventh game. Called in from the bull pen to face the Giants in the ninth inning, Johnson held them at bay until a string of bad luck for the Giants enabled Muddy Ruel to score the winning run from second in the 12th inning.

Washington repeated easily in 1925, finishing eight and a half games ahead of the Athletics, a team Connie Mack was patiently rebuilding. Walter Johnson turned in a 20-7 season, his 12th and last 20-game year, but for once (only the second time in his 19 years with the club) he was aided by another 20-game winner. Spitballer Stanley Coveleski was 20-5 as he registered his fifth consecutive 20-win year in 1925, his first year with the Senators.

Both pitchers received solid support from their batters, but even after a 3-1 lead in the Series, the Senators dropped the championship to the Pirates. Johnson won the first and fourth games, holding the Pirates to one run in each of these contests, but gave up 15 hits in the final deciding game. Bucky Harris was severely criticised for not pulling Johnson from this game by league president Ban Johnson, who accused the Washington manager of losing the Series for the sake of 'maudlin sentiment.'

Primarily because Babe Ruth suffered from an intestinal abscess which required surgery – 'the stomach-ache that was heard round the world' – and didn't return to the lineup until June, the Yankees finished seventh in 1925. This was the second and only other time in 14 years that the Great Man did not win or tie the league home run championship. Teammate Bob Meusel led the league in 1925 with 33, leading also in RBI's with 138. The best Ruth could do was 25, with a .290 season average (statistics that would cause modern players to ask for a raise).

The Bambino, who returned to his dangerous high-living as soon as he was able and sooner than he should have, aggravating his health problems and jeopardizing the Yankees' bid for the pennant, faced a serious showdown with manager Huggins, who sus-

Right: Brothers Joe and Luke Sewell played shortstop and catcher for Cleveland during the twenties.

pended him indefinitely and fined him $5000 (a new record). Outraged – more at the suspension than the fine – Ruth vowed that either he or Huggins must go ('either he quits or I quit'), but owner Ruppert stood behind his manager, forcing Ruth to back down and clean up his act.

Ill-health and suspension combined, Ruth missed about one-third of the 1925 season, playing in 98 games. It is a remarkable testimony to his popularity that in 1925 Yankee attendance also fell by about one-third, from slightly over one million in 1924 to just under 700,000 in 1925. Estimates of losses to the club due to his illness ranged as high as $500,000.

In 1926 Babe Ruth came back strong, hitting 47 home runs and averaging .372, and the Yankees began their second string of three consecutive pennants. Washington finished fourth as the great Walter Johnson, now 38, proved he was mortal and slumped to 15-16 in his last full season. It was a tight race, the sixth-place Tigers finishing only 12 games behind the Yankees. Third, six games behind, were Mack's Athletics; and second, finishing three games behind the Yankees, were the Indians, whose right-hander George Uhle completed 32 of 36 starts for a 27-11 record. Indian shortstop Joe Sewell, the man who couldn't be struck out, had an off year in 1926 with six strikeouts, a figure double his 1925 total.

The Yankee resurgence in 1926 owed much to some serious team rebuilding. Aging veteran Whitey Witt was replaced by outstanding center fielder and leadoff batter Earle Combs, and shortstop Everett Scott ended his record 1307 consecutive games in May, replaced by rookie Mark Koenig. Rookie Tony Lazzeri, who had never even seen a major-league game before he came up to the Yankees from the Pacific League to play second base in 1926, quickly became known as 'Push Em Up Tony' for his ability to hit with men on base, and in his rookie year registered an RBI total in the American League second only to Babe Ruth's. With Ruth, Meusel and Joe Dugan still in top form, the winning combination was completed by the addition of 23-year-old New Yorker Lou Gehrig.

In a story that has now become legend, Gehrig got his start as a Yankee regular on 2 June 1925 when

Hall of Famer Earle Bryan Combs – 'The Kentucky Colonel' – played center field for the Yankees from 1924 to 1935, ending his 12-year career with a .325 batting average and a .350 Series batting average.

veteran first baseman Wally Pipp, who hit .295 and led the league in triples the year before, told manager Huggins he had a headache. Gehrig played as a substitute, and from that day on this great hitter compiled the unsurpassed record of playing in 2130 consecutive games, ending on 2 May 1939, when he benched himself. Two months later he learned he had a fatal illness. Pipp never got in the starting Yankee lineup again, and was soon traded to Cincinnati.

Known as the 'Iron Horse' for his strength, durability and consistency, the courteous Gehrig, whose mother, until he married, sometimes accompanied him on road trips, and who had left engineering studies at Columbia to join the Yankees, was far removed in personality from the flamboyant Babe Ruth, in whose shadow he played for most of his career, but his record needs no apology. In the 11 years 1927-1937, his home run totals were 47, 27, 35, 41, 46, 34, 32, 49, 30, 49 and 37. Gehrig five times led the league in RBI's, twice in homers and hit as many as 52 doubles and 18 triples a season.

When he retired due to an illness rare enough to be named after him, Gehrig's 493 home runs and 1991 RBI's were second only to Babe Ruth's career totals. Only Ruth and Hank Aaron have ever surpassed his RBI's; and only Ruth and Ted Williams have ever bettered his lifetime slugging percentage of .632. Gehrig's lifetime batting average of .340 places him among the very best hitters in baseball. If he had not been cut down in his prime at 34, some statistics might now be written differently.

Despite four homers by Ruth, including three in one game, and a .300 Series average, complemented by a .348 average from Gehrig in his first Series appearance, the Yankees lost the 1926 championship to the Cardinals in one of the most dramatic Series on record. Pitching for the Cards, National League great Grover Cleveland Alexander turned in a virtuoso performance, fanning Tony Lazzeri in a memorable seventh-inning, seventh-game cliffhanger to save the day for St Louis.

In 1927 the Yankees were so hot that there was no American League pennant race. Considered by many the greatest team ever, the 1927 Yankees never fell from first place, and ended the season a league-record 19 games ahead of the second-place Athletics. Their 110 wins and .714 percentage remained the best in league history until the amazing Cleveland victory of 1954. Their team total of 158 home runs was almost three times that of the next best, the Athletics' 56. Even Philadelphia's seven future Hall of Famers, with a .303 team batting average and 91 wins, were no match for New York's incredible machine.

Above: Playing in 2130 consecutive games, Yankee Lou Gehrig earned himself the nickname 'The Iron Horse.' More than any other player Gehrig embodied the spirit of baseball at its best. Although disease ended his career tragically in 1939, he was specially honored by being elected to the Hall of Fame that same year.
Right: Lou Gehrig congratulates Babe Ruth as he crosses the plate after hitting his 60th home run in 151 at bats, in 1927. During the 11 years Gehrig and Ruth played together, they averaged 78 home runs a year and boosted the Yankees to five World Series.

Far left: Washington right fielder Edgar Charles 'Sam' Rice (1915-1933) hits a long ball.

Left: Second baseman 'Poosh 'Em Up' Tony Lazzeri played for the Yankees from 1926 to 1937, earning his nickname by averaging 96 RBI's a year during that time. He ended his career with the National League, with a .292 batting average.

Each member of this superb New York team turned in one of his finest individual seasons. Ruth hit 60 home runs, four more than any other team in the league except the Yankees, drove in 164 runs, and batted .356. Lou Gehrig, 1927's MVP, led the league with 175 RBI's, and scored 149 runs for a .373 average. His 218 hits included 52 doubles, 18 triples and 47 homers.

Until late in the season, Yankee fans were gratified to watch an intramural home run contest between Ruth and Gehrig, who together accounted for almost 25 percent of the American League home runs hit that year. As late as mid-August, Gehrig was leading Ruth 38-36. The Yankees' Earle Combs batted .356 and got 231 hits. Lazzeri and Meusel joined Ruth and Gehrig in driving in over 100 runs each – 102 and 103 – and registered averages of .309 and .337 respectively. Gehrig hit behind Ruth in the lineup, the most devastating one-two punch in history, and was followed by Meusel and Lazzeri. This terrorizing Yankee lineup became known to pitchers throughout the league as 'Murderers' Row.'

The Yankee team of 1927 batted a combined average of .307. Ruth, Gehrig and Lazzeri were the top three American Leaguers in home runs; Ruth and Gehrig led the league in slugging; Gehrig, Ruth and Combs led in total bases; Gehrig and Ruth were first and second in RBI's; Combs and Gehrig were the top two in hits; Ruth, Gehrig and Combs were the top three in runs scored; Gehrig led in doubles; and Combs and Gehrig were the top two in triples.

The Yankees failed to secure only two offensive categories in 1927. George Sisler led the league with 27 stolen bases, and Harry Heilmann took the batting championship in an exciting duel with Al Simmons that was not resolved until the final day of the season. Going six for eight in a doubleheader against the Indians, Heilmann finally passed Simmons and ended the season with a .398 average, only one hit short of .400.

The Yankee sluggers were supported by one of the strongest pitching staffs of the era. Waite Hoyt went 22-7, Herb Pennock 19-8, spitballer Urban Shocker 18-6, Dutch Ruether 13-6, and George Pipgras 10-3. Sinkerball artist rookie Wilcy Moore turned in a sensational never-repeated year as the league's leading relief pitcher, 19-7, and led the league with an ERA of 2.28. Only the Yankees' catching, which was average, was less than outstanding in 1927.

The Bronx Bombers crowned their pennant success by flattening the Pirates four straight in the

World Series, the first time an American League club had taken the Series without a loss. The story goes that before the first game, the Pirates came out as the Yankees were taking batting practice, and were so awed by watching Ruth, Gehrig, Meusel and Lazzeri knock successive balls into the bleachers that they never recovered.

The Yankees repeated in 1928 but not without a struggle. Despite another outstanding season from both Ruth and Gehrig, the Yankees' early July lead of 13 and a half games slowly dissipated as Lazzeri, Dugan, Meusel and Koenig suffered injuries and missed games. Strong seasons from Hoyt and Pipgras, who won 23 and 24, saved the day, but Pennock, with 17 wins, developed arm trouble late in the season and never again performed as well as he had.

On 8 September Connie Mack's rebuilt Athletics pulled into first place with a half-game lead. But on 9 September, before a record crowd of 85,264 fans at Yankee Stadium, the Yankees proved they were still champions by taking both games of a doubleheader from the Athletics, 3-0 and 7-3. After taking another game from Philadelphia the next day, they stayed on top for the rest of the season, clinching the pennant two days before the season ended. The Red Sox finished last again.

Ty Cobb and Tris Speaker closed their active careers at the end of the 1928 season. Another era of sorts had ended the year before when American League President Ban Johnson resigned after losing his long power struggle with Commissioner Landis, and all-time great pitcher Walter Johnson quit the game with a lifetime total of 416 wins.

Cobb and Speaker and the third member of their famous batting trio, Eddie Collins, now relegated to pinch-hitting, were all playing for Connie Mack in 1928. Once again the Athletics lost to the Yankees despite seven future Hall of Famers, but this year they narrowed the Yankees' lead from 19 to two and a half games. If age had not caught up with Cobb in the final weeks of the season and if Mack had figured out exactly where to put twenty-year-old slugger Jimmie Foxx in the lineup, the story might have been different.

The Yankees vanquished the Cardinals 4-0 in the 1928 Series. Following their sweep of the Pirates the year before, this gave the club the new record of eight consecutive victories in two consecutive Series. But the real story of the Series was the still unequalled hitting of Ruth and Gehrig, who dominated the championship as no two men ever have. In an incredible display of slugging, Ruth hit .625, still the highest batting average in World Series history, launched three homers in one Series game, drove in four runs, and scored nine. Gehrig hit .545, banged out four homers, drove in nine runs and scored five.

In 1929 the team that had made the amazing Yankees sweat in 1928 was unstoppable. Connie

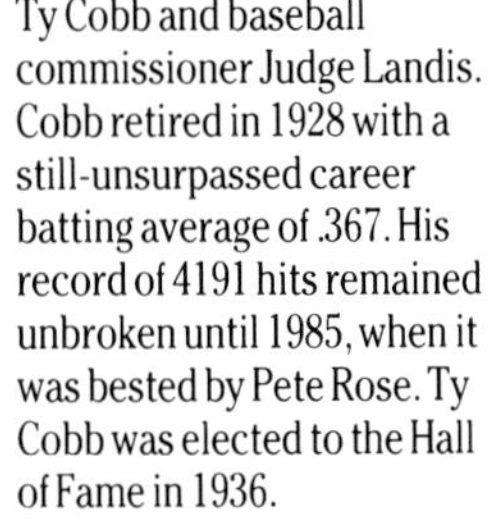

Ty Cobb and baseball commissioner Judge Landis. Cobb retired in 1928 with a still-unsurpassed career batting average of .367. His record of 4191 hits remained unbroken until 1985, when it was bested by Pete Rose. Ty Cobb was elected to the Hall of Fame in 1936.

Mack's Athletics took their first pennant in 15 years, beating out the second-place Yankees by a comfortable 18-game margin. The Yankees could muster only one league leader in 1929, Babe Ruth, who took the honors in homers and slugging. To complete the sad picture, New York manager Miller Huggins fell ill and died in September.

The team painstakingly assembled by Mack and the Shibes was the last dynasty formed exclusively from players purchased from minor-league clubs. Branch Rickey's farm system, which had done so well for the Cardinals, was well on its way to becoming accepted practice in the big leagues. The players Mack purchased from the minors finished second in 1925, third in 1926, second in 1927 and second in 1928 before all the pieces fell into place, and the Athletics took three pennants in a row.

Robert Moses 'Lefty' Grove and George Earnshaw, the mainstays of the Athletic pitching staff, both came from Jack Dunn's Baltimore club. Grove, possibly the best left-hander in history, threw a ball so fast it looked 'like a piece of white thread coming to the plate.' He came to Philadelphia in 1925 and quickly proved he was worth his $100,600 purchase price (Dunn wanted more than the $100,000 he'd received for Ruth) by leading the league in strikeouts for seven straight years, beginning in 1926.

In the Athletics' 1929-1931 championship seasons, Grove won a total of 83 games and lost only 15. When he did lose, which was rare, he was famous for smashing up the locker room and throwing anything that wasn't tied down. The 300-game-winning Hall of Famer was what was called a 'great competitor,' meaning he was mean. Grove had no compunction about throwing at opposing batters, including Babe Ruth, and even at his own teammates in batting practice. He did say that he never aimed for the head, and he never shaved Lou Gehrig, asserting 'It was best not to wake him up.'

George Earnshaw did not have the staying power of Grove, but at his peak he was right behind him, winning 67 and losing only 28 games in the A's three consecutive pennant years. Big left-hander Rube Walberg, another purchase from Dunn, also won

Hall of Famer Lefty Grove pitched for Philadelphia from 1925 to 1933. 20-, 28- and 31-game seasons in 1929, 1930 and 1931 helped bring the A's to the Series all three years.

At 6′ 11″ and 210 pounds, righthander George 'Moose' Earnshaw was an imposing pitcher. During the six years he pitched for the A's, he had three 20-game seasons, winning 98 games and losing 58.

Catcher Mickey Cochrane leaps for a tag in a close play. An essential component on one of Connie Mack's most laudable teams, 'Black Mike' played for the A's from 1925 to 1933, then for Detroit from 1934 to 1937. He was elected to the Hall of Fame in 1947.

many games. Max Bishop, regular second baseman during Mack's winning years, came from Dunn's Baltimore club, as did regular shortstop Joe Boley, who gave up his position in 1931 to the younger Dib Williams.

Catching for Grove in his heyday was Gordon 'Mickey' Cochrane. A Hall of Famer considered by many the best catcher of all time, Cochrane still holds the all-time highest lifetime average for a big-league catcher, at .320. Fast enough to bat third and occasionally first on a team with exceptionally good hitters, during the A's pennant-winning years Cochrane hit .331, .357 and .349, three of his nine .300-plus seasons. Even when he didn't hit outstandingly, as in his MVP year of 1928 when he hit .293, Cochrane's natural leadership inspired the team. His fire and dash – and occasional rage – were in every way on a par with Grove's.

Following Cochrane in the batting order were outfielder Al Simmons and first baseman Jimmie Foxx, a lineup almost as lethal as the Yankees' Murderers' Row. Foxx, a natural athlete with a temperament and outlook on life much like Ruth's, was perhaps the strongest man ever to play the game, crushing the balls he connected with out of shape. Known as 'The Beast,' his professional career began at age 16, and he was only 21 in 1929 when he finally became the regular on first base and turned in his first great season. That year Foxx hit .354, drove in 118 runs and launched 33 homers, the first of 12 consecutive seasons in which he hit at least 30 homers, a record unequalled even by Ruth. Only twice in those 12 years did his average fall below .300. In 1932 Foxx came close to breaking Ruth's 60-homer record, hitting 58; and in 1938, he hit 50, leading the league with 175 RBI's, a .349 batting average and a .704 slugging percentage. Foxx twice led the league in batting, and was three times elected Most Valuable Player. When he retired in 1945, one of the very few to hit over 500 homers, his 534 lifetime record was second only to Ruth's 714.

Testy Al Simmons, for whom Mack traded several players and $40,000 in 1924, paid out handsomely as a superb left fielder and one of the best right-handed hitters in baseball history. In his prime during his eight years with the A's from 1925 to 1932, Simmons four times topped .380, averaging .364, and drove in over 100 runs each year. He drove in over 100 runs in each of his first 11 years (as many as 165 per season), amassing a reputation as a great run-producer, and hit over 30 homers three times in the four years from 1929 to 1932. Simmons did all this with a batting style that was technically all wrong, breaking a cardinal rule of batting by stepping away from the pitch

Right-hander Howard Ehmke pitched for the Athletics from 1927 to 1930. Ehmke struck out 13 batters in the first game of the 1929 World Series, which the A's won 3-1. Philadelphia went on to defeat the Cubs four games to one.

instead of into it, supposedly robbing himself of power by 'putting his foot in the bucket.' His long bat and unorthodox style helped him to two league batting championships, the Hall of Fame, and a respectable .334 lifetime average.

Outfielders Bing Miller and Mule Haas also hit .300 for Mack's winning teams. Jimmy Dykes, a good fielder and solid hitter who had been with the club since 1918, held down first base, and the Athletics were well-supplied with reserves. All in all, the A's combination of Grove, Cochrane, Foxx and Simmons compares favorably with Yankee Hall of Famers Hoyt, Pennock, Ruth, Gehrig and Combs.

Beside the awesome ascendancy of the A's, what finally derailed the Yankee train in 1929 was the collapse of their pitching staff. Ruth was still hitting home runs and Gehrig was swinging into his prime, but Pennock was permanently weakened by his sore arm, Wilcy Moore never repeated his outstanding 1927 season and Hoyt just lost it. Other things being almost equal, Grove's 20 wins and Earnshaw's 24 did the trick. Finishing in second place, 18 games behind the A's, the Yankees, who introduced the use of numbers on players' uniforms in 1929, a helpful device soon adopted by all clubs, were still better off than the Boston Red Sox, who finished last again and scored fewer runs than any other club that season while playing in a park that was notoriously friendly to hitters.

Mack got off to a surprising start in the Series by using Howard Ehmke, instead of one of his regulars, to open against the Cubs. Ehmke kept the Cubs off-balance with his slowballs, winning 3-1 and setting a record of 13 Series strikeouts – a record that stood until Carl Erskine broke it in 1953. In the fourth game, Al Simmons banged out a homer to open a record-breaking Series inning in which the A's scored ten runs. Mule Haas, one of 15 A's who came to bat that inning, hit an inside-the-park three-run homer.

Two days later, with President Hoover in attendance, Haas hit another homer, and Bing Miller drove in the winning run with a double to clinch the Series. With Jimmy Dykes hitting .421 for the Series, Cochrane hitting .400, Miller hitting .368, and Foxx hitting .350 and slugging two homers, Mack crowned his first pennant of the decade with a 4-1 Series win, and showed that his boys had the stuff to move into the next decade with continuing dominance.

Aloysius Harry 'Bucketfoot Al' Simmons played left field for the Philadelphia Athletics from 1924 to 1932, winning the league batting title twice during those years and averaging .357. In the three Series he played for the A's, he smashed six homers, five doubles and 12 singles. Simmons was elected to the Hall of Fame in 1953.

Lou Gehrig, batboy John McBride and Babe Ruth at the 1933 All-Star game.

CHAPTER THREE
Heroes of the Depression

"To be considered great, a team must repeat."

Connie Mack

Repeat is what Mack's men did in 1930, and again in 1931. The Athletics who finished eight games ahead of the Senators in 1930 were the same team that left the Yankees 18 games behind in 1929, with Jimmy Dykes now playing third base on a regular basis. Al Simmons led the league with a .381 average, and he and teammate Jimmie Foxx together drove in 321 runs for Philadelphia – six runs less than the Gehrig-Ruth total – as they pushed their team to 102 victories in this hit-happy season.

In 1930 the owners, in response to the fans' enthusiastic reception to the hitting game, pumped more life into the ball than ever before. The American League batted .288 overall, with teams averaging better than five runs per game each – only the Red Sox failed to average over four runs per game. Three players registered slugging percentages over .700. Over in the National League, six clubs posted team batting averages of over .300. (By comparison, in 1968 only six players in the National League hit .300 or better.)

In the midst of this hitting carnage, the A's Lefty Grove won 28 games, lost five, and struck out 209 batters, posting a league-leading ERA of 2.54. Grove's ERA, remarkable for 1930, led Cleveland's Wes Ferrell, who posted a 3.31 ERA and won 25 games on his way to setting a record by winning over 20 games in each of his first four years in the majors, beginning in 1929. Ferrell, who with Detroit's 'Mechanical Man' Charlie Gehringer and Washington's shortstop Joe Cronin, turned in an outstanding performance in 1930, would take two more 20-game seasons, both with the Red Sox.

Right-hander Wesley Cheek Ferrell pitched for the Cleveland Indians for seven seasons (1927-33), then for the Boston Red Sox, Washington Senators, New York Yankees, Brooklyn Dodgers and Boston Braves, ending his career in 1941. The tall Southerner pitched six 20-game seasons during his 15-year career.

Babe Ruth, with 49 round trippers, was still the league's home run king in 1930. Hitting .359, his 153 RBI's were fourth-ranked in the league, following Philadelphia's Al Simmons (165) and Jimmie Foxx (156). Yankee teammate Lou Gehrig led the pack with 174 RBI's and hit .379. Combs hit .344, and catcher Bill Dickey, proving himself to be in the same league as catching great Mickey Cochrane, hit .339 in his second season with the Bombers. Once again it was the failure of New York's pitching staff that kept the hard-slugging Yankee club out of the race.

The Athletics followed up their 1929 Series victory by taking the 1930 Series from the Cardinals, 4-2, after dropping the first two games. This was the third time an American League club took four games in a row from their National League opponents. For Connie Mack, the win was his fifth world title, a record for a manager up to that date, but it was also to be his last. Despite an outstanding team that would repeat again in 1931, no one could have chosen a worse time to establish a dynasty. With the Wall Street failure cutting incomes everywhere, Mack found himself squeezed between the high salaries of his stars and a steadily declining attendance.

As the Depression deepened, attendance declined with the nation's financial health. Total baseball receipts of $17 million in 1929 slid to a low of $10.8 million in 1933, then climbed slowly to $21.5 million in 1939, followed by a wartime slump, then a new height of $68.1 million in 1948. During the hard years, baseball provided the public with a chance to at least temporarily forget the harsh realities of its economic winter and supplied superstars to fire the imagination. But this must have been small consolation for Connie Mack, who watched his team's attendance fall from 830,000 in 1929 to only 300,000 in 1933, the third straight year of serious decline. Mack also lost heavily in the market crash of 1929. Desperate for cash, he once again began dismantling his team and selling his stars.

In 1931, however, the Athletics were still intact. Spearheaded by an incredible MVP year from pitcher Lefty Grove, the club gave Mack his ninth and last pennant, placing him in position to become the first manager to win three straight World Series. The A's 107 victories were the highest win total of Mack's career, and their 1931 percentage of .704 was the second best in American League history. Al Simmons, chief accomplice to the A's star pitcher, led the league for the second straight year with a batting average of .390.

Lefty Grove won 31 games and lost only four. Not since Smokey Joe Wood's 34-5 season in 1912 and Walter Johnson's 36-7 record in the following year had an American League pitcher so outdistanced and outclassed all the competition. Grove's 16-game winning streak that season in fact tied the league record set by Wood and Johnson. Only one other pitcher in the league, New York's Lefty Gomez, with 2.63, posted an ERA under 3.00 in 1931. Grove's ERA was 2.05. He also led the league in wins, percentage (.886), complete games (27) and strikeouts.

The scores of the four games he didn't win were 7-5, 4-3, 2-1 and 1-0. His attempt at 17 straight victories was crushed when outfielder Jim Moore misjudged a fly ball. In a classic display of the Grove rage, the great competitor commemorated the occasion by ripping up his uniform and tearing steel lockers off the wall.

The Athletics of 1931 featured winning streaks of 17 straight in May and 13 in July. The Yankees, in their first season under manager Joe McCarthy, saw continued outstanding slugging from Ruth and Gehrig, who tied for league home run honors with 46 each. Gehrig set the all-time American League RBI record with 184. Teammate Lefty Gomez's 21 wins and 2.63 ERA helped keep the Yanks in second place, but with Red Ruffing having trouble adjusting in his first year after arriving from Boston, New York still fell short of the pitching it needed.

Despite some solid hitting from Al Simmons and Jimmie Foxx in the World Series, the Athletics dropped the championship to the Cardinals in a thrilling

Below: In the 17 years he played catcher for the New York Yankees (1928-46), Hall of Famer Bill Dickey played in eight World Series.

Above: Charlie Gehringer played for the Detroit Tigers for his entire 19-year career (1924-42). His outstanding defensive talent at second base was complemented by his superb batting. Gehringer won the league batting title in 1937 with a .371 average, and finished his career with a batting average of .320.

Above: Johnny Allen pitched for the New York Yankees from 1932 to 1935, then for Cleveland for five years. He finished up his career in the National League.

Opposite: Third baseman and sometime-shortstop Cecil Howell Travis joined the Washington Senators in 1933 and played his entire 12-year career with that team, finishing up in 1947 with a .314 batting average.

seven-game contest. In addition to the defeat of Mack's powerhouse team, 1931 was also marked, sadly, by the sudden deaths of American League president Ernest S Barnard and former president Ban Johnson. After 20 years of service as league secretary, Will Harridge became the new league president.

After the 1930 season, even the owners realized that their formula for success had been mixed a little too rich, and over the winter they squeezed some of the juice out of the ball. Not surprisingly, in 1931 team, league and individual batting averages declined dramatically. With the Great Depression tightening its grip on the land, contraction was felt everywhere. By 1933 American League attendance was off at least one and a half million from 1929, only 60 percent of what it had been in the heyday of the twenties. Forced to sell his stars to survive, Connie Mack began by shipping Al Simmons, Mule Haas and Jimmy Dykes to the White Sox for $150,000. By the 1936 season, practically all of his big names were gone except Jimmie Foxx, and Foxx soon went to the Red Sox, where he had some of the best years of his career.

The demise of the Athletics brought about a change in the balance of power in the American League. 1932 saw the Yankees back on top, ending the Athletics' three-year reign, just as the Athletics had ended the Yankees' three-in-a-row in 1929. Continuing the theme of reversal, the 1932 Bombers posted 107 wins – the same as Mack's boys in 1931 – and led the A's by 13 games, half a game less than the second-place A's had bested the Yanks in the preceding year.

The team Joe McCarthy steered to the championship in his second year of managing the Yankees was built largely of regulars from the Huggins regime, fortified with the pitching that had been lacking the three years previous. Babe Ruth, now 37, managed 41 home runs and a .341 average; Lou Gehrig continued to blast away with consistent excellence; and Combs, Lazzeri, Pennock, Pipgras and the more newly arrived Bill Dickey continued to turn in solid performances. But it was McCarthy's careful handling of the pitching that made all the difference. Vernon 'Lefty' Gomez compiled a 24-7 year, Red Ruffing went 18-7 and rookie Johnny Allen pitched 17-4.

Jimmie Foxx established himself as the league slugging king, hitting 58 home runs, and also led the league in runs (151) and RBI's (169). In 1932, the first of his three MVP years, he got 213 hits and averaged .364, just three points shy of league-leading Dale Alexander, (whom the Red Sox acquired from Detroit in mid-season). Philadelphia's Lefty Grove, who was 79-14 for the previous three years, actually lost 10 games in 1932, winning 25, and posting a league-leading ERA of 2.84.

The Yankees demolished the Cubs in the Series four games straight, the third straight Series sweep for the New York club. For Yankee manager McCarthy, who had been dropped by the Chicago club in the last week of the 1930 season for failing to bring owner Philip Wrigley a world championship, the victory must have been particularly sweet. The Yankees, hitting .313 as a team, averaged nine runs per game in their devastation of the Cubs.

Lou Gehrig turned in the greatest individual Series performance ever in 1932, hitting .549 for the championship games, his nine hits (he struck out once and walked twice) including three home runs and a double. He scored nine runs and drove in eight. New York's Lazzeri launched two homers too, but as usual it was Babe Ruth, hitting two homers in his tenth and last Series appearance, for a lifetime total of 15 Series homers, who really stole the show.

In the fifth inning of the third game, Ruth pointed to the most distant part of Wrigley Field, and after two strikes launched a homer into the center field bleacher at which he had apparently pointed. Manager McCarthy later insisted Ruth had merely pointed to the Cubs' dugout to silence hecklers, and the truth about the Babe's famous 'called shot' may never be known.

Although McCarthy's Yankees finished second the next three years, New York's purchase of the Newark team in the International League set the stage for a second era of Yankee domination. Placed under the gifted administration of George M Weiss, the Yankees' new farm system was to generate excellent Yankee replacements for years to come.

Batting .287 as a team, the Washington Senators surprised everyone in 1933 by finishing seven games ahead of a Yankee club torn by dissension, and 19 and a half games ahead of an Athletic club which was disappearing on the auction block. In New York, Babe Ruth, in his last season as a .300 hitter and seeking management of the Yankees, led a clique which refused to speak to McCarthy or to any player who did. Meanwhile, youthful Washington playing manager Joe Cronin spirited his club to a victory reminiscent of the Senators' 1924-1925 victories under 'boy wonder' Bucky Harris.

Pitching for the 27-year-old Cronin, a gifted leader who would one day become president of the American League, was Alvin 'General' Crowder, with 24 wins, and Earl Whitehill, with 22, backed up by the

Above: Right-hander Lynwood Thomas 'Schoolboy' Rowe pitched for the Detroit Tigers for nine years, moving to the National League in 1942. He helped the Tigers to three league championships, turning in season wins of 24, 19 and 16 during those years.

Right: Catcher Luke Sewell played for Cleveland from 1921 to 1932, for Washington for two years, for the Chicago White Sox from 1935 to 1938, for Cleveland again in 1939, and ended his playing career in 1942 with the St Louis Browns. As manager of the Browns from 1941 to 1946 he won one league championship, then managed four more years for the Cincinnati National League team.

best infield Washington had ever seen. Joe Kuhel covered first, Buddy Myer second, Cronin was at short, and Ossie Bleuge covered third with a dazzling display of defensive efficiency. Luke Sewell was solid behind the plate.

Cronin, batting .309 and driving in 118 runs, showed the way to the hard-hitting outfield of Heinie Manush, Goose Goslin and Fred Schulte. The Washington whackers launched few spectacular homers, but hit with a regularity and consistency sufficient to compile the league-leading team average.

Jimmie Foxx took another triple crown in 1933 and repeated as the league's Most Valuable Player, hitting 48 home runs, batting in 163 runs and scoring 125 runs. His batting average was .356. Teammate Lefty Grove, in his last year with the A's, led the league in wins for the last time with a 24-8 season, and former teammate Al Simmons, now with the White Sox, became the last American Leaguer to record 200 hits five years in a row in what was his last 200-hit season. The Philadelphia Athletics had already won their last flag. Despite the presence of President Franklin Delano Roosevelt at the third game of the World Series to throw out the first ball, the Senators, who would never win another pennant, dropped the world championship to the New York Giants, four games to one.

In 1934 the Detroit Tigers took their first pennant in

25 years, a win that marked the first time a club outside the eastern division had taken an American League championship since Cleveland in 1920. The key to the Tigers' success was the purchase of catcher Mickey Cochrane from cash-hungry Connie Mack in 1933. As playing manager, Cochrane justified his $100,000 price tag by solving Detroit's pitching problems, turning Lynwood 'Schoolboy' Rowe and Tommy Bridges into certified stars. Rowe took 24 games in 1934, including a 16-game winning streak in midsummer that tied him for the league record with Johnson, Wood and Grove. Bridges, featuring the league's best curve ball, added 22 wins to the Tigers' tally.

Cochrane's hurlers were backed up by the flawless Charlie Gehringer at second, Billy Rogell at short, Marv Owen at third and the hard-hitting outfield of Goose Goslin, Pete Fox, Jo-Jo White and Gerald 'Gee' Walker. Veterans Gehringer and Goslin churned out base hits, but the batting of a young first baseman named Hank Greenberg proved instrumental in compiling the team's .300 average.

Big (6′ 3½″ tall and weighing 210 pounds), awkward, slow and never more than adequate at his defensive position, Hank Greenberg nevertheless realized his boyhood ambition and became one of baseball's all-time great sluggers. Rising above his physical limitations through unremitting hard work, Greenberg as a youth practiced batting until his hands bled, and in the majors once stayed after a night game for more batting practice.

His first season in the big leagues was relatively undistinguished, although he hit .300 or better for each of the first seven seasons of a career interrupted by four and a half years of military service. In 1934, his second year with Detroit, he began to show his stuff, knocking out 26 homers and 63 doubles, only four below the major-league record. The RBI totals for which he was known also began to swell. In 1935, he led the league with 170 RBI's, tied Foxx for home runs with 36, and averaged .328. Playing with Detroit from 1933 to 1946 (he ended his career with Pittsburgh in 1947), Greenberg four times led the league in home runs, socking 58 in 1938, and ended his career with 331, then fifth on the all-time list, and a .313 average. After playing in only 12 games in 1936 because of a broken wrist, Hank turned in his best year in 1937. His 200 hits that season included 40 homers, 14 triples, 49 doubles, 137 runs scored, 183 RBI's – one less than Gehrig's league record – and a .337 average.

The Yankees, who finished seven games behind the Tigers in 1934, featured a triple crown year from Gehrig (49 homers, 165 RBI's, a .363 average), and a fizzle-out from Babe Ruth. For anyone else, 22

Tiger first baseman 'Hammerin' Hank' Greenberg smashes a liner through the gap. During the 12 years he played for Detroit, Henry Benjamin Greenberg helped bring his team to four league championships and two Series victories. Apart from his batting achievements during the season, he turned in a career post-season batting average of .318, with a .624 slugging percentage.

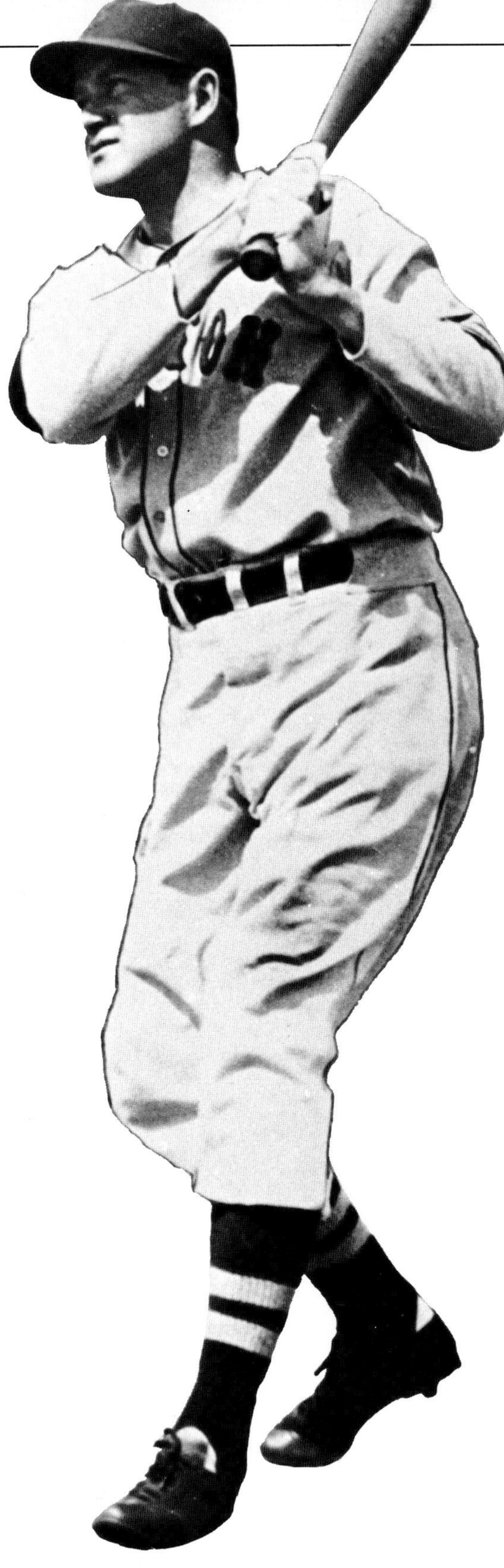

The sparkling shortstop Joe Cronin played the last 11 years of his 20-year career with the Boston Red Sox, and managed the team from 1935 to 1947. He was elected to the Hall of Fame in 1956.

Opposite: Joe DiMaggio touches the plate after blasting a homer out of the park. The legendary 'Joltin' Joe' DiMaggio hit in 56 consecutive games, was named the league's Most Valuable Player three times, clinched the batting title twice and led the league in home runs twice. The Yankee Clipper boosted his team to nine World Series victories. He ended his career with a .325 batting average, and was elected to the Hall of Fame in 1955.

homers, 84 RBI's and a .288 average would have been nothing to sneer at, but for the Babe these numbers spelled the end of the line. After the season, the Yankees let him go, and he ended his career with the National League's Boston Braves in June 1935, after three more homers. Across town, in tribute to the expense and energy lavished upon the club by new owner millionaire Tom Yawkey, the Red Sox, Babe's first major-league team, finished in the first division in 1934 for the first time since 1918.

But the real news in the Yankee camp in 1934 was the performance of four-time 20-game winner Lefty Gomez, who led the league with a 26-5 season and a 2.33 ERA, and also led in winning percentage, complete games, innings pitched, strikeouts and shutouts. A gifted comedian who attributed his success to 'clean living and a fast outfield,' Gomez was troubled by a sore arm throughout his career, but pitched with excellence when his ailment left him alone. After retirement he did well on the banquet circuit with a great stock of baseball stories, and teammates recall he used to speak of inventing a revolving goldfish bowl to save fish the bother of doing all the work.

919,000 enthusiastic spectators jammed Detroit's Navin Field in 1934, setting baseball's season attendance mark (and tripling the Tigers' 1933 total), but Detroit was unable to follow through in the Series, losing to the Cardinals, 4-3. In the final game, which Detroit dropped 11-0, Commissioner Landis was forced to remove Cardinal Joe Medwick from action after an incredible display of vegetable-throwing by loyal Tiger fans who disapproved of Medwick's aggressive slide into third baseman Marv Owen.

Detroit repeated with the same team in 1935. Over one million loyal fans filled Navin Field, a display of support unmatched by any other club in the dark decade. In a close struggle with the Yankees, Detroit's pitching staff paved the way. Bridges was 21-10, Rowe 19-13, Eldon Auker 18-7 and General Crowder 16-10. Hank Greenberg's league-tying 36 homers and league-leading 170 RBI's helped push his team to a .290 overall average. Charlie Gehringer, who rattled pitchers by not swinging until he had two strikes, struck out only 16 times in 610 at bats, hit .330 and drove in 108 runs. Manager Cochrane and outfielder Pete Fox both had .300 seasons. Despite owner Yawkey's outlay of $250,000 for manager-shortstop Joe Cronin and 45 wins from Wes Ferrell and Lefty Grove, the Red Sox finished fourth.

Detroit faced the Chicago Cubs in the 1935 World Series. Both clubs had lost their last four Series matches and were determined to win, but even with the loss of Hank Greenberg due to a broken wrist in the second game, Detroit was victorious this time, 4-2, setting off a celebration in Motor City that did not end until the following morning.

Even without Ruth, the Yankees had finished only three games behind Detroit in 1935. In 1936, with Greenberg's wrist keeping him out for the season, Schoolboy Rowe experiencing a sore arm, and manager Cochrane suffering a nervous breakdown, the Tigers fell 19 and a half games behind New York, and the Yankees took the first of four consecutive pennants. In this string, they would finish 19 and a half, 13, nine and a half, and 17 games ahead of their runners-up. New York manager Joe McCarthy, a perfectionist who had rankled under his three second-place finishes since 1932, put together a team in 1936 that had six men batting over .300 and five men achieving over 100 RBI's, and was propelled by the first of four consecutive 20-win seasons from hurler Red Ruffing. In the next eight seasons, the Yankees would take seven pennants and four consecutive World Series. To the solid Yankee lineup of Lou Gehrig, Tony Lazzeri, Frank Crosetti and Red Rolfe in the infield, with catching great Bill Dickey behind the plate, and George Selkirk and Ben Chapman in the outfield, McCarthy in 1936 added the final ingredient to one of the greatest clubs of all times, a young outfielder named Joe DiMaggio.

In his rookie year, 1936, on a team that averaged seven runs per game and clinched the pennant on 9 September, the earliest date in American League history, Joseph Paul DiMaggio, son of a fisherman, got 206 hits, including 44 doubles, 15 triples and 29 home runs. He scored 132 runs and had 124 RBI's. His batting average was .323, and his virtuoso performance

EW YORK

style and grace, which still captivate spectators on Old-Timer Days, created a following and a mystique second only to that of Babe Ruth, who must remain the most idolized ballplayer of all time. But DiMaggio, whose chemistry with the crowd contained nothing of the salt-of-the-earth appeal of Babe Ruth, must rank as a close second to the Bambino, and he was the object of such hero worship as only a handful of sports stars is ever likely to receive.

Above: Luke Appling, the quiet and efficient shortstop for the Chicago White Sox, played for them his entire 20-year career, during which time he clinched the batting title twice. For a shortstop, his 2218 games and 1424 double plays are second only to Luis Aparicio's record. He ended with a .310 batting average and was elected to the Hall of Fame in 1964.

Right: Speedster and center fielder Ben Chapman played for the Yankees from 1930 to 1936, when he moved to the Senators, then played for several different teams.

in left field, which he played most of the season, revealed a throwing arm that enabled him to lead all American League outfielders in assists, an unusual accomplishment from this position. The next year he improved, hitting .346, driving in 167 runs, scoring 151 times and launching 46 home runs.

In 1933 DiMaggio had been the most desired minor-league player in the country. His San Francisco Seals club decided to hold onto him for another year, figuring his price could only rise, but DiMaggio suffered a knee injury which scared off most would-be purchasers. Yankee scout Bill Essick convinced the Yankees to gamble $25,000 to acquire the 21-year-old player, and in 1935 DiMaggio proved he was not quite damaged goods by batting .398 and collecting 270 hits in 172 Pacific Coast League games.

McCarthy and DiMaggio, who eventually joined Ruffing, Gomez, Gehrig and Dickey in the Hall of Fame, together revamped the Yankee image from one of Ruthian brute strength to one of cool, efficient dominance. McCarthy not only expected his Yankees to win, he expected them to be dignified as well, and got rid of Ben Chapman, a southerner who played outfield with DiMaggio, because he was too emotional.

DiMaggio didn't need to be told to be cool. No one has ever been able to determine whether DiMaggio's enigmatic off-the-field behavior was attributable to snobbishness or insecurity, but his performance on the field renders such considerations inconsequential. His seemingly effortless mastery of the game, his

It is appropriate that the Yankees' precedent-setting four consecutive pennants and four consecutive world championships should begin with the arrival of DiMaggio, but in 1936 he had a lot of help. Most Valuable Player Lou Gehrig led the league with 49 home runs and 130 RBI's; 'Push Em Up Tony' Lazzeri, in his last big year, pushed in 109 runs; and right fielder George Selkirk knocked in 107. Hurler Monte Pearson added 19 wins to Ruffing's 20. The Yanks' ace catcher Bill Dickey knocked in 107 runs and set the American League season record for hits by a catcher, posting an average of .362.

Hitting was heavy throughout the American League in 1936, with five teams hitting over .290, and 18 players driving in over 100 runs. Luke Appling of Chicago led the league with a .388 average, the highest by a shortstop in the century. Leading in RBI's with 162 was Hal Trosky, a regular on first with Cleveland, the American League's strongest second division team, whose Earl Averill led the league in hits and was second only to Appling in batting.

Above: First baseman Hal Trosky swung a heavy bat for Cleveland for nine years (1933-41), averaging .310 and 113 RBI's a season during that time.

Left: Hall of Famer Bob Feller, who took four years out of his brilliant career for combat duty in World War II, became baseball's leading pitching prodigy when he signed on with Cleveland in 1936, at the age of 17. The strong and self-confident farmboy struck out 15 batters in his first major league appearance and broke the major league record for strikeouts with 18 the following year, quickly earning the nickname of 'Rapid Robert.' He pitched 3 no-hitters and finished up in 1956 with a career won-lost record of 266-162.

The Yankees lost the first and the fourth World Series games to the New York Giants, but came out on top to take the first of four consecutive Series. They would lose a total of only three games in all four Series, sweeping their last two championship contests. In 1936 the Yankees took one game from the Giants 18-4, and another 13-5, with seven-run innings in both these lopsided contests. To add insult to injury, the second seven-run inning was the last inning of the sixth and final game. In the second game, Tony Lazerri became the second player ever to hit a World Series grand slam.

Not all the news in the American League in 1936 came from New York. That year also saw the debut of a young player named Bob Feller, pitching for the Cleveland Indians. On 23 August Feller started his first big-league game, and made headlines when he struck out 15 batters, two short of the then-major-league record. On 13 September he struck out 17 Philadelphia Athletics, setting a new American League record and tying Dizzie Dean's major-league record. According to Feller, 'I guess that's when people began to realize I was for real.' Then Feller, at 17 the only real prodigy in baseball history, went home to Van Meter, Iowa, to finish high school.

Feller was mid-America personified, a product of the Iowa corn belt and a former semipro father who tutored him on a baseball diamond he and his father carved out of their farm when Feller was 12. By 1935

Right: Tommy 'Old Reliable' Henrich played outfield for 11 years for the Yankees.

Below: Third baseman Pinky Higgins turned in a .303 batting average and batted in 106 runs during his two years with the Red Sox in 1937 and 1938. Although he played mainly for the A's and Tigers, he ended his career in 1946 with Boston, who came up with the pennant that year.

Feller was pitching semipro ball in Des Moines. In a sequence of events that has since become legendary, Cleveland general manager Cy Slapnicka, in town to look at another player, finally gave in to months of pestering by Feller fans, went to Van Meter to see him play, and wired back that he had just signed 'the greatest pitcher he had ever seen.' The on-the-spot deal was sweetened with an autographed baseball and a dollar bill.

Feller later claimed it took him three years to learn how to pitch in the big leagues. In 1936 he walked 47 men in 62 innings, but he also struck out 76, and recorded his 15- and 17-strikeout games. Two years

later, when he was 19, he set a major-league record by striking out 18 men in one game. His fastball was called by many better than Johnson's, and he also had a curve which moved nearly as fast. By the time he was 22 he had won 107 games, including his first no-hitter.

Although four years in the service robbed him of spectacular career statistics, Feller recorded more low-hit games than any pitcher in baseball, including 11 one-hit games. No other pitcher has recorded more than five. His three no-hitters tied Cy Young's record. In his day he set major-league records for most strikeouts in a season (348 in 1946) as well as for most strikeouts in a single game. Ranked with the greatest American League pitchers, Johnson and Grove, Feller was one of the most exciting players since Babe Ruth, and a major draw. Fellow players considered him in a class by himself, and held him in particular awe. According to Ted Williams, 'He had more stuff than anybody.'

The Yankees repeated in 1937, winning 102 games for the second straight season and finishing 13 games ahead of the Tigers. Despite outstanding individual players who led the majors in hitting – including MVP Charlie Gehringer, who took league honors with a .371 average – the Tigers suffered from pitchers who skidded after manager-catcher Mickey Cochrane was severely beaned in May. The incident, reminiscent of Chapman's death, ended Cochrane's playing career. Elsewhere in the league, the Browns stirred memories of their 1922 power as each of their three regular outfielders hit above .325.

But it was the Yankees all the way. Gehrig had his last great year with 37 homers, 159 RBI's and a .351 average, and DiMaggio, in his second year with the Yanks, led the league with 46 home runs. New to the Yankees' indelible cast of characters was Tommy Henrich, an outfielder who personified the solid Yankee players who stood behind their superstars and gave the team its depth. Acquired as a free agent after a fierce bidding war, 'Old Reliable' Henrich was always capable of making the big play or getting the clean hit when it was needed. He hit .320 in 67 games in 1937, and played through 1950.

Although the Giants took one game from the Yankees in the 1937 Series, McCarthy's boys breezed to a 4-1 victory that ranks as one of the easiest Series wins ever for an American League team. Chalking up a total of 20 victories out of 22 Series games since 1927, the Bombers became the first club to take six world championships. Tony Lazzeri, in his last World Series with the Yanks, led both teams with a .400 average, including one homer, and Lou Gehrig hit his tenth and last homer in World Series play. For many, the highlight of the Series was Lefty Gomez's pause on the mound to observe a plane pass overhead.

Hank Greenberg, one of the greatest in Detroit's long history of great hitters, riveted attention throughout the 1938 season by methodically compiling a total of 58 homers. With five games left to play in the season, he was only two round trips short of Babe Ruth's 1927 record total. Big Henry failed to hit any long ones in the first three of these games, and had the misfortune to face Bob Feller in the fourth, the opener of a doubleheader against the Indians. Although Feller lost the game 4-1, he set a major-league record by fanning 18 players, and kept all of Greenberg's balls in the park. In the second game, Hank managed three singles, but that was all he wrote. Jimmie Foxx, now with Boston, also turned in an outstanding year, winning his third MVP, launching 50 home runs, and leading the league in average (.349), RBI's (175) and in slugging percentage (.704).

The 1938 Yankees, in manager McCarthy's opinion the best team he ever fielded, finished nine and a half games ahead of the Red Sox. Once again they had little on their minds through September. The Yankee farm empire, patiently assembled by George Weiss, began to pay off, adding such players as Joe Gordon to New York's durable veterans. In fact, some felt the Yankees' Newark farm team was so good it belonged in the majors. In his rookie year, Gordon, who replaced Lazzeri at second, hit 25 homers and established a great double-play combination with Frankie Crosetti. Henrich was now a starter in right field, and pitching was solid throughout, with Red Ruffing winning 21, Lefty Gomez 18, Monte Pearson 16 and farmer Spud Chandler 14. Relief pitcher Johnny Murphy recorded his first big year with 11 saves.

Lou Gehrig, who had complained of lumbago at the 1937 World Series and had for the first time turned in a championship performance that was less than extraordinary, recorded his weakest year since his first with the Yankees. Lou's 29 homers, 114 RBI's and .295 average were considerably more than a feeble effort, but were ominously low by his standards.

Hall of Famer Red Ruffing pitched 14 years for the Yankees (1931-46), achieving four consecutive 20-game seasons from 1936 to 1939.

Above: Spud Chandler worked his right-handed magic for the Yankees for 11 years, ending with a .717 winning percentage.

Left: Outfielder Doc Cramer played mainly for the A's, Red Sox and Tigers, finishing with a .296 career batting average.

The Yanks, who swept the Cubs 4-0, experienced difficulty only in the second game, when Dizzy Dean pitched his club to a 3-2 lead in the eighth inning. McCarthy, who now had the satisfaction of taking the world championship from his former team twice, also became the first manager in baseball history to win three consecutive World Series. Bill Dickey and Joe Gordon both hit .400 for the Series, with Gordon, in his first Series appearance, driving in six runs.

For the first time in Series competition, Lou Gehrig did not get an extra base hit or drive in a run. At spring training in 1939, his clothes hung on him like a sack, and his reflexes were shot. In the eight games he played at the start of the season, he managed only four singles in 28 at bats. When his teammates praised him for handling a routine play without error, Gehrig considered his .143 average and asked manager McCarthy to take him out of the game. McCarthy, who feared Gehrig wouldn't be able to get out of the way of a pitched ball, had been unwilling to take captain Gehrig out of the lineup. When the crowd at the stadium on 2 May 1939 heard that Gehrig was ending his record of 2130 consecutive games, they gave him a standing ovation. Lou sat down and wept, as did some of his teammates, until Lefty Gomez rallied them out onto the field. Gehrig remained in uniform for the rest of the season, but never played another game.

Two months later Gehrig learned he was suffering from amyotrophic lateral sclerosis, a rare neuromuscular disease with no known cure. On 4 July 1939 before a crowd of 60,000 which had gathered at

Yankee Stadium for a doubleheader and a special occasion called Lou Gehrig Appreciation Day, the Iron Man received a bear hug from Babe Ruth, and announced in a simple speech that despite the doctors' predictions, 'I consider myself the luckiest man on the face of the earth.' He lived to see himself voted into the Hall of Fame, and was the first Yankee to have his number retired. Lou Gehrig died on 2 June 1941.

The arrival of Charlie Keller from the Yankees' Newark farm team helped somewhat to replace the gap left by Gehrig. Hitting over .300 in his rookie season, 'King Kong' Keller took up position in left field, and with DiMaggio in center and Henrich in right formed one of the great outfields in baseball history. By midseason the Yankees were back on track, ending the year with 106 wins – the most of any year of their four-year streak – and a finish 17 games in front of a strong Red Sox team.

Strong on offense, the 1939 Yankees had five .300 hitters, and four players – DiMaggio, Gordon, Dickey, and Selkirk – who each hit more than 20 home runs and drove in more than 100 runs. MVP DiMaggio led the league with a .381 average, his first title and lifetime best, and after flirting with .400 became the last right-handed hitter to clear the .380 mark. Ruffing won 21 games, but with Gomez suffering a sore arm and slumping to 12, New York lacked a solid number-two starter, making it impossible for McCarthy to establish a set rotation. Individual performances made the difference, strong contributors including farm system sprouts Atley Donald – who won 13 games, including his first 12 – and Spud Chandler.

Left fielder Charlie 'King Kong' Keller joined the Yankees in 1939, contributing to a strong defensive outfield which was also tough on pitchers. He went to the Series four times with the Yanks, collecting his share of runs, homers, hits and RBI's along the way.

In early July a Red Sox team strong on slugging took five games straight from the Yankees at Yankee Stadium. Speaking for Boston that year was Jimmie Foxx, with a league-leading 35 homers, 105 RBI's, and a .360 average; Joe Cronin with 107 RBI's and a .308 average; Doc Cramer with a .311 average; Bobby Doerr with a .318 average, and a 20-year-old rookie named Ted Williams who batted .327, achieved a league-leading 145 RBI's, launched 31 homers, and nearly overtook Harlond Clift for the lead in walks – a remarkable testimony to the rookie's eye. Not to be forgotten was Lefty Grove, throwing a 15-4 season for the Red Sox, and taking his record ninth ERA title. Only lack of pitching depth prevented the Red Sox from giving New York a better run for its money.

The Yankees followed up their fourth consecutive pennant with a 4-0 sweep of Cincinnati in the Series, becoming the first club ever to win four consecutive world championships. No other club had ever been able to take more than two championships in a row. Charlie Keller exhibited a real Gehrig Series touch, batting .438, and driving in six runs with seven hits that included three home runs, a triple and a double.

The Yankees, with four pennants and four World

Red Rolfe scores for the Yankees in the 1939 World Series, while Joe DiMaggio, the batboy and umpire look on, and Cincinnati catcher Ernie Lombardi waits for a late throw. The Yanks blanked the Reds four games to none.

Series victories in as many years, were now in the middle of a period of dominance that would see them take seven pennants in eight years. They failed to repeat in 1940, but their third-place finish found them only two games behind the league-leading Tigers. That is how close they came to eight straight pennants. Most significant of all, in none of the years they won was there ever any question of their dominance after midseason.

With the steadily increasing use of radio and night games raising attendance and interest across the country, by the end of the decade baseball had not only recovered from the decline of the Depression, but had established itself on the American scene more securely and profitably than ever before. Stars like Joe DiMaggio, Jimmie Foxx, Hank Greenberg, Bill Dickey, Ted Williams and Bob Feller propelled the American League to what was probably the peak of its supremacy, a dominance that extended not only to the playing field but to the box office. By the first year of the new decade, the American League outdrew the National League by over one million paying spectators, outhomered the senior circuit by almost 200 runs, outscored it by over 700 runs, and outbatted it by an average of seven points. Not until a second world war and a social revolution called Jackie Robinson would its supremacy slacken.

Hall of Famer Jimmie Foxx, who played first base for the Philadelphia A's from 1925 to 1935, played for Boston from 1936 to 1942. In 1938 'The Beast' took the batting title for the second time, with a .349 average, leading the league in RBI's and bases on balls as well. Foxx's statistics are a testament to his power: during his 20-year career he belted 534 homers and batted in 1921 runs, ending up with a .609 slugging percentage.

On 29 April, 1944 a number of former major leaguers serving in the Navy played against a Hawaiian All-Star team (and won in 12 innings, 4-2) raising over a million dollars in war bonds.

CHAPTER FOUR

The Fighting Forties

"I don't think either of them can win."
Warren Brown, *Chicago Tribune* sportswriter, asked to pick a winner in the 1945 World Series.

As major league baseball embarked on the 1940s, things never looked better – assuming, that is, that baseball stadiums could be isolated from the world around them. In fact, various events beyond the confines of the stadiums were going to infringe heavily upon baseball before the decade was over. The most important event in the mainstream of history was, of course, World War II, but in retrospect it had relatively little effect on organized baseball as a whole, although it undeniably affected the careers of individual players. Much is made of the fact that World War II disrupted major league baseball, but in fact its impact was mainly confined to three or four seasons. Although Europe was at war by 1940, it was only in 1942 that American ballplayers began to go into the armed services in any numbers, and by 1946 almost all of them would return with just about as much talent as before.

Right-hander Bobo Newsom pitched for the Detroit Tigers from 1939 to 1941, winning two games (including a fifth-game shutout) and losing one for them in the 1940 World Series.

Another event that would have a more far-reaching impact on baseball had actually occurred on 27 August 1939. A doubleheader at Ebbets Field in Brooklyn between the Dodgers and the Reds was the first televised major league game, and although there were only a handful of sets to receive it, the newspaper account marveled over the fact that people 'as far away as 50 miles viewed the action and heard the roar of the crowd.' That televised game, even more so than the bombing of Pearl Harbor, would be the 'shot heard round the [baseball] world.' Television would wait until after World War II was over to make its pitch, but once it began to deliver in the late 1940s, baseball would never be the same.

Night baseball, too, which had been played only occasionally since the first night game on 24 May 1935, began to catch on after the war. By 1948 every major league club's stadium would have lights – except for Wrigley Field in Chicago. And 40 years later Chicago's North Side ball club would still be defying the trend to 'produce' baseball for the convenience of the television audience.

World War II was bigger than baseball, it was irresistible. Television was also bigger than baseball, but baseball chose to get aboard. But there was still another event in the 1940s that major league baseball, to its everlasting credit, may take some little pride in helping to bring about: that is, the acceptance of black Americans into the mainstream of society. Regrettably, it was not the American League that commenced the process: that honor belongs to the Brooklyn Dodgers and their owner, Branch Rickey, who in 1947 brought up Jackie Robinson from the Montreal farm team and put him in the lineup. But during the 1947 season, Bill Veeck, owner of the Cleveland Indians, put the second black player on the field, Larry Doby, and before the season was out the St Louis Browns fielded two blacks, Henry Thompson and Willard Brown. It must be admitted that thereafter the American League fell behind the National League in signing on black players – the Boston Red Sox waited until 1959 – but major league baseball can take some satisfaction in knowing that it helped to speed up the long overdue process of integrating America.

But as the 1940 season got underway, none of these revolutionary events was on the minds of most Americans, whether ballplayers or fans. In fact, the world seemed to be going on as usual, which meant that among other things the Yankees would probably win the American League pennant for the fifth consecutive year. Joe DiMaggio was as hot as ever – his .352 average would lead the league for 1940 – and there was Charlie Keller and Joe Gordon and Spud Chandler. The Indians, however, signaled a tight race to come when their 21-year-old ace, Bob Feller, pitched against the White Sox the first and only no-hitter on an opening day. Feller also went on to have a superb season, winning 27 games and leading all other pitchers in the league in virtually every category.

But in the end, the Yankees could only come in third, two games out, and Cleveland could only come in second, one game out, as the Detroit Tigers surprised everyone and took the pennant. Manager Del Baker had cleverly shifted the team's home run producer, first baseman Hank Greenberg, to left field in order to move backup catcher Rudy York into the starting lineup; Greenberg's 41 homers and 150 RBI's and York's 33 homers and 134 RBI's more than justified the switch. Charlie Gehringer and Barney

McCoskey also hit over .300, while Bobo Newsom (21-5) and Schoolboy Rowe (16-3) provided the necessary pitching skills. Newsom was a colorful character of the old school of baseball. His real name was Louis Norman Newsom, but he was known only as 'Bobo' because of his own habit of addressing everyone else as just that. (He is said to have called even the Olympian 'Mr Mack,' 'Bobo' on first meeting him.) Whether it was his rough manners or his lack of discipline, Newsom would pitch for 18 different teams during 26 years in the majors, but the fact is he won many games for those teams, finally retiring with a career total of 211-222.

In the World Series, the Tigers found themselves facing the Cincinnati Reds. Newsom pitched and won the first game, 7-2, with his father watching in the stands; the very next day, Mr Newsom died of a heart attack. The teams were tied, two games each, when Newsom returned to pitch in the fifth; he gave up only three hits, while his teammates gave him 13, so the Tigers went ahead in the Series. The Reds tied up the Series in the sixth game, so Newsom was asked to pitch the seventh (after only one day's rest – the teams' cities being so close that no travel days were allowed). Newsom did wonders, giving up no runs through the sixth inning while the Tigers tiptoed along on one unearned run; then in the seventh, when the Tiger shortstop cut off a throw that might have been a putout at home, the Reds tied up the game and a sacrifice fly brought in a second run. The Reds won game seven, 2-1, and the Series.

During the 1941 season, the war in Europe loomed ominously, but interfered with American baseball players very little. The notable exception was Hank Greenberg, who enlisted in the Army shortly after the season began. For two all-time greats of the American League, 1941 was a banner year. For one, it began on 15 May: Joe DiMaggio got one single in his four at bats – hardly much for any player, let alone the Yankee Clipper, to write home about. But he hit in the next game, and the next game, and the next game. . . . By 29 June he had hit in 42 consecutive games, breaking George Sisler's old American League record. A few days later he broke the all-time record for hitting in consecutive games, 44, set by Wee Willie Keeler back

Above: Catcher Rollie Hemsley played for Cleveland from 1938 to 1941, turning in four solid years out of his 19-year career before moving to the Reds, Yankees, and finishing up with Philadelphia's National League team.

Left: Birdie Tebbetts taps one into center field. Catcher George Robert Tebbetts played for the Tigers from 1936 to 1947, then moved to the Red Sox, and finished his career with the Indians.

in 1897. By now the whole country was waiting for each day's news report – and fans were showing up in record-breaking numbers at each Yankee game. Then on the night of 17 July, the Yankees played the Indians and 60,000 fans showed up in Cleveland. It took two pitchers, Al Smith and Jim Bagby, Jr, and some incredible catches by the Indians' third baseman Ken Keltner, to shut the mighty Joe down. Yet his hits in 56 consecutive games remains as of this day one of the most secure all-time records.

Meanwhile, another American League player was enjoying a good year at the plate, a 22-year-old in his third year with the Red Sox – Ted Williams. Williams was hardly an unknown; in his first season with the Sox, Williams had batted .327, hit 31 homers and led the league with 145 RBI's. Indeed, great things had been expected of Williams almost from the moment the Red Sox's general manager Eddie Collins had discovered him in San Diego in 1936. Collins had gone to California primarily to seek out a promising second baseman, Bobby Doerr, but Collins had been so impressed with the tall, 17-year-old, left-handed hitter that he signed up Williams too. It was 1938 before the Sox brought Williams to spring training, and even then he was confident to the point of cockiness. (One story goes that when someone said to him, 'wait till you see Foxx hit,' Williams' cool retort was, 'wait till Foxx sees me hit.')

But Williams had an eye and a bat that could more than support his mouth and his manner. The Sox had such a strong outfield in 1938 that he was sent to Minneapolis for another year of seasoning, but in 1939 he joined the Red Sox and proved that Eddie Collins had not been seeing double. And then in 1941, Williams was truly hot. By the time he came into the final day of the season, his average was .3995 – good

Theodore Samuel Williams – 'The Splendid Splinter' – played left field for the Red Sox for his entire 19-year career, with three years out for military service. Named the league's Most Valuable Player twice, in 1946 and 1949, and winning the Triple Crown twice, in 1942 and 1947, Teddy Ballgame ended his playing career in 1960 with a home run in his last at-bat. He was elected to the Hall of Fame in 1966.

the fourth game with the Yankees leading two games to one, and it was considered either team's Series to win. The Dodgers were leading 4-3 in the top of the ninth and relief pitcher Hugh Casey had set down the first two Yankees and then gone to a full count with Tommy Henrich. Casey pitched a curve (which some would insist was a spitter), Henrich swung and missed and Dodger fans were about to celebrate – when their usually fine catcher, Mickey Owen, let the ball get away. Henrich sprinted safely to first and before the inning was over, the Yankees picked up four runs. The Yankees won that fourth game, 7-4, and then went on to take the fifth, 3-1, and win their ninth World Series.

By the time the 1942 season got underway, America had formally and fully entered the war, and players were beginning to go off to the armed services. Bob Feller was one of the first of the stars to enlist. Just as

Left: Outfielder Sam Chapman played for the Philadelphia Athletics for 11 years, turning in his best year in 1941, with 106 RBI's and a .322 batting average.

Below: Ken Keltner played third base for Cleveland for 12 years, and ended his career in 1950 with the Red Sox.

enough to go into the record books as .400. The last major leaguer with a season average .400 or better was Bill Terry of the Giants, who had ended up with .401 in 1930. The Red Sox manager, Joe Cronin, told Williams he could sit out the doubleheader against the Athletics and preserve his .400 average, but Williams insisted on hitting his way into the record-book. In the first game, he went 4 for 5, and in the second game he went 2 for 3, ending the season with a .406.

In team play, however, the Red Sox could not match the Yankees. By 4 September and their 136th game, the Yankees were setting their own record by clinching the league pennant on the earliest date ever. The Yankees then went into the Series to face none other than the Brooklyn Dodgers; the Yankees and the Giants had met in five World Series but this was a first for these two New York rivals. The teams went into

Above: Yankee shortstop Phil 'Scooter' Rizzuto makes a putout at second base. Rizzuto played in nine Series contests during his 13 years with the Yankees. Phil Rizzuto continued in baseball after retiring from his playing career in 1956 by becoming a well-known and well-liked announcer.

Right: Right-hander Tex Hughson turned in a .640 winning percentage and a 2.94 ERA after his eight-year career with the Red Sox, including two 20-game seasons. He led the league in strikeouts in 1942, and averaged 125 strikeouts per season during his most active years.

in World War I, there was some suggestion that perhaps it wasn't right for grown men to be playing and watching a game while others were dying in battle. But President Franklin Delano Roosevelt himself wrote to the Commissioner of Baseball, Judge Landis, not long after Pearl Harbor: 'I honestly feel that it would be best for the country to keep baseball going.' In general, everyone agreed that major league baseball would help to keep up morale at the homefront and overseas, so the teams continued playing. But in the next two years, over 300 major league players would go into the armed services, and those who stayed had legitimate exemptions. Although many of the players were put into 'safe' positions, this was mainly because their commanding officers wanted to keep celebrities on their staffs. Many players refused such cushy assignments and found themselves sent off to the frontlines. Meanwhile, ball park attendance gradually declined as the public declined in numbers and had less time available for sports. Several teams began to suffer financially, but the major leagues continued.

There was little surprise when the Yankees came back in 1942 to take the pennant for the sixth time in seven years. The Yankees had such oldtimers as Joe DiMaggio, Charlie Keller, Joe Gordon, Bill Dickey, Red Ruffing and Lefty Gomez, but they also had some newcomers from their own farm system, including Phil Rizzuto at shortstop and a pitcher, Ernie Bonham, who would end the season with 21 wins. Forty-one-year-old pitcher Ted Lyons of the White Sox, however, won 14 and lost 6, leading the league with his 2.10 ERA. The Red Sox's Ted Williams won the triple crown, batting .356, with 36 homers and 137 RBI's. (Both Lyons and Williams would enter the armed forces after this season.)

The Yankees went into the World Series in 1942 highly favored to beat the inexperienced St Louis Cardinals, whose superb farm system, built up by general manager Branch Rickey, had yielded a crop of fine rookies. In the first game the Cardinals couldn't even get a hit off Yankee Red Ruffing until the eighth inning, and they lost 7-4. But the Cards came back in the second game to win 4-3. In the third game, before 70,000 fans at Yankee Stadium, everyone assumed that the Yankee bats would come alive, as they did – but Cardinal outfielders Terry Moore, Stan Musial and Enos Slaughter took turns making spectacular catches and the Cardinals upset the Yankees, 2-0.

Washington outfielder George Case led the league in stolen bases six times, and scored a league-leading 102 runs in 1943.

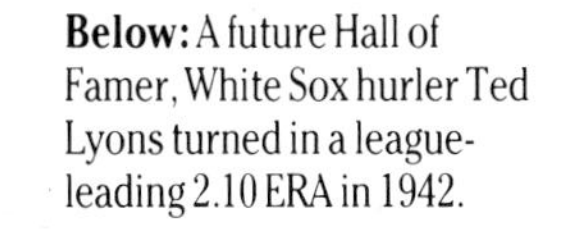

Below: A future Hall of Famer, White Sox hurler Ted Lyons turned in a league-leading 2.10 ERA in 1942.

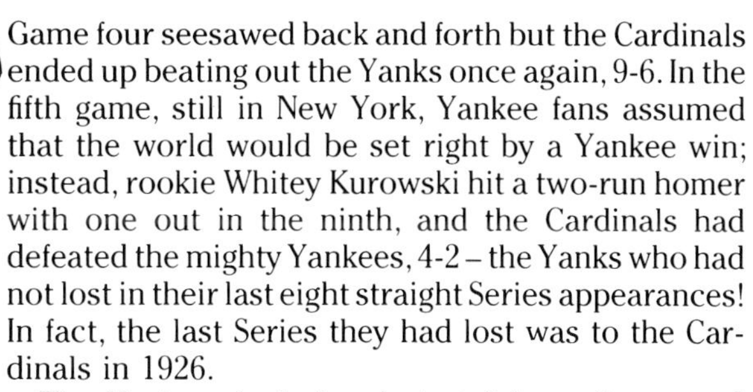

Game four seesawed back and forth but the Cardinals ended up beating out the Yanks once again, 9-6. In the fifth game, still in New York, Yankee fans assumed that the world would be set right by a Yankee win; instead, rookie Whitey Kurowski hit a two-run homer with one out in the ninth, and the Cardinals had defeated the mighty Yankees, 4-2 – the Yanks who had not lost in their last eight straight Series appearances! In fact, the last Series they had lost was to the Cardinals in 1926.

The Yankees had already lost Johnny Sturm and Tommy Henrich to the armed forces during the 1942 season; then in 1943 they lost Joe DiMaggio, Phil Rizzuto, Red Ruffing and Buddy Hassett. But all the other teams were losing players, too. Still, 1943 seemed like a season 'on hold' and it was probably no coincidence that both the Yankees and the Cardinals repeated in their leagues and met again in the World Series. And just as in 1942, the Cards lost the first game and then won the second. The Cardinals' Mort Cooper pitched in this game – with his brother Walker Cooper catching. Even more extraordinary was the fact that their father had died that very morning. In the third game (played in Yankee Stadium to cut down on travel during the war) the Yankees came back and won, 6-2, to make the game count 2-1. The teams then moved on to St Louis where the Yankees repeated with a 2-1 win. In the fifth game Mort Cooper gave up only a two-run homer to Dickey, but Spud

Right: The St Louis Browns' shortstop Vern Stephens led the league in RBI's with 109 in 1944, helping to boost his team to the league and world championships that year.

Opposite top: Pitching great Bob Feller poses with Walker Cooper at the Great Lakes Naval Training Center.

Opposite bottom: First baseman George McQuinn demonstrates his stretch. McQuinn, who played in the Series for both the Browns and the Yankees, finished his 12-year career in 1948.

Chandler shut down the Cardinals, and the Yankees won the Series four games to one, the seventh time they won it under manager Joe McCarthy.

The 1944 season was probably the nadir for major league baseball as far as the available talent was concerned. It was in this year, for instance, that the Cincinnati Reds actually used a 15-year-old pitcher, Joe Nuxhall. Virtually all the great players were off in the armed forces by now, so at least all teams were playing at about the same level. The Tigers and Yankees found themselves racing for the pennant, however feebly, with the St Louis Browns in hot pursuit. The Browns had never won a pennant, but in 1944, managed by Luke Sewell, and aided by veteran hitters Mike Kreevich and Vern Stephens, and pitchers Jack Kramer and Nelson Potter they defeated the Yankees and clinched the pennant on the last day of the season.

Below: Nelson Potter pitched for the Philadelphia A's until 1941, when he went to Boston and St Louis, finishing his career in 1949 with the Boston Braves.

As if to cooperate with the wartime restrictions on travel, the Cardinals won again in the National League, so there was to be not even a subway series but a staircase series, as both St Louis teams played in Sportsman's Park. The Cardinals, of course, were veterans at Series play, but the Browns surprised everyone by taking the first game, 2-1, on a two-run homer by George McQuinn. The Cardinals came back in the second game but the Browns once more astonished everyone with a win in the third game, 6-2. Then the Cards took the next three games, although hardly by routs – the scores being 5-1, 2-0 and 3-1. The Cardinals got to fly the World Series flag above Sportsman's Park, but the Browns could be

equally proud of their American League pennant, the first and only championship the team would win in St Louis.

The war would not end until August 1945, so the 1945 season was almost as devoid of the big stars as 1944 had been. No All-Star game was held in 1945, both because of the lack of all-stars and the wartime restrictions on travel. During the season, though, as the war was winding down first in Europe and then in the Pacific, several players were able to rejoin their teams. One of these was Hank Greenberg, who had been among the first to go into the armed forces. He rejoined the Tigers in June after completing his service with the Air Force in Europe, while pitcher Virgil Trucks got out of the Navy after the Japanese surrendered in August and also got into a Tiger uniform – just in time to pitch the final game of the season against the Yankees. And it was this final game that clinched the pennant for the Tigers, who had also relied on the talents of Rudy York and left-hander Hal Newhouser.

The Tigers went into the Series against the Chicago Cubs, and both teams were regarded as so light on talent that sportswriter Warren Brown quipped, 'I don't think either of them can win.' In fact, it was an exciting Series, with the lead swinging back and forth and taking the teams into a seventh and deciding game. Hal Newhouser gave up 10 hits to the Cubs but spaced them so that they produced only three runs, and the Tigers won the last game, 9-3, to become World Champions.

Right: One-armed Pete Gray appeared in 77 games for the St Louis Browns in 1945 and batted .218.

Below: Senator catcher Rick Ferrell puts out Yankee second baseman George 'Snuffy' Stirnweiss in a close play at home. Stirnweiss led the league in hits, triples, runs and stolen bases in 1944 and 1945.

The year 1945 will also be remembered as the year that the St Louis Browns fielded a one-armed outfielder, Pete Gray. Gray had lost his right arm in an accident at the age of six, but he had taught himself both to catch and bat with his one good arm. He manipulated a glove with such dexterity that he could make a catch and throw almost as fast as the average outfielder. As for his batting, by 1944 he was hitting .333 for Memphis in the Southern Association, so the Browns decided to bring him up. Gray played in 77 games during 1945 and hit .218 – an amazing feat even allowing for the fact that he wasn't facing the best pitchers of all time.

Another unique figure in the history of major league baseball was conspicuous in 1945 – but by his absence: Judge Kenesaw Mountain Landis, the first, most colorful and most powerful of the commissioners of baseball. He had died in November 1944 after having served since 1920, and for his occasionally autocratic ways, he was generally conceded to have made modern major league baseball a respectable institution. His successor was Albert Benjamin 'Happy' Chandler, a former governor and senator from Kentucky.

The year 1945 in baseball history will always be remembered as the year that Branch Rickey signed Jackie Robinson – although Robinson did not actually

Left: Second baseman Bobby Doerr played for the Boston Red Sox for 14 years, ending his career in 1951. In the 1946 World Series, Doerr had nine hits, a home run and three RBI's.

play for the Dodgers until 1947 – and true students of the sport will remember 1946 as the year of the Mexican League. A fabulously wealthy Mexican, Jorge Pasquel, decided to start a league that would compete with the two in the United States, and he went about building it up the way new teams and leagues had always tried to break into the bigtime – by offering players more money. Relatively few major league players went for the offers and most of these were from the National League – Sal Maglie, Max Lanier, Mickey Owen and others. The new Commissioner, 'Happy' Chandler, showed that he could be unhappy when someone intruded on his territory and immediately declared that any players who went down to Mexico would be barred from the two major leagues for five years if they tried to return. The players, in fact, were soon dissatisfied with conditions in the Mexican League and began to come back (the league soon folded). Chandler relented somewhat by letting them back in the majors in 1949.

The 1946 season also saw the return of almost all the prewar stars and major league baseball once again expressed the spirit of the country, as the fans turned out in record-breaking numbers to cheer on their teams. Hank Greenberg was back in form for the Tigers and hit 44 homers, while Bob Feller, after four years of service in the Navy, not only led the league in all kinds of pitching statistics, he set an all-time league strikeout record of 348. (Although research would later establish that Rube Waddell had actually struck out 349 in 1904.) Feller also completed 36 games, the most in the American League since Walter Johnson completed 38 in 1910.

But neither of these stars were enough to carry their teams to the top of the league. That honor fell to another returned serviceman, Ted Williams, whose .342 average, 38 homers and 123 RBI's led the Boston Red Sox to win the pennant for the first time since 1918. But Williams had plenty of help from such players as Dom DiMaggio, who hit .316, Johnny Pesky, with .342, Rudy York and Bobby Doerr. For the World Series, the Red Sox had to wait until the Cardinals and Dodgers went through a three-game play-off to break the tie – the first in major league history – for first place in the National League. The Cardinals emerged the winner, then promptly lost the first game in the Series to the Red Sox on a tenth-inning homer by Rudy York. The Cardinals took the second game, but the Red Sox, now on their home field, took the third – again paced by Rudy York's three-run homer. The Cards took the fourth game, 12-3, but the Red Sox took the fifth, 6-3, so the teams headed back to St Louis with the Cardinals needing to win two straight. They did win the sixth, so now it came down to the final game. Murray Dickson who had been so crucial in the Cardinals' wins, pitched this last game and went into

Below: Rudy York played catcher and first base for the Tigers from 1934 to 1945, when he went to the Red Sox, then the White Sox, and ended his 13-year career with the A's. During his year with the Tigers York averaged 27 home runs a season.

and the Dodgers. The Yankees had set a record-equaling (to that of the 1906 White Sox) 19-game winning streak, thanks to some old veterans such as Joe DiMaggio and Tommy Henrich, and a new young pitching staff that included Allie Reynolds (19-8) and reliever Joe Page.

The 1947 World Series produced three instant stars and two unforgettable plays by the Dodgers. Going into the fourth game, the Yankees were leading two games to one. The Yankees started Bill Bevens on the mound, despite his 7-13 record for the season, and although he was occasionally wild he came into the bottom of the ninth with a no-hitter and the Yankees leading 2-1. Bevens' ninth walk of the game put Carl Furillo on, but Bevens then got his second out. Yankee manager Bucky Harris signaled for Bevens to walk

Above: Shortstop Johnny Pesky played for the Red Sox from 1942 to 1951, then for the Tigers and Senators. During his first three years with the Sox he led the league in hits, and he finished his career in 1954 with a .307 batting average.

Right: 'Fireman' Joe Page pitched for the Yankees for seven years and went to the Series with them twice. In 1947 he set relief pitching league records in all three categories by winning 14, losing 7 and saving 17.

the eighth inning with a 3-1 lead; then he allowed Boston to tie it up and had to be relieved by Harry 'The Cat' Brecheen. In the bottom of the eighth, Cardinal Enos Slaughter led off with a single – a remarkable feat, considering that his elbow had actually been broken during the fifth game. The next two Cardinals went down, and then Harry Walker hit what was probably a reasonable single; Boston's Leon Culberson fielded it and threw to shortstop Johnny Pesky – who hesitated just long enough to allow Slaughter to go for broke and beat the throw to home plate. The Cardinals kept their 4-3 lead and won the 1946 World Series. For years afterwards, Pesky would be hounded by this split-second hesitation, but it seems fairer to just accept that Slaughter's gutsy running beat the throw.

Although Ted Williams enjoyed another outstanding season in 1947 – becoming the first American League player to take the triple crown of batting for the second time – the Red Sox could not repeat. The season started with a verbal war between the Yankees and the Dodgers – who were furious when the Yankees hired their coach Chuck Dressen – that led to a series of penalties from Commissioner Chandler, the most extreme being the suspension of Dodger manager Leo Durocher for the entire season, for 'conduct detrimental to baseball.' And the season ended with a baseball series between the Yankees

Pete Reiser in order to bring up the lighter-hitting Eddie Stanky, and Dodger manager Burt Shotton then put in a pinch hitter, Cookie Lavagetto, who promptly hit a double off the right-field wall and drove in the winning runs.

The Yankees came back and won the fifth game, so now the Dodgers had to do or die. In the bottom of the sixth, the Dodgers had a fairly solid 8-5 lead, but the Yankees got two men on base. Then Joe DiMaggio hit what looked like a sure homer toward the left-center bullpen, but Al Gionfriddo – who had just entered the game as a replacement – snagged the ball with a spectacular catch against the fence. The Yankees lost 8-6, but with Joe Page pitching five shutout innings in relief, the Yankees took the seventh and deciding game. Everyone agreed that the heroes of the Series had been Bill Bevens, Cookie Lavagetto and Al Gionfriddo – yet they never played in a single major league game again.

The Cleveland Indians led off the 1948 season as the only American League team with a black player, Larry Doby, who had played 29 games for the team in 1947.

Larry Doby forged the way for black players in the American League, joining the Cleveland Indians in 1947. He played outfield for them until 1956, when he went to the White Sox. Doby led the league twice in home runs, and ended his career with a .285 batting average.

Satchel Paige's pitching helped the Indians win a league pennant in 1948. Leroy Robert Paige pitched for the St Louis Browns from 1951 to 1953. He was elected to the Hall of Fame in 1971.

Then in midseason 1948, the Indians signed on a living legend from the old black leagues, 41-year-old Satchel Paige (his nickname coming from the fact that he had carried satchels, or luggage, as a boy). Even allowing for a certain amount of exaggeration, there was no denying that Paige was one of the fastest and most effective pitchers who had ever played the game. Paige was clearly well past his prime, but he would appear in 21 games for the Indians and end up 1948 with a 6-1 record and an ERA of 2.47. This was also the year that the Indians went all the way to take the pennant. Their shortstop-manager Lou Boudreau led the way with his .355 average and although Bob Feller ended up with only a 19-15 record, rookie Gene Bearden had a superb 20-7 record while Bob Lemon pitched ten shutouts to end up with a 20-14 season.

But it was hardly a walkaway for the Indians. As they came into the final weekend of the season, they appeared to have the pennant nailed down with their one and a half game lead over both the Red Sox and

the Yankees. The Red Sox eliminated the Yankees, but then on the final day of the season, the Red Sox won and the Indians lost – forcing the first play-off in American League history. The league used a single-game play-off, to be played in Boston's Fenway Park. Ted Williams, with his .369 average, was looked to as the potential tie-breaker, but it turned out to be Lou Boudreau who hit two homers and two singles, and behind the cool pitching of Gene Bearden the Indians won 8-3, and went into the Series for the first time since 1920.

In the Series the Indians found themselves confronting another team that were a bit rusty in Series play – the Boston Braves, who hadn't been there since 1941. The first game featured a hotly disputed call when the umpire ruled that pitcher Bob Feller had not picked off Phil Masi at second base – and then Masi went on to score the one run of the game and leave the Braves the winner, 1-0. As if to revenge themselves for what they regarded as an unearned win, the Indians came back and took the next three games straight. A record-setting crowd of 86,288 fans showed up in Cleveland's stadium for the fifth game to watch Bob Feller pitch what everyone assumed would be the decisive fifth game, but the Braves were able to hit him and ended up beating the Indians, 11-5. In the sixth game the Indians went ahead 4-1, but the Braves scored two more in the bottom of the eighth and had the tying run on third. Then Indian reliever Gene Bearden got the last out and the Indians took their first World Series in 28 years.

Right: Hall of Famer, shortstop and clutch hitter Lou Boudreau played for Cleveland from 1938 to 1950. **Below:** Indian pitcher Gene Bearden doubled and scored in the shutout he pitched in the 1948 Series.

Second baseman Joseph Lowell 'Flash' Gordon blasted a home run for Cleveland in the sixth game of the 1948 Series. Gordon played for the Indians for four out of his eleven years in the majors.

The Yankees had finished in third place in 1948, and that was enough to cost manager Bucky Harris his job. In his place the Yankees hired Charles Dillon 'Casey' Stengel. Hardly a household name at the time, Stengel had played as an outfielder with National League teams between 1912-25. He had gone on as a not very successful manager of the Dodgers and Braves during the 1930s, then had had considerable success managing the Oakland Oaks of the Pacific Coast League. Even so, Stengel hardly seemed to fit the Yankee 'image'; for those familiar with his public image thought of him as a slightly garrulous clown who spoke his own brand of English, dubbed 'Stengelese.' But Stengel wasted no time in demonstrating that if he was a clown, it was Pagliacci – a serious man behind the exterior. He had some veterans to draw on, although both DiMaggio and Berra were lost in the early season to injuries, but to the likes of Tommy Henrich and Phil Rizzuto he added new talents such as Hank Bauer, Jerry Coleman and Bobby Brown. For pitching Stengel could count on Vic Raschi, Allie Reynolds, Eddie Lopat and reliever Joe Page. Up the coast, though, another savvy manager, Joe McCarthy, had a powerful team in the Red Sox, with Ted Williams, Bobby Doerr, Dom DiMaggio, Johnny Pesky and Vern Stephens. As so often, though, the Red Sox couldn't come up with the pitching, so even though they led the Yankees coming into the final weekend, the Yankees beat them twice and took the pennant on the final day of the season.

And so the Yankees went into the 1949 Series to face their now archrival, the Dodgers, whom the Yankees had beaten in 1947. The Yankees took the first game, 1-0, but the Dodgers won the second by the same score. The third game went into the ninth inning with the score tied, 1-1. In the top of the inning the Yankees scored three runs, but then the Dodgers came back with two homers to make it 4-3; then Joe Page got them out before the score could be tied up. In the fourth game, Eddie Lopat and Allie Reynolds kept the Dodgers from winning again, and in the sixth game, the Yankees won 10-6, taking the first of ten pennants they would win under Casey Stengel and the first of five consecutive World Championships.

The 1940s had begun with the clouds of war hanging over major league baseball; they were ending with only the cloud of the Yankees hanging over the American League. A lot of good baseball had been played between those two thresholds, and although some statistics had been slightly skewered by the interruption of wartime service, this was a small enough price to pay to keep the world safe for baseball.

Right-handed hurler Allie Pierce 'Superchief' Reynolds threw for the Yankees from 1947 to 1954 and won seven out of nine World Series games – including two shutouts – during that time.

In the 12 years he managed the Yankees, Casey Stengel brought his team to ten league pennants and seven World championships. He was elected to the Hall of Fame in 1966.

CHAPTER FIVE

The Fabled Fifties

"I have one helluva ball club but it's underrated. And we're going to get better."

Casey Stengel referring to his 1953 Yankees.

The American League's 1950s were dominated by the New York Yankees. They won nine pennants and eight world championships. For much of the decade the other American league clubs were like fodder feeding the Yankees' championship stampede. There were years of challenge and disappointment for New York, and great performances from athletes of other clubs. Nonetheless, it was the rise and fall of the seemingly unbeatable New York franchise which stands out the most. The Yankees won the world championship seven times in the decade. From 1949-1953 Casey Stengel led the Bombers to five straight championships – a new record in the annals of the game. This was the same Stengel who was found deficient as manager of the Boston and Brooklyn clubs in the National League.

The first bang of the 1950 season took place off the field. Club owners refused to renew Happy Chandler's contract as Commissioner of Baseball. This opened the way for Ford C Frick to become baseball's third commissioner. Frick enjoyed a three-year contract at $65,000 a year. This was also the year that the Yankees introduced a sensational new southpaw, Whitey Ford. The year 1950 saw the end of one of the longest careers in the game. Connie Mack managed his beloved Athletics for the last time.

Mack's final stint in the Philadelphia dugout took place on 1 October 1950, as the A's closed out the season by beating the Senators at Shibe Park, 5-3. Mack's lifetime record of managing the same major league team for 50 years may never be broken. Although 17 of his later teams wound up in a disappointing last place, in his career Mack had experienced the thrills of glory, winning a total of nine pennants. It seemed that an era was ending when, on 16 October, Mack announced his resignation as manager. Although he continued as club president, Jimmy Sykes replaced him on the field.

The closing out of the 1950 season found New York struggling for the pennant. They finally took it in the last two games of the season. The best Boston's Red Sox could do was second place again, as Yankee rookie pitcher Whitey Ford provided his team with their winning edge. The club's management had plucked him from the Kansas City farm team and brought him to the varsity; Ford responded by winning nine out ten games. Sluggish hitting by Joe

Left-hander Whitey Ford – The Chairman of the Board – pitched for the Yankees for 16 years, turning in a won-lost record of 236-106 for an all-time second-best winning percentage of .690. Charles Edward Ford led the league in games won and in winning percentage three times, and twice in games saved and innings pitched.

Big Vic Raschi contributed to the Yankees' much-feared pitching staff from 1946 to 1953, with a won-lost record of 120-50 for those years, and an impressive career winning percentage of .667.

DiMaggio contributed to the difficulty the Yankees faced in winning the league championship. The usually dependable batter had been temporarily benched because of weak hitting, but later picked up and ended the season with an average of .301.

The Yankees faced the Philadelphia Phillies in the 1950 World Series. The National League champs had just beaten out the Brooklyn Dodgers for the pennant. Delaware millionaire Bob Carpenter had invested heavily in the Phillies, signing a number of prospects with hefty bonuses on the order of $50,000 each. The Philadelphia 'Whiz Kids' won their first pennant in 35 years and, wrote a New York baseball scribe, 'will now prepare to play a World Series against men who smoke cigars and chew tobacco.' The tough guys soundly spanked the kids in four straight, but the games were in fact very close. Philadelphia lost by only one run in each of the first three games 1-0, 2-1 and 3-2. Only in the final game in this pitchers' series was there any show of power. Even then the score was low by Yankee standards, 5-2, behind the 21-year-old rookie Whitey Ford.

This was the second straight World Series win for Casey Stengel, the 'wise old clown' who substantially changed professional baseball. He strengthened the bench by eliminating the old utility player – the 'jack of all trades, master of none' – from his club. In the off season he worked on developing a dozen or so of the

In 1951 Yankee pitcher Allie Reynolds won 17 games – including seven shutouts – and lost only eight. The following year he would whiff 160 batters to lead the league in strikeouts. Reynolds finished up with a career ERA of 3.30 and a .630 winning percentage.

best minor league players in the Yankee farm system. Casey concentrated on the most apt youngsters, a distinct departure from Rickey's assembly line approach. In line with this philosophy, Stengel founded the Yankees' first 'instruction school' in 1951, staffed by a distinguished faculty, including baseball deans Frank Crosetti, Ed Lopat, Bill Dickey and Ralph Houk. These old pros were assisted by Johnny Neun, Bill Skiff, Steve Souchak and Randy Gumpert. Although Casey delegated the drilling and most of the teaching, he kept a sharp eye on his students and teachers, overseeing the whole processs as well as the details. Dickey, Houk and Skiff worked with the catchers, Lopat and Gumpert with the pitchers, and Souchak and Crosetti taught the infielders.

Casey hoped to polish future superstars quickly in order to move them from the farm team circuit to the majors in the fastest possible time. The 1951 school, which was held in Phoenix, Arizona, included such luminaries as Mickey Mantle, Gil McDougald and Tom Morgan. Two American League Rookies of the Year, Bob Grim (1954) and Tony Kubek (1957), came directly into the majors from Casey's course of instruction. Mickey Mantle's Cinderella experience owes much to Casey's career-building approach. Practically overnight he was transformed from an unheralded shortstop on the Joplin, Missouri farm squad in the Class C association to playing next to Joe DiMaggio in the Yankee outfield.

Coach Bill Dickey remembers the 18-year-old's arrival at Phoenix. 'I was pitching batting practice when he took his first swings,' related Dickey. 'The kid hit the first six balls nearly 500 feet, over the lights and out of sight.' Mantle was later asked to take spring training with the varsity. He jumped overnight from Class C to Triple A and then to the major leagues.

Stengel turned many long-established baseball conventions inside out. This maverick studied people and situations while many of his opponents followed static guidelines with an almost biblical faith. In tight situations Casey astounded the pundits. He used left-handed batters against southpaws, and vice versa. The cherished 'percentages' mandated doing otherwise; Casey knew better. 'People alter percentages,' Stengel countered in defense of his moves against the book. 'Johnny Fredericks and Andy High were two left-handed batters with the Dodgers who could wear out a southpaw. And Carl Hubbell, one of the greatest left-handers in history, had more trouble with left-handed batters than he did with the right-handed ones.' Casey pulled things apart and put them together in new, exciting forms which effectively devastated a generation of opponents. He knew both his players and his opponents better than anyone else.

The St Louis Browns found their off-field excitement in the person of Bill Veeck, who purchased the club from Bill and Charlie DeWitt. Veeck added spice to the league's 1951 season in ways that were more exotic than some of Casey's most unconventional decisions. The club owner stationed contortionist Max Patkin to whoop it up on the coaching lines. Veeck's most famous stunt, filled at first with comedy, probably broke the heart of the man wearing uniform number '1/8,' Eddie Gaedel.

Gaedel's day in the sun occurred on 9 August 1951. The American League was celebrating its golden jubilee with gala festivals in all the parks. A crowd of 18,369 turned out to see St Louis play a doubleheader against Detroit. Gaedel, the Brown's first batter, strode to the plate. He stood three feet seven inches tall and weighed 65 pounds! Pitcher Bob Cain looked wide-eyed in astonishment and the plate umpire Ed Hurley glared suspiciously. Gaedel proudly stood his ground, holding a strong batter's stance. Zack Taylor, the Browns' manager, walked to the plate with a copy of Gaedel's playing contract and Hurley told everyone to play ball. Cain couldn't zero his pitches in the strike zone between the neophyte batter's shoulders and knees. The pitcher launched four balls. Triumphant, Gaedel trotted to first base. Jim Delsing went in to run for him.

Unfortunately Eddie Gaedel's career as a big league utility man ended there. The next day American League President Will Harridge refused to honor Eddie Gaedel's contract. According to Harridge, Gaedel's 'participation in an American League Championship game comes under the heading of conduct detrimental to baseball.' Gaedel responded that 'this is a conspiracy against little people,' but Harridge's decision held and Gaedel lost his $100-a-game job.

Not even the Eddie Gaedel affair could distract fans from the fact that the Yankees were on their way to winning their third straight pennant in 1951. The highlights of the season included the pitching feats of the 'Superchief,' Yankee Allie Reynolds, who further emphasized the fact by blazing a pair of no-hit games. The first occurred on 12 July in Cleveland, with George Woodling connecting for a Yankee home run to win the game 1-0. The second came against the Red Sox at Yankee Stadium, by a score of 8-0. Reynolds walked the first three batters in the first game and four in the second. These were the first no-hit games pitched by a Yankee since a Monte Pearson triumph in 1938. Reynolds' second win captured the pennant and a place in history: no other pitcher had thrown a no-hit game to nail down the pennant.

The Yankees squared off against the Giants in the 1951 World Series – but it might well have been the Dodgers for the National League except for one of the most exciting moments in baseball. The Giants and Dodgers had finished the regular season in a tie, and in the third play-off game, the Dodgers were ahead, 4-2, with the tying runs on second and third in the bottom of the ninth. Bobby Thomson came to bat and the Dodgers put in relief pitcher Ralph Branca, but Thomson sent his second pitch out of the field for a three-run homer that gave the Giants the series and the pennant. At first it seemed as if the Giants would continue their 'miracle' drive and sweep past the Yankees, as they won two of the first three games. Then they began to lose steam. The Yankees went on to win three straight and the title. During the strenuous pennant drive the Giants heavily relied on two 23-game winners, Sal Maglie and Larry Jansen. Worn out from the battle to the Series, neither pitcher won a game against the Yankees. Yankee rookie Mickey Mantle, however, didn't perform especially well either, batting an even .200. Willie Mays, the future Giant great, performed meagerly, batting only .182 during the Series. Veteran Joe DiMaggio, whose batting average during the regular season had reached a new low of .263, tapped in a modest .261 in the championship bouts.

DiMaggio did achieve yet another distinction in 1951. Playing in his tenth World Series had tied Babe Ruth's record for participation in championship games. His greatness on the field, however, was beginning to fade, and the Yankees needed some transfusions in their lineup. Added power came not only from Mantle but from a more sensational rookie, Gil

Left: Left-hander Ed Lopat warms up before a game. Edmund Walter 'Steady Eddie' Lopat performed consistently well for the Yankees, turning in 109 wins and only 51 losses during the seven years he pitched for them.

Below: Sportsman's Park, home field of the St Louis Browns since their entry into the American League in 1902, and of Chris van der Ahe's famous St Louis Browns even before that.

Above: Joe DiMaggio bids farewell to Casey Stengel and Yankee Vice-President Del Webb in Yankee offices in December, 1951.
Right: First baseman Mickey Vernon takes a cut during practice. James Barton Vernon played for the Senators for 13 and a half years, ending his 20-year career in 1960 after two years in the National League. His hitting won him the batting title twice, and he led the league in doubles three times.

McDougald. Gil, who was primarily a second baseman in his rookie year in 1951, moved to third base in 1952. Despite his rather strange batting stance, he led the team in batting with .306 in 1951. He also tied a record during the Series for the most runs batted in during an inning – four, by hitting a grand slam home run. He was the only rookie ever to hit a grand slam in the Series. In addition to hitting, McDougald proved an effective fielder.

Mickey Mantle, of course, was another young blood who was to revitalize the Yankee organization. The former shortstop on the Joplin farm team could hit the baseball a proverbial mile from either side of the plate. Mantle proved an apt replacement for Joe DiMaggio, although his powerful style was more reminiscent of the fabled Babe Ruth than of DiMaggio. The latter, slowed by injuries, decided to retire despite an offer of $100,000 from the Yankees in return for wearing the team uniform while viewing most of the next season from the dugout. Joe had collected over $700,000 in his 13 years with the team and now felt ready to move on to other careers. Naturally, a place had been reserved for him at the Baseball Hall of Fame in Cooperstown, New York.

At the press conference announcing his retirement, DiMaggio was asked who was the greatest hitter he had ever seen. 'That's an easy one,' he replied. 'Ted Williams, without a question.' One of the greatest players of all times, Ted was known as 'Mr Baseball,' or the 'Splendid Splinter.' During the 1950s he enjoyed the highest lifetime average for any active player. In nine All-Star games he held a .409 batting average. He also captured the batting and RBI crowns four times. He stood six foot three inches tall and weighed in at 205 pounds. Batting left-handed, he threw with his right.

In 1952 Ted Samuel Williams left the Red Sox to fly as a Marine jet pilot in Korea. His last game of the 1952 season was against Washington on 30 April 1952. As a farewell gesture he blasted a two-run game-winning homer against Detroit. The fighting and turmoil on the Korean Peninsula decimated other American League contenders. The Bronx Bombers lost Whitey Ford, infielders Gary Coleman, Bobby Brown and hurler Tom Morgan to the draft. Coleman was a sparkling second baseman, especially adept as an acrobatic pivot man in exciting double plays. For the 1952 season, scrappy Billy Martin replaced Coleman on the Yankees and Mantle opened his first full season by hitting the ball where it had never gone before, over the left-center wall in Washington. In his first full season with the Yankees he led the club with a batting average of .311 and was the team's second-best home run artist with 23. The 20-year-old blond wonder boy was a switch hitter who could slug, not slap from either side of the plate. He also struck out often from either side, sometimes kicking the water

Above: Shortstop Phil Rizzuto and second baseman Billy Martin polish up on their double-play maneuvers in a Yankee infield practice session.

Left: The great Mickey Mantle – 'The Commerce Comet' – began his blazing 18-year career with the Yankees in 1951. Three times selected as the league's Most Valuable Player, in 1956, 1957 and 1962, Mantle's fiercely competitive nature drove him to win the Triple Crown in 1956 as well. Besides his legendary batting skills with which he led the league in homers four times, in runs scored six times and in RBI's once – Mantle inspired a great team to even further greatness.

cooler on his return to the dugout. Pitchers, nonetheless, feared him and he soon led the club for free trips to first on balls.

Stengel relished winning the 1952 pennant and Series. The Yankees beat the Cleveland Indians by a narrow two games in the American League race before facing the Dodgers in the Series. Brooklyn battled gallantly, but suffered defeat for the sixth straight time. It took seven games, the Yankees taking the final one, 4-2, with a home run by Mickey Mantle clinching it.

Competition for the batting title in 1953 turned into a race between rookie slugger Mantle and the returning veteran Ted Williams. On 29 July, the discharged Marine Corps jet pilot zoomed into Fenway Park. Not quite 35 and a veteran of two wars, he returned to Boston with a boyish grin and, as usual, without a necktie. He was in no shape to play in the game against the White Sox that day, but a crowd of 19,083 nevertheless turned out just to catch a glimpse of their Red Sox idol. His first day on the field, 6 August 1953, proved dismal. He popped out while pinch-hitting, thereby ending a rally against the Browns. Three days later he stepped in to hit for Johnny Lipon. Mike Garcia wound up and threw the ball. Williams unleashed his swing and drove the ball into the sky and out of Fenway Park. All who had seen him knew that Ted was off and running. 'It's nice to know I haven't lost my batting eye,' remarked the Boston idol. In the 37 games remaining that season, he batted a searing .407 and smashed 13 home runs. Neither age nor the time in Korea adversely affected his performance.

Around the time of Williams' return, Mickey Mantle, 13 years his junior, was photographed chewing bubble gum while playing center field. By 1953 Mickey Mantle was fully at home. The Yankees rolled over the rest of the American League to take an unprecedented fifth straight pennant. It was the easiest of the five championships. The Bombers had one 18-game-streak that practically ended the race. In the final standings they led second-place Cleveland by eight and a half games. In the Series the Yankees met the Dodgers again and beat them again, four games to two. The exciting finish came in the sixth game, bottom of the ninth, when Billy Martin singled to score Hank Bauer and win the game 4-3. 'I have a helluva ball club, but it's underrated,' remarked Stengel following the game. 'And we're going to get better.' A week later the Yankees' front office underlined the comment by announcing the team would introduce its first black player. His name was Elston Howard and he could both catch and play the outfield.

Two startling moves would soon leave St Louis and Philadelphia without American League representation. Although Bill Veeck, in his first full season as owner of the Browns, managed to increase attendance from 293,790 to 518,796, the enlarged gate still wasn't enough to pay the bills, and Veeck desperately tried to get permission to move his club to Baltimore. Twice fellow club owners turned down his request for the new venture. During the 1953 season, hard up for cash, he stopped promotion and was reduced to selling players.

Something had to happen, and it did. On 29 September 1953 the American League announced that

Mickey Mantle slides in a close play at homeplate.

attorney Clarence W Miles and a syndicate had purchased the Browns and were moving the club to Baltimore (the team name was changed to the 'Orioles'). The reported price was $2,475,000. A year later Arnold Johnson would buy the Philadelphia Athletics for $3,500,000 and move them to Kansas City. Both clubs drew well in their initial season, the Orioles pulling 1,060,910 fans in 1954, and the sixth-place Athletics attracting 1,393,054 in Kansas City the next year.

Baltimore opened the 1954 season with the greatest parade in the city's history. Vice-President Richard Milhouse Nixon rode in an open car as did Connie Mack and Clark Griffith. An estimated 500,000 people turned out to watch the floats, marching bands and celebrities. Mrs John J McGraw, widow of the Orioles' manager a half century before, had a place of honor among those present. The season-opener saw the Orioles face off against Detroit. Baltimore was blanked 3-0 before a disappointed crowd of 46,354 fans. Baltimore lost 100 games that season, winning only 54. That, however, was good enough to land them into seventh place, leaving the cellar to the stumbling Athletics. In September, Baltimore managed to lure Paul Richards away from the White Sox to take over as the Baltimore manager. From then on the Orioles began to strengthen their wings for the eventual flight to the top.

The year 1954 proved momentous in the world of sports. England's Roger Bannister broke the most important track barrier by running the mile in under four minutes. His exact time was three minutes, 59.4 seconds. In baseball the Cleveland Indians achieved something of similar greatness. They shattered the nearly universal belief that baseball belonged to the Yankees. Author Douglas Wallop's novel *The Year the Yankees Lost the Pennant* was published that year. It was supposed to be a humorous fantasy with a

Above: Vice-President Nixon throws out the first ball in Baltimore at the American League's first game of the season, on 15 April 1954.

Left: Yankee right fielder Hank Bauer catches a long ball. Bauer's 14-year playing career included nine World Series contests, in which he scored 21 runs and batted in 24 more. He went on to manage Kansas City, Baltimore and Oakland for eight years after retiring from active play.

Above: Right-hander Early Wynn warms up before a game. A future Hall of Famer, Wynn pitched for the Cleveland Indians for nine years (1949-1957) during his 23-year career, turing in four 20-game seasons during that time.

Faustian theme. The seemingly unreal became fact and Mr Wallop was on his way to fame and fortune with *Damn Yankees* eventually becoming a successful Broadway musical and motion picture.

Ironically, the Yankees won more often in 1954 than in any previous term in Stengel's career as manager. They won 103 and lost 51, which was brilliant but not good enough. A fully inspired Cleveland Indian team broke the American League record by winning 111 games, losing only 43. The previous record of 110 games was assembled by the 1927 Yankees, who were considered the mightiest team in the history of the sport. Cleveland manager Al Lopez, who formerly played for Stengel in the National League, beat out his old teacher. The magical Indians simply had a better team. Their fine pitching staff included two 23-game winners, Bob Lemon and Early Wynn. Good performances on the mound from Mike Garcia (19-8) and 35-year-old Bob Feller (13-3) rounded out the pitching staff. Their best hitters were second baseman Bobby Avila and Al Rosen, batting .341 and .300 respectively. The club played excellent defense, particularly in the outfield.

In their last meeting the Indians defeated the Yankees twice on a balmy Sunday afternoon. After the drubbing, Hal Lebovitz, the baseball writer for the Cleveland *News*, offered Stengel a ride from the park to his hotel room. Stengel gruffly refused and was snappish in answering the reporter's questions. 'Stengel is a poor loser,' declared Lebovitz. After all, he and the Yankee club had never learned how to accept defeat.

The Indians faced Willie Mays and the Giants in the 1954 World Series. In the first game the score stood at 2-2 in the top of the eighth when Indian first baseman Vic Wertz stepped to the plate. Wertz, who batted .500 in the Series, faced a game-winning opportunity with two runners on base. He blasted a pitch high and long down the Polo Grounds' deep center-field alley. Willie Mays turned his back on the infield and ran like a gazelle. He seemed destined to crash against the out-

Right: Power-hitter Vic Wertz played first base for Cleveland from 1955 to 1958. Wertz's outstanding performance in the 1954 Series – smashing eight hits, scoring two runs and batting in three more – was not enough to bring his team the championship.

paid their way into Shibe Park in 1953. Owners Roy and Earle Mack, the sons of Connie Mack, were struggling to buy control from each other. Rumors surfaced that the A's were destined for far away places. A 'Save the A's' committee formed in hope of attracting enough local enthusiasm to warrant keeping the franchise in the city of brotherly love.

Then the Mack dynasty came to an end. Fifty-four years earlier, Ban Johnson had moved the A's to Philadelphia, and now another Johnson, businessman Arnold Johnson, was taking them out. Spry 92-year-old Connie Mack flew to Kansas City for the opening game. The crowds adored him, paying tribute with applause at the airport and later with an ovation at Municipal Stadium. Lou Boudreau was recruited away from Boston to manage the team. He stopped the A's almost certain fall to the basement, bringing them up to sixth place.

Facing the pennant-winning Indians was not the only challenge the Yankees had in the 1955 season. Their biggest trouble appeared in the depletion of their pitching staff. Both Allie Reynolds and Vic Raschi were gone and Eddie Lopat was clearly slipping. To reconstruct their pitching staff, the Yankee

Far left: Cleveland third baseman Al Rosen (1947-56) stands ready at bat.

Left: Cleveland's Mike Garcia – 'The Big Bear' – pitched his way to a league-leading 2.64 ERA in 1954.

field barrier. He caught the ball over his left shoulder in football fashion, a full 450 feet from home plate. The outfielder's grace, speed and precision cost the Indians the game. The Giants went on to win the opener in the bottom of the tenth. Sweeping the Series four games to none, they ended seven consecutive seasons of American League dominance.

The 1954 Series was staged in each league's biggest park. Cleveland's municipal stadium was the largest, with 74,000 seats, and the Polo Grounds had seating for 55,131 fans. Consequently an attendance record was set in this Series with a four-game total of 251,507 paying fans. They proved to be the most lucrative series to date for the players. The winning Giants were paid $11,147.90 for a full share and the Indians got $6,712.50. In contrast, poor attendance was undermining another once-proud team. The westward expansion of the American League began with the move of the Philadelphia Athletics to Kansas City.

In 1952 because of the solid pitching of Bobby Shantz, the A's had pulled up to fourth place. They then lost footing and continued to decline to seventh in 1953, ending up in the basement in 1954. Attendance drooped like performance, as only 362,113 fans

Indian pitcher and future Hall of Famer Bob Lemon won 207 games and lost only 128.

organization would have to pull a rabbit out of the hat. Although the kinds of winners they required were a scarce commodity, the New York front office waved a magic wand and created one of the most massive trade deals in history. The Yankees gave the Orioles Jim McDonald, Harry Bird and Bill Miller, pitchers; Hal Smith and Gus Triandos, catchers; Don Leppert, Willie Miranda and Kal Segrist, infielders; and Gene Woodling, an outfielder. In return the Orioles gave the Yankees Bob Turley, Don Larsen and Mike Blyska, pitchers; Darrell Johnson, a catcher; Dick Kryhoski, a first baseman; Billy Hunter, a shortstop; and Ted del Guercio and Jim Fridley, outfielders. Turley and Larsen were the key men for Stengel. They provided him with the pitching strength he needed. Baltimore gained a future star in Triandos, and Woodling proved very useful in a future trade with Cleveland. The Yankee farm system, in the meanwhile, turned up a pair of good hurlers in the persons of Johnny Kucks and Tom Sturdivant. They joined Ford, Grim, Byrne, Turley and Larsen as Stengel's winning pitchers.

American League fans enjoyed an exciting four-way contest in 1955 between the Yankees, White Sox, Indians and Red Sox. Early in the season, only three games separated the four teams, with the Indians in the lead. The Yankees put on a spectacular finishing run, winning 15 consecutive games and clinching Stengel's sixth pennant flag in seven seasons. At the finish the Yankees led the Indians by three games, although Cleveland had tried hard. Bob Feller was at the end of his career, splitting his eight decisions. A new strikeout ace, left-hander Herb Score, won 16 games and struck out 245 batters, more than one an inning. His wins recalled Feller's earlier glories.

This was not a great season for pitchers. The American League, for the first time in its history, could not boast of a single 20-game winner. Yankee Whitey Ford, Frank Sullivan of the Red Sox, and Bob Lemon of Cleveland won 18. Increased reliance on the use of relief pitchers may have accounted for the shift in statistics. In Cleveland relief specialists Ray Narleski and Don Mossi were considered the most valuable members of the staff after Herb Score. It was, however, another great season for Yankee catcher Yogi Berra. Berra was named the American League's Most Valuable Player for the third time, a distinction he shared with Joe DiMaggio and Jimmie Foxx.

The 52nd World Series finally caught up with Stengel. On the morning of 30 September 1955, only the most dedicated Brooklyn fans gave the Dodgers a chance against their rivals from across the river. The Dodgers were already down by two games, and it seemed yet again that they would be the bridesmaid instead of the bride for the eighth time. Brooklyn manager Walter Alston picked blue-eyed Johnny Podres, with his nine wins and ten losses, in desperation. His two aces, Don Newcombe (20-5) and Billy Loes (10-4), had just flunked the test against the Yankees. Podres' appearance on the mound coincided with his 23rd birthday. He celebrated it in style, holding the Bombers to seven hits as the Dodgers took the game, 8-3.

Thus began a three-game rally that shook the baseball world and brought seemingly limitless joy to the borough of Brooklyn. The Yankees tied the Series, taking game six behind the four-hit pitching of Whitey Ford. Yankee Stadium was the site of the seventh and deciding game. Johnny Podres, now 23 years and four days old, took up the pitching assignment. In a thrilling breathtaking performance, including 'el Catch' by Cuban speedster Sandy Amoros, Podres and the

Bums from Brooklyn blanked the Yankees 2-0. Tommy Byrne was the losing pitcher. Stengel characteristically accepted blame for the loss. 'Podres hadn't pitched a complete game since July,' remarked Casey, 'and I figured he couldn't last, so I had the hitters taking pitches. But he lasted so I guess I should've had the boys swinging.'

The American League was spreading out and reached a new attendance record with the completion of moves to Baltimore and Kansas City. The 1955 gate surpassed the 1953 gate by more than two million. The Washington Senators, however, were serious losers; the number of paying fans dropped from 595,594 in 1953 to 425,238 in 1955. In 1956, attendance at Washington's Griffith Stadium plunged even further. More and more commentators raised the question of whether the national capital could support a major league franchise.

The great leftie Whitey Ford pitched 18 Series games for the Yankees, winning a record 10 games. He was elected to the Hall of Fame in 1974.

Big Milt Pappas pitched for Baltimore for nine years and went to the Cincinnati Reds in 1966. He then pitched for Atlanta and for the Cubs, ending his career in 1973 with a won-lost record of 209-164 and a 3.40 ERA.

The Yankees opened in Washington on 17 April 1956. President Eisenhower threw out the season's first ball. But it was Mickey Mantle who proved to be the day's commander-in-chief by unleashing his batting arsenal. Up against veteran Camilo Pascual, he hit two home runs over the centerfield fence, the first time any batter had slugged two in the same game in that direction. Yoga Berra smacked four hits that game, including a homer, and the Yankees destroyed hapless Washington, 10-4.

Hall of Famer and former Yankee Bill Dickey had this to say in the clubhouse after the game: 'Mantle's got more power than any hitter I ever saw, including Babe.' By now the 24-year-old slugger was a national celebrity more for his potential than for what he had actually accomplished. Mantle had not won the American League batting honors in the 1955 season, those kudos going to Detroit sophomore outfielder, Al Kaline. Mantle, however, hit more home runs than anyone in the league that year with 37, and some rocketed farther than a ball had ever flown before. Yet he remained green and continued to struggle. He had not developed the consistency or the confidence needed to reach his full potential.

On that same opening day of 1956 Ted Williams showed that he planned to stay in the batting contest. He splashed two doubles and a single to the left side of second base, signaling that the baseball veteran was still out to break a few records of his own. But as the season progressed, it became clear that the batting honors would belong to Mickey Mantle. The homers he started hitting in Washington continued in profusion. Mantle set his sights on the Triple Crown – leading the league in batting percentage, home runs and runs batted in. Batting right- or left-handed he elicited fear in the hearts of pitchers. His strikeout percentage declined. He increasingly drew walks as pitchers fretted about throwing in the batting zone while he stood at the plate.

By the time of the All-Star game, the Yankees held on to first place. The White Sox, however, were having a sensational season and stayed uncomfortably close to the leaders. Freshman shortstop Luis Aparicio breathed life into the club. The team stressed speed with Aparicio, Minnie Minoso and Jim Rivera. The

Left: Outfielder and powerhitter Gus Zernial played for the Philadelphia, then the Kansas City Athletics from 1952 to 1957.

Below: Baltimore Oriole catcher Gus Triandos tries in vain to catch a ball fouled into the Yankee dugout by Gil McDougald.

Third baseman Ray Boone played for Detroit from 1953 to 1958. He led the league in RBI's with 116 in 1955.

White Sox led the league in steals and boasted an outstanding second baseman in Nellie Fox. Larry Doby and Sherman Lollar generated the team's batting power.

Rocky Colavito led the Indian attack. An outfielder, he had a great arm and fabulous power. Colavito hit 21 home runs that season, showing the promise of his future greatness. The Red Sox, revolving around Ted Williams, were on their way to a fourth-place position for the fourth straight time. On 6 August, Ted tied one of Babe Ruth's records, albeit a dubious one. Having dropped a Mickey Mantle fly ball, Williams fumed on his way to the dugout when the side was retired. He then spat in the direction of the box seats to show his disdain for the jeering fans, and was fined $5000, equaling the one received by Ruth. Williams was repentant and in his next game blasted a home run against Baltimore as a heroic apology.

In the summer of 1956 Mantle appeared to be threatening another Babe Ruth record. Few players had approached Ruth's 60 home runs in one season before 1956; Mickey had 47 going into September, but at this critical time he entered a slump and only produced five more during the season. He won the Triple Crown with 52 home runs, a .353 batting average and 130 RBI's, helping his Yanks capture the pennant. Mantle, in fact, led both major leagues in all three categories, a feat accomplished only four times.

The Yankees avenged their World Series defeat of the previous year by beating the Dodgers in seven games. With the series tied at two–all, the fifth game proved to be of great significance. Casey decided to gamble on pitcher Don Larsen, whose record was only 11 wins and 5 losses for the season. The burly

Left: Speedster shortstop Luis Aparacio led the league in stolen bases for nine consecutive seasons, including the seven he played for the White Sox (1956-62). He ended his 18-year career in 1973 with 506 stolen bases under his belt, and was elected to the Hall of Fame in 1984.

Below: Second baseman Nellie Fox played most of his 19-year career for the White Sox, leading the league four times in hits.

pitcher stood six feet tall and weighed 230 pounds. His opponent on the mound was Sal Maglie, the veteran former Giant. Both men were pitching flawless games until Mantle belted a home run in the fourth. Larsen, however, continued to down batters like flies.

Earlier Larsen had switched to pitching without a wind-up, after suspecting that third base coaches were reading him correctly and signaling his intentions to batters. Going into the ninth inning not a single Dodger had even made it to first base, and Larsen was only three out from pitching a perfect game. There had never been even a no-hitter in a World Series, and regular season perfectly pitched games had occurred only six times in the 75 years of major league history. Excitement grew as the Dodgers came up to bat.

Carl Furillo opened the inning by flying out. Then Roy Campanella grounded to Billy Martin, who threw the Dodger catcher out at first. Next Dale Mitchell came to bat as a replacement for Maglie. Larsen's first pitch was a ball, the second was called a strike, and the third was swung at and missed for strike two. Larsen picked up the resin bag, rubbed his hands, and threw. The ball was fouled back. He pitched again, Mitchell half swung, then checked his swing, and the umpire called strike three. Yogi Berra rushed out to the mound and leaped into Larsen's arms. Larsen had made history, pitching a perfect game before 64,519 Yankee Stadium fans in World Series play.

Brooklyn went on to win the sixth game but was clobbered by the Yankees 9-0 in the seventh and deciding game. With men on base, Yogi Berra belted

Yankee right-hander Don Larsen pitched five Series games for New York, but his most memorable was on 8 October 1956, when he pitched the only perfect game in World Series history.

two home runs off Don Newcombe, the outstanding Dodger game-winner who always lost his touch in World Series play. Berra's homers came in the first and third innings, giving the Yankees a 4-0 lead. Manager Alston thought Newcombe would settle down and allowed him to come out and begin the fourth inning as well. But when the first Yankee batter, Elston Howard, promptly hit one into the seats to make it 5-0, that was all for Don, who later received a telegram of condolence from President Eisenhower. Yankee pitcher Johnny Kucks (18-9) pitched a superb shutout.

The Cleveland Indians threatened the Yankees in the 1957 season. Rocky Colavito performed as one of

Outfielder Rocky Colavito played for Cleveland from 1955 to 1959 and from 1965 to 1967. Rocco Domenico Colavito hammered 21, 25, 41 and 42 homers in consecutive seasons, beginning in 1956.

Rookie of the Year in 1955, left-hander Herb Score pitched two brilliant seasons for Cleveland, leading the league in strikeouts both years, before he was hit in the eye by a line drive in 1957. His winning percentage declined dramatically after that, and he finished his career pitching for the White Sox in 1962.

the league's steadiest hitters, and pitcher Herb Score seemed destined for a legendary career. Pitching with blinding speed and a wicked curve ball, he won 16 games in his rookie year, and 20 in his second year out. He led the league in strikeouts in his first two professional seasons. Then, on 7 May 1957, Score was struck in the right eye by a line drive hit by Gil McDougald. He was 23 years old. The accident ended his season. Although he returned to baseball, he never regained his greatness. McDougald was sleepless after the accident. Not permitted to visit the pitcher in the hospital, he talked to all the doctors caring for the injured pitcher. 'If Score loses his eye, I might quit the game,' McDougald told Cleveland reporter Hal Lebovitz. 'It isn't worth it.'

Ted Williams had a momentous year with the Red Sox. Now 39 years of age and a four-time holder of the Triple Crown, he became the oldest batting champion in American League history. He averaged a searing .388 for the season. Although early in the season he suffered a slump and had numerous rows with the press, in two games (8 May and 13 June) he thumped three home runs. His previous three-homer game had been 11 years earlier in 1946. Toward the end of the 1957 season it seemed as if the Boston superstar could *not* be silenced. In September he went through six games and reached base 16 consecutive times without being retired. The Senators' Hal Griggs finally ended that remarkable string of successes. Home run honors for 1957 belonged to Roy Sievers, Washington's strongman, who belted 42 of them and had 114 runs batted in. He also led the league in total bases.

The first half of the 1957 season had found the Yankees in a meager third place, playing without verve. Then they came to life, winning ten straight, and moved into first place on 30 June. In the World Series that year the Yankees faced the Milwaukee Braves. Warren Spahn lead the Braves' pitching staff

with a 21-win season. Behind him were stellar performers center fielder Hank Aaron, who batted .322, and the league's home run king with 44, veteran Red Schoendienst. Third baseman Eddie Mathews was another Braves' long-ball hitter; he had slugged 32 home runs during the season.

The Yankees had rarely faced a team with such an awesome combination of batting and pitching power. The Series opened at Yankee Stadium, with Spahn facing Whitey Ford. Ford held the Braves to five hits and one run, and the Yanks won 3-1. The battle had begun, and in the Milwaukee locker room later that day the silence bespoke of a grim determination. In the second game Brave Wes Covington's spectacular second-inning catch ended a Yankee rally, and Milwaukee pitcher Lew Burdette held the Bombers to only seven hits, pulling out a 4-2 victory. Then in the first game at Milwaukee County Stadium the Yankees crushed the Braves 12-3 as six Brave pitchers allowed 11 walks. The defeat was even more bitter because of the performance of a home-town boy in a Yankee uniform, Tony Kubek. The rookie led the onslaught with two home runs and four RBI's.

Next it was the Braves' turn, with a 7-5 Warren Spahn victory in an exciting and controversial ten innings. With the Series tied at two games each, game five featured another clutch catch by Covington as Lew Burdette pitched his way to a slim 1-0 victory. Hank Aaron's homer in game six tied the score at two all in the top of the seventh, but New York went on to take the game 3-2. Lew Burdette pitched again in the crucial, winner-take-all seventh game, shutting down the Yanks 5-0. In Burdette's three games, all wins, he had allowed only two runs and 21 hits. The Yankees lost the Series for only their second time since 1942.

The irony for Casey Stengel was that Burdette, only the fourth pitcher to win three games in a World Series, had been traded from New York. He was also

Outfielder and first baseman Roy Edwards 'Squirrel' Sievers played for Washington from 1954 to 1959 and in 1964 and 1965. His best season was 1957, when he led the league in homers with 42, and in RBI's with 114.

Shortstop Tony Kubek hit two home runs in the World Series in his rookie year, and was named Rookie of the Year. He played a total of five Series during his nine years with the Yankees (1957-65).

the only pitcher ever to win three Series games from the Yankees. Casey's reaction was a mixed one, as he commented, 'How many runs did we score off that fellow? Two? Well that's the story.' He was quick to threaten, however, that the Yankees would be 'heard from again.'

Yogi Berra's season's performance raised speculation that he might be sliding toward an early retirement at age 32. At .251, his batting average was the lowest it had been in 12 seasons, although even in this off-year he managed to hit 24 home runs and bat in 84 runs. A colorful and irascible character, Berra had been named the American League's Most Valuable Player in 1951, 1954 and 1955. When he was named

Catcher Yogi Berra played his entire 19-year career for the New York Yankees, beginning in 1946. The 14 World Series he played in brought him four all-time firsts in the Series record books: most games played (75), most at-bats (259), most hits (71) and most doubles (10). His Series career statistics also include 12 home runs, 41 runs scored, 39 RBI's and 32 bases on balls. During the fifties Berra averaged 26 homers a season, and he was a fine defensive player as well, with a lifetime 175 double-plays to his credit. Three-time MVP Lawrence Peter Berra, who managed the Mets from 1972 to 1975 and the Yankees in 1965 and 1984-85, was elected to the Hall of Fame in 1971.

the MVP the third time, an umpire exclaimed 'Most Valuable Player! They ought to call him most voluble player.' For all his nagging about plate umpires' calls, Yogi rarely got tossed out of games and never drew a fine from the league president's office. Fears of his retirement were premature, as Berra quickly bounced back, eventually moving from his catching position to the outfield.

By now the impact of television on attendance was beginning to show at the gate. The Yankees, for example, had the vast New York metropolitan area to themselves after the Dodgers and Giants moved west, yet they were getting fewer fans through the turnstiles. In 1958 their attendance would drop 68,000 from the 1957 totals.

In the winter of 1958, American League president Will Harridge announced his plans for retirement. Seventy-two years old, he had served the League for 28 years. Joe Cronin was elected to the job on 31 January 1959 for a seven-year term of office. Cronin's successful election followed another bonanza season for those 'Damn Yankees.' But the season also featured bright stars throughout the league. The phenomenon of Ted Williams was still batting his way into baseball history. Already the oldest batting champion, Williams won his sixth batting championship in 1958, finishing at .328. Next in line was his Boston teammate Pete Runnels, who hit .322. White Sox slammer Rocky Colavito blasted four home runs in consecutive trips to the plate on 10 June. He managed to do this in Baltimore's Memorial Stadium, the toughest park in the league for home runs. Lou Gehrig has been the first American League player – back in 1932 – to hit four in a game.

In 1958 the Yankees gained their fourth straight pennant, their ninth in ten years. Stengel tied Connie Mack's record for managing nine league championships. Although New York ended up ten games ahead of the second-place White Sox, there were signs that the Yankee dynasty was beginning to crack. Early in the season the club had appeared unbeatable; they even had a 10-game winning streak, which ended when Tiger pitcher Frank Lary beat them. (Lary had an impressive 27-10 record in his contests with the Yankees.) Then the Yankees slowed down, not even maintaining a .500 win-loss margin in the last two months of the season. Their prime hitter, Mickey Mantle, was bothered by a shoulder injury and ended up with a .304 average.

The 1958 World Series was a repeat of 1957 – the Yankees against the Milwaukee Braves. Neither team had faced much serious opposition all season from within their leagues and both were looking forward to this ultimate contest. The Braves quickly moved into the lead by taking the first two games in Milwaukee, but the Yankees came back in their home stadium to win the third game. Then the Braves took the fourth game to gain what seemed like an unsurmountable lead of three games to one. But Yankee Bob Turley pitched a five-hitter, Elston Howard made a spectacular diving catch, and Gil McDougald hit a homer that proved to be the winning run as the Yankees took the fifth game, 7-0. With the Braves ahead three games to two, an exciting sixth game went into the end of the ninth inning with a 2-2 tie. Then McDougald's homer did it for the Yankees again as they won in ten innings, 4-3, tying up the Series at three games each. The seventh game pitted the Yankees' ace Don Larsen

From left to right: Warren Giles, National League President and Ford Frick, baseball commissioner, welcome Joe Cronin as the new American League President.

against the Braves' ace Lew Burdette. Larsen had to be relieved by Bob Turley, but Bill Skowron's three-run homer in the eighth put the Yankees on top, 6-2, and gave them another World Championship.

The 1959 season was distinguished by the Red Sox's introduction of their first black player, infielder Elijah (Pumpsie) Green. Now all 16 major league teams had been integrated. This decade-ending year was also unique in Yankee performance, as the club that had won nine of the previous ten pennants went through a frustrating series of slumps and injuries. By late May the World Champions were in the cellar, and by Labor Day they were eliminated from the American League race.

The fight for top place in the league centered on the White Sox and the Indians. Al Lopez, now with Chicago, relied on outstanding pitching, speed and defense to sweep a four-game series at Cleveland which began on 28 August. That spelled the end for the Indians and the White Sox ended up with a five-game lead. The White Sox went on to lose in a tight Series with the Dodgers.

And so ended the decade. Although subsequent decades brought a seemingly endless march of record-breaking performances, the fifties would be fondly remembered as an era bearing such legendary names as Joe DiMaggio, Ted Williams, Gil McDougald and Willie Mays.

Gil McDougald is congratulated by teammate Tony Kubek, after belting a third-inning solo homer in the fifth game of the World Series. The Yankees won this game and went on to take the Series, four games to three.

PEOPLES
OUT 0
STRIKE
BALL
INN 1
AT BAT 24
0 0 0
0 0 0
NATIONAL
AMERICAN
The Washington Post

CHAPTER SIX

The Sensational Sixties

"I'll never make the mistake of being 70 years old again."

Casey Stengel, after being fired from the Yankees.

Brooks Robinson graced third base with his sparkling performances for 23 years, playing for the great Baltimore Orioles from 1955-77. In 1964, when he was selected as the league's Most Valuable Player, Robinson led the league in RBI's with 118, and batted for a .317 average. On a team that won two out of four World Series contests and played in five league championships between 1966 and 1974, Brooks Robinson batted .500 and .583 in his first two play-offs, and batted .318 in the 1970 Series. He holds the all-time records at third base for fielding average, most games played, most putouts, most assists and most double plays. He was elected to the Hall of Fame in 1983.

The sixties began with the collapse of the Continental League – an idea whose time had never come. The venture had been the brainchild of attorney William A Shea. Branch Rickey was slated to serve as the league's president. Though stillborn, this challenge woke up the National and American Leagues to the fact that there was no shortage of interest and money for major league expansion. On 2 August 1960 Shea and Rickey announced in Chicago that the existing major leagues would absorb their franchises. The National League had already decided to add New York and Houston to its playing circuit. The American League quickly raced to parity. Calvin Griffith's Washington team was granted permission to relocate in Minneapolis-St Paul and a new franchise for the nation's capital was approved. General Elwood Quesada, chief of the Federal Aviation Administration, led the group investing in the new Washington team. Cowbow Gene Autry and tycoon Bob Reynolds rounded out the process by acquiring the new Los Angeles franchise. All the new clubs then had to scramble for players to field in time for the season's opener just four months away. In order to accommodate this, the other American League clubs created a players pool by each contributing 15 players from the 40-man reserve. The new clubs would pay $75,000 for each athlete they selected. The Angels invested in 30 players and the Senators invested in 31.

One gentleman clearly not for sale was Ted Williams, who passed an epic milestone during the 1960 season. Facing Wynn Hawkins, a Cleveland right-hander, he blasted his 500th home run at Cleveland Municipal Stadium, thereby joining the immortal Babe Ruth (714), Jimmie Foxx (534) and Mel Ott (511). Williams' triumph was witnessed by American League President Joe Cronin, who had managed the slugger when he hit his first professional home run. In another Red Sox-Indians match on 10 August Williams passed Ott by hitting number 512, again off a Cleveland pitcher Barry Latman, in the fifth. He slugged another in the sixth off Johnny Klippstein. The Red Sox won, 6-1. Following the game Williams announced that he was leaving baseball at the end of the season. He went out with a bang, batting .316 in his last year and hitting 29 home runs. Ending his baseball career on a fitting farewell note, Williams hit a home run in his last at bat, in Fenway Park on 28 September in a 5-4 Red Sox victory over the Orioles. Williams' career home runs totalled 521.

The 1960 season found the Yankees pulling themselves together after the previous season's slump. The Yankees went on to claim the pennant, completing Stengel's tenth win in 12 years, a feat which tied him with John McGraw for the most championships in a major league career. The Baltimore Orioles came in second place with fine performances by manager Paul Richards' pitching staff. They finished eight games behind the leaders.

The World Series found New York pitted against the Pirates. Although New York had greater cannon power, outhitting Pittsburgh 91 to 60 and outscoring them 55 to 27, the Pirates made their hits count. The Bucs won the first game despite the fact that the Yankees had 13 hits to Pittsburgh's six. The Yankees wreaked revenge in the next two games, however, punishing an assortment of Pirate pitchers. Game two of the Series, with a final score of 16-3, featured two Mickey Mantle home runs, including a blast that soared 478 feet. It was the first time in the 51-year history of Forbes Field that a right-handed batter had hit a homer over the center-field wall.

The Yankees cleaned up in the third game with a score of 10-0, as Whitey Ford held Pittsburgh to four hits – three singles and a double. Despite their two resounding defeats, the Pirates fought their way back in a tense and exciting fourth game, winning by a score of 3-2. With the Series tied at two all, the Pirates went ahead the next day, beating the Yankees 5-2 with sure relief pitching by Elroy Face. But in the next game Casey's boys opened up another slugfest, winning 12-0, the biggest margin for a shutout in World Series history.

The final game, played before 36,683 fans, epitomized baseball at its most dramatic. Rocky Nelson drove in a first-inning homer to put the Pirates ahead, 2-0. The Bucs earned two more runs in the second. Then Bill Skowron broke the ice for the Yankees, hitting a solo home run in the fifth. The next inning New York exploded as Bobby Richardson singled, Tony Kubek walked, Mickey Mantle singled and Yogi Berra belted a homer. The Yankees moved ahead, 5-4, then added two more runs off relief pitcher Elroy Face in the eighth. The score was 7-4 when Pittsburgh came to bat in the eighth. Gino Cimoli, pinch-hitting

First baseman Bill 'Moose' Skowron averaged .294 during his nine years with the New York Yankees (1954-62), and popped more than 20 homers four times in those years.

for Face, singled to right. Then centerfielder Bill Virdon sliced a grounder at Kubek who was ready for the easy double play; the ball, however, took a bad bounce, striking the shortstop in the throat and knocking him to the ground. He required first aid and was forced to leave the game. Dick Groat then singled Cimoli home, a sacrifice and a hit scored another run, and part-time catcher Hal Smith got hold of a low pitch for a three run-homer, putting Pittsburgh ahead, 9-7. The Yankees came back in the ninth to tie the score at 9-9.

The big right-hander Art Ditmar pitched for the Yankees for four and a half years, playing in three World Series, before moving to Kansas City in mid-season 1961.

Ralph Houk replaced Casey as the Yankee manager. Houk was a clear-headed man committed to professional baseball, and an excellent field manager. The club in his charge was so powerful no obstacle could stand in its way. Most serious baseball talk of the 1961 season buzzed about the awesome power of the so-called 'M&M' boys, the Mantle and Maris combination. The Yankees had acquired the talented Roger Maris in 1960. He and Mantle chased Babe Ruth's 60-homer record all summer long, keeping in stride with the master's accomplishments of the 1927 season. Injuries ended Mantle's run in September at 54, but Maris persevered, hitting number 60 on 26 September against right-hander Jack Fisher. He belted record-breaking number 61 on 1 October, the closing game of the season.

Ever since Babe Ruth hit 60 big ones in 1927, baseball theologians weighed the implications of his record being matched or broken. In 1930 Hack Wilson of the Chicago Cubs had walloped 56; Jimmie Foxx and 'Hammerin Hank' Greenberg subsequently nailed 58 outside of the fence, in 1932 and 1938 respectively. Then, when Roger Maris nearly vaporized Tracy Stallard's pitch with his 61st homer, he was not immediately canonized. Instead the high priests and a vocal segment of the baseball congregation were calling for a major league inquisition. Earlier, anticipating a possible schism, Commissioner Ford Frick ruled that Ruth's record would remain exalted unless it was topped within the 154 games of the traditional baseball calendar. Secularists like Joe Cronin reacted against the pontiff, seeing 'no logic to the ruling.' The addition of new clubs had indeed extended the season to 162 games. But Ruth himself took the home run title after playing 44 more games than Ed Williamson who hit 27 during 112 games of the 1884 National League season. Maris himself never suggested that he equalled the greatness of Ruth, who hit his home runs when few other players managed to do so. In 1927 the

Above: Roger Eugene Maris played right field for Cleveland and Kansas City before joining the Yankees in 1960. When he hit next to Mickey Mantle in the line-up, the two batting giants became known as the 'M&M boys,' lethal to pitchers. Maris, who was selected as the league's Most Valuable Player in 1960 and 1961, smashed a record-shattering 61 homers in 1961. A farm boy from North Dakota at heart, Roger Maris never enjoyed the limelight, and played the last two years of his 12-year career with the St Louis Cardinals.

The Pirates came up in the bottom of the ninth with Bill Mazeroski leading off. Although not considered a dangerous hitter, the second baseman connected with a high fast ball that sailed over the left-field fence, to clinch the game and the Series for Pittsburgh. In the locker room following the game Mickey Mantle sat down and cried. It was a tough Series for the Yankees to lose, and soon heads began to roll.

Five days after the final game Casey Stengel announced that he had been fired because of his age. 'I'll never make the mistake of being 70 years old again,' said the disgruntled Stengel. The decision to fire him was called 'cold blooded' by the press. Columnist Arthur Daley in *The New York Times* wrote: 'Casey imparted warmth to a cold organization and gave it an appeal that couldn't be bought for a million dollars. He was priceless. From a public relations standpoint the Yankees have done great damage to themselves.... It's a shabby way to treat a man who has not only brought them glory but also has given their dynasty firmer footing than it ever had. So long, Case, you gave us 12 unforgettable years.'

General Manager George Weiss also lost his job that November. He was the other person most responsible for putting together the teams that had won so many pennants and championships. Happily, he and Stengel were soon reunited in their old capacities in the New York expansion franchise, the Mets. In another shake-up, managers Jimmy Dykes of the Tigers and the Indians' Joe Gordon switched jobs in the league's first managers' trade.

Right: On 4 July 1957 Yogi Berra belted a home run, the 250th of his career, to score Tony Kubek and Mickey Mantle. Berra finished the day with eight runs batted in as the Yanks swamped the Red Sox, 10 to 0.

entire American League produced only 439, so that Babe's 60 accounted for some 14 percent of all the home runs in the entire league. In 1961 the American League yielded a record of 1,534, making Maris's clout a mortal four percent. Maris's beatification did occur, though, and he shares the official record, albeit with an asterisk next to his name.

Meanwhile, the Yankees devoured their opponents in 1961, winning the pennant under manager Ralph Houk. New York hit a record 240 home runs, with Bill Skowron, Yogi Berra, Elston Howard and Johnny Blanchard joining Mantle and Maris in hitting over 20 each. Even so, the Yankees did not lead the league in runs; the second-place Tigers scored 841 to the Yankees' 827.

New York's pennant victory was the second straight. The club enjoyed pitching support from Whitey Ford, whose reliable right arm produced a 25-4 season. Ford was clearly worth his $50,000 salary. Other clubs demonstrated powerful hitting during the 1961 season. Third in batting were Minnesota's Harmon Killebrew and Baltimore's Jim Gentile, both hitting 46 homers. Rocky Colavito bashed 45, while Norm Cash, his Detroit teammate, powered 41 over the fence. In his most sensational season, Cash won the league's batting title, the first in his 17-year league career.

In the 1961 World Series contest between the Yankees and Reds, Whitey Ford put to rest Babe Ruth's most cherished record of pitching 29 and two-thirds consecutive scoreless innings in World Series play. Shutting out Cincinnati in the opening game, 2-0, Ford extended his streak of scoreless pitching to 27 innings. Pitching again in the fourth Series game, Ford went five scoreless innings before his ankle gave out, thereby setting a record of 32. The Yankees won the Series in five games.

The Yankees brought aboard their first black player in 1955 when they signed Elston Howard. The big man played outfielder, then catcher for them until 1967, ending his career the following year in Boston. He played 10 World Series during his 14-year career.

The 'M&M' batting fusillade nearly eclipsed Yogi Berra's yeoman records. By now he had played in 14 World Series, including 75 games, with 259 times at bat. He would make the World Series record books with runs scored (41), total bases (117), hits (71), doubles (10), home runs (12), runs batted in (39), and walks (32).

President John F Kennedy threw out the first ball of 1962 as the Senators opened in their new $24 million stadium built at the taxpayers' expense. A throng of 44,383 watched the home squad inaugurate their magnificent palace by beating Detroit, 4-1. Kennedy stayed for the whole game, leaving Laotian Ambassador Tiao Khampan back at the White House meditating on the inscrutability of American presidents.

The ebbs and flows of the 1962 season may have differed from the previous year but the Yankees again rose to the top. The batting hurricane of the previous year was tempered, with Maris dropping to 33 and Mantle to 30 home runs for the year. Harmon Killebrew surged to 48, thereby winning the second of the six home run titles he would garner. The greatest surprise of the season was the ferocity of the two new clubs, the Minnesota Twins and the Los Angeles Angels. Like nimble sharks, they gashed the league leader until the final two weeks of the season, when New York burst to the surface. The Angels were the most surprising club in the game. General manager Fred Haney netted some astounding deals to keep his team in the water.

In the 1962 Series, the Yankees faced the Giants, who forced them to play seven games before they could wring out a victory. Whitey Ford's record-breaking pitching streak was stopped in the second inning of the first game. Ford had little trouble winning, 6-2, but the game ended his scoreless Series total at 33 and two thirds consecutive innings. But the most memorable episode in the 1962 Series came in the seventh game, in the bottom of the ninth, with the Yankees leading only 1-0 and the Giants at bat. The Giants got two men on, one on second, the other at third, with two out, when Willie McCovey came to bat. Ralph Terry was pitching – the very Ralph Terry who two years before had delivered up the fateful pitch to Bill Mazeroski. McCovey was a far more powerful hitter than Mazeroski, and sure enough, he got hold of Terry's third pitch and sent a line drive rocketing toward right center field. But this time Yankee second baseman Bobby Richardson snared it – and the Yankees had done it again.

Early Wynn might have been the most tragic figure of the 1962 season. At the year's end he stood one game short of the cherished goal of winning his 300th lifetime victory. The White Sox released him at the end of the season, then allowed him to join spring training in 1963 and attempt to win a berth. Failing to do so, he nonetheless stayed in shape, hoping for another opportunity. Finally the Cleveland Indians offered him a contract. Years before Wynn had pitched his best games with Cleveland; he had taken more than 20 scalps in four great seasons. Now, aching with gouty arms, legs and feet, his dream eluded him his first four times out. He used painkillers to ease the suffering. In July, in his fifth try, he crossed the line, capturing the big gold watch in a game against Kansas City. In the last victory of his major league career he led the Indians to a 7-4 triumph over the Athletics. Wynn became the fourteenth major league pitcher to win 300 games and the first in the American League since Lefty Grove went over the top in 1941.

Within weeks of the opening of the 1963 season, the league witnessed another record-shattering performance by the explosive Minnesota Twins. Playing in a doubleheader against Washington, they slugged eight home runs in the first contest and four in the second. The 1939 Yankees had been the only other American League team to hit eight homers in a single contest. Harmon Killebrew and Vic Power (true to his name) hit a pair each and Bob Allison, Jimmie Hall, Bernie Allen and Rich Rolling connected for one each.

Below left: Hall of Famer Harmon 'Killer' Killebrew led the league in homers six times during his 22-year career.

Below: Pitcher Camilo Pascual won 20 and 21 games for the Twins in 1962 and 1963.

All this was chickenfeed to the Yankees, who gobbled up the pennant despite injuries to Mickey Mantle, and Roger Maris's bad back. Mantle was badly hurt when he crashed into the center-field fence while chasing a Brooks Robinson home run. He played in only 65 games and Maris appeared in 90. Nonetheless the team did have something to crow about. They finished 10 and a half games in front, their largest margin since 1947. New York then went on to lose four straight against the cocky Los Angeles Dodgers. They lost two to Sandy Koufax, and one each to Don Drysdale and Johnny Podres. New York was held to four runs, 22 hits and a team batting average of .171. Yogi Berra made his last active appearance as a Yankee player in game three, when he lined out while pinchhitting for Jim Bouton.

Berra came back in a Yankee uniform as manager and Houk replaced Roy Hamley as the club's general manager. 'My big problem as manager will be to see if I can manage,' commented Yogi from his new vantage point. Before his selection he had closely eyed every one of Houk's moves in anticipation of the moves by the front office.

Opposite top: In 1962 right-hander Ralph Terry led the league in wins with 23 and in innings pitched with 298.2. He helped the Yankees to a Series victory that year by winning two of the three games he pitched.

Opposite bottom: On the last day of the 1961 season, Roger Maris blasted his 61st homer to break Babe Ruth's landmark record.

The 1964 season opened as usual in Washington. President Lyndon B Johnson took obvious delight in being the tenth Commander-in-Chief to throw out the first game ball. (Johnson confided to the Senators' manager Gil Hodges that before entering politics he played first base back in Texas.) The Senators lost to the Angels, 4-0, with pitcher Claude Osteen making the only hit, a double. During the fourth inning the stadium's loudspeakers blared the announcement that there was a quorum call on the floor of the Senate over the Civil Rights Bill. Several Senators – politicians, not players – raced out of Johnson's box and to the exits.

Right: The big right-hander Dean Chance, who pitched for Los Angeles from 1961 to 1964, had a phenomenal season in 1964, turning in 20 wins and only 9 losses, with a 1.65 ERA and 11 shutouts.

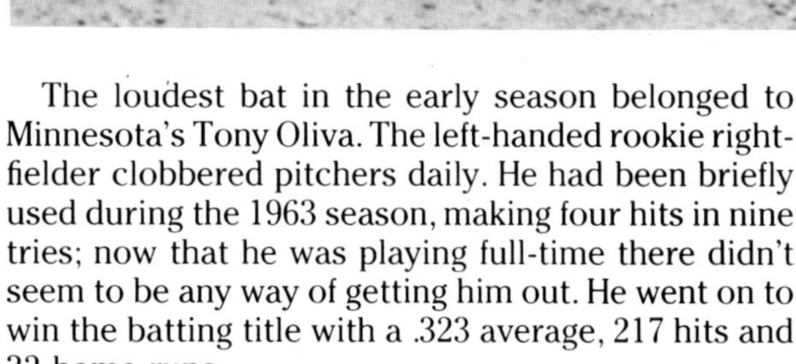

Right: Outfielder Tony Oliva played for the Minnesota Twins for his entire 15-year career, during which time he won the batting title three times. In 1964 he was selected as Rookie of the Year, leading the league in hits with 217, in doubles with 43 and in runs scored with 109. He retired from active play in 1976 with a .304 lifetime batting average.

The loudest bat in the early season belonged to Minnesota's Tony Oliva. The left-handed rookie right-fielder clobbered pitchers daily. He had been briefly used during the 1963 season, making four hits in nine tries; now that he was playing full-time there didn't seem to be any way of getting him out. He went on to win the batting title with a .323 average, 217 hits and 32 home runs.

In Boston and elsewhere in the league a new crop of talent put on some outstanding performances. Nineteen-year-old outfielder Tony Conigliaro and Dick Radatz, an outstanding relief pitcher, were stirring up the crowds in Boston's Fenway Park. Conigliaro played furious ball until he was hit by a pitch that broke his arm late in July; he returned late in the season, showering a total of 24 home runs and achieving a .290 batting average. Radatz, known as 'The Monster,' came in almost every other day to shut down batters in late innings of play. A workhorse, he appeared in 79 games – only two shy of the American League record of 81 appearances on the mound. Radatz, in fact, appeared in 29 more innings than John Wyatt, the record-holder, and earned an astounding 16 wins in games he did not start.

A fine defensive player, Jim Fregosi played shortstop for the California Angels from 1965 to 1971, when he was traded to the Mets in exchange for Nolan Ryan. Fregosi finished his 18-year career in the National League with Pittsburgh, in 1978.

Below: The big power-hitter Boog Powell played outfield and first base for the Baltimore Orioles from 1961 to 1974, finishing his 17-year career with the Indians and the Dodgers. During the five seasons he went to the league championships with the Orioles, he averaged 23 home runs and 85 RBI's each year.

Meanwhile Baltimore fans were having a love affair with John 'Boog' Powell, who walloped 39 homers. A large man, left-hander Powell had trouble keeping his weight under 225 pounds. His season's batting average was a respectable .290. Angels fans were singing the praises of Jim Fregosi at shortstop and Dean Chance on the mound. Luis Tiant, a fine Cleveland pitcher, and Bert Campaneris, a Kansas City infielder, were also part of the crop of new young players who had earned respect during the season.

Early in 1964, Charles O Finley, the owner of the Kansas City team, tried to raise a storm about the lay-out of Yankee Stadium. According to Finley, New York gained an unfair advantage because the Stadium favored left-handed pull hitters. To prove his point he raised a replica of the barrier at Yankee Stadium in his park, calling it the 'pennant porch.' League officials ordered the contraption dismantled and the matter was soon forgotten. Gabe Paul, general manager of the Cleveland Indians, summed things up when he said, 'We have more important things to worry about than that. The Yankees have won several pennants not because of the dimensions of their park but because of their great talent.'

The Yankees were indeed the subject of the '64 season question.' Could the New York club reinflate again after being so badly stomped by the Dodgers? After all, only the 1940 Cincinnati Reds had recovered from such a rout to take the pennant again. The Yankees somehow won the American League title instinctively, as if their chromosomes were programmed to play the cycle of World Series fall after fall. Through most of the summer they played sluggish baseball, and it seemed as if Yogi Berra, who had taken over as manager, couldn't maintain control. A headline-making scuffle over Phil Linz's harmonica seemed to knock the team out of its stupor and they started a serious race for the pennant. Rookie pitcher Mel Stottlemyre came up from the minors in August and played a key role by supplementing the pitching of Whitey Ford and Jim Bouton. Yogi Berra had had Stottlemyre brought up from Richmond farm club out of desperation. Whitey Ford had developed a bad hip and the Yankees had sunk to third place. In his debut, Stottlemyre went the distance, defeating Chicago, 7-3. His overhand sinker had helpless batters swinging at the ground. Soon veterans Mickey Mantle, Roger Maris, Elston Howard and Joe Pepitone put their shoulders to the wheel in order to power the Yankee drive. The Yankees got back on track, grabbing the pennant on their way to the World Series against the St Louis Cardinals.

Whitey Ford's contribution to New York's 29th league championship deserves special comment. In 13 seasons he had won 216 games while losing only 84 for a .720 percentage. This surpassed Spud Chandler's old mark of .717. It was the highest win ratio in major league history for any pitcher who had won more than 200 games.

Once again the Yankees entered the contest burdened by injuries. A bad leg left Mantle limping and Tony Kubek couldn't play in the classic because of a sprained wrist. Ace Whitey Ford opened for the Bombers against Ray Sadecki. Ford let in five runs before being relieved by Al Downing, then Rollie Sheldon and Pete Mikkelsen. The Cardinals won 9-5. The Series then seesawed, with the Yankees winning the second and third games, and St Louis winning the

Yankee Elston Gene 'Ellie' Howard batted .274 for his 14-year career. In 1964 he helped hit his team to the Series, with a .313 batting average and 84 RBI's. In the Series itself he went 7 for 24 as the Yanks lost a close contest to St Louis, four games to three.

James Timothy 'Mudcat' Grant pitched for Cleveland for six years, turning in an unimpressive 64 wins and 59 losses. He moved to Minnesota in 1964, however, and in 1965 won 21 games, losing only seven, to help his team to the World Series.

fourth and fifth games. Consecutive homers by Maris and Mantle, and Joe Pepitone's grand slam in the eighth inning clinched a Yankee victory in the sixth game, tying the Series at three games each. For the decisive seventh game, Berra picked Stottlemyre to pitch against Bob Gibson. The Cards scored three times in the fourth and three times in the fifth to run up a 6-0 lead. Mantle then belted a three-run homer, putting the Yankees back in the race, but St Louis scored again in the seventh inning. New York went down fighting as Clete Boyer and Phil Linz hit solo home runs in the ninth before Gibson tied up a 7-5 victory for the Cards. The day after the Series ended, the front office fired Berra, while Johnny Keane quit as manager of the Cardinals; both decisions had been reached during the midsummer doldrums. Ironically, the Yankees later recruited Keane to manage the team.

In 1965, the New York Yankees couldn't get going. Age and injuries had humbled baseball's premier club into the mire of sixth place. It was their lowest finish since 1925. Now a rainbow of possibilities awaited the other American League clubs, and the Minnesota Twins won the championship for the first time ever. For decades they had played as the lowly Washington Senators before moving to the far north in 1961. Managed by modest Sam Mele, the Twins gained their laurels by hitting the long ball. Harmon Killebrew, Bob Allison, Don Mincher and Jimmie Hall swung heavy-duty bats, while Tony Oliva won the league's Most Valuable Player award with his solid hitting and play at shortstop. Ace 21-game winner Jim 'Mudcat' Grant and the other Minnesota pitchers were buoyed by such hitting prowess.

The Series opened in Minnesota on Yom Kippur, a Jewish High Holy day, which prevented Sandy Koufax from pitching for the Dodgers. To the horror of Los Angeles fans their starting pitcher, Don Drysdale, was swept from the mound in the top of the third and the Twins won, 8-2. Koufax took the mound the next day and again the Dodgers were stunned as their ace was tagged for two in the sixth and pulled for a pitch hitter; the Twins went on to win, 5-2. Gloom hung over Los Angeles like smog as the teams approached game three. Dodger pitcher Claude Osteen, who had an unimpressive 15-15 record, turned the Series around by papering the Twins, 4-0. Drysdale then triumphed in game four as the Dodgers plastered their opponents, 7-2. The next day Koufax shut down Minnesota, 7-0. The Twins' Mudcat Grant then beat Osteen on the mound and hit a three-run homer to win the game 5-1, bringing the Series race down to the wire. Sandy, with two days rest, faced Jim Kaat going for the Twins. The two southpaws staged a thrilling

In 1966 the Orioles went all the way, helped by such outstanding talent as pitcher Dave McNally (above), who had a .684 winning percentage that year, the future Hall of Famer at third base, Brooks Robinson (opposite top), and outfielder Frank Robinson (opposite bottom), who won the batting title that year.

duel, which could have gone either way. Kaat was then replaced by a string of relievers as Koufax, who kept a slight edge by allowing only three hits, sealed the Series with a 2-0 victory.

In 1966 the American League pennant belonged to the Baltimore Orioles. They ran off a 13-game lead by the end of July and sashayed to their first pennant since rising from the ashes of the 1954 St Louis Browns. Frank Robinson, an outfielder obtained the previous winter from Cincinnati, fired up the club. An outstanding hitter, Robinson set out to burn every opposing American League pitcher while he ignited his teammates into action. Slugging first baseman Boog Powell, and clutch hitter and third base wizard Brooks Robinson grilled mounds of determined pitchers. Fielding stars Luis Aparicio and Paul Blair joined a well-balanced pitching staff to close the lid on the teams that found themselves on the Baltimore skillet.

Both Robinsons, Frank and Brooks, had been outstanding ballplayers for a decade before Baltimore made it to the Series. Yet they were hardly what one could call household names. Frank came into the majors with the Cincinnati Reds in 1956 and was voted Rookie of the Year. He earned the Most Valuable Player of the Year Award in the National League in 1961, but his triumphs were overshadowed by the Mantle and Maris performance that year. The Reds inexplicably gave Baltimore a wonderful gift by trading Robinson while he was still in his prime. Robinson promptly earned the American League Triple Crown and was named the league's Most Valuable Player in 1966, thereby becoming the only person to garner that title in both leagues. He eventually became the first black to manage a major league team.

Brooks Robinson's talent had also been overlooked for years by fans and sports commentators. He finally gained the reputation of being the finest third baseman of his time and possibly in history. Upon retiring after 20 years with Baltimore he held just about every fielding record a third baseman could hold. Even old-timers had begun comparing him with vintage heroes Pie Traynor and Billy Cox.

While Baltimore blazed, the Yankees fell from their sixth place purgatory to the bottom. This was only the third time in the club's 64-year history that they had sunk so low. Keene was dropped as manager, and Houk left the front office to resume his old position. In mid-September Don Topping sold his shares of the club to CBS; Mike Burke, a network vice-president and former University of Pennsylvania football player, was named the club's president. A month later Lee MacPhail, son of the old baseball magnate, joined the front office as general manager. Other developments in the American League in 1966 included the unveiling of the California Angels' new park in Anaheim. The triple-decker structure was built in less than two years at a cost of $24 million.

The 1966 Series looked like it was going to be a test of Baltimore's hitting power against Los Angeles' pitching. The Orioles began blasting early in the

Left fielder Carl Yastrzemski whacks a long line drive. Yaz played his entire 23-year career with the Boston Red Sox, powering the team to the World Series in 1967. He won the Triple Crown and was selected as league MVP that year, with 44 home runs, 112 runs scored and 121 RBI's. The Sox won the pennant on the last day of the season as Yaz went 4 for 4 against Minnesota. Then, despite Yaz's three homers, his team lost a close Series to St Louis, four games to three.

Right: Dave Boswell pitched for Minnesota from 1964 to 1970, ending his career in 1971 with the Tigers and Orioles. His best season was 1969, when he turned in 20 wins and his team won the division.

Far right: The big right-hander Jim Lonborg pitched for Boston from 1965 to 1971, striking out a league-leading 246 batters in 1967 to win 22 games and the Cy Young Award. Lonborg won two of the three games he pitched in the '67 Series, including a one-hit shutout.

opener against pitcher Don Drysdale. In the first inning with one man on base, Frank Robinson tagged the Dodgers for a home run. Then even before many of the fans had found their seats, Brooks Robinson, the next batter, hit another homer. Each team picked up a run in the second and the Dodgers one more in the third – their last run in the entire Series! Paralyzed, they suffered through an excruciating 33 consecutive scoreless innings – the most of any team in championship history. Los Angeles made six errors in one game, three of them in one inning. The Orioles responded by playing errorless ball throughout the Series, with Jim Palmer, Wally Bunker and Dave McNally pitching consecutive shutouts. They gave Baltimore its first World Series victory as well as the first pennant since the old National League Baltimore Orioles of 1896.

The Boston Red Sox, only one step away from the basement in 1966, fought their way to the top in 1967. Under the leadership of Carl Yastrzemski, a modern-day Samson, they muscled their way up to take the pennant on the final day of the season. 'Yaz,' a moody leftfielder, won the Triple Crown with more pith than even Frank Robinson. Yastrzemski seemed to win games daily with his home runs as he tied the Twins' Harmon Killebrew with 44, and led with 121 RBI's and a .326 batting average. Boston came out on top of a furious four-team contest, which included Minnesota, Detroit and Chicago.

Just how Boston won the pennant has been the subject of a great deal of ironic commentary. Some of the team showed up at spring training overweight, and it seemed unlikely that they would climb higher than ninth or tenth place. Yet by the start of the season manager Dick Williams' coaches were boasting that their squad was in 'the best physical shape ever.' The starting nine players averaged only 24 years of age, but were fast on their feet. A number of pundits predicted a secure last-place finish for the club, and any suggestion that they would win the pennant would be have been met with charges of lunacy. Boston seemed as allergic to the pennant title as some people are to goldenrod.

The new-found Boston strength developed in part through the promotion of a group of capable rookies from the Red Sox's Toronto farm club. In 1967, Toronto manager Dick Williams had been moved to Boston to harness the calves he had nourished down on the farm. Williams was a strict disciplinarian who was not afraid to crack the whip during training and in the regular season, on or off the field. In the past, Red Sox players had been protected from harsh criticism by Tom 'Papa' Yawkey, the club's owner. Dick Williams and a bit of luck changed all that.

Billy Rohr pitched in Boston's first contest against the Yankees. The youngster had spent a sleepless night the evening before, thinking about his first major league start. He won the game, pitching a one-hitter, and then found himself on the Ed Sullivan show being touted as the best in the league. Boston sportswriters were rhapsodic and fans began celebrating in the first weeks of the season, only to be disappointed when the club became sloppy and started losing

games. As smiles turned to frowns, the manager and players started calling each other names. Williams scolded pitcher Jim Lonborg for 'throwing the ball right down the pipe' on a two-strike count with bases loaded. He questioned George Scott's brain power for swinging at a pitch when he had been given the 'take' sign. Williams himself muddled things up by moving outfielder Reggie Smith to second base, and playing first baseman George Scott in the outfield. After everyone tired of name-calling and Scott and Smith regained their positions, the team started winning again. Yastrzemski and Tony Conigliaro blasted balls out of everyone's reach, and Williams reserved his name-calling for umpires and league officials.

By the end of April, Boston was tied with New York for first place. Fans were ecstatic, and the players' dreams of glory pulled the team together. Williams imposed a jailhouse routine, insisting that every member of the club, star or not, had to attend morning practice and obey strict curfews, complete with bed checks. Every time the players grew restive, the rebellion was smothered by a string of victories.

Yaz experienced ups and downs as did other team members. He was benched for a while in the midst of a slump. Russ Gibson, the promising catcher, never caught fire, and Reggie Smith struck out 13 times in 25 visits to the plate. To make matters worse, Rico

Right: Red Sox outfielder Tony Conigliaro became the youngest player ever to hit 100 home runs. In his rookie season (1964) he belted 24 homers, then led the league the following year with 32. With 104 homers under his belt at age 22, in August 1967 a fastball hit him in the face, sidelining him for the rest of the season and curtailing his rise to greatness.

Below: Outfielder Al Kaline played for the Detroit Tigers for his entire 22-year career (1953-74). His outstanding hitting won him acclaim early on, as he won the batting title in 1955 with a .340 average. In 1967 he batted .308 with 25 homers as his team finished the season tied with the Twins for second place, one game behind the Red Sox.

Petrocelli suffered acute tendonitis and catcher Bob Tillman accidentally beaned his teammate, pitcher John Wyatt.

Then in a game against Boston's archrival, the Yankees, Red Sox infielder Joe Foy hit a bases-loaded home run which seemed to turn the tide, starting Boston's rise into orbit. Some have claimed that criticism only served to kindle the Boston fire. White Sox manager Eddie Stanky remarked of Carl Yastrzemski: 'Maybe an all-star ball player, but only from the neck down.' Outraged fans showered Stanky and his team with beer cans, paper cups and an array of garbage when they next visited Fenway Park. Perhaps it was the trade that brought the Red Sox catcher Elston Howard that catalyzed the pennant. Howard, briefly heartbroken by the deal, soon was coaxing winning games out of Boston's often shaky pitching staff.

Opponents argued that it took more than Howard's catching experience to boost the Boston pitching staff. Joe Pepitone of the Yankees bluntly stated, 'John Wyatt has so much Vaseline on him that if he should ever overslide second base he'd keep on going to the fence.' The Boston team faced constant complaints about Wyatt's Vaseline ball and other teammates' spitballs. One day umpire Hank Soar asked to examine the ball but found it wiped clean; he threw it back – but not before indicating that he knew very well what Wyatt was pitching by first spitting on it himself.

Playing with grit and sheer determination, Boston stayed in the 1967 race despite the fact that Tony Conigliaro, who had hit 20 homers and knocked in 67 runs, was tragically hit in the face by a pitch in August that would end his season and ruin his exceptional career. He would play for four more years after sitting out the 1968 season, but would never regain his former level of brilliance. On 7 September four clubs were virtually tied at the top: Chicago and Minnesota shared first, while Boston and Detroit shared second, only one percentage point behind. Chicago was the first to drop out, only two games before the season's finish. Detroit and Minnesota held on tenaciously until the last day. Boston defeated Minnesota twice and then had to wait for the outcome of the Tigers' doubleheader against California. The Tigers took the opener, but the Angels then turned Detroit's pennant dream into a nightmare by taking the second game. Boston had done the impossible.

Right-hander Denny McLain hurled his way to 31 wins in 1968, winning the Cy Young Award and helping the Tigers become world champs.

The 1967 World Series lasted seven games. Cardinal pitcher Bob Gibson struck out 10 as St Louis won a close first game 2-1. Although the Red Sox, fired by two Yaz homers and Lonberg's superb pitching, stomped the Cardinals 5-0 in game two, Boston's hopes began to fade as St Louis racked up impressive victories in the next two games, shutting down the Sox 6-0 in game four. They now led the Sox by three games to one, but Boston kept alive with a 3-1 victory in game five, then switched on their power for game six. Three fourth-inning home runs by Yastrzemski, Smith and Petrocelli set a World Series record, as eight St Louis pitchers tried to douse the Boston fire. With an 8-4 win, the Red Sox tied the Series at three games each. But in the decisive seventh game, Gibson again struck out 10 for the Cardinals, winning the game and Series for St Louis.

Although Yaz batted .400 for the Series with 10 hits, including two doubles and three homers, Cardinals Roger Maris, Lou Brock (who hit .414 and stole a record seven bases) and Bob Gibson (who won three games, striking out 26 and giving up only 14 hits) proved unbeatable.

Thwarted in 1967, the Tigers devoured their opponents in the 1968 season, smoothly running to a 12-game lead by the finish of the pennant race. Their pitching ace Denny McLain was the first 30-game winner since Dizzy Dean in 1934. Winning 31 games and losing only six, McLain was voted the league's

Left-hander Mickey Lolich's superb pitching complemented McLain's, as he worked his magic for the Tigers as well. In the '68 Series Lolich hit a home run and won all three of the games he pitched. After 13 years with Detroit, Lolich pitched for the Mets and Padres, ending his career in 1979 with a lifetime won-lost record of 217-191.

Most Valuable Player and the winner of the Cy Young award. Denny enjoyed tremendous batting power to back him up: Al Kaline, Norm Cash, Dick McAuliffe, Jim Northrup, Willie Horton, Mickey Stanley, Gates Brown and Bill Freehan were all capable of getting runs across the plate. In addition, the Tigers had another pitching ace in Mickey Lolich, a pleasant and paunchy southpaw who, though overshadowed by McLain, could throw a fast ball as close to the speed of sound as any Denny propelled.

The year's batting records were the inverse of the ones in pitching. The combined batting average for both leagues amounted to a mere .236, the lowest ever recorded. Only one American League player batted better than .300: Carl Yastrzemski passed a hair's breadth over that mark by taking the batting title with an average of .3005, the lowest league-leading average in the history of the majors. Mickey Mantle had a moment in the sun during the 1968 season. His 18 home runs moved him past Ted Williams' 521 and Jimmie Foxx's 534 into third in the all-time home run contest with 536. Another notable event of the year was the move of the Kansas City Athletics to Oakland, where some future greats – including Reggie Jackson, Bert Campaneris, Jim 'Catfish' Hunter and Joe Rudi – would work toward making history.

The Tigers won the World Series in seven games. Affable Mickey Lolich pulled the contest out from under the seemingly unbeatable Cardinals. St Louis' Brock and Gibson tormented their opponents on offense and from the mound. Brock hit .464 with two home runs, and stole seven bases. Gibson shut out the Tigers in the opener with a record 17-strikeout performance. Denny McLain, who faced Gibson in the opener, had trouble controlling the ball and left after five innings.

Lolich pitched a six-hitter in game number two, winning 8-1. He surprised everyone, himself included, by hitting the first home run in his six-year major league career. The Cardinals went on to win the next two games, first behind Ray Washburn and then as Gibson fanned 10 batters to take his seventh straight World Series victory, 10-1. Again McLain was the loser, and the Cards were ahead, three games to one.

Lolich came back to win the fifth contest for the

Tigers, 5-3. The Tigers then exploded in the sixth game, including a ten-run inning; McLain was the winning pitcher as the Tigers roared to a 13-1 victory. In the final match Lolich faced Gibson. The score was 0-0 with two outs in the seventh inning when Gibson gave up singles to Tigers Norm Cash and Willie Horton. Next Jim Northrup hit a line drive that center fielder Curt Flood misjudged and it flew over his head for a triple. Northrup then scored on a Bill Freehan double. Each team scored once in the ninth and when the game ended at 4-1, Detroit catcher Bill Freehan ran out to the mound and hugged Lolich, lifting him off his feet.

The 1969 season saw the expansion of both the major leagues to 12 teams each, adding the Montreal Expos and the San Diego Padres to the National League, and the Kansas City Royals and the Seattle Pilots to the American. The leagues were then split

into two streamlined divisions, each with six teams, playing a 162-game schedule. Under the new system the league championships were decided in favor of the team that passed a new hurdle, a best-of-five play-off. The American League Eastern Division was comprised of New York, Boston, Baltimore, Detroit, Washington and Cleveland; the Western included Oakland, Minnesota, California (as Los Angeles renamed itself), Chicago, Seattle and Kansas City.

In addition to these changes, new rules were devised to help batters in their confrontations with pitchers. Pitching in both leagues had become so dominant that too few runs were being scored to keep fans watching television or coming to the stadiums. Batting averages were slipping as games seemed to creep along with all the action of a cricket match. In order to rectify this situation, the pitching mound was lowered five inches and the strike zone reduced in size: instead of being from the top of the shoulder to the bottom of the knee, it was contracted to the area between the armpit and the top of the knee. These measures provided an aid to batters while making even greater demands on pitchers.

The outstanding Tiger outfielder Al Kaline demonstrates his swing. Kaline put his swing to good use in the '68 Series, going 11 for 29 and popping two homers. Al Kaline finished up his career in 1974 with 3007 hits, and was elected to the Hall of Fame in 1980.

Below: As part of Detroit's unstoppable team, Tiger outfielder Willie Horton smashed 36 homers in 1968, then batted .304, with one round-tripper, in the World Series.

Baltimore shortstop Mark Belanger makes a double play. Belanger played for the Orioles for 17 years, ending his career in 1982 after one season with the Dodgers. Belanger went to the play-offs six times and the Series four times with the Orioles. His .977 fielding average rates him an all-time second place.

The Orioles, under skipper Earl Weaver, won the American League Eastern Division pennant in 1969 with a solid 109 victories. They left defending champions Detroit 19 games behind in second place. Baltimore allowed their opponents an average of only 2.38 runs per game all year. Their distinguished pitching staff included Mike Cuellar (23-11) as well as Dave McNally (20-7) and Jim Palmer (16-4). Palmer pitched a no-hitter, while the other two came close by not allowing men on before the final inning of nearly perfect games. Six Orioles batted .280 or better with 'Boog' Powell and Frank Robinson most successful at the plate. In addition, the club enjoyed the best defense in the league. Shortstop Mark Belanger handled a glove with the finesse of Luis Aparicio. Second base belonged to Dave Johnson, while Paul Blair controlled center field. It seemed all a Baltimore pitcher had to do was let the opponents hit the ball and his colleagues make the out.

The Minnesota Twins won the Western Division title after a season-long fight against the Oakland A's. The heated contest left the managers of both teams without jobs. Hank Bauer lost his because the Athletics failed to win, while victorious Billy Martin was kicked out because of frequent conflicts with the Twins' front office. Harmon Killebrew's 49 home runs and 140 RBI's led the Minnesota offense, and teammate Rod Carew's .322 batting average foreshadowed his future achievements. Other outstanding performers included Oakland's Reggie Jackson, who hit 47 home runs, and Washington's Frank Howard, who sent 48 balls over the fence. Pitcher Denny McLain

came through with an impressive 24-9 season for Detroit, but it proved to be his last winning season.

Baltimore won three straight in the American League's first play-offs, shutting out Minnesota for the pennant. The first two games went into extra innings, the Orioles winning the first 4-3 in 12 innings, and the second 1-0 in 11. The final game was a romp, ending at 11-2.

Baltimore was clearly the favorite going into the 1969 World Series. They faced the New York Mets, a relatively inexperienced club that stood eighth in National League batting at .241. Despite their low overall batting, some on the squad managed to pull off a game-winning hit with almost daily regularity. Their strong pitching staff was led by Tom Seaver, a 25-game winner, and Jerry Koosman, who finished with 17-9. They were rich in depth and spirit and led by the rarest of managers, Gil Hodges, the former Brooklyn first baseman.

The Orioles won the first game, 4-1, as Mike Cuellar

Left: Second baseman Davy Johnson played for Baltimore from 1965 to 1972, turning in a respectable .280 batting average in 1969.

Below: Left-handed hurler Mike Cuellar pitched his best years for Baltimore, beginning in 1969 when he tied Denny McLain for the Cy Young Award. For half of his eight years with the Orioles, Cuellar won at least 20 games, helping bring his team to five league play-offs and three Series.

beat Tom Seaver. New York won the second game, 2-1, on Jerry Koosman's two-hit pitching. From then on the Mets didn't stop winning until the Series was over. They took the third game behind the pitching of Gary Gentry, 5-0. Tommie Agee, the Mets' center fielder, put on an incredible one-man show that game. He blasted a homer in the first; then in the fourth, with two Baltimore runners on base and two out, he sprinted to the 396-foot marker and made an unbelievable back-handed, finger-tip catch against the wall. In the seventh inning, with two out and the bases

loaded, Baltimore's Paul Blair smacked a line drive to right center that seemed a certain triple until Agee snared it with a diving catch. Both plays ranked with the most sensational in Series history. Agee by himself saved six runs, and Gary Gentry, the rookie pitcher, was credited with the 5-0 win. Seaver came through in the fourth game by pitching a six-hit game, winning 2-1 in the tenth inning. Then the Mets took the final game 5-3, despite the fact that Baltimore clobbered Koosman for two home runs and three runs in the third. Regaining his cool, he pitched scoreless ball for the rest of the game.

The sixties were closing with Ted Williams' return to the sport. The last .400 hitter ended nine years of self-imposed exile by accepting the position of manager of the Washington Senators in 1969. The team offered him a $1 million stock deal and a partnership with owner Robert Short. Williams went on to lead the Senators to their first winning season in 17 years and was voted the American League Manager of the Year. In this way the torch of tradition was handed on to the seventies.

Opposite: The Orioles' pitching phenomenon, Jim Palmer won 16 games – including a no-hitter – and lost only four in 1969, giving him a league-leading .800 winning percentage.

Above: Baltimore outfielder from 1964 to 1976, Paul Blair hit 26 homers and scored 102 runs in 1969.

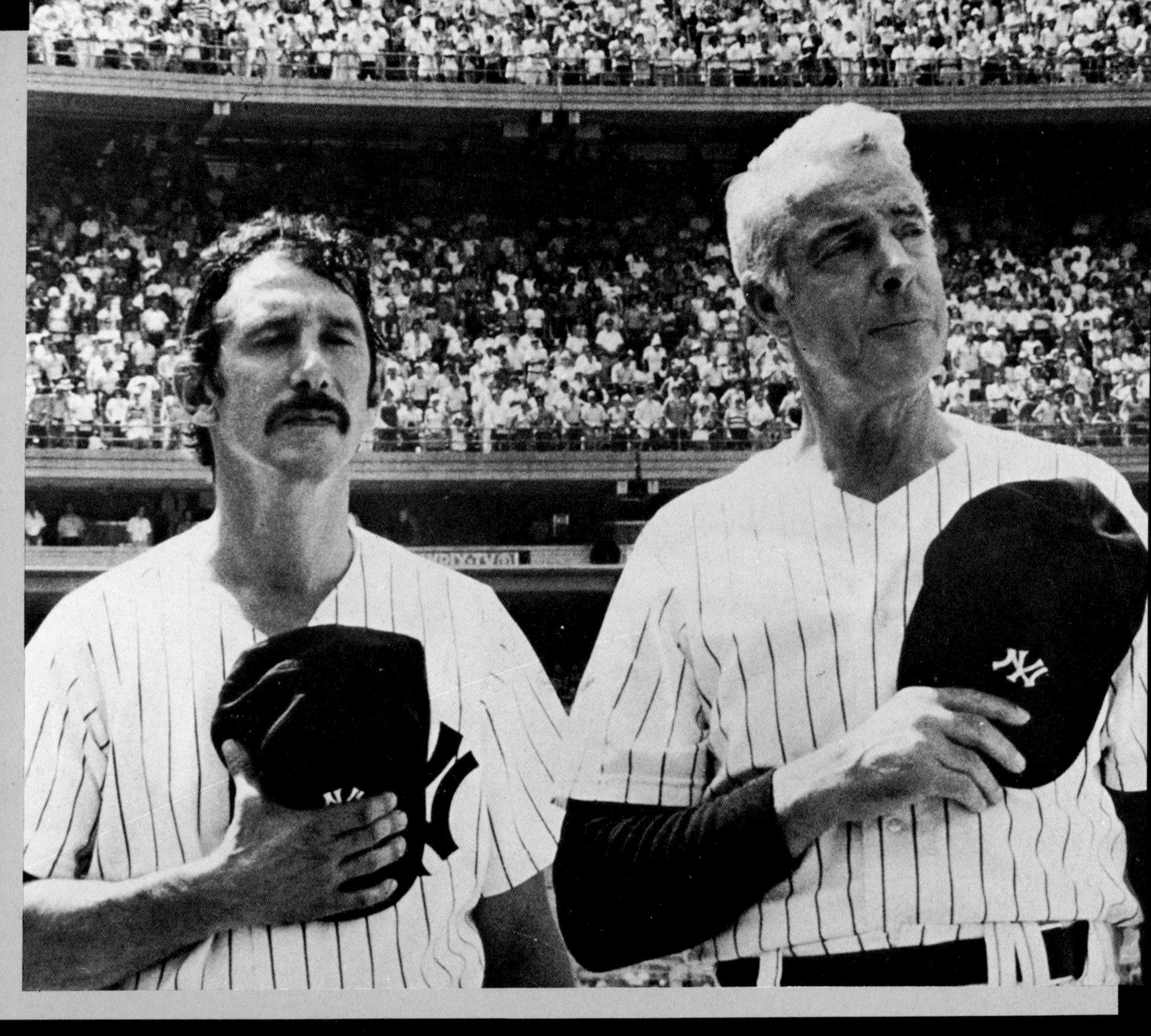

Billy Martin and Joe DiMaggio pause for the National Anthem.

CHAPTER SEVEN

The Seditious Seventies

"I only regret that I didn't sell more of them. I hope to wake the stupid owners to the facts of reality."

– Charles O Finley, owner of the Oakland A's, reacting to the beginning of the free-agent era in 1976.

The Red Sox left fielder Carl Yastrzemski entered the seventies with a bang, batting .329 with 40 home runs, 102 RBI's and a league-leading 125 runs scored.

Opposite: Jim Palmer would win the Cy Young Award three times, in 1973, 1975 and 1976, turning in eight 20-game seasons for the Orioles during the decade.

Any decade of major league baseball is apt to combine some changes with stability, some innovations along with traditions, but by any measure the seventies must stand out as one of the most revolutionary in the history of baseball. As so often since it first challenged the senior National League at the outset of the twentieth century, the American League seemed to take the lead in assaulting tradition. There was nothing much new about the various shifts of American League franchises to different cities, but its expansion to 14 teams was a novelty that the National League chose not to adopt. Far more upsetting to many students of the game was the American League's adoption of the designated hitter in 1973, a change that continues to divide fans of both leagues.

However, it must be admitted that the most radical of all changes in the 1970s did not start within the American League. It began with Curt Flood of the St Louis Cardinals when he challenged the reserve clause in 1970, for although Flood's case would be rejected by the nation's courts, it led the way for the eventual dislodging of what had come to be accepted as the keystone of organized baseball's great superstructure. Baseball, of course, survived the blow, but there is no denying that the relationships of players to their clubs, cities and fans would never again be quite the same – not to mention the impact it would have on the economics of organized baseball.

The reserve clause that had become so crucial was never formally promulgated as such at one single moment. What had become known as 'the reserve clause,' in fact, was a group of clauses or terms that had become part of the standard contract of virtually every player in professional baseball since the early twentieth century. Originally the newborn American League had challenged the concept of total ownership of a player and had successfully raided the estab-

lished National League. But as soon as it was accepted as a second major league, the American League's club owners were only too willing to accept and enforce these terms. And under the terms that became known as 'the reserve clause,' each player was legally bound to his original contracting team until he was sold or traded to another team, which then retained total control of the player. There was, to be sure, the possibility that a club might release a player, who would then be free to sign on with another team – but in practice a club was not apt to release a player until he was either too old or inept to be of interest to other teams. If a player, for whatever reason, didn't want to play with a team that held him under contract, essentially his only option was to retire from professional baseball. By their absolute adherence to these conditions, the major league club owners effectively owned the players.

If it was not exactly a form of slavery – to the extent that the players had entered into these contracts of their own free will – it seemed suspiciously like a monopoly and restraint of trade of the kind that the American legislatures had been trying to eliminate during the twentieth century. But the Supreme Court, although it had never actually ruled on the reserve clause as such, had, since 1922, in a series of decisions, ruled that organized baseball was exempt from the antitrust laws that applied to the rest of the businesses of America. Ironically, this exemption was a tribute to the special standing of baseball in American society, because the Supreme Court ruled that other organized sports – boxing, hockey and professional football – did have to comply with the antitrust laws. But irony was of little consolation to players who saw their salaries and careers, almost their entire lives while active professionals, controlled by the owners. Meanwhile, the owners had long convinced many that the reserve clause was necessary to keep the richest clubs from buying up all the better players and thus tearing apart the network that had allowed so many teams to remain competitive for so many years.

Then, on 16 January 1970, Curt Flood filed a suit against organized baseball's sacred cow, the reserve clause, and in so doing began what might be called the seditious seventies. Flood was a 32-year-old outfielder who had just finished his 12th year with the St Louis Cardinals. Regarded as one of the better players in the majors, he had just been paid $90,000 for the 1969 season – at that time, one of the highest salaries in either league. When the 1969 season ended, however, the Cardinals decided to trade Flood to the Philadelphia Phillies. This type of deal had been occurring in organized baseball for decades, but Curt Flood now charged that the reserve clause was 'a contract for perpetual service' and he refused to be treated as 'property . . . a chattel . . . a slave for a team against his will.' Backed by the Major League Baseball Players Association, Flood brought a suit for $3 million against organized baseball club owners in the United States District Court in New York City. The District Court quickly ruled that it could not go against the decisions of the Supreme Court; after the US Circuit Court of Appeals also turned down Flood's suit, he appealed to the Supreme Court. It was 1972 before the Supreme Court ruled that the reserve clause was binding since organized baseball had always been treated as exempt from antitrust laws; but the majority of opinion did call this exemption an 'aberration' and suggested that Congress reconsider this situation.

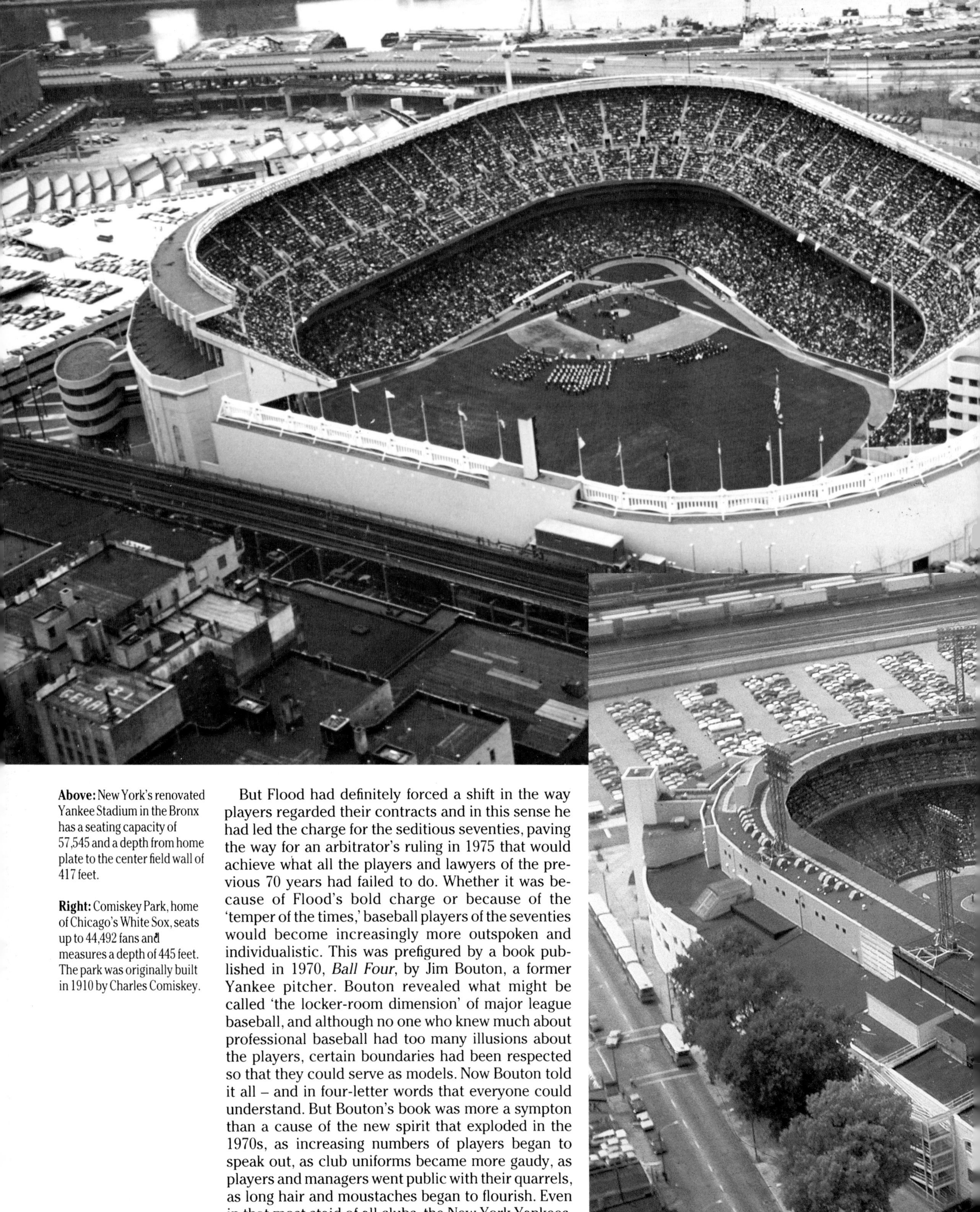

Above: New York's renovated Yankee Stadium in the Bronx has a seating capacity of 57,545 and a depth from home plate to the center field wall of 417 feet.

Right: Comiskey Park, home of Chicago's White Sox, seats up to 44,492 fans and measures a depth of 445 feet. The park was originally built in 1910 by Charles Comiskey.

But Flood had definitely forced a shift in the way players regarded their contracts and in this sense he had led the charge for the seditious seventies, paving the way for an arbitrator's ruling in 1975 that would achieve what all the players and lawyers of the previous 70 years had failed to do. Whether it was because of Flood's bold charge or because of the 'temper of the times,' baseball players of the seventies would become increasingly more outspoken and individualistic. This was prefigured by a book published in 1970, *Ball Four*, by Jim Bouton, a former Yankee pitcher. Bouton revealed what might be called 'the locker-room dimension' of major league baseball, and although no one who knew much about professional baseball had too many illusions about the players, certain boundaries had been respected so that they could serve as models. Now Bouton told it all – and in four-letter words that everyone could understand. But Bouton's book was more a sympton than a cause of the new spirit that exploded in the 1970s, as increasing numbers of players began to speak out, as club uniforms became more gaudy, as players and managers went public with their quarrels, as long hair and moustaches began to flourish. Even in that most staid of all clubs, the New York Yankees, the Board of Directors took to carrying on like a circus. Major league baseball in the 1970s, it might be said, had caught up with America of the 1960s.

The 1970 season itself did not produce any revolutionary surprises. Indeed, in the American League it was an exact repeat of the 1969 season, with the Orioles again winning the Eastern Division and the Twins again winning the Western Division. The Orioles achieved this with essentially the same team as in 1969, managed by the same feisty Earl Weaver. With such superb players as Boog Powell and Brooks Robinson, and three 20-game winners – Mike Cuellar, Dave McNally and Jim Palmer – the Orioles won 108 games and left the Yankees in second place, 15 games behind (even though the Yankees had the league's Rookie of the Year in Thurman Munson and the Manager of the Year in Ralph Houk). In the Western Division, the Twins left the Oakland A's nine games behind, thanks to such achievements as Jim Perry's 24 victories and Harmon Killebrew's 41 homers, and despite the fact that a knee injury kept Rod Carew out for much of the season.

As in 1969, the Orioles wiped out the Twins in the play-offs in three straight (10-6, 11-3, 6-1), scoring their 27 runs on 36 hits. This year, though, the Orioles went into the Series not against 'The Amazing Mets' but against 'The Big Red Machine' from Cincinnati. But the machine had some mechanical problems – specifically, its pitchers were suffering from injuries, and the Orioles swept the first three games. It looked like it would be a clean sweep in the ninth game when in the eighth inning, with two Reds already out, Lee May hit a three-run homer and the Reds won, 6-5. But

the Orioles took the fifth game, 9-3, and their Brooks Robinson not only was named the Series Most Valuable Player, the glove that he wore in making several spectacular catches was acquired by the Baseball Hall of Fame.

Another American Leaguer who had a stand-out year was Luis Aparacio, shortstop for the Chicago White Sox, who set a league record of 2219 games at his position (on his way to his all-time career record of 2581 games as shortstop). But one player who would probably prefer to forget the 1970 season was Denny McLain of the Detroit Tigers. After his spectacular 31 wins in 1968, McLain had never quite been able to live up to his image, but throughout 1970 he was constantly being suspended for everything from investing in a bookmaking operation to tossing water on sportswriters to carrying a gun. When the season ended, the Tigers traded McLain to the Washington Senators, but it was all downhill for McLain from this point on. 1970 was the year, too, that the Seattle Pilots, after one disastrous season in that city, moved to Milwaukee where they became the Brewers.

The next season, 1971, saw another American League team go through its own time of troubles. The Washington Senators – not the original Senators, which had gone to Minnesota as the Twins in 1961 – had been steadily losing support, despite all the rhetoric about the nation's capital needing a major league team. In 1971, the Senators became most notable for having the controversial Curt Flood and Denny McLain on their roster. Flood left the team after the first three weeks to avoid the publicity that had surrounded him ever since his suit challenging the reserve clause. Denny McLain would stay to pitch for the Senators, but he ended up losing 22 games. After the season ended, the Senators left town, reappearing in Texas as the Rangers in 1972, but the complaints that the nation's capital required a major league team would continue in the years ahead.

In the 1971 pennant race, the Baltimore Orioles won the Eastern Division of the American League for the third straight year, this time leaving the Tigers 12 games behind. Once more, too, the Orioles relied heavily on their strong pitching, as this year Pat Dobson (20-8) joined Cuellar (20-9), McNally (21-5), and Palmer (20-9) to give Baltimore only the second team in major league history (the White Sox of 1920 was the first) with four 20-game winners. In the Western Division, 1971 was the year that the Oakland A's finally broke through the pack, with Kansas City 16 games behind in second place. The A's had several stars, including Reggie Jackson with his 32 home runs

Opposite: Catcher Thurmon Munson played for the Yankees from 1969 to 1979, when he died in an airplane crash. Voted Rookie of the Year in 1970, Munson helped his team win three pennants by batting .339 in league championship, and he averaged a whopping .373 in his three World Series batting performances.

Below: Reggie Jackson booms a long one. Jackson played outfield (and some DH) for the Oakland A's from 1968 to 1975, leading the league in home runs twice, in runs scored twice and in RBI's once during that time. He helped power the A's to three pennants, and was selected as the league's Most Valuable Player in 1973.

Left-hander Vida Blue pitched for Oakland from 1969 to 1977, ending up with a won-lost record for those years of 124-86. Blue, who had pitched a no-hitter at the end of 1970, went on in 1971 to win 24 games and lose only eight, with a 1.82 ERA, and walked away with both the Cy Young Award and the league's Most Valuable Player designation.

and 'Catfish' Hunter with his 21 wins and Rollie Fingers and his numerous saves in relief. But much of the excitement was generated by their 22-year-old left-handed fastball pitcher, Vida Blue, who, after losing his season's opener, went on to win 10 straight. He ended up with a 24-8 record, and such other impressive stats as 24 complete games, eight shut-outs, 301 strikeouts and an ERA of only 1.82. Blue not only took the American League's Cy Young Award – as the youngest pitcher to ever achieve such an honor – but also claimed its Most Valuable Player Award. Everyone agreed, though, that Manager Dick Williams (formerly of the Red Sox) deserved a lot of the credit for disciplining a group of often unruly individualists into a true team.

In the play-offs, however, Baltimore's experience proved too much and the A's were defeated in three straight. The Orioles' sweep of the play-off completed their fourth pennant in six years. The Orioles then went on to the Series heavily favored over the Pittsburgh Pirates, who despite such solid players as Roberto Clemente and Willie Stargell lacked a strong pitching staff. The Orioles won the first two in Baltimore, but the Pirates took the next three in Pittsburgh

– including the fourth game, the first night game in World Series history. Back in Baltimore, the Orioles won the sixth game, 3-2, on Brooks Robinson's sacrifice fly in the 10th inning, but Steve Blass held the Orioles to four hits in the seventh and deciding game, and the Pirates won 2-1 to become the champions.

The 1972 season began in a way that prefigured an increasingly – some would say depressingly – familiar phenomenon within the major leagues: a strike – the first general strike by players in organized baseball. The issue was one of pension and medical benefits. Refusing to play all their spring training exhibition games, by the time the strike was settled on 13 April, the players had missed 86 regular season games as well. These games were never made up, the result being that different teams played different totals of games. Further signs of the growing unrest and temerity among the players was Vida Blue's temporary 'retirement' from baseball in order to see if he could obtain a better salary after his previous spectacular season. He ended up returning for far less than he wanted and having a losing season (6-10) as well. This was also the year that the Supreme Court upheld the lower courts in preserving the reserve clause, and suggested that Congress reconsider allowing organized baseball to remain exempt from antitrust legislation.

In the 1972 pennant race, the Oakland A's repeated in the Western Division, beating out Chicago by 5 and a half games. The A's claimed a formidable team, with such as Reggie Jackson, Bert Campaneris, Joe Rudi, Sal Bando and Gene Tenace to back the pitching of Catfish Hunter and Rollie Fingers. On the other hand, the A's seemed to have a 'fifth wheel' in the person of their owner, Charles O Finley, an irascible and often irritating millionaire from Chicago. The only real contest in the majors in 1972 was in the American League's Eastern Division, where even as late as Labor Day four

Above: Hall of Fame third baseman Brooks Robinson relaxes between innings in the Baltimore dugout. Although Robinson sacrificed in the winning run in game six of the 1971 World Series, the Orioles lost the final, deciding game by one run.

Left: Sal Bando takes a big cut. A solid third baseman, Salvatore Leonard Bando played for the Oakland A's from 1968 to 1976. He played the last five seasons of his 16-year career with Milwaukee.

Above: The Detroit Tigers' left-hander Mickey Lolich turned in two superb seasons in 1971 and 1972, winning 25 and 22 games. Lolich's career won-lost record is 217-191.

teams – Boston, Baltimore, Detroit and New York – were separated by only half a game. With only five days to go, Baltimore was finally eliminated; with four days to go, New York was eliminated and with three days to go, the Red Sox led the Tigers by half a game. In the final series of the season, Detroit took the first two games so that even though Boston won the final game, the Tigers squeaked by with its half-game lead.

With spunky manager Billy Martin and with such hot pitchers as Mickey Lolich and Joe Coleman, the Tigers felt they had a solid chance of deposing the A's, but in five hard-fought games Oakland ended up winning the last and deciding game. Once again, though, the exuberant A's found themselves facing a disciplined and experienced team, the Big Red Machine of Cincinnati. Yet the A's took the first two games of the Series, with Oakland's Gene Tenace making Series history by hitting homers his first two times at bat. The Reds won the third by a close 1-0, but the A's came back and took the fourth by a slim 3-2 victory, scoring two of their three runs in the ninth inning. When the Reds rebounded to win the fifth and sixth and tie up the Series at three games each, it seemed that experience would win out. But in the seventh game, played in Cincinnati, the A's came through with a 3-2 victory and the World Championship – their first since 1930, when the franchise was in Philadelphia. For most of the players on both teams, it was a lean Series: six games were decided by only one run, while the A's team batting average was .207 and the Red's was .208. The notable exception was the amazing performance of the A's Gene Tenace, who hit four homers (having hit only five all season), batted in nine of the A's 16 runs, and ended up with a slugging average of .913. Other American League players who enjoyed a banner season in 1972 included the Cleveland Indians' Gaylord Perry (obtained from the San Francisco Giants) who had a 24-16 season, and Richie Allen (obtained from the Los Angeles Dodgers) who played for the White Sox and led the league in home runs (37) and RBI's (113).

The 1973 season will always remain in the history of baseball as the year that the American League adopted the rule allowing a designated hitter for the pitcher. Originally it was to be merely a three-year trial, but after this first year when the statistics showed that the American League teams had higher team batting averages, scored more runs and drew more crowds, the rule was adopted permanently. The National League refused to go along even with the trial year – and National League fans would never let American League supporters forget that they regarded this as 'kid stuff' from the junior league. (Almost everyone would forget that the founder of the American League, Ban Johnson, had earlier in the century said the same thing about pinch-hitters.)

As it happened, despite all the predictions that the designated hitter would wipe out pitchers' records, the 1973 season turned out to be 'the year of the pitcher' for the American League. Twelve of the league's pitchers won 20 or more games, and there were five no-hit games in the league. The most remarkable records were those compiled by Nolan Ryan, acquired by the California Angels in a trade with the New York Mets. His win-loss record was a respectable 21-16, but this included two no-hitters and two one-hitters, plus an ERA of 2.87. Going into his final game of the season, Ryan needed 15 strikeouts to tie Sandy Koufax's all-time one-season (1965) record of 382 strikeouts – and although he needed 11 innings

Right: Shortstop Bert 'Campy' Campaneris played for the Oakland A's from 1968 to 1976, averaging 44 stolen bases per season during that time. In the 1973 World Series he went 7 for 21, smashing a homer in the seventh game to help his team clinch the title.

to get them, Ryan ended up with 16, thus taking over the major league record with 383 strikeouts.

In the end, though, this didn't help the Angels in their Western Division, won again by the Oakland A's for the third consecutive year. The A's had 20-game winners in Catfish Hunter, Vida Blue, and Ken Holtzmann, backed by Rollie Fingers in relief; they also had the solid hitting of Bert Campaneris and Gene Tenace and the superlative hitting of Reggie Jackson, whose 32 home runs and 117 runs batted in were enough to make him the Most Valuable Player in the league (although Rod Carew of the Twins had the highest

Nolan Ryan, after his record-setting 383rd strikeout on 27 September, 1973.

Right: Rollie Fingers pitched for the Oakland A's from 1968 to 1976, helping them to five consecutive league play-offs and three Series during that time. In his last Series for the A's in 1974, Fingers turned in a 1.93 ERA. Fingers moved to San Diego in 1977, then to Milwaukee in 1981.

Below: A young Rod Carew waits on deck. Voted Rookie of the Year in 1967, Carew quickly lived up to his promise by winning the batting title seven times during his 12 years with the Minnesota Twins (1967-78).

batting average with his .350). In the Eastern Division, the Baltimore Orioles returned to the top spot, eight games over the Boston Red Sox, thanks in large part to their stellar pitching trio, Palmer, Cuellar and McNally. But in the play-offs, Oakland beat the Orioles, although it took them all five games to do so.

The World Series again required all seven games to produce a winner. The National League's team was the New York Mets, who had surprised everyone by winning their division on the last day of the season. Inevitably, many fans began to think that the 'Miracle Mets' were going to pull a replay of their 1969 season. But although it took all seven games and Oakland had to win the last two of these, the A's did again win the Series. The most extraordinary episode of the Series was in the second game, which had gone into 12 innings with the teams tied 6-6. The Mets came up in the top of the inning and scored four runs, three of them due to two errors by the A's substitute second baseman, Mike Andrews. When the A's could only pick up one run in the bottom of the inning, that meant the game. The A's owner Charles Finley, excitable in the best of circumstances, announced after the game that second baseman Andrews had a 'sore shoulder' and was being put on the disabled list – so that the A's could activate another player – but Andrews almost immediately revealed that Finley had pressured him into signing the statement about his 'injury.' Baseball fans and the Oakland players protested Finley's blatant effort to punish Andrews, and Commissioner Bowie Kuhn ordered that Andrews be reinstated – and fined Finley $5000. As this was just one of many instances of Finley's interference, little wonder that Dick Williams quit as manager of the A's, despite leading them to the World Series championship for the second year in a row.

For the 1974 season, Oakland was managed by Alvin Dark – although Finley was literally on the phone much of the time trying to call plays – and the A's continued their winning ways, despite all the headlines about the flamboyancy and fights. With their especially strong pitching staff of Hunter, Blue, Holtzmann and Fingers, they beat out the Texas Rangers by five games to take the Western Division title again. The Baltimore Orioles also repeated in the Eastern Division, winning 27 of their last 33 games to beat out the Yankees by two games. In the league play-offs, however, the Orioles were no match for the A's, losing three games to one. Oakland's superb pitching staff held the Orioles to only one run in the final 27 innings of the four-game series.

In the 1974 World Series, the A's found themselves facing a rival from down the coast, the Los Angeles Dodgers, and although the A's sometimes seemed like escapees from a situation comedy, when it came to the crunch, 'They play the game the way it should be played.' That was how the Dodgers' manager Walter Alston put it after the Series, and he should know, for the A's took the Series four games to one. Not that it was a breeze for the A's as four of the five games were decided by 3-2 scores. The heroes for the A's were Rollie Fingers, who came on in relief in all four of the A's wins, and Joe Rudi, whose homer won the last game.

The 1974 season was marked by a number of record-breaking performances – the most notable, of course, being Hank Aaron's breaking of Babe Ruth's lifetime home run record. Nolan Ryan pitched his third no-hitter while compiling a 22-16 record; he set a record by striking out 19 in a nine-inning game and struck out 367 for the season (with his fastball timed at 100.9 mph). Gaylord Perry of the Cleveland Indians pitched 15 consecutive wins – and then lost six in a row; Al Kaline of the Tigers became the 12th player in modern major league history to get 3000 hits and Rod Carew of the Twins took his third straight American League batting championship with .364. Catfish Hunter of the A's won over 20 games for his fourth straight season. Declared a free agent at the end of the season, he was signed by the Yankees (for over $3 million on a five-year contract). Hank Aaron, after his record-breaking season, also left his team. Dissatisfied with the Braves' refusal to appoint him as manager, he got himself traded to the Milwaukee Brewers (thus reversing the route taken by Babe Ruth, who after setting his records in the American League went on to end his career in the National League).

Had Aaron been appointed manager of the Atlanta Braves he would have been the first black to manage a major league team and it would have complemented the National League's pioneering appointment of Jackie Robinson as the first black player. Instead, the honor of the first black manager came to the Cleveland Indians, who signed on Frank Robinson from the California Angels at the end of the 1974 season. Robinson had experience as manager of the Santurce team of the Puerto Rican Winter League, and the Indians' front office gave him a one-year contract for 1975. At the end of the season the Indians had won almost half their games (.497 to be precise), which was only good enough for fourth place in the Eastern Division, but Robinson would be offered a second year's contract. The last major barrier to blacks in major league baseball had come down.

Cleveland Indian manager Frank Robinson argues with the home plate umpire. Hall of Famer Frank Robinson was the first black manager in the major leagues. After a 21-year playing career he managed Cleveland from 1975 to 1977, when he moved to San Francisco.

But the 1975 season in the American League belonged to another club, the Boston Red Sox. On paper, the Orioles appeared to be a much stronger team; the Red Sox, starting with their manager, Darrell Johnson, were largely unknowns. The exception was Carl Yastrzemski, but he was more a Boston favorite than an American League power. And there was the now-aging pitcher, Luis Tiant. But after that came some relative unknowns such as Dwight Evans and Carlton Fisk and a couple of rookies named Fred Lynn and Jim Rice. These rookies were soon to become household names, as Rice hit .309 with 22 homers and 102 RBI's, while Lynn hit .331 with 21 homers and 105 RBI's – earning Lynn not only the league's Rookie of the Year Award but also the Most Valuable Player title, the first man in major league history to win both in the same year. Baltimore did well, with Jim Palmer and Mike Torrez winning over 20 games each, but Boston did even better and took the division by four and a half games over the Orioles. In the Western Division, it was the A's once again, this time by seven games over the Kansas City Royals. But in the pennant play-offs, whether it was because they missed Catfish Hunter or not, the A's went down three straight to the Red Sox.

Certainly the Red Sox were hardly a team top-heavy with pitchers, despite the solid efforts of Tiant, Rick Wise and Bill Lee. On the other hand, their opponent in the World Series, the Cincinnati Reds, wasn't

Although an injury kept him out of post-season play, Red Sox outfielder Jim Rice sparked the team to a league championship in his rookie year (1975), batting .309 with 22 homers and 104 RBI's. Selected as the league's Most Valuable Player in 1978, Rice took over left field from Carl Yastrzemski to carry on a tradition of greatness that began over three decades earlier with Ted Williams.

Left: Red Sox right fielder Dwight 'Dewey' Evans stands ready at the plate. Dewey joined the Sox in 1972, and became a perennial Golden Glover with his sure glove and his rifle arm. In the 1975 World Series, Evans batted .292 with five RBI's.

Below left: Luis Tiant pitched for the Red Sox from 1971 to 1978, turning in three 20-game seasons during that time. In 1975 he won 18 games, then won one playoff game and two Series games. Win or lose, Tiant always entertained the fans with his variety of colorful pitching motions.

Below: Centerfielder Fred Lynn joined the Red Sox in 1974. The following year he helped carry the team to the Series with outstanding performances at the plate and in the field, becoming the only player ever to win both Rookie of the Year and Most Valuable Player awards in the same season. He went on to have five more good years with Boston and was then traded to the California Angels.

Above: Catcher Carlton 'Pudge' Fisk joined the Red Sox in 1972, and was selected Rookie of the Year. He played for Boston through 1980, then was lost to free agency through a front office error, to the chagrin of hometown fans. The most memorable hit of his career is perhaps the game-winning twelfth-inning home run that sent the 1975 World Series into a seventh game.

Opposite: George Brett entered the major leagues in 1974 and quickly warmed up to American League pitchers. In his first three years he accrued 539 hits, twice led the league in hits and triples, and won the batting title in 1976 with a .333 average. A skilled third baseman, Brett has played his whole career for the Kansas City Royals.

especially strong in pitching either. But what the Reds did have was power and experience – embodied in such players as Pete Rose, Johnny Bench, Joe Morgan and Tony Perez. In what many fans would long remember as one of the most exciting Series, Boston extended the Reds to every last inning and it took Joe Morgan's single in the ninth inning of the seventh game to sneak the Reds by with a 4-3 victory and the World Championship. This was the Series with a controversial incident in the third game: the Reds Ed Armbrister bunted to sacrifice a teammate to second and then didn't move fast enough as Boston's Carlton Fisk leaped forward to pick up the ball. As Fisk collided with Armbrister, then threw wildly to second, the upshot left Reds safe on second and third and led to a game-winning single by Joe Morgan.

There were several more positive moments in the 1975 season. Rod Carew won his fourth consecutive batting title with a .359 average, while Nolan Ryan pitched his fourth no-hitter (tying Sandy Koufax). On 28 September, four Oakland A's pitchers pooled their talents to win a no-hitter against the Angels – the first time that more than two pitchers had won a no-hitter.

But all of this action on the diamond was overshadowed by a ruling made at the end of the 1975 season, a ruling that was to have a major impact on major league baseball. It had really begun in 1974 with the owners' agreement to submit various issues regarding salary and contracts to binding arbitration. At the end of 1974 arbitrator Peter M Seitz had ruled that Jim 'Catfish' Hunter was a free agent because the Oakland A's owner Charles Finley had broken his contract. Then in 1975 pitcher Andy Messersmith played the full season for the Los Angeles Dodgers without any contract while Dave McNally played only part of the season for the Montreal Expos, also without a contract. When the season ended, both pitchers claimed they were free agents because they had played out their option. Needless to say, the owners recognized this as yet another assault on the reserve clause, but unlike Curt Flood, who had made a frontal assault, McNally and Messersmith came around from behind by treating their claim as one for arbitration rather than for the courts. And on 23 December 1975 Seitz ruled that players, after completing their contracts, were free to sign with any club. It was, in effect, the end of the reserve clause.

The impact was both immediate and long-term. Two federal courts would uphold the arbitrator's ruling. Meanwhile, with the expiration of the club owners' overall contract with the Major League Baseball Players Association, the owners and players failed to reach an agreement on how to handle this new development, so the owners refused to open the spring training camps on 1 March. By 17 March, the players indicated they would be willing to negotiate certain points, so Commissioner Kuhn ordered the camps to open while negotiations proceeded. Agreement on a four-year contract incorporating the new phenomenon of free agents was finally reached on 12 July, the very eve of the 1976 All-Star Game. The terms attempted some compromise between total freedom and the old reserve clause: after five years in the major leagues, a player could ask to be traded (and could veto up to six clubs); if he was not traded, he became a free agent. After six years in the majors, a player became a free agent, although he could only negotiate with 13 clubs, including his latest owner, that participated in a draft.

Although the owners signed this agreement, they were not alone in predicting that it would mean the end of organized baseball, as it seemed that the richer clubs would buy up all the star players. But the results in the first year were somewhat mixed. It was November 1976 before the first free-agent draft was held, and it was true that many of the 24 players who participated were able to get contracts for much more money than they had been earning, but they did not all go to the so-called rich clubs. Meanwhile, fearing that they might lose good players once they became free agents, clubs began to offer present players multi-year contracts at much better salaries. Not unexpectedly, though, the most extreme response came from Charles Finley, owner of the Oakland A's. Even before the agreement of July, he began to dismantle his team before his star players could become free agents. He traded Reggie Jackson and Ken Holtzman to the Baltimore Orioles in April. Then in June he tried to sell Vida Blue to the Yankees and Rollie Fingers and Joe Rudi to the Red Sox, but Commissioner Kuhn immediately voided the sale of these three on the grounds that it was 'inconsistent with the best interests of baseball.' Finley sued Kuhn, but Kuhn was upheld by the courts.

After such a start to the season, the amazing thing was that the Oakland A's did as well as they did. They played hard-driving ball, stealing a record-setting team total of 341 bases, and they made a late-season charge against the leaders, the Kansas City Royals. But the Royals – led by George Brett and his league high .333 batting average – came out ahead by two

5
CITY

KC

and a half games in the Western Division. Over in the Eastern Division, the teams found themselves confronting, of all things, the new Yankees. Billy Martin had taken over as manager in the middle of the 1975 season, and the team was back in a renovated Yankee Stadium, after playing in New York's Shea Stadium for two years. The Yankees' prime owner, George Steinbrenner, had assembled the team with a fair amount of cash, including such outstanding players as Thurman Munson, Mickey Rivers and Chris Chambliss, as well as the two recently acquired former Oakland A's, Catfish Hunter and Ken Holtzman. Inspired by Billy Martin's aggressive style, the Yankees ended up in first place, 10 and a half games ahead of the Orioles (even though at one point the Orioles enjoyed a 20-game winning streak).

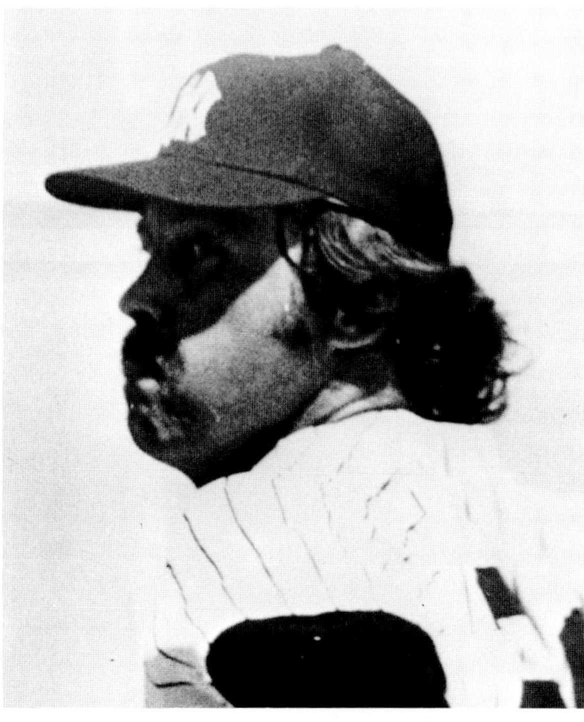

The 1976 league play-offs between the Yankees and the Royals went the full five games, with the Yankees winning the fifth and decisive game on Chambliss's ninth-inning homer. (Chambliss hit .524 in the five games.) Having won their first pennant since 1964, however, the Yankees lost the World Series to the Cincinnati Reds in four straight games. About the only point the fans had to argue over, it being such a swift and decisive Series, was that the second game was played on a Sunday evening, instead of the traditional Sunday afternoon, to satisfy the preferences of the television audience. Since the temperature fell to 40 degrees, the ballpark fans – and players – really felt they had been shut out in the cold. One image that warmed the cockles of all baseball fans' hearts during the 1976 season, though, after all the legal and financial squabbles, was the performance of the Detroit Tigers' rookie right-hander, Mark Fidrych. It was not only his fine record of 19-9, nor his leading ERA of 2.34, it was his spontaneous and high-spirited antics on the mound that reminded everyone that baseball was still a game for the young at heart.

The American League took another step on its own away from the National League when in 1977 it expanded to 14 teams; the Mariners were established in Seattle and the Blue Jays set up in Toronto. Not unexpectedly, the Blue Jays came in last in their Eastern Division, but the Mariners came in only next to last in the Western Division – a half game ahead of the Oakland A's. Whether the A's precipitous decline was due to the behavior of the free agents or Charles Finley himself would be debated by students of baseball, but in fact it was still far too early to say whether the movement of free agents was having much effect on any baseball statistics other than individual player's salaries.

But the big story, if not scandal, of the 1977 season was provided by the Yankees, which seemed to have taken on not only some of the Oakland A's players – including now Reggie Jackson – but also the A's unruly manners. George Steinbrenner, thanks to the emergence of free agents and his own checkbook, had assembled what was dubbed 'the best team that money could buy,' and he had put them under the feisty Billy Martin. What resulted was an often incredible spectacle of arguments, confrontations and actual fights involving principally Martin, Reggie Jackson and Steinbrenner, but drawing several other players into the maelstrom. Yet just as the Oakland A's had managed to play ball when it counted, so now these bickering Yankees managed to come through. As late as 7 August, the Yankees were five games out of first place, but they won 13 of the next 14 games and 38 of their last 51 – ending up two and a half games ahead of both the Red Sox and the Orioles in the Eastern Division. The Red Sox had 213 home runs, the fourth highest team total in American League history, but they lacked the pitching of the kind that Ron Guidry, Catfish Hunter and Don Gullet provided for the Yankees.

Opposite: Golden Glove second baseman Frank White turns a double play. White has played an important role in Kansas City's winning tradition since joining the team in 1973.

Left: After seven successful years with the Oakland A's, in 1974 Catfish Hunter became one of the first players to enter the open market as a free agent. George Steinbrenner won the bidding war, signing Hunter to a $3-plus million contract. The investment paid off as Hunter won 23 games, pitching 328 innings and completing 30 games in 1975. In 1976 he aided a Yankee run to the World Series.

Below: Left-hander Ron Guidry – 'Louisiana Lightning' – won 16 games in his first full season with the Yankees in 1977, and the following year won the Cy Young Award with his league-leading 25 wins and 1.74 ERA.

Outfielder Bobby Bonds played for the California Angles in 1976 and 1977, batting in 115 runs in the latter year.

In the Western Division the Kansas City Royals repeated their victory of the previous year, beating out the Texas Rangers by eight games. Considering that the Oakland A's had been effectively dismantled, their last-place finish was not totally unexpected. More surprising was the fifth-place finish – 28 games out – of the California Angels, but it was at least partially explained by the injuries suffered by Joe Rudi and Bobby Grich and by the fact that Nolan Ryan somewhat canceled out his 341 strikeouts with 204 walks, thus ending up with a respectable but not overly-impressive 19-16 record.

The American League play-offs were a re-run of 1976, pitting the Yankees against the Royals again and also going into a fifth and deciding game. Once again, too, the Yankees took that fifth game, this time with three runs in the ninth inning. The Yankees thus found themselves back in the World Series for a second successive year, this time facing the Los Angeles Dodgers. With four 30-home run hitters, the Dodgers were top-heavy with hitters, but it was Yankee home runs that beat them, particularly Reggie Jackson's five home runs, including three consecutive homers on only three pitches – both Series records (for Babe Ruth's three homers in two different Series games, 1926 and 1928, involved more pitches). The Yankees won the Series, four games to two, with Jackson taking the honors as Most Valuable Player.

But for the regular season of 1977, the most impressive batting performance was that of Rod Carew, who won his sixth American League batting title with his average of .388 – the highest since Ted Williams' .388 in 1957 – and a total of 239 hits, the most since Bill Terry's 254 in 1930. Another remarkable performance was given by Dennis Eckersley of the Cleveland Indians, who pitched a total of 22 and a third consecutive hitless innings over three games.

In the 1978 season the same four teams won the league's four divisions as had the year before, and 1978 featured the same Yankee turmoil as well. Gone were the austere, pinstriped Yankees of former years, the team that seemed so superior to the ordinary sweating ballplayers that it was dubbed 'the Board of Directors.' Once again, most of the controversy revolved around Martin, Steinbrenner and Jackson, three of a kind in a territory where there was probably room for only one (and a need for none). Aside from the verbal brickbats, Jackson and Martin almost came to blows. Their showdown came on 17 July, when Martin signaled Jackson to hit at three successive pitches but Jackson tried (unsuccessfully) to bunt each time. Jackson was then suspended for five days. But instead of letting it go at that, Martin made a crack

Left: Reggie Jackson is congratulated on a home run as Lou Piniella looks on.

Below: Cleveland's designated hitter and first baseman Andre Thornton leaps back to first base as Kansas City's Pete LaCock awaits the attempted pick-off throw.

Above: The Yankee whiz at third base Graig Nettles leaps for a low line drive. Nettles worked his magic for the Yankees from 1973 to 1983, when he joined the Padres. He helped his team win the division and the pennant in 1978, smashing 27 homers during the season and batting .333 in the play-offs.
Opposite top: Red Sox right-hander Mike Torrez fires a fastball. Torrez came from the Yankees in 1978 as a free agent. That same year he started and lost the memorable one-game play-off in Boston that sent the Yankees to an eventual World championship.
Opposite bottom: Don Baylor, designated hitter and outfielder for the California Angels from 1977 to 1982, waits in the on-deck circle. Baylor was named the league's Most Valuable Player in 1979, when he powered 36 homers, batted in 139 runs and scored 120. In 1983 he moved to the Yankees.

to sports reporters on 23 July about Jackson and Steinbrenner: 'One's a born liar, the other's convicted.' (This last a reference to the fact that Steinbrenner had pleaded no contest to federal charges of making illegal political contributions.) By the next day, Martin was reading a resignation statement: 'I owe it to my health and my mental well-being to resign.' Bob Lemon took over as manager for the rest of the season – although to thoroughly confound everyone, on 29 July, the Yankees announced that Martin would return as manager in 1980.

By the time Lemon took over, the Yankees were 10 and a half games behind the division-leading Red Sox, who looked unbeatable with their combination of hitting and pitching. But now the Yankees seemed to want to play ball instead of games, and led by such pitchers as Ron Guidry, Ed Figueroa, Rich Gossage and Sparky Lyle, the Yankees began to win. Then in September the Red Sox lost 14 out of 17 games and the Yankees took over the lead. When the Red Sox won their last eight games, however, they pulled even with the Yankees, and both teams ended the regular season with 99-63 records. A tie-breaker game was necessary, and the Yankees put in Ron Guidry, whose season record was already 24-3, the highest win percentage for a 20-plus game winner in major league history. Helped by Bucky Dent's three-run homer and Reggie Jackson's game-winning home run, Guidry raised that percentage to an astounding .893 and the Yankees had the championship of the Eastern Division.

In the Western Division it was the Kansas City Royals for the third consecutive year; with strong pitching from Dennis Leonard, Paul Splittorff, Larry Gura and Rich Gale, and with the powerful bat of George Brett, the Royals left the California Angels five games behind. In the play-offs, however, despite Brett's three homers, the Yankees beat the Royals three games to one. The World Series also turned out to be a rematch between the Yankees and the Dodgers, with the Dodgers slightly favored. And when the Dodgers took the first two games, it seemed that the Yankees were doomed, but with the strong bats of Reggie Jackson, Lou Piniella, Bucky Dent and Thurmon Munson, and some superb fielding by third baseman Graig Nettles, the Yankees rebounded to take the next four games and the World Series – the first team to lose the opening two games and then end up winning the Series in six games.

Ron Guidry's record-breaking win percentage of .893 was one of the personal highlights of the 1978 season. Another was Rod Carew's seventh American League batting title with a .333. This seventh title tied him with Rogers Hornsby and Stan Musial, with only Ty Cobb's 12 and Honus Wagner's 8 holding the lead. The Red Sox's Jim Rice also had an extraordinary year, with 46 home runs and 139 RBI's, giving him the league's lead in each category.

Right: The California Angels' great Rod Carew holds a career batting average of .330.

Below: Don Baylor looks on imploringly after umpire Durwood Merrill called him out.

The 1979 season was one of those 'turnover' years. Just when it seemed that a few teams were settling down as permanent dynasties, new teams took over first place in all four divisions. In the case of the American League's Eastern Division, the Yankees fell from first place, 13 games down into fourth place. It

seemed that all the headlines finally caught up to them. The trouble began in April when Rich Gossage, the relief pitcher, got into a fight in the shower with catcher Cliff Johnson. Gossage tore a ligament in his right hand and was out of the lineup for three months. (Johnson was traded to the Cleveland Indians.) Then in June, with the team going nowhere, Bob Lemon was fired as manager – only to be replaced by none other than Billy Martin. In August, the Yankee catcher, captain and sparkplug Thurman Munson died in the crash of a jet plane he owned and was piloting. Finally, in October, Billy Martin was fired after he was caught covering up his involvement in a barroom brawl.

But by then it was too late for the Yankees to do anything with the 1979 season. The Baltimore Orioles had won 102 games and beat out two hard-hitting challengers, the Milwaukee Brewers (by eight) and the Boston Red Sox (by 11 and a half) to give manager Earl Weaver his sixth division title win in 11 years. The Orioles themselves, with such as Ken Singleton and Eddie Murray, were no slouches at bat and had a team total of 181 homers, and when Jim Palmer injured his elbow and was out for two months, Mike Flanagan came through with a 23-9 record. But if Baltimore's being in first place was no great surprise, the California Angels in first place in the Western Division was: they had been finishing an average of 23 and a half games down for the previous 18 seasons! With the old cowboy star Gene Autry as owner and Jim Fregosi as manager, the Angels were able to field an impressive if not overpowering team, including Don Baylor, Dan Ford, Brian Downing and Bobby Grich. They also could boast of Nolan Ryan, who struck out 223 batters that year; and although they had acquired Rod Carew from the Twins and he hit a respectable .318, he was out for much of the season due to a finger injury.

In the league's play-offs, however, the Angels were beaten out by the Orioles, three games to one. The Orioles then found themselves in what was billed as a 'railroad series' because the National League's winner was the Pirates of nearby Pittsburgh. And it was a good thing that the teams didn't have to fly because the foul weather might have grounded them. As it was, the rain and cold affected several key plays. But it was as bad for one team as the other, and when the Orioles took three of the first four games, they were sure that the pot of gold was just the other side of the gray clouds. Instead, the Pirates took the last three games – as remarkable as it seems, as only three other teams had previously done this – and became the World Champions.

But if such upsets are hard for the losers, they are good for the game. Attendance figures for 1979 broke the record for the fourth straight year, with the total for the major leagues being 43,548,450 – up 46 percent from 1975 – and observers agreed that this was at least in part due to the new winners. Whatever the reasons, the American League, designated hitters and all, was ready to take on the 1980s.

Oriole Ken Singleton cracks a rightfield hit in the 1979 World Series against Pittsburgh. Despite Singleton's 10 for 28, Baltimore lost the Series four games to three.

A multiple exposure shows the Royals' relief pitcher Dan Quisenberry's characteristic sidearm motion.

CHAPTER EIGHT

The Unsettled Eighties and Into the Nineties

"My goal is to take the club to arbitration when I'm 50 – and win."

Jerry Koosman, 42-year-old pitcher

Below: Outfielder Steve Kemp joined the Tigers in 1977 and quickly rose to stardom. The Tigers, wary of his impending free agent status, traded him to the White Sox in 1981. The following year he left the White Sox as a free agent and signed with the Yankees. After two years of mediocre performances, Kemp was traded to the Pirates along with Tim Foli and $400,000 for Dale Berra and a minor league pitcher.
Opposite: Yankee outfielder Dave Winfield begins a powerful swing. Winfield played for San Diego for eight years before he signed a 10-year, $15-plus million contract with the Yankees in 1981. In his first four years with New York he racked up 390 RBI's, and won three Golden Glove Awards.

As the American League entered the 1980s, most longtime observers of the major leagues would probably agree that organized baseball would continue to change. True, there had been all kinds of changes in the sport even since the first professional teams had agreed on the rules and operations in the last quarter of the ninteenth century. But in the 1970s, a different kind of change seemed to be occurring, some fundamental shift in the relations among all the participants, including the fans. The striking down of the reserve clause in the 1970s undoubtedly was the major and most tangible blow to the old arrangements, but the role of television was arguably even more influential.

Television, after all, disconnected organized baseball from the simple financial link between ballpark attendees and available income. Television brought in a whole new source of money – and lots of it. Given the spirit of the country in the 1960s, with many formerly consenting groups demanding to renegotiate their contracts with society at large, it should be no surprise that baseball players insisted on renegotiating theirs, too, so that they could get what they considered their fair share of the new and large sums of money. Thus followed the free agents, the drafts, the arbitration, the agents, the million-dollar contracts – and the strikes.

Between 1978 and 1981, 43 players negotiated contracts worth over $1 million each; the peak would be reached by outfielder Dave Winfield when in November 1980 the New York Yankees signed him to a 10-year contract worth at least $13 million (and a cost-of-living clause that made it worth a possible $20 million). All players were riding the coattails of the major free agents and superstars, too, and the average salary of all major-league players went from $50,000 in 1976, when the reserve clause was still in effect, to $200,000 by 1981. Inevitably, the owners of the major league clubs decided that they should obtain some advantage from the free-agent inflation. When the owners' agreement with the players expired on 31 December 1979, the owners demanded a new condition: any club that lost a player when a free agent moved must be allowed to obtain a player from the club that signed the free agent.

The players immediately recognized that this would put a brake on the free agent system and they refused to accept this condition. During the final week of spring training in 1980, the players staged a walkout and threatened to go on strike on 23 May if there was no agreement with the owners. Minutes before the deadline, the club owners and the Players Association agreed to set up a committee – formed of two player representatives and two general managers – that would study the whole issue of free agents; if they

NE

could not come up with a solution that received the endorsement of all parties by 31 January 1981, each side could take whatever action it chose to. So the conflict between the owners and players was set aside and the 1980 season was played out. The American League fans did not seem too upset about the squabbles over terms and money, for a record-breaking 22 million turned out for just this league's games during 1980.

In the American League's Eastern Division, an exciting and hard-fought battle developed between 1979's winner, the Orioles, and 1978's winner, the Yankees. The Orioles could not count on their old pitching trio of Cuellar, Palmer and McNally, but they came up with two 20-game winners in Steve Stone and Scott McGregor. The Yankees had three equally strong pitchers in Tommy John, Ron Guidry and Rudy May, along with relievers Rich Gossage and Ron Davis. And where the Orioles could take to the attack with Ken Singleton and Eddie Murray, the Yankees could counter with Reggie Jackson and Dave Winfield. (Jackson's 41 homers tied him with the Brewers' Ben Oglivie for the league's lead.) The Brewers also remained a threat – as a team, they hit 203 home runs – but in the end the Yankees prevailed.

Opposite: Yankee ace Tommy John winds up. John helped his team to the division title in 1980, winning 22 games and losing only nine.

Opposite (inset): The Texas Rangers' third baseman Buddy Bell batted .329 in 1980, with 83 RBI's. Bell joined the Rangers in 1979 after seven years with the Indians.

Left: Ben Oglivie takes a cut. The power-hitting outfielder joined the Milwaukee Brewers in 1978 and led the league the following year in homers, with 41. In 1982 his 102 RBI's helped bring his team the pennant.

Below: The Oriole first baseman Eddie Murray fields a ball. Murray, who joined Baltimore in 1977 and was named Rookie of the Year, wields a heavy bat and is known for his excellent defensive play as well.

In the Western Division in 1980, however, it was hardly a contest, as the Kansas City Royals left the Oakland A's 14 games behind in second place. The Royals were paced by two truly hot players, George Brett and Willie Wilson. Brett looked like he might end up with a .400 batting average but had to settle for .390 (still the highest since Ted Williams' .406 in 1941), a .664 slugging average and 118 RBI's, while Wilson got 230 hits on his way to a .326 batting average. But one Oakland A was positively sizzling: Rickey Henderson broke Ty Cobb's 1915 league record of 96 stolen bases when he ran off with 100.

In the league play-offs, the Royals met the Yankees for the fourth time in five years; the Yankees had won three of these, but 1980 was the Royals' turn. The Royals, in fact, beat the Yankees three straight, with one of those storybook confrontations coming in the third game. In the seventh inning with the Yankees ahead, 2-1, George Brett with his .390 average came to

bat against Rich 'Goose' Gossage with his 100-mph pitches. Brett hit a homer with two on and this assured the Royals their victory. In the World Series, though, the Royals fell to the Phillies, four games to two.

All of which was quite cut-and-dried compared to what happened in the 1981 season – which may or may not go down as a major watershed year in the history of organized baseball. The January 1981 deadline proposed in the May 1980 agreement had come and gone without the owners and players coming to terms over the issue of compensating teams that lost free agents. The players maintained their position that any form of compensation would undermine the value of a free agent. The owners' final offer as the 1981 season got underway was that for every 'premium' player who left a club as a free agent, that club was to get a replacement choice from a select roster of players from the club that signed the free

Opposite top: Ace relief pitcher Goose Gossage fires a fastball. Gossage led the league in saves twice during his six years with the Yankees.
Opposite bottom: During the years speedster Rickey Henderson played for Oakland, he led the league in stolen bases five times.
Left: Outfielder Willie Wilson joined the Royals in 1976, led the league in stolen bases in 1979, and won the batting title in 1982.
Below: George Brett readies himself to tag out the runner. Brett's defensive skills and astounding .390 average earned him the batting title and MVP honors in 1980.

NEW YORK

agent. (A 'premium' player was defined by a complex formula involving his statistics in relation to other players at his position.) Although rejecting this compromise, the players began the season but made it clear they would strike if some progress wasn't made in negotiations.

So the 1981 season got underway on schedule, and also as if on schedule, the Yankees and the Orioles came rolling into mid-June in first and second place, respectively, in the Eastern Division. In the Western Division, Oakland was once again leading, with the Texas Rangers one and a half games behind them on 11 June. And then, just as they had threatened to do, all players in both major leagues went on strike, starting on 12 June. Day after day it went on, and soon Americans accepted that there was not going to be any major league baseball in the immediate future. Minor league and other teams found themselves with unexpectedly large crowds, and countless words were written about the role of baseball in American life. All the major league players went unpaid, of course, while the owners lost all the profits for those days. Seven hundred and fourteen games were eventually cancelled during the 49 days the strike lasted – the longest strike in the history of organized sports – but finally, on 31 July, the club owners and the players arrived at a compromise. Teams that lost a 'premium' free agent could be compensated by drawing on a pool of players formed by players contributed from all the clubs, not just the signing club; the teams that lost players through this pool system would be compensated from a fund supported by all the clubs; the net effect was to disperse the impact and cost so that owners would not lose the incentive to bid large sums for the premium free agents.

This, at least, was the essence of the compromise and when it was announced that the players would report for a 10-day summer 'training session' before resuming play, fans were ready to forgive and forget. 'Let's play ball!' was the cry. Then came the outcry when it was learned that the owners had decided to 'split' the season: namely, first-place teams in each division at the end of the first half would play the first-place teams at the end of the second half to settle division winners. If the same team happened to win both halves, it would play the runner-up from the second half only to determine the winner. That did not occur, but something else that was predicted

Opposite: Willie Randolph readies himself at the plate. Since joining the Yankees in 1976, the second baseman has played in four league play-offs and three World Series.

Below: Minnesota's third baseman John Castino dashes in for a bloop hit.

might happen did occur: the two National League teams that had the best overall records, the Cincinnati Reds and the St Louis Cardinals, both came in second for each 'season' and thus did not get a chance at a play-off slot.

With a certain amount of grumbling from various sides, then, 1981's second season got underway on 10 August. This time, the Milwaukee Brewers won in the Eastern Division, beating out the Red Sox by only one and a half games and then only by winning 11 of their last 17 games. In the Western Division, the Kansas City Royals edged out the Oakland A's by only one game. But by the irony of the system, Oakland, as winner of the first half, came right back and defeated the Royals in three straight to win the Western Division play-offs. In the Eastern Division play-offs, the Yankees beat the Brewers, three games to two. After all this, the pennant race was still not over, and for the American League, this saw the Yankees facing the A's – with Oakland now managed by Billy Martin, late of the Yankees. If Martin was supposed to jinx the Yankees, it didn't work as New York beat the A's in three straight games. Actually, Yankee Graig Nettles almost singlehandedly beat the A's, with his nine RBI's – three of them coming off his double in the ninth inning of the final game.

In the World Series the Yankees came up against their archrivals, the Dodgers, for the 11th time. Although the Yankees had taken eight of these Series, this was not to be the year for the ninth. The Dodgers lost the first two, then came back and won the next four (only the second team to achieve this, the first

being the Yankees, who did exactly the same thing to the Dodgers in 1978). All in all, 1981 had been a topsy-turvy season. Because the teams had played only about two-thirds of their games, the records for the season included such feats as Eddie Murray's 78 RBI's. But one player who would never complain of the 1981 season being too short was Len Barker of the Cleveland Indians, who on 15 May pitched a perfect game against the Toronto Blue Jays – only the 11th perfect game in major league history.

For the 1982 season, the strike seemed to have been totally forgotten and baseball was back to normal – which by now meant a fair amount of intramural fighting among the Yankees. George Steinbrenner, it might have been thought, got rid of one of his sparring partners when he let Reggie Jackson, once more a free agent, sign with the California Angels for 1982. (Jackson immediately announced he had no intention of becoming the 'team leader' – but he did end up with 39 homers, the sweetest of which was certainly the one he hit in his first game against the Yankees. Steinbrenner, meanwhile, tried to get even by accusing the Angels at one point of using 'illegal bats'). Stein-

Above: Reggie Jackson cracks a long ball. Jackson led the league in home runs and in strikeouts in 1982, his first year with the Angels.

Left: Sal Bando waits in the on-deck circle. Bando played third base for Milwaukee from 1977 until his retirement in 1981.

Opposite top: Dwayne Murphy rounds second base. Outfielder Murphy joined the A's in 1978. In the Western Division play-offs in the 1981 strike season, Murphy went 6 for 11.

Opposite bottom: Manager Billy Martin signals from the dugout. Martin managed the A's from 1980 to 1982.

brenner displayed his insensitivity to the players when he wrote a letter urging them to come to spring training three weeks early and then he tried to cut pitcher Tommy John's salary for failure to produce enough wins. When he announced that the Yankees were considering playing their first home games in Denver, Colorado – because Yankee Stadium's renovations might not be ready – he drew the wrath of all New Yorkers. Kicking a process server out of his office one day did not enhance Steinbrenner's image as a cool executive, either.

And since the Yankees also went through three managers during the 1982 season, it is no wonder that they didn't finish in first place in their division. (The Yankees began with Bob Lemon; on 25 April, Gene Michael took over, and on 3 August Clyde King got the nod.) But two teams did produce an old-fashioned race in the Eastern Division – the Brewers and the Orioles. The Brewers had an imposing array of power players in Paul Molitor, Cecil Cooper, Robin Yount, Ben Oglivie, Gorman Thomas and Ted Simmons, and had several respectable pitchers, while the Orioles had a more seasoned and balanced team playing under their longtime manager Earl Weaver. As occasionally happens with the chance of scheduling, the Orioles and Brewers found themselves in a four-game series in the final days of the regular season, but the Brewers had a three-game lead and looked virtually safe. Then the Orioles took the first three games, drew up to a tie, and turned it into a one-game season. The Brewers had acquired Don Sutton near the end of the season for just such a crisis, and in the final game he came through and the Brewers took over first place by winning 10-2.

In the Western Division, the California Angels took first place, but not without a struggle with the ever-threatening Kansas City Royals. Even with the likes of Willie Wilson and George Brett the Royals weren't able to overcome the Angels' power-packed lineup that included Reggie Jackson, Don Baylor, Fred Lynn

and Rod Carew – all former winners of the Most Valuable Player Award. In the play-offs, the Angels beat the Brewers in the first two games – perhaps because they were at Anaheim. But in Milwaukee the Brewers took all three, the first time a team had come from being down by two games to win a five-game play-off. In the World Series, though, the Brewers ran up against an equally powerful Cardinals, and after the two teams had scored a total of 72 runs through seven games, the Cardinals emerged as World Champions. But everyone recognized the Brewers' work and talents, and their Robin Yount was voted the league's Most Valuable Player, their Pete Vukovich won the Cy Young Award and their Harvey Kuenn, who took over only in June, was American League Manager of the Year.

Several other American Leaguers would long recall the 1982 season. Rickey Henderson of the Oakland A's first broke Lou Brock's 1974 record of 118 stolen bases and then went on to steal a total of 130. Meanwhile, Gaylord Perry started out the 1982 season with 297 career wins, but no team to pitch for; finally the

Opposite top: Outfielder Gorman Thomas contributed to the Brewers' power line-up. Thomas' league-leading 39 home runs in 1982 helped bring Milwaukee the pennant that year.

Opposite bottom: Milwaukee's shortstop Robin Yount was selected as the league's Most Valuable Player in 1982, the year he cracked 210 hits and 46 doubles for a league-leading .578 slugging percentage. Despite Yount's becoming the first player in World Series history to have two four-hit games, Milwaukee lost the Series in seven games to St Louis.

Left: First baseman Cecil Cooper stretches for the throw. Cooper joined Milwaukee in 1977 after six years with Boston. The big power-hitter led the league twice in RBI's and twice in doubles for the Brewers, maintaining a solid .305 batting average.

Left: Paul Molitor turns a double play. Molitor joined the Brewers in 1978, playing mainly second and third base. In 1982 he scored a league-leading 136 runs, and popped two homers in the league playoffs.

Right: At age 21 Rickey Henderson breaks Ty Cobb's American League single-season stolen base record of 96.

Below: Yankee phenomenon Dave Winfield pumps his way around the bases for a stand-up triple.

Seattle Mariners signed him on and on 6 May Perry got his 300th win, only the 15th major league pitcher to achieve this. And just in case anyone feared that baseball was running out of traditions to maintain, the Oakland A's fired Billy Martin when the season was over – and the Yankees would take him on to manage for 1983.

Every so often, major league baseball has one of those seasons where all kinds of sideshows seem to overshadow the main events at center ring – and 1983 was such a season. There was the ongoing saga of the decline and fall of Bowie Kuhn, Commissioner of Baseball for the previous 15 years. Kuhn had failed to satisfy some of the club owners and in November 1982 they had managed to get enough votes to oust him. However, they asked him to stay in office until his successor could be found, and throughout 1983 Kuhn openly lobbied in every way possible to see if he couldn't get the owners to re-appoint him. (He would hang on through 1983 – but would ultimately fail.) Ironically, one of the charges against Kuhn was that he didn't exercise sound financial judgment – i.e. the owners wanted to make more money. This charge came at a time when two of the television networks, NBC and ABC, signed a new contract for televising baseball games that guaranteed the teams some $1,100,000,000 over the next six years.

Speaking of television, a poll of active players showed that most of them opposed the use of television's instant replay to resolve disputes over controversial calls by umpires – a proposal that often surfaces. A more disconcerting development was the increasing number of players who were being charged with using drugs – cocaine in particular. Four members of the Kansas City Royals alone were found guilty of cocaine use in 1983, and there were several others already serving prison sentences for drug cases. A somewhat lighter moment came on 4 August when Dave Winfield of the Yankees was arrested in Toronto for 'cruelty to animals': he had thrown a baseball at one of the numerous seagulls that hover over the Blue Jays' home field – and killed the bird. (Winfield would explain that he had intended only to frighten it away and the charge was dropped.)

There had been a close race within the Eastern Division well into July, with the Yankees, Tigers and Orioles all in contention, while in the Western Division the Kansas City Royals were giving the division-leading Chicago White Sox a run for their money. Although the Yankees were having yet another of their tempestuous seasons under Billy Martin, they were on the verge of taking first place away from the Orioles. As for the White Sox, everyone was aware that it was not the first time the team had been on a hot streak, only to collapse. So when the Yankees met the Kansas City Royals at Yankee Stadium on 24 July, each team was needing every win it could get. It was the top of the ninth with the Yankees leading 4-3 and two Royals out when George Brett stepped up and hit a homer off reliever Rich Gossage that gave the Royals two runs and a 5-4 lead. At that point, Billy Martin stepped out of the dugout and pointed out to the umpire that Brett had used a bat with more than the 18 inches of pine tar allowed by the rules. Once the umpire was convinced, he ruled that Brett's homer didn't count, that he was out – and the Yankees thus won the game. (What was not generally known at the time was that Gaylord Perry, on the Kansas City team, tried to sneak the bat away during all the commotion at the plate, but the umpire chased him all the way into the runway between the dugout and the locker room and retrieved the bat.) The Royals naturally protested the umpire's ruling, and four days later Lee MacPhail, president of the American League,

Tiger right-hander Dan Petry hurls a pitch. Petry joined Detroit in 1979, turning in 19 wins for them in 1983 and 18 wins (with a .692 winning percentage) the following year to help bring the Tigers to the Series.

Main picture: Oakland catcher Mike Heath goes into the stands for a foul ball.
Inset: A catcher's profile.

Opposite: The Orioles' shortstop Cal Ripken fires a throw to first base. Ripken was named Rookie of the Year in 1982, and the following year was selected as the league's Most Valuable Player as his team went all the way to win the World Series.

Above right: The Angels' outfielder Fred Lynn perches in the California dugout. In the 1982 league play-offs Lynn batted 11 for 18, and the following year he gained acclaim with his All-Star grand slam.

Below: Lou Whitaker fields a grounder. As Detroit's second baseman, 'Sweet Lou' was named Rookie of the Year in 1978. His solid play has contributed to the Tigers' rise to the top.

overruled the umpire: 'Games should be won and lost on the playing field – not through technicalities of the rules.' The game was to be replayed from the moment after Brett's homer. On 18 August, before 1245 fans, one more Royal came up, then the final three for the Yankees – and the game ended in 9 minutes and 41 seconds with Kansas City on top, 5-4.

But by then, the damage had been done. The Yankees had been tied for first place with the Orioles on 28 July, but they had gone into a slump after the disputed game and by the time the final innings were played, the Yankees were in fifth place. The Orioles then went on to hold off the Detroit Tigers and take first place in the Eastern Division. In the Western Division, the White Sox finally held on to a lead and for the first time since 1959 qualified for post-season play. In the playoffs, the Orioles beat the White Sox in three straight, taking the third game on Tito Landrum's homer. The World Series was billed as another 'railroad series,' since it pitted the Orioles against their neighbors up the line, the Philadelphia Phillies. The Phillies seemed loaded with talent with the likes of Mike Schmidt, Joe Morgan, Pete Rose and Steve Carlton, but the Orioles had their own talents such as Eddie Murray and Cal Ripken, Jr. (What they couldn't count on, though, was their star designated hitter, Ken Singleton, since this was an odd year, and thus the Series didn't allow for the DH.) Although the Phillies took the first game, the Orioles went on to sweep the next four and take the Series.

So all in all, 1983 turned out to be a successful year for most of the members of the American League. After more losses in the All-Star Game than anyone could remember, the American League won the 50th anniversary game, 13-3, with Fred Lynn hitting the first grand slam home run in the history of All-Star games. The Texas Rangers set a record of sorts in 1983, too, when they got 12 runs in an extra inning, the most ever in major league history. And in the same season the Brewers played the White Sox for four hours 11 minutes, the longest game in American

SOX
SOX

Padres – which Goose Gossage had already left the Yankees to join. Meanwhile, Dave Righetti, considered one of the hottest pitchers around, was assigned to be a relief pitcher for the Yankees. And in one of the more surprising moves, the Yankees signed up the oldest active player in the major leagues, 44-year-old Phil Niekro, the famed knuckleballer who had worked for the Braves, first in Milwaukee and then in Atlanta, for 19 years.

One of the more astounding developments of the 1984 season was when Tom Seaver, long a National League ace pitcher, suddenly appeared on the roster of the Chicago White Sox. This came about through a simple error on the part of the Mets' front office, which neglected to put Seaver's name on their list of 'protected' players – those not eligible for the pool

Opposite: After 17 years in the National League, pitching great Tom Seaver was lost to the Chicago White Sox, in 1984. 'Tom Terrific' won 15 games for the Sox that year. His career ERA stands at about 2.80.

Left: The Royals' ace reliever Dan Quisenberry helped them clinch the 1985 World championship title with his steady performances.

League history. (The Brewers won, 12-9.) Dan Quisenberry set a major league record when he posted 39 saves for the Kansas City Royals; Dave Righetti pitched a no-hitter for the Yankees (over the Red Sox, 4-0), the first for the team in 27 years and Carl Yastrzemski of the Red Sox set a new American League record of 3058 appearances, and then retired on 1 October. Lee MacPhail also retired as president of the American League at the end of 1983 – and Billy Martin was fired by the Yankees again.

The Yankees started out the 1984 season, in fact, with numerous changes. Aside from having Yogi Berra as manager, Steinbrenner decided to shake up a team he felt wasn't producing what he expected for his money. This left several players fed up, and when Graig Nettles publicly criticized Steinbrenner's changes, he was promptly traded to the San Diego

draft. The alert White Sox noticed this and immediately claimed Seaver; at first Seaver threatened to retire rather than go, but he realized that he was more interested in his career than his location, so in February he settled with the White Sox.

Another major personnel change for major league baseball came about in March 1984 when the club owners finally agreed on a successor to Bowie Kuhn as Commissioner of Baseball. Their choice was Peter Ueberroth, president of the Los Angeles Olympic Organizing Committee who, even before the Olympics were held, was recognized for his mastery of its financial and organizational complexities. It would be 1 October 1984, however, before he would actually take over as commissioner for a five-year term.

But the really exciting news of 1984 was made on the playing field. In the Eastern Division, the Yankees were a threat as usual, but although Dave Winfield and Don Mattingly raced each other down to the last

Above: Knuckleballer Phil Niekro throws a pitch. After 20 years in the National League, Niekro signed with the Yankees in 1984, winning 16 games for them and losing eight.

Left: First baseman Don Mattingly, who joined the Yankees in 1982, won the batting title in 1984 with a .343 average.

FISK

day for the individual batting title – with Mattingly just sneaking into the lead with his .343 – the team couldn't get it all together. The World Champion Orioles were also picked as a good prospect to repeat but they also didn't make it. Instead, the Detroit Tigers opened the season with a win, like 12 other major league teams; but unlike the other 12, Detroit just went on winning and winning, setting a record by winning 35 out of their first 40 games. At one point they also won 17 straight games on the road, and Tiger Jack Morris pitched a no-hitter on 7 April. By 18 September, the Tigers had clinched first place in the Eastern Division, and their manager, Sparky Anderson, would end the season as the first manager to lead two different clubs with 100-plus victories.

In the Western Division the Chicago White Sox seemed like the top prospect when the season began, but instead it was the Kansas City Royals, with the Twins in second. It hardly made any difference to the Tigers, since they took the playoffs in three straight. And the story in the World Series was not much different, although the Padres did manage to win the second game. Detroit took the Series, four games to one, with the same well-balanced team that had been winning all season – including such as Kirk Gibson, Alan Trammell and Willie Hernandez (who ended up winning both the Cy Young Award and the Most Valuable Player Award). The only thing that marred Detroit's spectacular season was the riotous celebration that occurred in Detroit after their Series clincher – and which left one innocent bystander dead.

With a season such as that, it might be assumed that Detroit was picked to be an easy winner for 1985, but the experts thought better. They decided that Detroit simply couldn't maintain the pace – and that another team was due to get hot. The team they picked for the Eastern Division was the Toronto Blue Jays, and indeed the Blue Jays got off to a good start

Opposite: White Sox catcher Carlton Fisk slams a home run. Fisk, who joined the Sox in 1981, hit 37 home runs in 1985.

Above: Shortstop Alan Tramell joined the Tigers in 1977. In 1984 Tramell's .314 batting average helped the Tigers' unstoppable run to the Series, and his pair of two-run homers in game four of the Series helped Detroit take the championship.

Left: The World Champions in 1984 – the Detroit Tigers.

Right: George Brett handles a smash down the third base line with ease. Brett's sparkling 1985 post-season performance helped the Royals take it all.

Far right: In 1986 Boston Red Sox pitcher Roger Clemens led his team to the pennant with his 24-6 performance. Clemens, whose 20 strikeouts in one game set a new major-league record on 29 April 1986, won the Cy Young Award and was voted American League MVP.

Below: Red Sox third baseman Wade Boggs won the batting title in 1985 with his .368 batting average.

and by mid-season were in first place, two and a half games ahead of the Yankees. The Yankees started out the season under Yogi Berra but were doing so poorly that in May he was replaced – by Billy Martin! The Yankees now had, in addition to such hitters as Mattingly, Winfield, and Don Baylor, none other than Rickey Henderson, newly signed from the Oakland A's to a generous five-year contract. The Red Sox had high hopes at the outset, with such players as Jim Rice, Wade Boggs, Dwight Evans, and Bob Stanley, but with a shortage of pitching talent the team couldn't get the wins. The Baltimore Orioles also looked good, having just acquired Fred Lynn to go with an already strong lineup, but by June the Orioles were doing so poorly that Earl Weaver came out of retirement to manage them again.

Over in the Western Division, the Kansas City Royals had been picked to repeat, but at mid-season they were seven and a half games down in third place, with the Angels in first, six games ahead of the A's. The Brewers, incidentally, had decided to try a new tactic and signed on a star pitcher from Japan, Yutaka Enatsu, but he never really felt at home with American baseball and was soon dropped.

Two players who were at home with American baseball and who had been exiled for some years were Mickey Mantle and Willie Mays; both had taken jobs as public relations 'greeters' for gambling casinos, and Commissioner Bowie Kuhn had thus

21

Above: The Royals' pitching ace Bret Saberhagen, who joined the team the year before, hurled his way to a victory in game seven of the 1985 World Series.

banished them from any association with major league baseball. The new commissioner Peter Ueberroth reinstated Mantle and Mays and won the instant approval of most baseball fans. But Ueberroth did not gain the approval of all active players when he also called for mandatory urine tests by everyone connected with major league baseball, as an attempt to end the ongoing drug use by players.

In the end, all of the controversies over drugs and salaries were swept away by the threatened strike by all major league players due to their inability to negotiate a new basic agreement with the club owners. The players insisted that the owners were making profits and should share more of these profits with the players. The owners insisted that many of the clubs were losing large sums. And so as the weeks passed and threat of a strike drew nearer, finally 6 August was set by the players as the absolute deadline for an agreement.

The players did strike, but for barely a day and a half; by 8 August the players were back on the fields, and all missed games were made up during the rest of the season. The differences that caused the strike were resolved by compromise and the strike was quickly forgotten as the annual race for the pennant moved into the final laps. In the American League, the Toronto Blue Jays won the Eastern Division, in an excitingly close race with the Yankees, who ended up two games behind. In the Western Division the first-place Kansas City Royals came in one game ahead of the California Angels. The Royals won the playoffs in seven games and went on to meet the St Louis Cardinals in the 1985 World Series, which the Royals won, repeating their playoff feat by coming from behind 3 games to 1 to win 4 to 3.

As the 1986 season began to emerge from hibernation, the conventional wisdom was that the Kansas City Royals would repeat – at least to take the Western Division if not go all the way. In the Eastern Division, the Yankees seemed to come out on top in most of the predictions, with the California Angels projected at about third place and the Red Sox even farther down by these same measures. While these predictions proved, of course, to be wildly off-base, few other changes would come about in the league. Lou Piniella replaced Billy Martin as manager of the Yankees, and when Dick Williams left the San Diego Padres in the National League he soon showed up as manager of the Seattle Mariners in the American League West. Kirk Gibson, the Tigers' star, threatened to move on if he didn't get a better salary offer, but in the end he signed on – the fact was that no teams were showing any interest in high-salaried free agents – as did Carlton Fisk with the White Sox and Don Mattingly with the Yankees. One crucial swap during the season occurred when Don Baylor of the Yankees went over to the Red Sox in return for Mike Easler; both were to serve as their teams' designated hitters, and Baylor would turn out to be his team's sparkplug as well. And Phil Niekro, at 46 the oldest active pitcher, hoped to play the season with his brother Joe on the Yankees, but he was soon let go and signed on with the Cleveland Indians.

At first it looked as though Phil Niekro had made a lucky move as the Indians took an early lead (after leading the American League in losses in 1985). Then the spotlight suddenly shifted to the Red Sox on 29 April as a hitherto not widely acclaimed young pitcher, Roger Clemens, astonished baseball fans by setting a new modern major-league record of 20 strikeouts in a nine-inning game against the Mariners. And in case it seemed that this was one of those flash-in-the-pan performances, Clemens continued to win and win and win – his first 14 games, in fact. Not an all-time record but good enough to help the Red Sox take over first place in the Eastern Division by 15 May.

By the mid-season All-Star game (which the American League won, 3-2), there were the Red Sox, still in the first, with a solid seven-game lead over the favored Yankees. (Making some wags swallow that old chestnut about 'June is the month when both the basketball and baseball seasons end in Boston.') And in the Western Division, instead of the highly-touted

Red Sox catcher Rich Gedman rips a line drive in the 1986 American League playoffs against the California Angels.

Royals, there were the California Angels – with only a one-and-a-half-game lead, but still not bad for a team of senior citizens. Two of the latter had done quite well. On 14 May, Reggie Jackson hit his five hundred thirty-seventh home run, taking over sixth place from Mickey Mantle among career home run hitters; and on 18 June, Don Sutton won his three hundredth game.

During the second half of the season, the Red Sox found themselves challenged at various times – by the Yankees, the Orioles, the Tigers and the Blue Jays – while the Angels had to hold off the Texas Rangers. But despite all the predictions, the Red Sox and the Angels ended up on top of their divisions. Going into the playoffs, it seemed the two teams were fairly evenly matched. Boston finally had what it had lacked for so many years – pitchers to support their hitters. Not only did Clemens come through with the best record in the majors (24-6), but there was Bruce Hurst and Oil Can Boyd. (Tom Seaver, who had come over to the Red Sox from the White Sox during the season, didn't figure that much in the team's victory, and injuries kept him out of the playoffs.) For hitting, the Red Sox could count on Wade Boggs (who had taken the league's batting championship with his .357), Jim Rice, Dwight Evans, Rich Gedman and Don Baylor. The Angels, meanwhile, could point to Mike Witt, Kirk McCaskill, John Candelaria and Don Sutton as pitching aces, while at bat they relied on Doug DeCinces, Bobby Grich, Brian Downing and the rookie sensation, Wally Joyner (although injury also kept him out of the playoffs).

The Angels took the first game of the playoffs, collapsed in the second and came back to take the third. In the fourth game the Red Sox took a 3-0 lead into the ninth inning, blew it, and then lost in the eleventh – it seemed that the Angels were unstoppable. The Red Sox went into the fifth game, down 3-1 in games, and sure enough, when the ninth inning came round, the Angels had a 5-2 lead. Buckner got on first and Don Baylor ripped a home run, but this still left the score 5-4 and soon there were two outs. Then Gedman got hit by a pitch and went to first, and up came one Dave Henderson, a Red Sox only since being acquired from the Mariners in August and hardly a known quantity to even many Boston fans. Henderson soon had two strikes on him and in the Angels' clubhouse the champagne was one pitch from being poured – when Henderson hit a home run, giving the Red Sox a 6-5 lead. The Angels tied it up in the bottom of the ninth, but Boston went on to take the game in the eleventh inning, 7-6. After that, anything might seem anticlimactic, but the Red Sox went on to win the sixth and seventh games – depriving the Angels' manager, Gene Mauch, of yet another pennant (in his 25 years as a manager, he had never won one) but providing baseball fans with a tale to recount over many a winter.

Now on to the World Series, where the Red Sox – in their first since 1975 – found themselves facing the New York Mets, generally conceded to be the strongest team of 1986, with the winningest record (108 victories). Few would give Boston much chance in the first two games at Shea Stadium, but the Red Sox took them both. Then just to prove how baseball continually defies the statistics, the Mets went up to Fenway Park and took the first two there. The Red Sox won the fifth game, though, and the teams returned to Shea Stadium with the Red Sox holding a 3-2 lead in games. In the sixth game, the Red Sox went into the ninth inning with a 2-0 lead and it looked like they were finally going to take their first Series since 1918. But the Mets managed to get two runs and send the game into extra innings; again, the Red Sox came through, first on a homer by Henderson and then on some hits that gave them an insurance run. The Mets came back in the bottom of the tenth with three runs and won 5-4, tying the Series at three a piece. In the seventh, deciding game Boston took an early 3-0 lead, but the Mets caught up, went ahead on a homer by Ray Knight, and won the game 8-5. But the Red Sox had more than exceeded expectations, and true baseball fans agreed it was a season to be proud of and one that proved yet again just what an intricate and unpredictable game baseball truly is.

The American League began the 1987 season with no particular shakeups or scandals: The road was clear for a classic season of old-fashioned baseball. True, there were those free agents – Rich Gedman and company – who held out, found no takers and ended up rejoining their teams in May. This was part of the larger issue of alleged collusion among the team owners to cease bidding for free agents: It was 21 September when an arbitrator ruled that there had been collusion at least since 1985, but no one knew quite

Right: Hard-hitting Kirby Puckett, who joined the Twins in 1984, was one of the factors that led the team to the World Championship in 1987.

Below: Ace hurler Willie Hernandez was in his tenth year with the Tigers in 1987.

what to do with that conclusion. Likewise, the issue of racism that emerged during the celebration of the 40th anniversary of Jackie Robinson's breaking down the color barrier in the major leagues: It was quite clear that blacks and Hispanics were still being denied any significant role in management or administrative positions – a few coaches, a couple of front-office slots, and that was about it. Although it was a profoundly serious issue and was going to have to be resolved before too many more seasons, it did not seem to affect the play on the field during 1987.

When the season began, some students of the game thought that Cleveland was going to take the American League's Eastern Division, although others predicted that the Yankees were going to claim the crown. One thing all agreed on: The Red Sox could not repeat. In the Western Division some thought the Texas Rangers were due, some picked the Angels again, some the Kansas City Royals and still others the Oakland As. One thing they all agreed on: The Minnesota Twins didn't have a chance.

In the event, Cleveland never even made a serious bid. The Brewers set a major-league record by winning their first 13 games, but by mid-July the Yankees had taken over first place in the East. And they did have a lot going for them – Don Mattingly was having an especially good year – but they also had George Steinbrenner as owner, and he ended up keeping the team and its manager, Lou Piniella, in almost constant turmoil. Meanwhile, Rickey Henderson, from whom so much was expected, never got over a series of physical and 'social' afflictions (and by the end of the season was talking of moving on). The result was that the Yankees were constantly being pressed by both the Tigers and the Blue Jays. By mid-August the Blue Jays had taken over the lead. Then, in one of those coincidences of scheduling, the Blue Jays found them-

Above: Frank Viola (seen here), along with teammate Bert Blyleven, was one of the Twins' regular starters in 1987.

Left: A pulled hamstring kept daunting Yankee baserunner Rickey Henderson from having one of his better seasons.

selves coming into the last days of the season with two series against the Tigers – seven games altogether. In the first set, at Toronto, the Blue Jays took the first three and lost the fourth, leaving them with a 2½ game lead over the Tigers. During the week, however, the Blue Jays proceeded to drop three more games to Milwaukee, so when they came up against the Tigers on the final weekend in Detroit their lead had been reduced to one game. The Tigers won that first game and were tied for first; they won the second and took a one-game lead; then they won the third and clinched the Eastern Division title.

Over in the Western Division things went a bit differently. Outfoxing the experts, the Twins gained first place relatively early on, but they were constantly pressed by Oakland, the Angels and the Royals. By mid-September only 3½ games separated the fourth-place Royals from the first-place Twins. But the Twins fooled everyone and stayed on top. Much credit was given to their new manager, Tom Kelly, at 37 the youngest in the majors, but it was nevertheless a true team effort. The Twins had no superstar pitching, but Frank Viola and Bert Blyleven came through, and the Twins had acquired Jeff Reardon and Juan Berenguer who delivered in relief. Kirby Puckett had a good year, and non-headline-grabbers such as Kent Hrbek, Tom Brunansky, Gary Gaetti and Dan Gladden came through when needed.

Right: In 1987 the Brewers' Paul Molitor had a 39-game hitting streak.

Above: The Twins scored two firsts in the 1987 Series. They won all their home games, and they brought the Championship home to Minnesota.

The Tigers, meanwhile, had many of their veterans from the spectacular 1984 season – Alan Trammell, Lou Whitaker, Kirk Gibson and Darrell Evans – and under veteran manager Sparky Anderson they were generally conceded to have the advantage over the Twins. But in the playoffs the Twins' pitching pretty much shut down the Tigers' hitters, while the Twins came through with the runs when they needed them. With some ace relieving by Reardon and Berenguer, the Twins managed to defeat the Tigers by an impressive four games to one.

So the Twins went into the World Series with their first pennant since 1965 to meet the St Louis Cardinals. Once more, the smart pickers seemed to favor the seasoned Cardinals, although they had two injured stars, Jack Clark and Terry Pendleton. When the Twins took the first two games in the Metrodome, the smart ones began to wonder, but when the Cardinals swept the three games in St Louis they began to relax. But the Twins went on to do something no other team had done in the 31 times a World Series has gone into seven games – win all of their home games. True, the unusual environment of the Metrodome – its distracting lighting and the ear-splitting noise level – played some part, but the fact is that all the Twins came through, while the Cardinals never quite found their level. Thus, against all predictions, the Minnesota Twins won their first World Series.

So the 1987 season ended – nothing spectacular, but baseball as it is supposed to be: defying the odds, statistics and predictions. Several American League players had a season they would not soon forget. Paul Molitor made one of the most successful assaults on Joe DiMaggio's 56-game hitting streak, but he finally stopped at 39. Don Mattingly, however, set a new major league record with six grand-slam homers for the season, and he homered in eight consecutive games, tying Dale Long's 1956 record. Bob Boone took over a major-league record long held by Al Lopez, the most games caught in a career. And Don Baylor took over a record of dubious achievement: awarded first base the most times (255) by being hit. (Most observers agree that Baylor generously helped himself to this record.) The MVP award, after being debated all season as due either George Bell of the Blue Jays or Alan Trammell of the Tigers, went to George Bell, while the Cy Young award went to Roger Clemens. Rookie of the year went to Mark McGwire of the Oakland As, who not only broke the major-league record of most homers for a rookie but went on to win the league's home run record with his 49. With rookies like that, the future of the American League seemed more than secure.

The 1988 season in the American League began with one of those major league records teams prefer not to set: the Baltimore Orioles lost their first 21 games. Little wonder the Orioles finished last in their division, with a 52-107 record. But the rest of the Eastern Division more than made up for this with one of the classic surprises in recent major league history. The Yankees had been predicted to go all the way, but by the All-Star Game (which the American League won, 2-1)

Detroit was in the lead, with the Yankees and Brewers close behind. The Red Sox were 8½ out, but no one except a few diehard Red Sox fans thought of them as a contender. Indeed, things were so bad in Boston that John McNamara was fired during the mid-way break and an obscure third-base coach, Joe Morgan, was named manager of the Red Sox in what looked like a mere holding operation. Instead, the Sox began to win game after game – 24 consecutive wins at Fenway Park – and by Labor Day were in first place, ending up with a one-game lead over Detroit even though they lost 7 out of their last 10 games.

In the Western Division, it was another story, with the Oakland A's quickly moving into first place and never being seriously threatened; with the aid of Jose Canseco's 42 homers and 40 stolen bases (the first such 40/40 man in major league history) and the likes of Dave Henderson and Mark McGwire, they cruised to a 13-game lead over the Twins. No wonder, then, that this Oakland team crushed the Red Sox four straight in the playoffs. No wonder, either, that the A's were generally picked as favorites in the World Series. But the surprises that make baseball the game it is came around – surprises named Kirk Gibson and Orel Hershiser – and the Los Angeles Dodgers won the Series, four games to one.

The year 1988 was notable for several other events off the field. Most notably, the major leagues decided to enforce the balk rule – instructing umpires to watch closely that pitchers paused at the 'set' position before proceeding to throw. This led to a record number of balk calls throughout the season. Although many complained that this new stringency would distort the game, the balk rule did not seem that crucial in subsequent seasons as pitchers made sure they came to a halt.

The 1989 season seemed to be one of those in which events off the field at times overshadowed the game itself – specifically the scandal over charges that Red manager Pete Rose had gambled on baseball games, and the tragic death of baseball's recently appointed commissioner, A. Bartlett Giamatti. On a more positive note, Jim Abbott, the young onc-handed pitcher from Michigan and a hero of the 1988 Olympics, joined the California Angels and ended up with an ERA of 3.92 to go with his 12-12 record. Meanwhile, another hard-to-match event took place when Ken Griffey, Sr., and

Above: With 42 homers and 40 stolen bases in 1988, Oakland's Jose Canseco became major league baseball's first 40/40 man.

Left: Homer-hitting Mark McGwire of Oakland was a clear choice for 1987 Rookie of the Year.

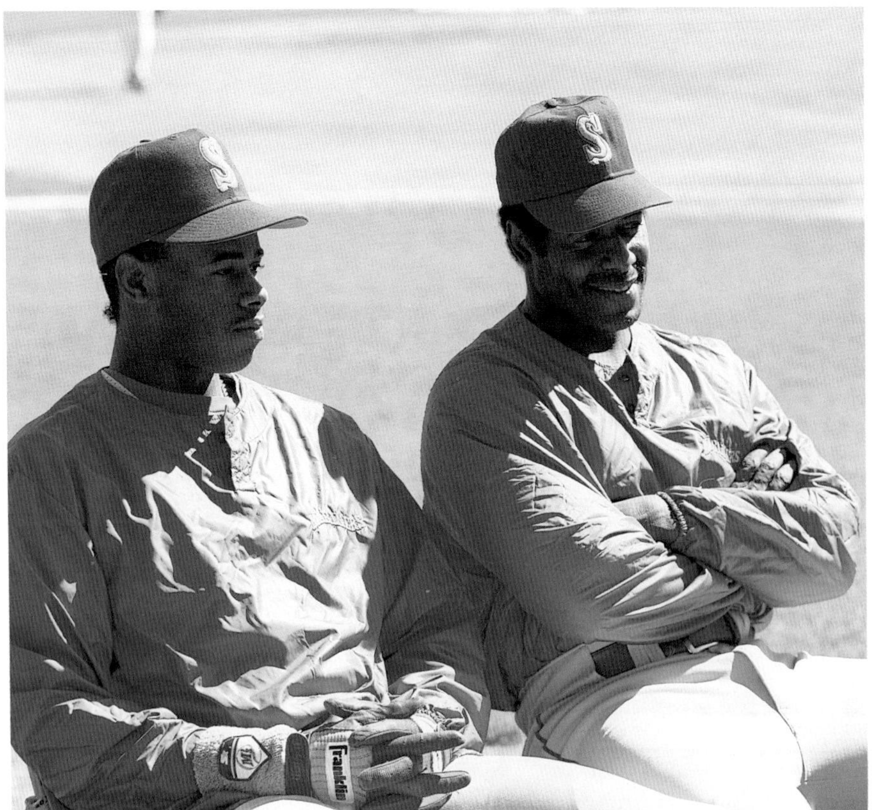

Top: Seattle Mariners Ken Griffey, Sr. and Ken Griffey, Jr., played together in 1989.

Above: A's fans hold brooms to signify their hopes for a sweep of Boston during the fourth game of the 1990 ALCS.
Right: Oakland's Dave Stewart turned in his third straight 20-win season in 1989. In 1990 he was one of nine pitchers who threw a no-hitter.

Ken Griffey, Jr., both played for the same team, the Seattle Mariners.

Meanwhile, the Oakland A's were picked to win the Western Division and with the aid of Dave Stewart's third straight 20-win season – and after Jose Canseco came back from an injured wrist – the A's did indeed pull away, beating the Kansas City Royals by seven games. In the Eastern Division, Toronto inaugurated its new Skydome in July and with record-breaking crowds cheering them on, the Blue Jays caught up to the amazingly rejuvenated Baltimore Orioles and squeaked into first place with a two-game lead.

In the playoffs, although the Blue Jays were the sentimental favorites, they couldn't compete with the likes of Canseco, McGwire, and now Rickey as well as Dave Henderson, and the A's took the league crown four games to one. Because the A's were to play their neighbors, the San Francisco Giants, the World Series was soon dubbed the 'BART' Series – a pun on the nickname of the late 'Bart' Giamatti (to whom the Series was dedicated) and the Bay Area's Rapid Transit system – but the Series became memorable for another reason. The A's won the first two games in their ballpark, then on October 17, as game three was about to begin at Candlestick Park, an earthquake hit the Bay Area. Not only did the Series halt, there was even some suggestion that it should be canceled, but the Series did resume on October 27, and the A's two aces – Dave Stewart and Mike Moore – supported by the team's heavy hitters, completed their sweep.

As the 1990 season began, the accepted wisdom was that the Oakland A's were now a full-fledged dynasty, and indeed they did dominate the Western Division again, beating out the Chicago White Sox by nine games. The A's were greatly aided by Rickey Henderson's MVP performance. In the Eastern Division, Toronto once again looked like it was going to meet the A's at the showdown; with eight games to play, Toronto led the second-place Red Sox by one and a half games. Then the Blue Jays lost six of their last eight games, while the Red Sox managed to win most of theirs and ended up in first place, two games ahead of Toronto. The exciting Jays could be partially consoled by having an all-time record with over four million fans in their Skydome.

In the playoffs, Oakland repeated its 1988 sweep of Boston, but the tables were turned when the A's came

Left: In game four, Oakland players celebrate the ninth-inning double play that sealed their 1990 ALCS victory.

up against the Cincinnati Reds, and in one of the biggest upsets in recent World Series, the A's fell in four straight games.

Off the field, 1990 was the year that the controversial George Steinbrenner was forced to give up his post as the chief owner and managing partner of the New York Yankees for 'the best interest of baseball.' Among the player standouts were Cecil Fielder – just back in the American majors after a season in Japan – who hit 51 homers for Detroit. Chicago White Sox reliever Bobby Thigpen set a new major league record by making 77 appearances, during which he pitched 88 innings and had an 1.83 ERA. Veteran reliever Dennis Eckersley of the A's had 48 saves (second all-time) with his astounding 0.61 ERA.

The 1991 season began with the A's once more perceived as the team to beat in the American League, but plagued by injuries, Oakland never got off the ground; instead virtually every team in the division took turns at first place until finally the race settled down to one between the Twins and Chicago. Gradually the Twins pulled away, taking first place by eight games – the first time a team had come from last place to first place in one year. In the Eastern Division, many people picked the Red Sox, what with Roger Clemens and a pack of strong hitters. And they did start strong, with an 18-9 record, but by 7 August the Red Sox were 11½ games behind the Blue Jays. Then the Bosox took four games from Toronto, and went on to win 31 of 41 games so that by 22 September they were only a half game out – only to collapse again by losing 10 of their last 13 games. By the end, the best the Red Sox could do was to salvage a tie for second place with Detroit, both seven games down from the Blue Jays, who had shaken their reputation for 'choking.' Many attributed the Jays' rise to the top to their new acquisitions, such as Joe Carter, Roberto Alomar, Devon White, Tom Candiotti, and Candy Maldonado.

In the playoffs, there was no single dominating favorite. Although it was pointed out that the Twins had never lost a postseason game in their Metrodome, there's always a first time in baseball, and after losing the opener, the Blue Jays did beat the Twins in the Metrodome. But in the next three games, the Twins proved too strong and took the division crown, four games to one. In the World Series, the Twins came up against the Atlanta Braves, thus setting up a historic confrontation between two teams that had come from last place the year before. The Twins were generally favored – among other reasons because they had never lost a World Series game in their home field, and they had the advantage of playing the first two and the last two there. Indeed, the Twins did take the first two from the Braves, but the games were close, and when the Series moved to Atlanta, the Braves astonished all but their most dedicated tomahawk-wielding fans by sweeping the three games there. Two were tight games, but the third was a 14-5 blowout, and when the teams headed back to the Twin Cities with the

Left: Minnesota's 1991 World Series MVP Jack Morris waves his hat after pitching the 10-inning seventh game over the Braves.

Below: The Blue Jays' Roberto Alomar helped Toronto win their division in 1991, as the Jays drew a record four million fans.

journeymen Braves leading the old-masters Twins, three games to two, fans sensed that this could be one of those great Series in which nothing was decided until a final pitch. In the sixth game, the teams matched each other run for run through the ninth inning, and it took Kirby Puckett's homer in the bottom of the twelfth to give the Twins a win. It was a record-breaking third Series game decided by a final pitch. And so the season came down to a World Series seventh game between two evenly matched teams. And that's the way the finale went, inning by inning with scattered hits and brilliant fielding, as each team went scoreless until the bottom of the tenth, when the Twins got one run across and became the 1991 World Champions. Minnesota's Jack Morris, who pitched all 10 innings for his second win, was chosen Series MVP. The Twins players were the first to agree that the Braves had nothing to apologize for, that this was one of those World Series in which the teams were so evenly matched it was hard to call one team losers.

The American League's 1991 season was especially memorable for seeing Rickey Henderson's inevitable takeover of the all-time major league career stolen base record, Nolan Ryan's seventh no-hitter, and Cal Ripken, Jr.'s pursuit of Lou Gehrig's record of consecutive games played. With records like this, the American League seemed certain to continue to provide many more thrills in the years to come.

So, too, in the final decade of the American League's first century of existence, the 25-year difference between the two major leagues came to seem less and less significant. And if major league baseball faced some serious problems – from drug abuse to financial crises – it was only because baseball is inseparable from the fabric of American life. With its new generation of players and fans, the American League is assured of moving into the 21st century as a leading player in the national pastime.

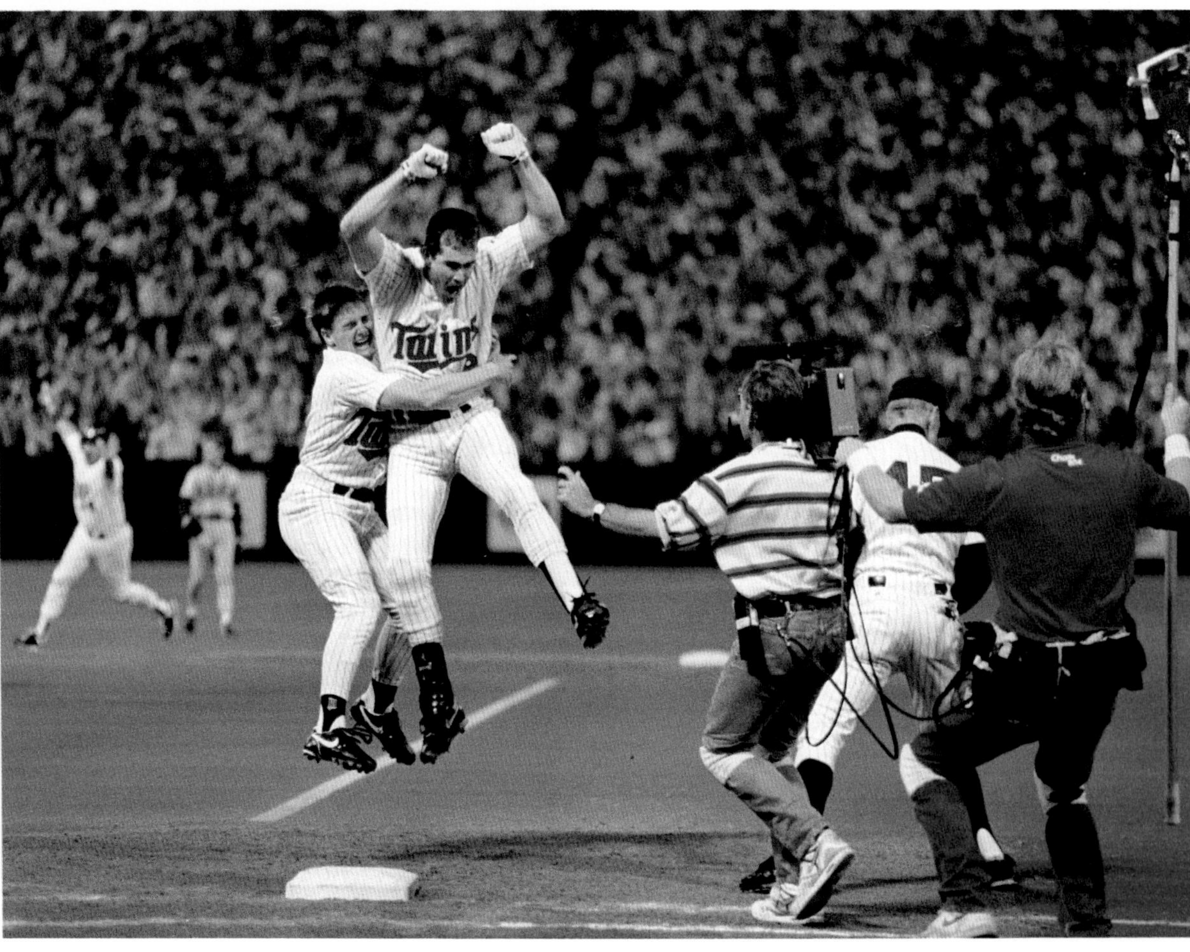

Above: The Rangers' Nolan Ryan pitched an unprecedented seventh no-hitter in 1991, at age 44. **Right:** Minnesota's Gene Larkin and Chuck Knoblauch celebrate the thrill of victory after Larkin knocked in the winning run in the seventh game of the 1991 World Series.

INDEX

Numbers in *italics* indicate illustrations

Aaron, Henry 99, 102, *102*, 103, 104, 108, 114, 125, 132, *136*, 139, 142, 147-48, 153, 197, 299, 341
Abbott, Jim 385
Adock, Joe *99*, 99
Agee, Tommie 326, 327
Alexander, Dale 247
Alexander, Grover C 34, *35*, 37, 39, 41-2, 45-50, *49*, 51, 94, 216, 236
Allen, Richie *141*, 338
Allen, Johnny *246*, 247
All-Star Game (50th), 372
Alomar, Roberto 387, *387*
Alston, Walter 98, 124, 150, 153
American Association (Players) 201, 203
American League 22, 99, 108, 146, 156; attendance 222, 223, 232, 246, 259; formation 200-03; franchises 203, 204, 205 (moving 287, 306; expansion 330, 347. *See also* baseball leagues); players switch to 203; profitability 205, 363, 368; recognition of 205
Anderson, 'Sparky' *134*, 139, 144, 150, 377
Anson, Adrian 17, 18
Aparicio, Luis 293, *295*, 316, 335
Appling, Luke 252
Armbrister, Ed 151
Atlanta Braves *2-3*, 112, 125, 132, 147, 169-71, 196, 197, *197*, 387-88
Auker, Eldon 250
Avery, Steve 197
Averill, Earl 253
Avila, Bobby 288

Bagby, Jim 225
Baker, Frank *212*, 212, 215
ball; cork-centered 212; lively 222, 223, 225, 244
Baltimore Orioles 21, 22, 114, 124, 125, 132, 141, 143, 159, 204-05, 287, 316-18, 324, 325, 333, 335-37, 340, 341, 342, 347, 353, 359, 363, 366, 372, 377, 384, 386
Bando, Sal *337*, 365
Banks, Ernie *106*, 108
Barber, Red *65*
Barker, Len 337
Barrow, Edward 226
Barry, Jack *211*, 212, 215
bases stolen, records 116, 118, 128, 148, 156, 197
baseball game: attendance 54, 56, 57, 61, 62, 85, 97, 104, 105, 107, 108, 166, 244, 250, 266, 271, 275, 289, records 133, 146, 156, 159, 384, 385; balk rule 192-93, 385; in Civil War *13*; early history *8*, 8-11, *198*; fans 22, 147, 168; innovations in 15, 33, 61-62, 66; longest running 43, 122, 372; night games, 194, *194*, 262; no-hitters 14, 39-40, 67, 78, 96, 103, 116, 121, 124, 168, 177, 262, 282, 296, 338, 344, 375, 378, 388; as power game 222, 224, 244, 246; Presidential opening/ involvement 33, *43*, 56, 61, 136, 222, 229, 233-34, 248, *287*, 287, 292, *304*, 309, 311; popularity 18, 22, 42, 45, 66, 77, 78, 112; public image 200, 205, 262, 332; radio/television coverage of 62, 66, 72, 77, 96, 112, 148, 174; rules 42-3, 50, 112, 129-31, 136, 146, 223, 224; standardization 9, 17-18. *See also* balls: lively ball: designated hitter
baseball leagues: competition 204; expansions 289, 306, 323, 347; financial crises 388; and National agreements 201-02, 204, 229; and St. Nicholas peace pact 205, 206, 207
baseball managers 21, 37, 39, 49, 57-8, 65, 85, 131, 280, 308, 317; black players as 341; owner conflict 83-4; strategy 18, 22, 28-9, 34, 68, 73, 94, 144, 246-47, 250, 252, 257, 262, 276-77, 281-82, 294-96, 313, 318
baseball players 200; accidents/injuries/illness/ deaths 64, 73, 75, 86, 107, 128, 214, 222-23, 225, 234, 236, 256-57, 272, 298, 314, 321, 353; alcoholism/drug abuse 20-1, 42, 174, 188, 197, 366, 380, 388; benefits 86, 142; blacklisting 83, 86; contracts 11, 12, 36-7, 59, 65, 73, 82, 127, 201, 204, and anti-trust laws 331, 337, and arbitration/ negotiation 162, 165-68, 337, 344, 356, 380, and 'free agents' 151-53, 194, 344, 361, and bonuses 93. (*See also* reserve clause); and corruption 14, 42, 47; as heroes 29; in military *40*, 40-1, *77* 77-8, 96, *260*, 265-66 267-69, *269*, 285; purchase prices of 239, 249, 252, 306; safety 102; raiding 203, 204, 271; salaries 22, 46, 82, 83, 138, 144, 153, 159, 162, 196, 203, 216, 218, 229, 309, 331, 344, 356; strikes 144, 162, 166, 186, 337, 356-59, 363; training 49, 62; unions/associations 9, 15, 17, 18, 83, 104, 132, 138, 162, 165, 202, 203, 331, 344; World Series shares 206, 210. *See also* black players
batting averages 57, 193. *See also* hitting records
Bauer, Hank *277, 287*, 323
Baylor, Don *351, 352*, 366, 380
Beardon, Gene 274, *275*
Bedient, Hugh 213
Belanger, Mark *324*, 324
Bell, Buddy *358*
Bench, Johnny *140*, 144, 146, 177
Bender, 'Chief' 207, *207*, 212, 215
Berenguer, Juan 383, 384
Berra, Yogi 100, 290, 292, 296, 300-02, *301, 308-09*, 309, 311, 313, 375, 378
Bevans, Bill 272-73
Bird, Harry 290
black baseball clubs 18-19, 78-80
black players 78, 80-2, 84, 86, 99-100, 194, 262, 270-73, 286, 303, 324
Black Sox. *See* Chicago White Sox, scandal
Blackwell, Ewell *84*, 85
Blair, Paul 316, 324, *326-27*, 327
Blanchard, Johnny 309
Blass, Steve *143*
Blue, Vida *336*, 336, 337, 340, 344
Blyleven, Bert *336*
Blyska, Mike 290
Boggs, Wade *378*, 381
Bond, Tom 19
Bonds, Bobby 195, *348*
Bonham, Ernie 266
Bonilla, Bobby 195
Boone, Bob 385
Boone, Ray *294*
Borowy, Hank 78
Boston Beaneaters 21
Boston Braves 34-6, *36*, 62, 85, 96, 215
Boston Pilgrims 28
Boston Red Sox 83, 128, 151, 189, 204, 206, 213, 214, 215, *216*, 226, 250, 258, 265, 271, 275, 277, 294, 303, 318-20, 321, 338, 342-43, 380-81, 382, 385, 387
Boswell, Dave *318-19*
Bottomley, Jim 47, 50, 57
Boudreau, Lou *274*, 274, 275
Bouton, Jim 136, 314, 332
Bradley, George 144
Bresnahan, Roger *30*
Brett, George *345*, 350, 360, *360-61*, 369, *378*
Bridges, Tommy 249
Briles, Nelson 128
Brock, Lou *123*, 128, 129, *148*, 148, 156, *156-57*
Brooklyn Excelsiors *10*
Brooklyn Dodgers 26, 37, 38, 43, 54, 61, 62, 67, 72, 74, 75, 83, 86, 90, 96, 98, 100, 103, 225, 265, 272, 277, 282-83, 286, 290-91, 294, 296-97; integration in 78, 80-1, 86; move 104. *See also* Los Angeles
Brouthers, Dan 20, 22
Brown, Bobby 285
Brown, Gates 322
Brown, Mordecai *31*, 31, 32, 36
Brown, Willard 262
Buhl, Bob 103, 104
Butler, Brett 195
Brunansky, Tom 383
Brush, John 201, 204, 205, 206, 207
Bunker, Wally 318
Burdette, Lew *98*, 103, 104, 108, 299-300, 303
Burkett, Jesse 22, *23*
Bush, Joe 226, 230, 231

Cadore, Leon 43, *44*
California Angels 306, 310, 348, 353, 365, 366-67, 381, 385
Camilli, Dolf 73, 74
Campanella, Roy 80, 86, *87*, 90, 97, *100*, 100, *101*, 107
Campaneris, Bert 313, 337, *338*, 339
Campanis, Al 189, 191
Candiotti, Tom 387
Candlestick Park, 195, *196*
Canseco, Jose *385*, 385, *386*
Carew, Rod 324, *340*, 341, 344, 348, 350, *352*, 353, 366
Carlton, Steve 138, 144, *145*, 153, 165, 168, 171, 174-75, *176*, 177, 189
Carrigan, Bill *211*
Carter, Gary *172-73*, 189
Carter, Joe 387
Cartwright, Alexander 9
Case, George *267*
Casey, Hugh 265
Cash, Norm 309, 322
catchers 230, 233, 244, *263*, *293*, 320, *370-71*
Cavarretta, Phil 78, *79*
Cepeda, Orlando *107*, 107, 127, 128
Chalmers Award 34
Chambliss, Chris 347
Chance, Frank 31, 32 210
Chandler, 'Happy' 78, *82*, 82, 83, 84, 94, 270, 271, 272, 280
Chandler, Spud *255*, 257, 262, 267-68, 314
Chapman, Ben *252*
Chapman, Ray 225
Chapman, Sam *265*
Chase, Harold *42*
Chesbro, Jack 28
Chicago Cubs, 26, 30-2, 33, 50, 54, 57, 58, 63, 67, 78, 83, 124, 127, 132, 144, 154, 178, 180, 186, 194, 195, *195*, 210-11
Chicago White Sox (Stockings) 17, 18, 19, 42, 80, 114, 180, 204, 207, 210, 216-17, *218*, 225-26, 293-94, *295*, 303, 372, 386, 387; scandal 217-19
Cicotte, Eddie 217, 218
Cincinnati Reds *10, 11*, 11, 42, 62, 67, 68, 72, 103, 116-17, 124, 139-41, 144, 146, 150-51, 153, 168, 171, 188, 191, 192, 194, 195, 196, 201, 338, 342, 344, 387
Clark, Will 195, *195*
Clemens, Roger *379*, 380, 381, 387
Clemente, Roberto 102, 125, *139*, 142, *143*, 143, 144, 146, 197
Cleveland Indians 99, 210, 225, 262, 273-74, 287-89, *289*, 294, 297-98, 303, 311, 349-50, 382
Continental League 108, 112
Cobb, Ty 26, 207-08, *208*, 209-10, 212, *213*, 214, 215, *216*, 225, *228*, 229, *238*, 238
Cochrane, Mickey *240*, 240, 249, 250, 255
Colavito, Rocky 294, *297*, 302, 309
Coleman, Jerry 277, 285
Coleman, Vince *186*, 192, *192*
Collins, Eddie 209, 212, 217, 238, 264
Collins, Jimmy 203, *203*, 206, 215, 217
Combs, Earle 235, 244, 247
Comiskey, Charles 200, *200*, 201, 218
Comiskey Park *332-33*
Cone, David 197
Conigliaro, Tony 312, *320*, 321
Continental League 306
Coombs, Jack 37, 212, 215
Cooper, Cecil 366, *366-67*
Cooper, Mort 75, 78, 267
Cooper, Walker *75*, 75, *269*
Corcoran, Larry 18
Coveleski, Stanley 222, *222*, 234
Covington, Wes 299
Cramer, Doc 258
Cravath, Gavvy 37
Crawford, Sam 212, *216*
Cronin, Joe 247, *250*, 258, 265, 302, *302, 306*
Crosetti, Frankie 255, 282
Crowder, Alvin 247, 250
Cuellar, Mike 324, *324-25*, 333, 334
Cuyler, 'Kiki' *49*
Cy Young Award 103, 172, 178, 195, *196*

Dark, Alvin *94*, 94, 96
Davis, Harry 212
Davis, Ron 359
Dawson, Andre *174*, 189, 192
Dean, Jerome 'Dizzy' *52, 56*, 56, *58-9*, 58-60, 63, 64, 67-8, 77, 78-80
Dean, Paul 58, *58-9*, 60
Delahanty, Ed 20-21
Delahanty, Jim 211
Del Guercio, Ted 290
Dent, Bucky 350
Derringer, Paul 68, *69*, 72
designated hitter 137, 146, 330, 338, 372
Detroit Tigers 129, 183, 209-10, 211, 229, 248-49, 255, 262, 269, 309,

321-23, 337-38, 377, *377*, 382, 383, 385, 387
Detroit Wolverines *20*, 20
Dickey, Bill 244, *245*, 253, 256, 282
Dickson, Murray 271-72
DiMaggio, Dom 271
DiMaggio, Joe 250-52, *251*, 255, 257, *258*, 262, 263-64, 273, 280-81, 283, *284*, 285, *328*
Dinneen, William *206*
Ditmar, Art *307*
Dobson, Pat 335
Doby, Larry 262, 273, *273*, 294
Doerr, Bobby 258, 264, *271*, 271
Donald, Atley 257
Donovan, Wild Bill 210, *215*
Douglas, Phil *46*, 47
Doyle, Larry 29, 37
Drabek, Doug *1*, 4, 195, *196*
Dressen, Charlie 98
Drysdale, Don 114, *114-15*, 116, 118, 124, 128, 315, 318
Duffy, Hugh 22
Dugan, Joe 226, 235
Durham, Leon *178*
Durocher, Leo 67, 73, *73*, *74*, 74-5, 83-84, 85, 86, 94, 96, 99, 103, 272
Dykes, Jimmy 241, 244

Earnshaw, George 239, *239*
earthquake, 1989 World Series, 386
Eckersley, Dennis *176-77*, 348, 387
Ehmke, Howard *240*, 241
Erickson, Scott *197*
Erskine, Carl 90, *92*, 96, 98, 241
Evans, Darrell 385
Evans, Dwight 342, *343*, 348
Evers, Johnny *31*, 35-6

'fair foul' rule 14
farm system 47, 57, 59, 75, 239, 247, 255, 257, 266, 280, 281-82, 290, 314, 318
Federal League 36, 214, 216
Feller, Bob *253*, 253-54, 262, 265, *269*, 271
Felsch, Oscar 217, *218*
Fenway Park 212
Ferrell, Wesley *244*
Fidrych, Mark 347
Fielder, Cecil 387
Fingers, Rollie 336, 337, *340*, 340, 344
Finley, Charles 313, 340, 344
Fisk, Carlton 342, *344*, 376
Flanagan, Mike 353
Flood, Curt *122*, 137-38, *138*, 330, 331, 332, 335
Forbes Field 306
Ford, Whitey *280*, 281, 285, 290, *291*, 306
Foster, George *154*, 154, *216*
Fox, Nellie 294, *295*
Fox, Pete 249, 250
Foxx, Jimmie 240, 241, 244, 246, 247, *248*
franchises 14, 22, 26, 72, 203, 204, 205
Frazee, Harry 226
Freedman, Andrew 22
Freehan, Bill 322
Fregosi, Jim *313*
Frick, Ford *78*, 80, 81, 94, 96, 103, 280, *302*
Fridley, Jim 290
Frisch, Frank *46*, 46, *50*, 50, 57
Furillo, Carl 86, 90, *90*, 93, 100

Gaedel, Eddie 282
Gaetti, Gary 383
Gandil, Arnold 217
Gant, Ron 196, 197, *197*
Garcia, Mike 288, *289*
Gardella, Danny 82
Garms, Debs 72, *77*
Garvey, Steve *151*, 157, *164*, 171, 175, 189
'Gashouse Gang'. *See* St. Louis Cardinals
Gedman, Rich *381*
Gehrig, Lou 50, *223*, 235-36, *236*, 237, 238, *242*, 244, 245, 247, 253, 255, 256-57, 388
Gehringer, Charlie 229, *245*, 249, 250, 255
Gentile, Jim 309
Gentry, Gary 327
Giamatti, A Bartlett 194, *194*, 195, 385
Gibson, Bob 37, *113*, 122, 128, 139, 321
Gibson, Kirk 193, *377*, 380, 385
Gionfriddo, Al 273
Gladden, Dan 383
Glavine, Tom 197
Gomez, Lefty 244, 245, 247, 250, 255, 257
Goldsmith, Fred 18
Gooden, Dwight 178-80, *180*, 187, 189, *190*, 191
Gordon, Joe 255, 257, 266 *276*
Grant, Charlie 80
Grant 'Mudcat' *314*, 315, 361
Gray, Pete *270*
Greenberg, Hank 54, 60, *249*, 249, 250, 255, 262
Griffey, Ken, Sr. & Jr. 385-86, *386*
Griffith, Clark *201*, 203, 204, *213*, 215, 287
Grim, Bob 282
Grimes, Burleigh 43, 47
Groat, Dick *114*, 115
Groh, Heinie *45*, *224-25*
Grove, Robert 'Lefty' *52*, *239*, 239, 244, 247, 248, 258
Guidry, Ron *347*, 347, 350, 359
Gwynn, Tony 191

Haas, Mule 241
Haddix, Harvey 107-08, *109*
Hafey, Chick 50, *51*, 57
Hall of Fame 20, 22, 64, 69, 146
Hanlon, Ned 20, 21, 22
Harridge, Will 246, 282, 302
Harris, Bucky *232*, 233, 234, 276
Hart, Jim 201, 202
Hartnett, Gabby *68*
Hatcher, Billy 196
Heilmann, Harry 225, *229*, 229, 237
Henderson, Dave 385, 386
Henderson, Rickey 386, 388
Herman, Babe 54
Herman, Billy 58, 63, 73
Hermann, August 205
Hernandez, Keith 159, *187*
Hernandez, Willie 377
Hershiser, Orel 192, 193, *193*, 194, 197, 385
Herzog, Whitey 177
Higgins, 'Pinky' *254*
hitting records 22, 26, 28, 34, 37, 39, 43-4, 48, 50, 51, 54, 59, 63, 64, 68, 72, 74, 75-6, 78, 83, 86, 98-9, 103, 104, 107, 114, 118, 121, 139, 146, 159, 169, 171-72, 183-86, 193, 195-96, 207, 209, 215, 223, 224-25, 228-29, 235, 238, 247, 248, 249, 250-52, 253, 256, 257, 265, 294, 311, 338, 341, 348, 350, 387
Hodges, Gil 86, 90, *91*, 93, 96, 98, 100, *130*, 131, *131*, 146, 326
Holmes, Tommy 78
Holtzman, Ken 340, 344, 347
home run records 43, 51, 59, 69, 85, 86, 93, 100, 103, 116, 128, 142, 147-48, 153, 156, 212, 217, 224, 225, 226-27, 229, 230, 232, 236, 237, 240, 245, 255, 293, 298, 302, 306, 311, 318, 322, 341, 348
Hooper, Harry 215, *228*
Horner, Bob 189
Hornsby, Rogers 39, 43-4, *45*, 46, 48, 50, 51, 58, 195
Horton, Willie 322, *323*
Houk, Ralph 282, 309, 317, 333
Houston Colt 45s (Astros) 112, 118, 144, 165, 168, 188, 189, 194
Howard, Elston 286, 297, 302, *309*, 309, *315*, 320
Hoyt, Waite *226*, 226, 229, 237, 238, 241
Hrbek, Kent *2-3*, *383*
Hubbell, Carl 56, *59*, 59, 63, 65, 85, 282
Hughes, Sam 80
Hughson, Tex *268*
Hulbert, William 12, *13*, 14
Hunter, Billy 290
Hunter, 'Catfish' 336, 337, 340, 341, 344, *347*, 347
Huston, T L 230

'inside baseball' 22
International League 247
Irwin, Monte 94, 96

Jackson, Joe 212, 214, *216*, 217, 218, *219*, 219
Jackson, Reggie 156, 324, *335*, 337, 339, 344, 348, *349*, 350, 359, 365, *365*, 367, 381
James, Bill 35-6
Jamieson, Charles *232*
Jenkins, Ferguson 124, *124*, 127, 139
Jennings, Hughey 22
John, Tommy *358*, 359
Johnson, Banford *200*, 200-01, 202-03, 204, 205, 207, 212, 234, 238, 338
Johnson, Cliff 353
Johnson, Darrell 290, 342
Johnson, Davy 324, *325*
Johnson, Howard *189*
Johnson, Walter 209, *210*, 212, 214, 215, 226, *232*, 233-34, 235, 238
Jones, Cleon 132-33, *191*, 191
Jones, Sam 226, 231
Jones, Tom 211
Joss, Addie 210, *210*
Justice, David *197*

Kaat, Jim 172, 177
Kaline, Al 293, *320*, 322, *323*, 341
Kansas City Athletics 287, 289. *See also* Oakland
Kansas City Royals 323, 344, 347, 348, *348-49*, 360-61, 364, 366, 369-72, 378, 382, 386
Keefe, Jim 20
Keeler, 'Wee Willie' 22, *22*
Keller, Charlie *257*, 257, 266
Kelly, Mike 18, *18*
Kelly, Tom 383
Keltner, Ken *264*
Kemp, Steve *356*
Killebrew, Harmon 309, 310, *311*, 324, 333
Killian, Ed 210, 315
Kiner, Ralph 83, *83*, 85, 94, 97
King, Clyde 366
Klein, Chuck 54, 59, *60-1*, 64
Kluszewski, Ted *102*
Knight, Ray 189, *189*
Knoblauch, Chuck *388*
Koenig, Mark 235
Konstanty, Jim 93
Koosman, Jerry 132, *132-33*, 325
Korean War 285
Koufax, Sandy *110*, 114, 116, 118, 120, 124, 125-26, *127*, 315
Kryhoski, Dick 290
Kubek, Tony 282, 299, *300*, 314
Kucks, Johnny 297
Kuhn, Bowie *112*, 112, 152, 168, 169, *174*, 174, 340, 344, 368

Labine, Clem 90
LaCock, Pete *348-49*
Lajoie, Nap 203, *203*, 204, 211, *211*, *213*
Landis, K M *36*, 36, 42, 43-4, 46, 47, 60, 69, 77, *78*, 78, 80, *218*, 219, 222, 229, 238, 239, 250, 270
Lardner, Ring 223
Larkin, Gene *388*
Larsen, Don 103, 290, 294, *295*, 296, 302-03
Lary, Frank 302
Lasorda, Tom *154*, 154, 157, 174, 194
Lavagetto, Cookie 273
Law, Vernon 115, *117*
Lazzeri, Tony 235, 236, *237*, 247, 253, 255
Leach, Tommy 26, 28
Leibrandt, Charlie 197
Lemke, Mark 197
Lemon, Bob 274, 288, *290*, 350, 353, 366
Leonard, Dutch 216
Leppert, Don 290
Lewis, George 'Duffy' 213
Lindstrom, Fred 54, 58
lively ball 31, 33, 34, 43, 50, 51
Lockman, Whitey 94, 96
Lollar, Sherman 294
Lombardi, Ernie 68-9, *69*, *258*
Lonborg, Jim *319*
Long, Dale 103, *104*
Lopat, Al 288
Lopez, Al *66*
Los Angeles Dodgers 107, 108, 114, 116-17, 121, 124, 125, 148-50, 154-56, 157-59, 165, 168, 171, 186, 187, 192, 193, *193*, 194, 196, 311, 315, 317, 340, 348, 350, 364, 381, 385
Lowe, Bobby 22
Lynn, Fred 342, *343*, 366, *372*, 378
Lyons, Ted 266, *267*

McAuliffe, Dick 322
McBride, John *242*
McCarthy, Joe 50, 245, 246, 257, 279
McCormick, Frank 68, *70*, 72
McCosky, Barney 262-63
McCovey, Willie *108*, 108
McDonald, Jim 290
McDougald, Gil 282, 284-85, 298, 302, *303*
McGinnity, Joe *28*, 29, *30*, *203*
McGraw, John J 22, *28*, 28-9, 34, 37-9, 43, 44, 45, 47, 57-8, *58*, 61, 80, 203, 204, 206, *207*, 287
McGraw, Tug *132-33*, 145, 146
McGregor, Scott 359
McGwire, Mark *385*, 385, 386
McLain, Denny, 128, *321*, 321-22, 324-25, 335
McMullin, Fred 217
McNally, Dave *150*, 151, *316*, 318, 324, 333, 340, 342
McNamara, John 385
MacPhail, Larry 61-2, *63*, 66, 67, *68*, *72*, 72, 73-4, 75, 77
MacPhail, Lee 317, 375
McQuinn, George *269*
Mack, Connie 22, *23*, 205, *213*, 215, 234, 238, 244, 246, 280, 287, 289
Maglie, Sal *82*, 82, 93, 94, 283, 296
major leagues: competition 153; expansion 108; organization (1981 season) 168; profitability 112. *See also* National

League; American League
Maldonado, Candy 387
Mantle, Mickey 115, 116, 122, 282, 283, 284, *285*, 285-86, *286*, 292-93, 294, 302, 306, 308, 310, 311, 314, 315, 378
Manush, Heinie 229, 249
Marberry, Firpo 233
Marichal, Juan 120, *121*, 125, 128
Marion, Marty 78
Maris, Roger 114, 116, 128, *308*, 308-09, 310, *310*, 311, 315
Marquard, Rube *34*, 34, 37
Marshall, Mike 148, *150*
Marshall, William *85*
Martin, Billy *285*, 286, 324, *328*, 338, 347, 348, 350, 353, 364, *364*, 368, 375, 378
Martin, 'Pepper' 57, 77
Masi, Phil 275
Mathews, Eddie 97, *98*
Mathewson, Christy *28, 29*, 29, 32, 34, 37, 48, 64, 197, 207, 213, 214
May, Rudi 359
Mays, Carl 229
Mays, Willie *94*, 94, 98-9, *100*, 107, 116, 124, 128, 139, *149*, 197, 283, 289, 378
Mazeroski, Bill *117*, 308
Medwick, Joe 58, 60, 63, *64*, 64, 73
Merkle, Fred 32, *34-5*, 210-11
Messersmith, Andy 151, *152*, 342
Meusel, Bob 226, 232, *234*, 234, 235
Meusil, Emil 45
Mexican League 82, 83, 271
Michael, Gene 366
Miller, Bill 290
Miller, Bing 241
Mills, A G *14*, 17
Milwaukee Braves 97, 103, 104, 108, 112, 120, 298, 302
Milwaukee Brewers 335, 359, 364, *366*, 366-67, *367*, 382, 383, 385
Minnesota Twins *2-3*, 124, 191, *192, 197*, 197, 310, 311, 315, 321, 324, 333, *363*, 382, 383, 384, 385, 387, *387*, *388*, 388
Minoso, Minnie 293
Miranda, Willie 290
Mitchell, Kevin 195
Mize, Johnny 64, *64-5*, 85
Molitor, Paul 366, *384*, 385
Montreal Expos 112, 118, 191, 323
Moore, Mike 386
Moore, Wilcy 237, 241
Morgan, Joe *144*, 146, 151, *163*, 171, 344, 385
Morgan, Tom 282, 285
Moriarty, George 211
Morris, Jack 377, *387*, 388
Most Valuable Player Award 47, 48, 51, 57, 59, 63, 72, 74, 75, 78, 85, 86, 93, 97, 98, 99, 100, 103, 104, 108, 115, 125, 139, 154, 159, 193-94, 195, 196, 386, 388; shared 168
Mueller, Don 94, 96, 99
Mullin, George 210
Munger, George 78
Munson, Thurman 333, *334*, 347, 353
Murphy, Dale *170*, 171
Murphy, Dwayne *364*
Murray, Eddie *359*, 365, 372
Murtaugh, Danny 138
Musial, Stan *75*, 75-6, *77*, 82, 83, 85-6, 94, 99, 104, *112*, 118, *120-21*, 121, 128, 197
Mutrie, Jim *20*, 20

National Baseball Commission 205, 210, 218: Commissioner 219, 270, 280, 375, authority of 229
National League: competition 17, 22, 36, 72, 82; expansion 17, 112, 131 (*See also* major leagues); franchises 14, 201, 202 and shifts 96-7, 104-5, 107, 112; monopoly of 200, 201, 204; organization 12, 26; playoffs 131, 132, 144, 146, 148, 157, 159, 165, 168; profitability 22, 39, 42, 66, 85
Nettles, Craig 350, *350-51*, 375
New York Giants 20, *21*, 26, 28-9, 30, 32, 34, 39, 46, 47, 50, 54, 57-8, 59, 61, 63, 69, 85, 94-6, 98-9, *105*, 206, 207, 212, 213, 217, 230, 234, 282, 310; move 104
New York Highlanders 205, 206
New York Knickerbockers *9*, 9
New York Mets 112, 118, 124, 127, 131, 132, 138, 146-47, 178, 188, 189, 191, 192, 193, 195, 197, 325-27
New York Yankees 47, 50, 68, 76, 78, 81, 86, 96, 114, 115-16, 118, 121, 153, 157-59, 168, 192, 226, 229-32, 235, 236-39, 244-45, 246-47, 249-50, 252-53, 255-59, *258*, *262*, 265, 266, 267-68, 272-73, 276, 277, 280, 281, 282, 285, 286, 287-92, 293-94, 297-98, 302, 306-10, 311, 313-15, 317, 347, 348, 350, 352-53, 359, 360, 363, 364, 369-72, 377-78, 381, 382, 384, 385; attendance at games 223, 235, 238, 302; instruction school 282; players bought and traded 226, 290; unrest in 347, 348-50, 365-66, 369, 375
Newcombe, Don 86, 90, *93*, 96, 100, 103, 297
Newsom, Bobo *262*, 263
Nichols, Charles *21*, 22
Nicholson, Bill *78*
Nicolau, George 194
Niekro, Phil *132*, 132, 159, 177, 375, *375*, 380
night games 61, *62*, 65-6, 67, 73, 83, 143, 180, *194*, 195
Nixon, Otis 197
Northrup, Jim 322
Nuxhall, Joe 268

Oakland A's 144, 150, 194, 195, 196, *196*, 322, 335, 337-39, 340, 344, 347, 348, 364, 382, 385, *385*, 386, *386*, 387, *387*
O'Connell, Jimmy 47, *47*
O'Day, Hank *33*
O'Doul, Lefty 51, *51*, 54
Oeschger, Joe 43, *44*
Oglivie, Ben *359*, 366
Oliva, Tony *312*, 312, 315
O'Malley, Walter 94, 105-06
Ott, Mel *4-5*, 59, *63*, 63, 83, 85
Owen, Marv 249, 250
Owen, Mickey 73, 82

Page, Joe *272*
Paige, Satchel 80, 274, *274*
Palmer, Jim 318, 324, *327*, 330, *331*, 342
Pappas, Milt *292*
Pascual, Camilo *311*
Pearson, Monte 253, 282
Pendleton, Terry 197
pennant races *17*, 18, 19, 21, *22*, 26, 30, 31-2, 34, 35, 37, 39, 42, 43, 45, 47, 48-9, 50, 56, 58, 59, 61, 62, 63, 67, 68, 72, 75, 78, 85, 90, 93, 94-6, 97, 98, 103, 108, 116, 118, 121, 124-25, 128, 172, 177, 188, 192, 194, 197, 204, 206, 210, 212, 213, 214, 215, 216, 225, 226, 229, 231, 232, 235, 237, 239, 248, 250, 258, 266, 268, 271, 274, 277, 280-81, 282, 286, 290, 302, 303, 306, 309, 311, 314, 316, 318-20; divisional rules 323; divisional titles 324, 333, 335, 337-38, 342, 344, 347-48, 350, 359, 360, 363, 364, 366, 369, 375-77; playoffs 275, 325, 333, 336, 338, 339-40, 342, 347, 348, 350, 353, 360, 367, 372, 377, (1981: 363-64)
Pennock, Herb 226, *231*, 231, 237, 247
Pepitone, Joe 315
Perez, Tony *146*, 151, *152-53*
Perry, Gaylord 125, 139, 177, 338, 341, 367-68
Perry, Jim 333
Pesky, Johnny 271, 272, *272*
Petrocelli, Rico 321
Petry, Dan *369*
Pfeffer, Fred 18, 37
Philadelphia Athletics *12*, 36, 205, 207, 212, 214, 215, 234, 236, 239-41, 244, 245-46; moving 287; rebuilding 238. *See also* Kansas City
Philadelphia Phillies 116, 121, 281, 372
Piniella, Lou 195
Pipgras, George 231, 237, 238, 247
pitching dominance 114
pitching records 19, 21-2, 29, 30, 31, 34, 37, 39, 47, 58, 59, 60, 66-7, 97, 108, 116, 118, 124, 128, 138, 142, 144, 159, 165, 174, 187, 204, 212-13, 214, 226, 233, 239, 241, 244, 254, 255, 271, 314, 336, 341, 365, 368; and shutouts 207, 274, 306, 309; trick pitches 222-23, 224, 320. *See also* baseball games: no hitters
pitching rules 42-3, 50, 131, 133, 323
Pittsburgh Pirates 26, 28, 46, 47-8, 50, 67, 80, 114, 115-6, 138, 141-43, 144, 148, 150-51, 159, 171, 174, 192, 195, *196*, 197, 206, 211, 234, 238, 306-08, 336, 353
Plank, Eddie *205*, 205, 207, 215
Podres, Johnny *125*, 290-91
Potter, Nels 268
Powell, John 'Boog' *313*, 313, 324, 333
Puckett, Kirby *382*, 383, 388
Pulliam, Harry 205

Quinn, Jack *222*
Quisenberry, Dan *354, 375*, 375

Radatz, Dick 312
Radbourne, Charles *19*, 19-20
Raines, Tim *160, 166*, 166, 188, *189*
Randolph, Willie *362*
Raschi, Vic *281*
Rawlings, Johnny 45
Reach, Albert 202, *202*
Reardon, Jeff 383, 385
Reese, Pee Wee 74, 86, 90, 100, *100, 174*
Reiser, Pete *74*, 74, 75
reserve clause 136-38, 144, 146, 151, 162, 330-31, 337, 344, 356
Reynolds, Allie *277, 282*, 282
Rhodes, James 'Dusty' *88*, 99
Rice, Jim *342*, 342, 378, 380
Rice, Sam 229, 233, *237*
Richards, Paul 287
Rickey, Branch 47, *49*, 49, 77, 78, 80-1, 90, 94, 108, 267
Riddle, Elmer *76*
Righetti, Dave 375
Rijo, Jose 196
Ripken, Cal 372, *373, 388*
Risberg, 'Swede' 217
Rivera, Jim 293
Rivers, Mickey 347
Rizzuto, Phil *266*, 266, 285
Robinson, Brooks *306, 316*, 316-17, 318, 333, 335, *337*
Robinson, Frank *103*, 103, *117, 316*, 318, *341*, 341
Robinson, Jackie 78, *80-1*, 80-1, 84, 86, 90, *97*, 100, 146, 197, 262, 270-71, 382
Robinson, Wilbert 22, 37, 57
Roe, Preacher *86*, 90
Rogers, Steve *168*
Rohe, Billy 318
Rohe, George 208
Rolfe, Red *258*
Rookie of the Year Award 84, 94, 107, 108, 127, 180
Roosevelt, Franklin D 61, 77,
Rose, Pete *129, 142*, 146, *147*, 151, *152-53*, 159, 165, *169*, 169, 171, *175*, 175, 183-86, *184-85*, 186, *191*, 191, 194, 196, 197, 385
Rosen, Al *289*
Roush, Edd *42*
Rowe, 'Schoolboy' 248, *249*, 250, 263
Rudi, Joe 337, 344
Rudolph, Dick 35-6
Ruel, Muddy 233, 234
Runnels, Pete 302
Ruppert, Jacob 226, 230
Rusie, Amos *20*
Ruth, Babe 50, 58, 62-3, 67, 215, *216*, 217, 219, *220, 223*, 225-26, *227*, 230, 232, 234, *236*, 237, 238, *242*, 244, 245, 247, 249-50; influence of 226-28, *227*, 235; as pitcher 226; suspension of 234-35
Ryan, Nolan *124*, 124, 146, 168, *169*, 175, 187, 189, 192, *192*, 338-39, *339*, 341, 344, 348, 353, 388, *388*

Saberhagen, Bret *380*
St. Louis Browns 205, 229-30, 255, 268, 269, 282, *283*. *See also* Baltimore Orioles
St. Louis Cardinals 26, *49*, 49, 50, 56, *57*, 59-60, *62*, 63, 72, 74, 75, 76, 83, 84, 121, 122, 125, 128, 129, 168, 172, 186, 187, 191, *192*, 267, 271, 321, 322, 381, 385
San Diego Padres 112, 171, 180, 183, 194, 323
San Francisco Giants *4-5*, 107, 108, 118-120, 122, 124, 125, 141, 142, 188, 189, 194, 195, *195, 196*, 386
Sandberg, Ryne 178, *179*, 195
Santiago, Benito 192
Schalk, Ray 217
Schang, Wally 226
Schmidt, Mike *153*, 154, *165*, 165
Schulte, Frank 34, 37
Schulte, Fred 248
Score, Herb 290, 298, *298*
Scott, Everett 226, 235
Scott, Mike 188, *188*, 194
Seattle Mariners 347, 368, 386, *386*

Seattle Pilots 323. *See also* Milwaukee Brewers
Seaver, Tom *126*, 127, 138, *138*, 142, 154, *155*, 168, 180, 325, 326, *374*, 381
Segrist, Kal 290
Selee, Frank 21
Sewell, Joe *235* and Luke *235, 248*
Sewell, Rip *76*
Shawkey, Bob 215, *230*, 231
Sherman Antitrust Act 36, 46, 138, 144
Shocker, Urban *229*, 237
Shore, Ernie *216*
Shotton, Burt *83*, 85
Sievers, Roy 298, *299*
Simmons, Al 229, 239, 240-41, *241*, 244, 248
Simmons, Ted 366
Singleton, Ken *353*, 359, 372
Sisler, Dick 93
Sisler, George *224*, 225, 226, 228-29, 230, 237
Skowron, Bill 303, 306, *307*, 309
Slaughter, Enos 272
Smith, Elmer 225, *225*
Smith, Hal 290
Smith, Lonnie 197
Smith, Ozzie *191*, 191
Smith, Zane 195
Smoltz, John 197
Snider, Duke 86, 90, *91*, 100
Spahn, Warren 85, *85*, 94, 97, 103, 104, 108, 116, 121, 298, 299
Spalding, Al *11*, 12
Speaker, Tris *209*, 209, 212, 213, 215, *224-25*, 225, 239
Spink, Taylor 201
Sportsman Park *283*
Stallings, George 215
Stanley, Mickey 322
Stargell, Willie 125, 142, *142*, *159*, 159, 171
Steinbrenner, George 347, 348, 365-66, 387
Steinfeldt, Harry 31
Stengel, Casey 37, 45, 63, 118, *118*, 276-77, *278*, 281-82, 286, 288, 289, 291, 299, 302, 306; firing of 208
Stephens, Vern 268
Stewart, Dave 195, 386, *386*
Stirnweiss, George *270*
Stone, Steve 359
Stoneham, Horace 85, 86, 105
Stottlemyre, Mel 314, 315
Stovey, George 19
Strawberry, Darryl 178, *182*, 189, 193
Sullivan, Frank 290
Summers, Ed 210
Sutcliffe, Rick *183*
Sutter, Bruce *172*
Sutton, Don 366, 381
Swoboda, Ron *131*, 131

Tebbetts, Birdie *263*
television, effect on baseball 262, 302, 347, 356, 368
Tenace, Gene 337, 338, 339
Terry, Billy *55*, 57, 59, 62
Terry, Ralph *310*, 310
Tesreau, Jeff *214*
Texas Rangers 335, 372, 381, 382, *388*
Thigpen, Bobby 387
Thomas, Gorman 366
Thompson, Henry 262
Thomson, Bobby *96*, 96
Thornton, Andre *348-49*
Tiant, Luis 312, 342, *343*
Tinker, Joe *31*, 36
'Tinker-to-Evers-to-Chance' 31, 33, 210
Toney, Fred *39*, 39
Toronto Blue Jays 347, 377-78, 381, 382, 383, 386, 387, *387*
Torrez, Mike 342, *351*
Trammell, Alan *377*, 377, 385
Travis, Cecil *247*
Traynor, Pie *48*, 48
Triandos, Gus 290, *293*
Trosky, Hal *253*, 253
Truman, Harry S 94
Turley, Bob 290, 302

Ueberroth, Peter 192, 194, 375, 380
Uhle, George 235
umpires 18, 22, 29, 32, 96, 133; altercations with 204, 230, *341*, 368, 369-72
uniform numbers: introduced 241; retired 257

Valenzuela, Fernando 166, *166-67*, 171, *171*
Vance, Dizzy 47, *48*, 54
van der Ahe, Chris 201
Vander Meer, Johnny *66*, 66-7, *67*, 85
Vaughan, Arky 58, *63*, 63
Vaughn, Jim 39, *40*
Veeck, Bill 282, 286
Vernon, Mickey *285*
Vincent, Fay 194, *194*
Viola, Frank 383, *383*

Waddell, Rube *204*, 205, 207, 271
Wagner, Honus 22, *24*, *26*, 26, 27, 31, 33, 39, 64, 197, 211
Waitkus, Eddie 86, *86*
Walker, Dixie 73, *73*, 81
Walker, Moses Fleetwood 19
Wallace, Bobby *26*
Walsh, Ed *208*, 210
Walters, Bucky *68*, 68, 72
Wambsganss, Bill 225
Waner, Lloyd 50, *50* and Paul 64, 77
Ward, John Montgomery 19, *19*, 22
Washington Senators 138, 209, 214, 232-34, 247-48, 270. *See also* Minnesota Twins; Texas Rangers
Weaver, 'Buck' 217, 219
Weaver, Earl 324, 333, 353, 366, 378
Weiss, George 247, 308
Wertz, Vic 289
Western League 201. *See also* American League
Whitaker, Lou *372*, 385
White, Bill 194, 197
White, Devon 387
White, 'Doc' *208*
White, Frank *346*
White, Jo-Jo 249
Whitehill, Earl 247
Whiteman, George 217
Wilhelm, Hoyt 96, *97*
Willett, Ed 210
Williams, Claude 217, 218
Williams, Cy 43
Williams, Dick 318-19, 336, 340
Williams, Ken 230
Williams, Matt 195
Williams, Ted 258, *264*, 264-65, 266, 271, 272, 285, 286, 293, 294, 298, 302, 306, 327
Wills, Maury 116, *116-7*, 118, *119*
Wilson, Lewis (Hack) 50, 54, *55*
Wilson, Willie *361*
Winfield, Dave *357*, 359, 368, 375
Woodling, Gene 290
Wood, Smokey Joe 212, 213, *214*
World Series 17, 20, 22, 28, 30, 36, 39, 41, 42, 47, 50, 56, 60, 64, 65, 76, 77, 78, 83, 86, 96, 99, 100, 103, 104, 108, 114, 115, 117-18, 120, 121, 122-24, 126, 128, 129, 132, 141, 142-43, 144, 146, 148-50, 151, 153, 154, 157-59, 165, 168, 172, 180, 187, 188, 189, 192, 200, 206; importance 211; rules 207, 211, 217; 1903: *206*, 206; 1905: 207; 1906: 208; 1907: 210; 1908: 210; 1909: 211; 1910: 212; 1911: 212; 1912: 213, *214*; 1915: 215-16; 1916: 217; 1918: 217; 1920: 225; 1922: 230; 1923: 232; 1924: 234; 1925: 234; 1926: 236; 1927: 238; 1928: 238; 1929: 241; 1930: 244; 1931: 245-46; 1932: 247; 1936: 253; 1937: *4-5*, 255-56; 1939: 258; 1940: 263; 1941: 265; 1942: 267; 1943: 267; 1944: 268; 1946: 271; 1947: 272-73; 1948: 275; 1949: 277; 1950: 281; 1951: 282-83; 1954: 289; 1955: 290-91; 1956: 294-97; 1958: 302-03; 1959: 303; 1960: 306-08; 1962: 310; 1965: 315; 1966: *316*, 317-18; 1967: 321; 1968: 322; 1969: 325-27; 1971: 336; 1972: 338; 1973: 340; 1974: 340; 1975: 342, 344; 1976: 347; 1977: 348; 1979: 353; 1980: 361; 1981: 364-65; 1982: 367; 1984: *377*, 377; 1985: 378-79; 1986: 381; 1988: 385; 1989: 195, 386; 1990: *196*, 196; 1991: *2-3*, 196-197, *197*, *387*, 387-88, *388*
World War II, effect on baseball 262, 263, 266, 267-68
Wright, Harry 11, 19, *19*
Wrigley Field 194
Wyatt, Whitlow 73, 74, *74*
Wynn, Early *288*, 288, 310-11

Yankee Stadium *230-31*, 231-32, 313, *332-33*, 366
Yastrzemski, Carl 151, *318*, 318, 319, 320, 321, 322, *330*, 375
York, Rudy *271*
Young, Cy 203, 204, 206, *211*, 211, 254
Young, Nick 202
Youngs, Ross *45*, 46
Yount, Robin *366*, 366

Zernial, Gus *293*
Zimmerman, Heinie 34, 212, 217
Zimmerman, Roy 82

Photo Credits

All photographs courtesy of the National Baseball Library, Cooperstown, New York, except the following:
The Baltimore Sun: 324.
Marcello Bertinetti: 158.
Chicago White Sox: 332-33 (bottom).
The Greer Studios, Inc., Baltimore, MD: 287 (top).
Nancy Hogue: 123, 129, 134, 136-37, 140, 144, 145, 147, 151, 152-53, 153, 154, 155, 157, 159, 162, 163, 164, 165, 168, 170, 171 (right), 174 (bottom), 175, 176, 313 (top), 318 (top), 330, 331, 334, 337 (top), 340 (bottom), 341, 342, 343 (all three), 344, 347 (bottom), 348-49 (all three), 351 (top and bottom right), 353, 357, 358 (inset), 359 (both), 361 (bottom), 362, 364 (bottom), 365 (both), 366-67 (two top), 369, 372 (bottom), 373, 376 (large picture), 377 (top), 378 (both).
Mrs. Al Kaline: 320 (bottom).
Library of Congress: 43.
Ron Modra: 160, 166, 167, 169, 171 (left), 172, 173, 177, 178, 179, 180, 181 (except bottom), 182, 183, 184, 185, 186-87, 188, 189, 190, 191 (all three), 192 (both), 345, 346, 350-51 (top), 352 (top), 354, 356, 358 (large picture), 360 (bottom), 361 (top), 363, 364 (top), 366 (bottom), 368, 370-71 (both), 374, 375 (right), 377 (bottom), 379, 380, 381, 382 (both), 383 (both), 384, 385 (both).
New York Yankees: 332-33 (top).
Ponzini Photography: 1, 193, 194 (bottom right), 195, 196 (bottom), 197 (left), 385 (top right), 386 (top left and bottom right), 387 (bottom), 388 (top left).
Bruce L. Schwartzman: 194 (bottom center).
UPI/Bettmann Newsphotos: 2-3, 4-5, 194 (top), 196 (top), 197 (right), 386 (center left), 387 (top left and center), 388 (bottom left).
US Navy: 260, 299 (top).
Angela White: 181 (bottom).

Acknowledgments

The author and publisher would like to thank the following people who have helped in the preparation of this book: Brooks Robards and Stephen Minkin, who contributed to the history; Design 23, who designed it; Barbara Paulding Thrasher, who edited it; Mary R Raho, who did the picture research; Cynthia Klein, who prepared the index. Special thanks also go to the following personnel at the National Baseball Hall of Fame and Museum, Inc.: Thomas R Heitz, librarian; Donna Cornell, manager, photo collection; Elizabeth Zayat and Paul Cunningham, summer interns.